6th Workshop on Research in Computational Typology and Multilingual NLP (SIGTYP 2024)

St. Julian's, Malta
22 March 2024

ISBN: 978-1-7138-9461-2

Printed from e-media with permission by:

Curran Associates, Inc.
57 Morehouse Lane
Red Hook, NY 12571

Some format issues inherent in the e-media version may also appear in this print version.

Printed with permission by Curran Associates, Inc. (2025)

For permission requests, please contact the Association for Computational Linguistics at the address below.

Association for Computational Linguistics
209 N. Eighth Street
Stroudsburg, Pennsylvania 18360

Phone: 1-570-476-8006
Fax: 1-570-476-0860

acl@aclweb.org

Additional copies of this publication are available from:

Curran Associates, Inc.
57 Morehouse Lane
Red Hook, NY 12571 USA
Phone: 845-758-0400
Fax: 845-758-2633
Email: curran@proceedings.com
Web: www.proceedings.com

SIGTYP 2024

The 6th Workshop on Research in Computational Linguistic Typology and Multilingual NLP

Proceedings of the Workshop

March 22, 2024

The SIGTYP organizers gratefully acknowledge the support from the following sponsors.

Supported By

Google

Association for Computational Linguistics (ACL)
209 N. Eighth Street
Stroudsburg, PA 18360
USA
Tel: +1-570-476-8006
Fax: +1-570-476-0860
acl@aclweb.org

Introduction

SIGTYP 2024 is the sixth edition of the workshop for typology-related research and its integration into multilingual Natural Language Processing (NLP). The workshop is co-located with the 18th Conference of the European Chapter of the Association for Computational Linguistics (EACL 2024), which takes place in St Julian's, Malta. This year our workshop features a shared task on Word Embedding Evaluation for Ancient and Historical Languages.

Encouraged by the 2019 – 2024 workshops, the aim of the sixth edition of SIGTYP workshop is to act as a platform and a forum for the exchange of information between typology-related research, multilingual NLP, and other research areas that can lead to the development of truly multilingual NLP methods. The workshop is specifically aimed at raising awareness of linguistic typology and its potential in supporting and widening the global reach of multilingual NLP, as well as at introducing computational approaches to linguistic typology. It fosters research and discussion on open problems, not only within the active community working on cross- and multilingual NLP but also inviting input from leading researchers in linguistic typology.

The workshop provides focused discussions on a range of topics, including the following:

1. Integration of typological features in language transfer and joint multilingual learning. In addition to established techniques such as "selective sharing", are there alternative ways to encoding heterogeneous external knowledge in machine learning algorithms?
2. Development of unified taxonomy and resources. Building universal databases and models to facilitate understanding and processing of diverse languages.
3. Automatic inference of typological features. The pros and cons of existing techniques (e.g. heuristics derived from morphosyntactic annotation, propagation from features of other languages, supervised Bayesian and neural models) and discussion on emerging ones.
4. Typology and interpretability. The use of typological knowledge for interpretation of hidden representations of multilingual neural models, multilingual data generation and selection, and typological annotation of texts.
5. Improvement and completion of typological databases. Combining linguistic knowledge and automatic data-driven methods towards the joint goal of improving the knowledge on cross-linguistic variation and universals.
6. Linguistic diversity and universals. Challenges of cross-lingual annotation. Which linguistic phenomena or categories should be considered universal? How should they be annotated?
7. Language-specific studies to support or contradict universals. Framing a study on 1-3 languages that would shed more light on common linguistic structures and properties.

The final program of SIGTYP contains 2 keynote talks, 5 shared task papers, 11 archival papers, and 2 extended abstracts. This workshop would not have been possible without the contribution of its program committee, to whom we would like to express our gratitude. We should also thank Chris Bentz and Ximena Gutierrez-Vasques for kindly accepting our invitation as invited speakers. The workshop is sponsored by Google. Please find more details on the SIGTYP 2024 website: https://sigtyp.github.io/ws2024-sigtyp.html

Organizing Committee

Workshop Organizers

Michael Hahn, Saarland University
Alexey Sorokin, Yandex and Lomonosov Moscow State University
Ritesh Kumar, Dr. Bhimrao Ambedkar University
Andreas Shcherbakov, University of Melbourne
Yulia Otmakhova, The University of Melbourne
Jinrui Yang, The University of Melbourne
Oleg Serikov, King Abdullah University of Science and Technology
Priya Rani, University of Galway
Edoardo M. Ponti, University of Edinburgh
Saliha Muradoğlu, Australian National University
Rena Gao, University of Melbourne
Ryan Cotterell, Swiss Federal Institute of Technology
Ekaterina Vylomova, The University of Melbourne
Oksana Dereza, University of Galway

Program Committee

Program Chairs

Michael Hahn, Saarland University
Alexey Sorokin, Yandex and Lomonosov Moscow State University
Ritesh Kumar, Dr. Bhimrao Ambedkar University
Andreas Shcherbakov, University of Melbourne
Yulia Otmakhova, The University of Melbourne
Jinrui Yang, The University of Melbourne
Oleg Serikov, King Abdullah University of Science and Technology
Priya Rani, University of Galway
Edoardo M. Ponti, University of Edinburgh
Saliha Muradoğlu, Australian National University
Rena Gao, University of Melbourne
Ryan Cotterell, Swiss Federal Institute of Technology
Ekaterina Vylomova, The University of Melbourne

Reviewers

Badr M. Abdullah, Aryaman Arora

Barend Beekhuizen, Claire Bowern, Miriam Butt

Giuseppe G. A. Celano

Richard Futrell

Rena Wei Gao

Borja Herce, Kristen Howell

Elisabetta Jezek, Gerhard Jäger

Ritesh Kumar, Kemal Kurniawan

Johann-Mattis List

Saliha Muradoglu

Joakim Nivre

Yulia Otmakhova, Robert Östling

Edoardo Ponti

Priya Rani

Oleg Serikov, Andreas Shcherbakov, Alexey Sorokin, Richard Sproat

Daan Van Esch, Giulia Venturi, Ivan Vulić, Ekaterina Vylomova

Jinrui Yang

Olga Zamaraeva

Keynote Talk: Zipfian laws across diverse languages

Christian Bentz
University of Tübingen
2024-03-22 09:00:00 – Room: **Radisson, Marie Loise 1**

Abstract: There are few - if any - universals which hold across all known languages. Promising candidates are quantitative laws such as Zipf's law of word frequencies and Zipf's law of abbreviation. This talk will review some of the current research into these laws from a cross-linguistic perspective. This includes a discussion of the methodological challenges when working with diverse languages, modalities, and writing systems, as well as the controversial question how "meaningful" the laws are given random baselines. Finally, an avenue for further research is explored: the challenge of defining a statistical fingerprint for human languages.

Bio: Christian Bentz is currently an Assistant Professor at the Department of General Linguistics, University of Tübingen. He received his PhD in Computation, Cognition, and Language from the University of Cambridge. His research interests include information theory, quantitative linguistics, language typology, and language evolution.

Keynote Talk: Text-based typology for modeling linguistic diversity in NLP

Ximena Gutierrez-Vasques
UNAM, Mexico City
2024-03-22 13:45:00 – Room: **Radisson, Marie Loise 1**

Abstract: During this presentation, I will elaborate on the importance of capturing the immense diversity inherent in natural languages. This extends beyond advancing language technologies; it also serves to answer interdisciplinary research questions and enrich the exploration of linguistic typology through computational lenses. By harnessing textual data and unsupervised NLP techniques, we can induce typological knowledge, thereby facilitating the expansion of existing typological databases and facilitating more comprehensive language comparisons for various NLP applications.
I will illustrate these concepts through a case study that demonstrates how simple techniques such as subword tokenization and the analysis of multilingual text corpora enable the study of the morphological typology of languages and the complexity of their morphological systems. We will also examine the implications and constraints associated with these methodologies.

Bio: Ximena Gutierrez-Vasques is a computational linguist with an interdisciplinary focus to deepen the study of human language. Her lines of research cover multilingual NLP, computational morphology, and NLP under-resourced languages of the Americas. She was a postdoctoral researcher at the University of Zürich where she specialized in approaches for modeling linguistic complexity and typology using text corpora and inspired by information theory. She recently joined an interdisciplinary research center in Mexico (CEIICH, UNAM), where she works in the interface between humanities and the field of AI.

Table of Contents

Program

Friday, March 22, 2024

08:50 - 09:00	*Opening Remarks*
09:00 - 10:00	*Keynote by Christian Bentz*
10:00 - 10:30	*Low-Resource NLP*
	GUIDE: Creating Semantic Domain Dictionaries for Low-Resource Languages Jonathan Janetzki, Gerard De Melo, Joshua Nemecek and Daniel Lee Whitenack
	Predicting positive transfer for improved low-resource speech recognition using acoustic pseudo-tokens Nay San, Georgios Paraskevopoulos, Aryaman Arora, Xiluo He, Prabhjot Kaur, Oliver Adams and Dan Jurafsky
10:30 - 11:15	*Break*
11:15 - 12:20	*Typology and Language Comparison*
	A New Dataset for Tonal and Segmental Dialectometry from the Yue- and Pinghua-Speaking Area Ho Wang Matthew Sung, Jelena Prokic and Yiya Chen
	Language Atlas of Japanese and Ryukyuan (LAJaR): A Linguistic Typology Database for Endangered Japonic Languages Kanji Kato, So Miyagawa and Natsuko Nakagawa
	A Call for Consistency in Reporting Typological Diversity Wessel Poelman, Esther Ploeger, Miryam De Lhoneux and Johannes Bjerva
	Are Sounds Sound for Phylogenetic Reconstruction? Luise Häuser, Gerhard Jäger, Johann-Mattis List, Taraka Rama and Alexandros Stamatakis
	The Typology of Ellipsis: A Corpus for Linguistic Analysis and Machine Learning Applications Damir Cavar, Ludovic Mompelat and Muhammad S. Abdo
12:30 - 13:45	*Lunch*

Friday, March 22, 2024 (continued)

13:45 - 14:45	*Keynote by Ximena Gutierrez-Vasques*
14:45 - 15:30	*Multilinguality*
	GTNC: A Many-To-One Dataset of Google Translations from NewsCrawl Damiaan J W Reijnaers and Charlotte Pouw
	ModeLing: A Novel Dataset for Testing Linguistic Reasoning in Language Models Nathan Andrew Chi, Teodor Malchev, Riley Kong, Ryan Andrew Chi, Lucas Huang, Ethan A Chi, R. Thomas McCoy and Dragomir Radev
	Compounds in Universal Dependencies: A Survey in Five European Languages Emil Svoboda and Magda Ševčíková
	Sociolinguistically Informed Interpretability: A Case Study on Hinglish Emotion Classification Kushal Tatariya, Heather Lent, Johannes Bjerva and Miryam De Lhoneux
15:30 - 16:15	*Break*
16:15 - 17:00	*Shared task on Word Embedding Evaluation for Ancient and Historical Languages*
	Findings of the SIGTYP 2024 Shared Task on Word Embedding Evaluation for Ancient and Historical Languages Oksana Dereza, Adrian Doyle, Priya Rani, Atul Ojha, Pádraic Moran and John McCrae
	TartuNLP @ SIGTYP 2024 Shared Task: Adapting XLM-RoBERTa for Ancient and Historical Languages Aleksei Dorkin and Kairit Sirts
	Heidelberg-Boston @ SIGTYP 2024 Shared Task: Enhancing Low-Resource Language Analysis With Character-Aware Hierarchical Transformers Frederick Riemenschneider and Kevin Krahn
	UDParse @ SIGTYP 2024 Shared Task : Modern Language Models for Historical Languages Johannes Heinecke

Friday, March 22, 2024 (continued)

	Allen Institute for AI @ SIGTYP 2024 Shared Task on Word Embedding Evaluation for Ancient and Historical Languages Lester James V. Miranda
17:00 - 17:30	*Typology and Human Language Processing*
	Syntactic dependency length shaped by strategic memory allocation Weijie Xu and Richard Futrell
	A Computational Model for the Assessment of Mutual Intelligibility Among Closely Related Languages Jessica Nieder and Johann-Mattis List
	Predicting Mandarin and Cantonese Adult Speakers' Eye-Movement Patterns in Natural Reading LI Junlin, Yu-Yin Hsu, Emmanuele Chersoni and Bo Peng
17:35 - 17:50	*Computational Morphology and Lexicography Modeling of Modern Standard Arabic Nominals (EACL Findings)*
17:50 - 18:00	*Best Paper Awards, Closing*

Syntactic dependency length shaped by strategic memory allocation

Weijie Xu
University of California, Irvine
weijie.xu@uci.edu

Richard Futrell
University of California, Irvine
rfutrell@uci.edu

Abstract

Human processing of nonlocal syntactic dependencies requires the engagement of limited working memory for encoding, maintenance, and retrieval. This process creates an evolutionary pressure for language to be structured in a way that keeps the subparts of a dependency closer to each other, an efficiency principle termed *dependency locality*. The current study proposes that such a dependency locality pressure can be modulated by the surprisal of the antecedent, defined as the first part of a dependency, due to strategic allocation of working memory. In particular, antecedents with novel and unpredictable information are prioritized for memory encoding, receiving more robust representation against memory interference and decay, and thus are more capable of handling longer dependency length. We examine this claim by analyzing dependency corpora of 11 languages, with word surprisal generated from GPT-3 language model. In support of our hypothesis, we find evidence for a positive correlation between dependency length and the antecedent surprisal in most of the languages in our analyses. A closer look into the dependencies with core arguments shows that this correlation consistently holds for subject relations but not for object relations.

1 Introduction

Language processing requires efficient use of bounded cognitive systems, creating evolutionary pressures that have been argued to shape the structure of human language (Gibson et al., 2019). In the domain of syntax, one source of evidence for this idea comes from the principle of dependency locality, which holds that linguistic units connected in a syntactic dependency tend to stay close in linear order, due to the limited resources of working memory (WM) to hold the subparts of a non-local dependency in working memory (Hawkins, 1994; Gibson, 1998, 2000; Ferrer-i-Cancho, 2004; Liu, 2008; Futrell et al., 2015, 2019; Temperley and Gildea, 2018; Futrell et al., 2020). With this basic finding, a natural next step is to see how far this efficiency-based account for dependency locality can go, with a more and more realistic characterization of the nature and constraints of WM.

We explore strategic memory allocation as one such constraint that may further shape the structure of syntactic dependencies. The idea is that limited WM resources are strategically allocated, subject to a trade-off between the economical investment of WM on each linguistic unit stored, and the minimization of potential cost in future processing tasks (Lieder and Griffiths, 2020; Lewis et al., 2014; Gershman et al., 2015). Specifically, we propose that linguistic units with novel and unpredictable information should receive prioritized WM resources for encoding and storage in memory, thus yielding more robust representation against memory interference and decay.

The result of this strategic memory allocation is that when an antecedent carries novel and unpredictable information, it can tolerate longer dependency length. In the current study, we test this hypothesis in 11 languages: Amharic, Danish, English, German, Italian, Japanese, Korean, Mandarin, Russian, Spanish, and Turkish. To preview the results, across all the dependency types, we find a general positive correlation between antecedent surprisal and dependency length for more than half of the languages in our analysis. A closer look into the dependencies with core arguments demonstrates that the effect consistently emerges for most of the languages in subject relations, but not in object relations.

2 Background

2.1 Dependency Locality

At the individual level, the processing of sentences with nonlocal dependencies requires active engage-

Proceedings of the 6th Workshop on Research in Computational Linguistic Typology and Multilingual NLP (SIGTYP 2024), pages 1–9
March 22, 2024

Language	Corpus	Genre	All Depends	Subject	Object
Amharic	ATT (Seyoum et al., 2018)	doc-by-doc	4,164	643	525
Danish	DDT (Johannsen et al., 2015)	sent-by-sent	45,976	4,203	3,963
English	GUM (Zeldes, 2017)	doc-by-doc	89,947	7,881	7,296
German	GSD (McDonald et al., 2013)	sent-by-sent	155,480	9,602	8,474
Italian	ISDT (Bosco et al., 2013)	doc-by-doc	208,939	10,323	11,735
Japanese	GSD (Tanaka et al., 2016)	sent-by-sent	113,771	5,005	4,018
Korean	Kaist (Chun et al., 2018)	doc-by-doc	154,609	9,855	24,690
Mandarin	GSDSimp (Nivre et al., 2020)	sent-by-sent	63,456	5,538	7,576
Russian	SynTagRus (Droganova et al., 2018)	doc-by-doc	329,745	32,822	25,065
Spanish	AnCora (Taulé et al., 2008)	doc-by-doc	333,728	21,472	31,143
Turkish	BOUN (Marşan et al., 2022)	sent-by-sent	45,914	3,861	4,680

Table 1: Dependency corpora used as datasets. 'Genre' refers to whether the texts in the corpus are organized as independent sentences (sent-by-sent), or as documents with larger coherent discourse size (doc-by-doc). 'All Depends' indicates the number of all the dependencies after data exclusion. 'Subject' is a subset of 'All Depends' and indicates the number of dependencies with subject relations. 'Object' indicates the number of dependencies with object relations.The original Russian corpus has over 1.2M tokens with over 600 documents; we randomly sampled 300 documents from the original corpus in our analysis in order to save the computational power.

ment of working memory. Consider the sentence with a nonlocal dependency as in (1b) compared to (1a). The language user needs to maintain the antecedent "nurse" active in WM for a longer period of time until it is retrieved later at the retrieval site "supervised." Under the Dependency Locality Theory (Gibson, 1998, 2000), the integration of the second part of the dependency should become increasingly difficult as the dependency length increases. This effect has been confirmed empirically in reading time studies (Bartek et al., 2011; Grodner and Gibson, 2005). This locality effect could be due to the memory decay of the antecedent's representation over time, or due to cumulative similarity-based interference introduced by the intervening materials between head and dependent (Lewis and Vasishth, 2005; Vasishth et al., 2019).

(1) a. The *nurse* supervised the administrator...

b. The *nurse* who was from the clinic in downtown LA supervised the administrator...

At the population level, this processing constraint functions as an evolutionary pressure that shapes language structure. It has been observed crosslinguistically that word order reflects the minimization of dependency length in general (Hawkins, 1994, 2004, 2014; Ferrer-i-Cancho, 2004; Liu, 2008; Futrell et al., 2015, 2020). For example, Futrell et al. (2020) point out the explanatory power of dependency locality principle for multiple typological phenomena, such as the contiguity of constituents, short-before-long and long-before-short constituent ordering preference, and the consistency in head direction.

2.2 Strategic Memory Allocation

Despite the general constraint of the limited memory capacity, WM is a highly flexible system that is dynamically optimized for the relevant cognitive tasks at hand or in the future (Sims et al., 2012; Sims, 2016; Van den Berg and Ma, 2018; Jakob and Gershman, 2023). One instantiation of this dynamic optimization of WM can be the strategic memory allocation: WM resources such as attention can be dynamically and strategically allocated in a way that prioritizes the information with novel and unexpected content given its context, resulting in higher memory precision and representation fidelity (Bruning and Lewis-Peacock, 2020).

Empirically, in the domain of language processing, deeper encoding for more informative referents have been shown to facilitate their retrieval later at the other side of the dependency (Hofmeister, 2011; Hofmeister and Vasishth, 2014; Karimi et al., 2019; Troyer et al., 2016). Theoretically, a more predictable unit is *a priori* more likely to be reconstructed successfully even if it is lost from memory, and thus if only a limited number of units can be stored, it would be less important to store the predictable ones, a dynamic observed in the sentence processing model of Hahn et al. (2022).

If WM resources can be dynamically and strategically allocated to prioritize novel and unexpected information, this can potentially shape the struc-

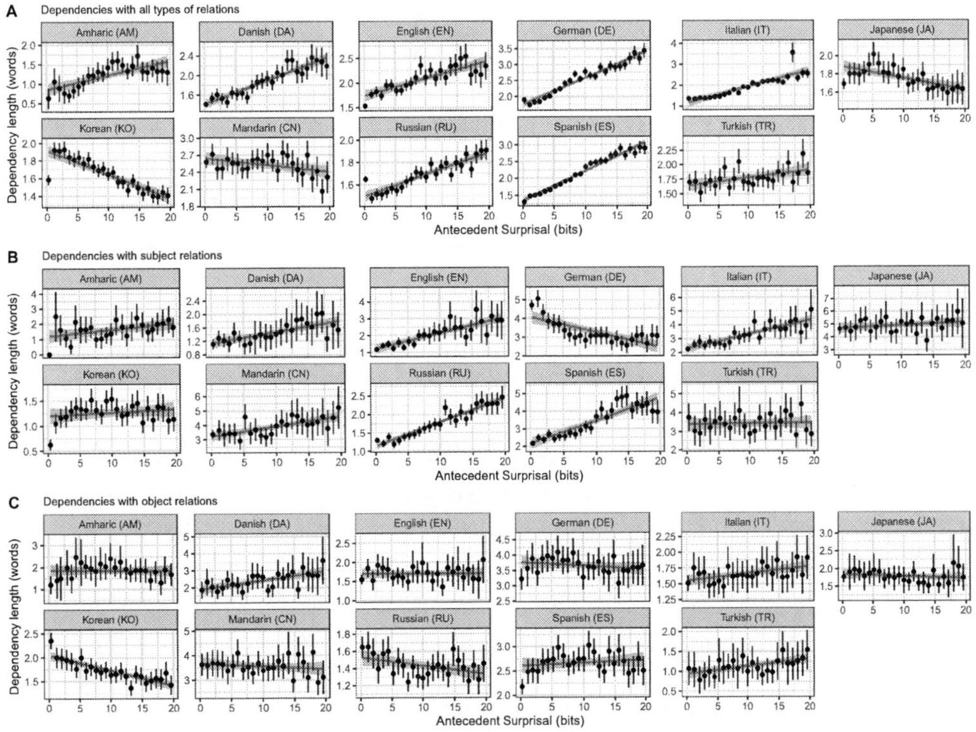

Figure 1: Average orthographic dependency length as a function of antecedent surprisal. Surprisal is binned into 25 categories, and the mean dependency length within each category is shown in black with a 95% confidence interval in blue. A linear fit to these points is shown in red.

ture of language by modulating the pressure of dependency locality. When the antecedent is less predictable but more informative, it should receive more WM resources and thus maintain a more robust memory representation, making it less likely to go through memory decay before it needs to be retrieved from memory at the other side of the dependency. Consequently, dependencies with less predictable antecedents are able to tolerate more intervening materials before the retrieval site, resulting in less pressure to put the subparts of a dependency local to each other, hence more likely to have longer dependency length.

3 Method

3.1 Data

We examine our hypothesis using the corpora taken from Universal Dependencies (UD) release 2.11 (Nivre et al., 2020), as described in Table 1. Some UD corpora consist of independent sentences, while others are organized document by document, thus providing longer and enriched discourse context for each token.

Token surprisal. For each token w in the dependency corpora, we obtain its surprisal $-\ln p(w|c)$ given the preceding context c using the GPT-3 base language model (`text-davinci-001`; Brown et al., 2020). We use the maximally allowed context window in the corresponding document or sentence. Due to the recent advancements in the performance of language models, they are increasingly applied to approximate human predictions in psycholinguistics literature (Levy, 2008). The surprisal generated from these models highly correlates with human processing difficulty indexed by behavioral measures such as reading times (Smith and Levy, 2013; Goodkind and Bicknell, 2018; Hao et al., 2020; Wilcox et al., 2020; Hoover et al., 2023), and this relationship has been shown to hold cross-linguistically (Wilcox et al., 2023; Xu et al., 2023).

Data transformation. Flat structures (e.g. foreign phrases, multiword proper names, fixed expressions, etc.) are merged such that the surprisal of the whole structure is the sum of all its components, and that the first word in the structure is treated as the head when calculating the dependency length with other sentence elements. Sen-

	Full Dataset		Subject Relations		Object Relations	
Language	L (words)	L (surprisal)	L (words)	L (surprisal)	L (words)	L (surprisal)
Amharic	$p = 0.175$	+	+	$p = 0.186$	−	$p = 0.876$
Danish	+	+	+	+	$p = 0.447$	+
English	+	+	+	+	$p = 0.743$	+
German	+	+	−	−	−	−
Italian	+	+	+	+	$p = 0.093$	+
Japanese	$p = 0.416$	$p = 0.775$	$p = 0.088$	$p = 0.985$	$p = 0.21$	$p = 0.94$
Korean	−	−	$p = 0.072$	$p = 0.156$	−	−
Mandarin	$p = 0.062$	$p = 0.331$	+	+	−	$p = 0.359$
Russian	$p = 0.395$	$p = 0.050$	+	+	−	$p = 0.454$
Spanish	+	+	+	+	$p = 0.058$	+
Turkish	$p = 0.161$	$p = 0.784$	−	$p = 0.59$	$p = 0.384$	$p = 0.083$

Table 2: Summary of statistical results for the effect of antecedent of surprisal on dependency length. "+" indicates a significant (at $p < 0.05$) positive correlation between antecedent surprisal and dependency length, while "−" indicates a significant negative correlation; p values are presented if the effect is not significant.

tences that are too short may have limited room for the dependency length to vary, so we exclude sentences containing less than five words. We exclude tokens that are punctuation. We also exclude tokens with a surprisal value greater than 20 bits. We then extract all the dependencies in which both the head and the dependent are spared from data exclusion. We also analyze two subsets of these dependencies: 1) a subset that only includes subject relations (marked as `nsubj` and `csubj`); and 2) a subset that only includes object relations (marked as `obj`, `iobj`, `ccomp`, and `xcomp`). These are considered core arguments in a sentence, whose head-dependent distance is less subject to grammatical constraints than other syntactic relations.

Dependency length. We analyze two variants of measures for dependency length L. The first variant takes L as the orthographic dependency length, measured as the number of intervening orthographic words between the head and the dependent. The second variant takes L as the sum of surprisal of all the intervening words. Instead of assuming that every word contributes to memory interference to the same extent, this information-theoretic dependency length is supposed to better handle low-informative words, such as function words, which induce less memory burden compared to high-informative content words (Gibson, 1998; Grodner and Gibson, 2005).

3.2 Statistical Analyses

For the full dataset, we fit linear mixed-effect models (Baayen et al., 2008) for each language to separately predict the two variants of dependency length L introduced above as a function of antecedent surprisal, with random slope and intercept by dependency type. We also include three control variables: sentence position in the text (if the corpus is doc-by-doc), sentence length (word counts of a sentence), and the antecedent position in the sentence. In the analyses of the two subsets of data with subject or object relations only, we fit a linear model with the same critical variable and control variables as above. All the continuous variables are z-scaled.

4 Results

Figure 1 shows the average orthographic dependency length as a function of antecedent surprisal, along with linear fits. The visualization for the information-theoretic dependency length yields similar patterns (see additional figure in Appendix). Table 2 summarizes the statistical results of all the six versions of analyses (two measures of dependency length L crossed with three datasets). The sign indicates the direction of the antecedent surprisal effect on dependency length, with a plus sign suggesting a significant positive correlation between antecedent surprisal and dependency length.[1]

For the analysis on the full dataset, Danish, English, German, Italian, and Spanish show significant positive effect of antecedent surprisal with both measures of dependency length. The effect is significant for Amharic only with the dependency

[1]Analysis code is available at `https://github.com/weijiexu-charlie/Dependency-length-strategic-memory-allocation`

length as surprisal. A significant negative effect of antecedent surprisal is found for Korean. The effect for other languages does not reach significance.

For subject relations, we find evidence for a positive effect of antecedent surprisal on dependency length for 7 out of 11 languages, namely Amharic, Danish, English, German, Italian, Mandarin, Russian, and Spanish. There is no significant effect for Japanese and Korean. For German and Turkish, however, the data support a negative antecedent surprisal effect. For object relations, there is little evidence for a positive antecedent surprisal effect on the orthographic dependency length, with the effect being significantly negative for Amharic, German, Korean, Mandarin, and Russian. For the dependency length as surprisal, there is a positive antecedent surprisal effect in Danish, English, Italian, and Spanish. But the effect is negative for German and Korean.

5 Discussion

In general, our results provide evidence for a positive correlation between antecedent surprisal and dependency length, indicating that dependencies whose antecedent is more surprising and informative are able to tolerate longer dependency length. This is especially true for subject relations, where 7 out of 11 languages in our analysis exhibit a positive antecedent surprisal effect on dependency length. For object relations, however, the data presents a mixed picture without clear support for an expected antecedent surprisal effect.

This asymmetry between the subject and the object can be due to the possibility that object relations may be under more grammatical pressure than subject relations to put head and dependent closer to each other. For example, according to the Accessibility Hierarchy proposed by Keenan and Comrie (1977) as a linguistic universal, the subject is more relativizable than the object crosslinguistically to form a relative clause.

It is worth noting that the correlation observed in the current study is compatible with some other theories as well. For example, the Uniform Information Density (UID) theory holds that language production should avoid abrupt fluctuation of information across linguistic units (Jaeger and Levy, 2006; Meister et al., 2021). Therefore, surprising antecedents may be followed by longer sequence of units for a smoother transition to the other side of the dependency, which is supposed to bear lower surprisal due to the high mutual information with its antecedent (Futrell et al., 2019). However, compared to UID, which is a computational-level theory (Marr, 1982), the strategic memory allocation proposed in the current study focuses on the processes more at the mechanistic level.

6 Conclusions

In a nutshell, we find empirical support for a positive correlation between the length of a dependency and the surprisal of its antecedent. A closer look into the dependencies with core arguments shows that this relationship consistently holds for subject relations, but not for the object, possibility due to the stronger grammatical constraint between the object and the verb. At the population level, this finding indicates that although working memory constraints exert a general pressure on language structure to organize in a way that minimizes dependency length, this pressure is further modulated by informativity. This crosslinguistic pattern is consistent with our hypothesis of strategic working memory allocation as an individual-level processing strategy, where less predictable but more informative linguistic units are prioritized in working memory to maintain a more robust representation against memory interference and decay, thus are more tolerant for longer dependency length.

Limitations

The results of the current study are contingent upon the reliability of the corpora and the language model we use. For the use of corpora, our analyses may be vulnerable to the potential inaccuracies in corpus annotations, especially for dependencies whose identity is ambiguous and controversial. In terms of the use of language model, as one of the state-of-the-art LLMs, GPT-3 provides high-quality estimation of token surprisal, especially in languages with substantial sample size, such as English. However, the accuracy of surprisal estimates may be compromised when the model's training data is limited, diminishing the extensibility of our analysis to understudied languages. This limitation is particularly relevant for languages of potential interest from a typological perspective.

References

R Harald Baayen, Douglas J Davidson, and Douglas M Bates. 2008. Mixed-effects modeling with crossed random effects for subjects and items. *Journal of Memory and Language*, 59(4):390–412.

Brian Bartek, Richard L Lewis, Shravan Vasishth, and Mason R Smith. 2011. In search of on-line locality effects in sentence comprehension. *Journal of Experimental Psychology: Learning, Memory, and Cognition*, 37(5):1178.

Cristina Bosco, Simonetta Montemagni, and Maria Simi. 2013. Converting Italian treebanks: Towards an Italian Stanford dependency treebank. In *Proceedings of the 7th Linguistic Annotation Workshop and Interoperability with Discourse*, pages 61–69, Sofia, Bulgaria. Association for Computational Linguistics.

Tom B Brown, Benjamin Mann, Nick Ryder, Melanie Subbiah, Jared Kaplan, Prafulla Dhariwal, Arvind Neelakantan, Pranav Shyam, Girish Sastry, Amanda Askell, et al. 2020. Language models are few-shot learners. *arXiv preprint arXiv:2005.14165*.

Allison L Bruning and Jarrod A Lewis-Peacock. 2020. Long-term memory guides resource allocation in working memory. *Scientific Reports*, 10(1):1–10.

Jayeol Chun, Na-Rae Han, Jena D Hwang, and Jinho D Choi. 2018. Building Universal Dependency Treebanks in Korean. In *Proceedings of the Eleventh International Conference on Language Resources and Evaluation (LREC 2018)*.

Kira Droganova, Olga Lyashevskaya, and Daniel Zeman. 2018. Data conversion and consistency of monolingual corpora: Russian UD treebanks. In *Proceedings of the 17th International Workshop on Treebanks and Linguistic Theories (TLT 2018)*, volume 155, pages 53–66.

Ramon Ferrer-i-Cancho. 2004. Euclidean distance between syntactically linked words. *Physical Review E*, 70(5):056135.

Richard Futrell, Roger P Levy, and Edward Gibson. 2020. Dependency locality as an explanatory principle for word order. *Language*, 96(2):371–412.

Richard Futrell, Kyle Mahowald, and Edward Gibson. 2015. Large-scale evidence of dependency length minimization in 37 languages. *Proceedings of the National Academy of Sciences*, 112(33):10336–10341.

Richard Futrell, Peng Qian, Edward Gibson, Evelina Fedorenko, and Idan Blank. 2019. Syntactic dependencies correspond to word pairs with high mutual information. In *Proceedings of the Fifth International Conference on Dependency Linguistics (Depling, SyntaxFest 2019)*, pages 3–13.

Samuel J Gershman, Eric J Horvitz, and Joshua B Tenenbaum. 2015. Computational rationality: A converging paradigm for intelligence in brains, minds, and machines. *Science*, 349(6245):273–278.

Edward Gibson. 1998. Linguistic complexity: Locality of syntactic dependencies. *Cognition*, 68(1):1–76.

Edward Gibson. 2000. The dependency locality theory: A distance-based theory of linguistic complexity. In Alec Marantz, Yasushi Miyashita, and Wayne O'Neil, editors, *Image, language, brain: Papers from the first mind articulation project symposium*, pages 94–126. The MIT Press.

Edward Gibson, Richard Futrell, Steven P Piantadosi, Isabelle Dautriche, Kyle Mahowald, Leon Bergen, and Roger Levy. 2019. How efficiency shapes human language. *Trends in Cognitive Sciences*, 23(5):389–407.

Adam Goodkind and Klinton Bicknell. 2018. Predictive power of word surprisal for reading times is a linear function of language model quality. In *Proceedings of the 8th Workshop on Cognitive Modeling and Computational Linguistics (CMCL 2018)*, pages 10–18, Salt Lake City, Utah. Association for Computational Linguistics.

Daniel Grodner and Edward Gibson. 2005. Consequences of the serial nature of linguistic input for sentenial complexity. *Cognitive Science*, 29(2):261–290.

Michael Hahn, Richard Futrell, Roger Levy, and Edward Gibson. 2022. A resource-rational model of human processing of recursive linguistic structure. *Proceedings of the National Academy of Sciences*, 119(43):e2122602119.

Yiding Hao, Simon Mendelsohn, Rachel Sterneck, Randi Martinez, and Robert Frank. 2020. Probabilistic predictions of people perusing: Evaluating metrics of language model performance for psycholinguistic modeling. In *Proceedings of the Workshop on Cognitive Modeling and Computational Linguistics*, pages 75–86, Online. Association for Computational Linguistics.

John A Hawkins. 1994. *A performance theory of order and constituency*. 73. Cambridge University Press.

John A Hawkins. 2004. *Efficiency and complexity in grammars*. Oxford University Press.

John A Hawkins. 2014. *Cross-linguistic variation and efficiency*. Oxford University Press.

Philip Hofmeister. 2011. Representational complexity and memory retrieval in language comprehension. *Language and Cognitive Processes*, 26(3):376–405.

Philip Hofmeister and Shravan Vasishth. 2014. Distinctiveness and encoding effects in online sentence comprehension. *Frontiers in Psychology*, 5:1237.

Jacob Louis Hoover, Morgan Sonderegger, Steven T Piantadosi, and Timothy J O'Donnell. 2023. The plausibility of sampling as an algorithmic theory of sentence processing. *Open Mind*, 7:350–391.

T Florian Jaeger and Roger Levy. 2006. Speakers optimize information density through syntactic reduction. *Advances in neural information processing systems*, 19.

Anthony MV Jakob and Samuel J Gershman. 2023. Rate-distortion theory of neural coding and its implications for working memory. *Elife*, 12:e79450.

Anders Johannsen, Héctor Martínez Alonso, and Barbara Plank. 2015. Universal dependencies for Danish. In *International Workshop on Treebanks and Linguistic Theories (TLT14)*, page 157.

Hossein Karimi, Michele Diaz, and Fernanda Ferreira. 2019. "A cruel king" is not the same as "a king who is cruel": Modifier position affects how words are encoded and retrieved from memory. *Journal of Experimental Psychology: Learning, Memory, and Cognition*, 45(11):2010.

Edward L. Keenan and Bernard Comrie. 1977. Noun phrase accessibility and universal grammar. *Linguistic Inquiry*, 8(1):63–99.

Roger Levy. 2008. Expectation-based syntactic comprehension. *Cognition*, 106(3):1126–1177.

Richard L Lewis, Andrew Howes, and Satinder Singh. 2014. Computational rationality: Linking mechanism and behavior through bounded utility maximization. *Topics in Cognitive Science*, 6(2):279–311.

Richard L Lewis and Shravan Vasishth. 2005. An activation-based model of sentence processing as skilled memory retrieval. *Cognitive Science*, 29:375–419.

Falk Lieder and Thomas L Griffiths. 2020. Resource-rational analysis: Understanding human cognition as the optimal use of limited computational resources. *Behavioral and Brain Sciences*, 43:e1.

Haitao Liu. 2008. Dependency distance as a metric of language comprehension difficulty. *Journal of Cognitive Science*, 9(2):159–191.

David Marr. 1982. *Vision: A Computational Investigation into the Human Representation and Processing of Visual Information*. Henry Holt and Co., Inc., New York, NY, USA.

Büşra Marşan, Salih Furkan Akkurt, Muhammet Şen, Merve Gürbüz, Onur Güngör, Şaziye Betül Özateş, Suzan Üsküdarlı, Arzucan Özgür, Tunga Güngör, and Balkız Öztürk. 2022. Enhancements to the BOUN Treebank Reflecting the Agglutinative Nature of Turkish. *arXiv preprint arXiv:2207.11782*.

Ryan McDonald, Joakim Nivre, Yvonne Quirmbach-Brundage, Yoav Goldberg, Dipanjan Das, Kuzman Ganchev, Keith Hall, Slav Petrov, Hao Zhang, Oscar Täckström, Claudia Bedini, Núria Bertomeu Castelló, and Jungmee Lee. 2013. Universal Dependency annotation for multilingual parsing. In *Proceedings of the 51st Annual Meeting of the Association for Computational Linguistics (Volume 2: Short Papers)*, pages 92–97, Sofia, Bulgaria. Association for Computational Linguistics.

Clara Meister, Tiago Pimentel, Patrick Haller, Lena Jäger, Ryan Cotterell, and Roger Levy. 2021. Revisiting the Uniform Information Density hypothesis. In *Proceedings of the 2021 Conference on Empirical Methods in Natural Language Processing*, pages 963–980, Online and Punta Cana, Dominican Republic. Association for Computational Linguistics.

Joakim Nivre, Marie-Catherine de Marneffe, Filip Ginter, Jan Hajič, Christopher D. Manning, Sampo Pyysalo, Sebastian Schuster, Francis Tyers, and Daniel Zeman. 2020. Universal Dependencies v2: An evergrowing multilingual treebank collection. In *Proceedings of the Twelfth Language Resources and Evaluation Conference*, pages 4034–4043, Marseille, France. European Language Resources Association.

Binyam Ephrem Seyoum, Yusuke Miyao, and Baye Yimam Mekonnen. 2018. Universal Dependencies for Amharic. In *Proceedings of the Eleventh International Conference on Language Resources and Evaluation (LREC 2018)*, Miyazaki, Japan. European Language Resources Association (ELRA).

Chris R Sims. 2016. Rate–distortion theory and human perception. *Cognition*, 152:181–198.

Chris R Sims, Robert A Jacobs, and David C Knill. 2012. An ideal observer analysis of visual working memory. *Psychological Review*, 119(4):807.

Nathaniel J Smith and Roger Levy. 2013. The effect of word predictability on reading time is logarithmic. *Cognition*, 128(3):302–319.

Takaaki Tanaka, Yusuke Miyao, Masayuki Asahara, Sumire Uematsu, Hiroshi Kanayama, Shinsuke Mori, and Yuji Matsumoto. 2016. Universal Dependencies for Japanese. In *Proceedings of the Tenth International Conference on Language Resources and Evaluation (LREC'16)*, pages 1651–1658, Portorož, Slovenia. European Language Resources Association (ELRA).

Mariona Taulé, Maria Antònia Martí, and Marta Recasens. 2008. AnCora: Multilevel annotated corpora for Catalan and Spanish. In *Proceedings of 6th International Conference on Language Resources and Evaluation*, volume 2008, pages 96–101.

David Temperley and Daniel Gildea. 2018. Minimizing syntactic dependency lengths: Typological/cognitive universal? *Annual Review of Linguistics*, 4:67–80.

Melissa Troyer, Philip Hofmeister, and Marta Kutas. 2016. Elaboration over a discourse facilitates retrieval in sentence processing. *Frontiers in Psychology*, 7:374.

Ronald Van den Berg and Wei Ji Ma. 2018. A resource-rational theory of set size effects in human visual working memory. *ELife*, 7:e34963.

Shravan Vasishth, Bruno Nicenboim, Felix Engelmann, and Frank Burchert. 2019. Computational models of retrieval processes in sentence processing. *Trends in Cognitive Sciences*, 23(11):968–982.

Ethan G Wilcox, Tiago Pimentel, Clara Meister, Ryan Cotterell, and Roger P Levy. 2023. Testing the predictions of surprisal theory in 11 languages. *Transactions of the Association for Computational Linguistics*, 11:1451–1470.

Ethan Gotlieb Wilcox, Jon Gauthier, Jennifer Hu, Peng Qian, and Roger P. Levy. 2020. On the predictive power of neural language models for human real-time comprehension behavior. In *Proceedings of the 42nd Annual Meeting of the Cognitive Science Society*, page 1707–1713.

Weijie Xu, Jason Chon, Tianran Liu, and Richard Futrell. 2023. The linearity of the effect of surprisal on reading times across languages. In *Findings of the Association for Computational Linguistics: EMNLP 2023*, pages 15711–15721, Singapore. Association for Computational Linguistics.

Amir Zeldes. 2017. The GUM corpus: Creating multilayer resources in the classroom. *Language Resources and Evaluation*, 51(3):581–612.

A Appendix

Additional figure:

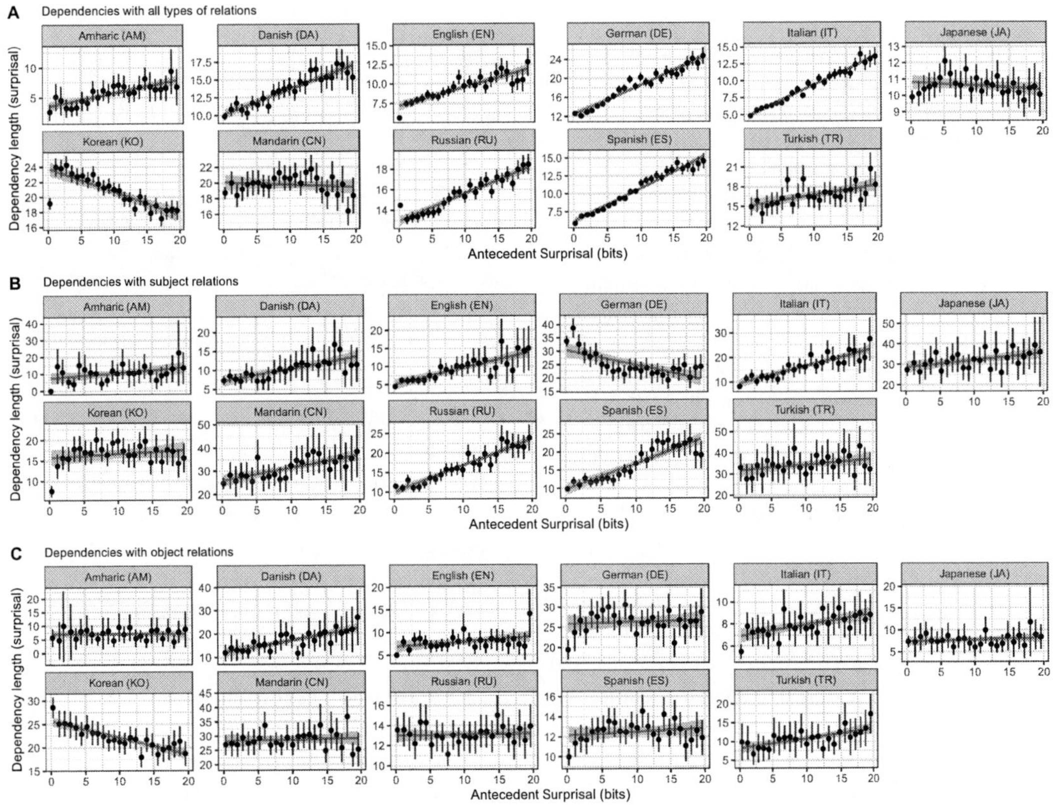

Figure 2: Average information-theoretic dependency length as a function of antecedent surprisal with subject relations. Surprisal is binned into 25 categories, and the mean dependency length within each category is shown in black with a 95% confidence interval in blue. A linear fit to these points is shown in red.

GUIDE: Creating Semantic Domain Dictionaries for Low-Resource Languages

Jonathan Janetzki[a], **Gerard de Melo**[a],
Joshua Nemecek[b], and **Daniel Whitenack**[c*]
[a]Hasso Plattner Institute / University of Potsdam
[b]SIL International, [c]Prediction Guard
jonathan.janetzki@student.hpi.de, gerard.demelo@hpi.de,
joshua_nemecek@sil.org, dan@predictionguard.com

Abstract

Over 7,000 of the world's 7,168 living languages are still low-resourced. This paper aims to narrow the language documentation gap by creating multiparallel dictionaries, clustered by SIL's semantic domains. This task is new for machine learning and has previously been done manually by native speakers. We propose GUIDE, a language-agnostic tool that uses a GNN to create and populate semantic domain dictionaries, using seed dictionaries and Bible translations as a parallel text corpus. Our work sets a new benchmark, achieving an exemplary average precision of 60% in eight zero-shot evaluation languages and predicting an average of 2,400 dictionary entries. We share the code, model, multilingual evaluation data, and new dictionaries with the research community.[1]

1 Introduction

There are 7,168 languages spoken on Earth according to the Ethnologue (Eberhard et al., 2023). Creating dictionaries is the first step toward documenting languages, and it is also one of the most effective ways to preserve languages and cultures (Abah et al., 2018). A successful approach to creating dictionaries for low-resource languages is *rapid word collection* (Boerger, 2017): A team of linguists travels to spend 2–3 weeks with around 60 indigenous people and guides them through a questionnaire. Each question pertains to a particular *semantic domain* (Moe, 2010) that groups words with related meanings. In the following, we call this membership word-*Semantic Domain Question* (SDQ) link. Since this manual collection process involves traveling, it is expensive and sometimes even impossible (e.g., due to the risk of spreading diseases). This work investigates to what extent automated solutions can be an alternative means to procure such dictionary information at a greater speed and lower cost.

(1) What are the parts of a bird?

- ***èfuwu, èkoa, àwàdawo,*** *nusuɖùtɔ,*
  (feathers, gizzard, wings, greedy)

  xèvia, ***àzì, àwàda,***
  (bird, egg, wing)

Figure 1: New dictionary entries: GUIDE linked seven words (bold) in the low-resource language Mina-Gen to an SDQ (top). Five are correct (blue), and two are incorrect (orange and underlined; labeled by a Mina-Gen speaker). Words in parentheses are translations.

The key idea of this paper is to automatically create semantic domain dictionaries for low-resource languages and fill in missing entries using a multilingual parallel text corpus of Bible translations, along with existing semantic domain dictionaries.

Our paper makes the following contributions:

- **Dictionary creation.** We propose the language-agnostic tool *Graph-based Unified Indigenous Dictionary Engine* (GUIDE), which links words in 20 languages and seven language families to their SDQs. It achieves state-of-the-art performance and has an average precision of 65% (see Figure 1). To the best of our knowledge, we propose the first automated approach to address this task.
- **Language flexibility.** To build a dictionary for a language, GUIDE requires only a Bible translation in that language, which is accessible in a verse-aligned format for at least 833 (Åkerman et al., 2023) languages. GUIDE can also be adapted to build dictionaries from any other parallel text.
- **Richer dictionaries.** We have predicted 32,000 new word-SDQ links for twelve languages with existing dictionaries that can en-

[*]Work done while the author was at SIL International.
[1]Repository: https://github.com/janetzki/GUIDE

Proceedings of the 6th Workshop on Research in Computational Linguistic Typology and Multilingual NLP (SIGTYP 2024), pages 10–24
March 22, 2024 ©2024 Association for Computational Linguistics

rich *FieldWorks Language Explorer* (FLEx)[2] (if verified by a native speaker). Three of these languages are low-resourced.

- **New dictionaries.** We have predicted 19,000 word-SDQ links for eight languages with little to no pre-existing dictionary entries (see Figure 1). While these require further validation by a native speaker, they can be a useful resource, given that seven of the languages are low-resourced.

2 Background

Before describing the task in more detail, we introduce key resources and terms.

2.1 SIL's Semantic Domains

SIL's semantic domains (Moe, 2010) are a language-agnostic, standardized taxonomy to create dictionaries that mirror arbitrary aspects of the world, arranging words in 1,783 semantic domains, which are in turn divided into one or more SDQs. For each SDQ, the dictionaries list corresponding words. Semantic domains, SDQs, and words form a tree-structured graph[3], shown in Appendix A.

Each semantic domain consists of an *identifier* (ID) (e.g., "*5.6.2*"), a name (e.g., "*Bathe*"), a short description, one or more SDQs, and a list of entries (matching words or phrases) for each SDQ. In the following, we use the notation "*5.6.2-4*" as SDQ ID for the 4th question of semantic domain 5.6.2.

2.2 Defining "Low-Resource Language"

We follow the NLLB Team's (2022) definition of "low-resource languages", assuming that every language that is not listed as one of the 53 high-resource languages in their FLORES-200 dataset (Goyal et al., 2022; Guzmán et al., 2019) is a low-resource language.

3 Related Work

Existing approaches to creating dictionaries address different sets of languages and map words to ontologies or words of other languages.

The *Universal Wordnet* (UWN) is a graph-structured knowledge base for more than 200 languages that de Melo and Weikum (2009) automatically generated. They used several data sources, especially existing bilingual dictionaries and to a limited extent also parallel corpora. As a scaffold, they used *Princeton WordNet* (Fellbaum, 2000), which provides a semantic hierarchy of English terms, and they enriched it with more than 1.5 million new semantic links for more than 800,000 words. Our work has a similar goal, as we investigate how to create and enrich another linguistic resource automatically. We use the semantic domains as a scaffold and focus on low-resource languages, for which we assume only a small amount of parallel text.

Alnajjar et al. (2022) show how to find new translations of words in three endangered Uralic languages. Their key idea is to construct a graph of words in these and other languages, with known translations as edges. An advantage of their approach is that it does not require parallel texts or word alignment. By predicting missing links in this graph, they built new bilingual dictionaries that help preserve these endangered languages. Similarly, we build a graph in which words in different languages are separate nodes. But there are two important differences:

1. GUIDE also builds dictionaries for languages without labeled data.
2. We group words by their SDQs instead of predicting word-to-word translations. This approach allows us to build highly *multiparallel* dictionaries because words often have no 1:1 translations across languages but have different semantic ranges. "*Multiparallel*" means that the dictionaries are not mono- or bilingual but follow the same structure in all languages. SDQs provide for this flexibility.

Based on the reviewed related work on dictionary creation, we can summarize the research gap as follows: There is a need to create highly multiparallel dictionaries for low-resource languages without labeled data. We address this gap by using existing parallel text.

4 Dataset

We next describe the source of our parallel text, the 20 languages that we selected for our dataset, and its size.

[2]FLEx is a tool to document and analyze languages and the most common tool used with Moe's (Moe, 2010) semantic domains. The FieldWorks page provides a more detailed description of FLEx: `https://software.sil.org/fieldworks/flex` (visited on 2023-10-16).

[3]The entire hierarchy of semantic domains can be explored at the official page: `https://semdom.org/v4/1` (visited on 2023-10-09).

	Language information				Bible translations		Dicts.
Language	ISO	# Speakers	Language family	Res.	Sample	# V.	# Entries
Development							
Bengali	ben	273M	Indo-European	High	আলো হোক (*āelā ehāka*)	31k	0.91k
Chinese (simplified)	cmn	1.14B	Sino-Tiebetan	High	要有光 (*yào yǒu guāng*)	31k	24k
English	eng	1.46B	Indo-European	High	Let there be light	37k	26k
French	fra	310M	Indo-European	High	Que la lumière soit	37k	30k
Hindi	hin	610M	Indo-European	High	उजियाला हो (*ujiyālā ho*)	31k	22k
Indonesian	ind	199M	Austronesian	High	Jadilah terang	11k	11k
Kupang Malay	mkn	350k	Creole (Malay-based)	Low	Musti ada taráng	9.8k	0.33k
Malayalam	mal	37.4M	Dravidian	Low	പ്രകാശം ഉണ്ടാകട്ടെ (*prakāśa uṇṭākaṭṭe*)	31k	25k
Nepali	npi	25.6M	Indo-European	Low	उज्यालो होस् (*ujyālo hos*)	31k	14k
Portuguese	por	260M	Indo-European	High	Que haja luz	31k	21k
Spanish	spa	559M	Indo-European	High	Sea la luz	37k	29k
Swahili	swh	71.6M	Niger-Congo	High	na kuwe nuru	31k	5.2k
Evaluation (zero-shot)							
German	deu	133M	Indo-European	High	Es werde Licht	31k	0
Hiri Motu	hmo	95.0k	Austronesian	Low	Diari ia vara namo	31k	0
Igbo	ibo	30.9M	Niger-Congo	Low	Ka ìhè dị	31k	0
Mina-Gen	gej	620k	Niger-Congo	Low	Kɛ̃klɛ̃ ne va e mè	35k	0
Motu	meu	39.0k	Austronesian	Low	Diari aine vara	31k	0
South Azerbaijani	azb	14.9M	Turkic	Low	Qoy işıq olsun	31k	0
Tok Pisin	tpi	4.13M	Creole (English-based)	Low	Lait i mas kamap	36k	0
Yoruba	yor	45.9M	Niger-Congo	Low	Jẹ́ kí ìmọ́lẹ̀ kí ó wà	31k	0

Table 1: Language information and dataset size: Language name, ISO 639 code (Eberhard et al., 2023), Number of speakers (Eberhard et al., 2023), Language family (Eberhard et al., 2023), and "resourcefulness" for the 20 languages in our dataset (defined in subsection 2.2). "Dicts." means "Semantic domain dictionaries" and "V." means "Verses". The matched number of words refers to the number of dictionary entries that also appear as words in the respective Bible translation. All samples have the same meaning. Text in parentheses shows transliterations of non-Latin scripts. Appendix B lists the Bible translations' source URLs.

4.1 The eBible Corpus

Åkerman et al. (2023) compiled the eBible corpus, which covers 833 languages from 75 language families, including languages that are considered extremely low-resourced. Each Bible translation in the eBible corpus is a text file with one line per verse (i.e., the corpus is verse-aligned).

Our dataset covers 20 languages in total: twelve development (i.e., training) languages and eight zero-shot evaluation languages. The difference between the two is that our dataset also contains semantic domain dictionaries for the development languages, which serve as labels, while there are no labels for the evaluation dataset.

4.2 Selected Languages

Table 1 displays the twelve languages that we use to train our model and the eight zero-shot evaluation languages that we use for testing. We chose languages based on the availability of data, the availability of language speakers for evaluation, and the language family (seeking to cover a broad spectrum).

4.3 Dataset Size

Table 1 further shows the size of our dataset for each of these languages, measured in terms of the number of verses in the Bible translations as a parallel text corpus and the number of semantic domains, which serve as labels. FLEx[4] provides the semantic domain dictionaries.

[4] A list of languages with existing semantic domain dictionaries is on this FieldWorks page: https://software.sil.org/fieldworks/download/localizations/ (visited on 2023-10-16).

5 Dictionary Creation with GUIDE

We now describe the GUIDE technique to induce dictionary entries for semantic domains based on a graph neural network.

5.1 Graph Induction

We transform our dataset into a graph, in which each node is a word in one of the 20 languages. The unique key of each node is its language code and the word itself (e.g., "*eng: grandchild*"). We hence use the term "*node*" as a synonym for "*word*" because each word becomes a node in the *Multilingual Alignment Graph* (MAG) (ImaniGooghari et al., 2022) that we build. The edges are the alignments between these words. We first create a *raw MAG*, which uses absolute word alignment counts from the parallel corpora as edge weights. We then transform it into the *final MAG*, which uses normalized edge weights and contains only a filtered subset of the raw MAG's nodes and edges.

Figure 2 shows the neighborhood of the Mina-Gen word "*màmayɔviwoa*" (grandchild of a female person, according to a Mina-Gen speaker) in the final MAG. Four words from the development languages have a link to an SDQ, while the Mina-Gen (zero-shot evaluation language) word does not.

GUIDE's preprocessing pipeline converts our dataset into the raw MAG and converts the raw MAG into the final MAG. Appendix C visualizes the individual steps. Note that we do not remove stop words.

5.1.1 Tokenization

The first step of our preprocessing pipeline is tokenization. Depending on the language, we use different tokenizers.

Stanza tokenizer. A *Stanza* (Qi et al., 2020) tokenizer exists for eight of the 20 languages in our dataset: Chinese (simplified), English, French, Hindi, Indonesian, Portuguese, Spanish, and German. All of them are high-resource languages.

SentencePiece. If the Stanza toolkit does not provide a tokenizer, we use a language-agnostic tokenizer. For six agglutinative languages (Bengali, Malayalam, Nepali, Swahili, South Azerbaijani, and Igbo), we invoke *SentencePiece* (Kudo and Richardson, 2018) to identify subwords. We train the SentencePiece tokenizer for each of these six languages with a vocabulary size of 10,000.

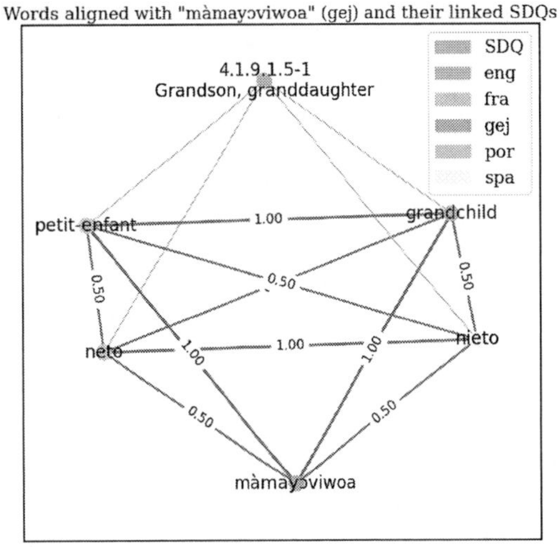

Figure 2: A subgraph from the final MAG showing the 1-hop neighborhood of the Mina-Gen word "*màmayɔviwoa*": The gray edges are word alignments with their normalized strength. Edges with higher strengths are thicker. The blue edges are SDQ links. The shown SDQ 4.1.9.1.5-1 is "*What words refer to the children of your children?*" The SDQ is shown here as a separate node, although it is technically part of the word nodes' feature vectors. To improve readability, the graph excludes some languages.

Punctuation mark splitting. If we cannot use Stanza, and the language is not agglutinative, we resort to simply splitting at punctuation marks (including whitespace). Specifically, we use such punctuation mark splitting for Kupang Malay, Hiri Motu, Mina-Gen, Motu, Tok Pisin, and Yoruba.

5.1.2 Term Normalization

Multi-Word Terms. For each language covered by the Stanza toolkit (Qi et al., 2020), we perform additional preprocessing steps: *Part-of-Speech* (POS)-Tagging, *Multi-Word Token* (MWT) expansion (only for French, Indonesian, Portuguese, Spanish, and German), and lemmatization. MWT expansion merges common combinations of tokens. It produces, for example, "*arc-en-ciel*" (rainbow) in French and "*guarda-costa*" (coastguard) in Portuguese.

Case Normalization. We normalize the words in all languages with Latin script by lowercasing them.

5.1.3 Edge Induction

Word-SDQ Matching. For all languages in our development dataset, we assign all matching SDQs to each word. We perform this matching by simply looking for exact matches in the semantic domain dictionary for the respective language.

Word Alignment. The core assumption of this paper is that words with similar meanings would be aligned. Similar to Imani Googhari et al. (2022), we use the Eflomal statistical word aligner (Östling and Tiedemann, 2016) to generate bilingual alignments for each language pair in our dataset, except for pairs of two zero-shot evaluation languages because both have no labels. We post-process the unidirectional alignments of Eflomal with atools[5] and the *grow-diag-final-and* (GDFA) heuristic (Koehn et al., 2005) to obtain symmetric bilingual alignments. We also aggregate all alignments by word, resulting in the raw MAG.

5.1.4 Graph Refinement

Three processing steps convert our raw MAG to the final MAG.

Edge Weight Normalization. In the raw MAG, each edge between two word nodes u and v has a weight $w_{\text{raw}}(u, v) \in \mathbb{N}^+$ that we convert to a normalized weight $w_{\text{norm}}(u, v) \in (0, 1]$:

$$w_{\text{norm}}(u, v) = 2\,\frac{w_{\text{raw}}(u, v)}{S_{L(v)}(u) + S_{L(u)}(v)}$$

where $S_{L(v)}(u)$ is the strength of node u concerning the language of v, specifically the sum of the edge weights of all edges from word u to a word in language v.

Edge Weight Filtering. To reduce noisy alignments, we remove all edges (u, v) with a weight $w_{\text{norm}}(u, v) < 0.2$.

Isolated Node Removal. As the final preprocessing step, we remove all words from the graph that have no edge to a word in the development dataset, including words from such development languages. We call such words *isolated* even though they may have neighbors in a zero-shot evaluation language. This process reduces the number of nodes in the MAG by 52% – from 414,964 to 199,605, which is the final number of nodes in the MAG.

5.2 Graph Neural Network

GUIDE uses a *Graph Neural Network* (GNN) (Scarselli et al., 2009) to perform a massively multi-class multi-label classification. Each class is one of 7,425 SDQs.

5.2.1 Node Features

We train the GNN by representing each node with a set of features, using two main types of node features (Duong et al., 2019): graph structural features and word meaning features.

Graph structural features. Inspired by Imani et al. (2022), we incorporate *node degree* and *weighted node degree* (i.e., the sum of adjacent weights) as additional graph structural information. These two features are continuous numbers.

Word meaning features. We further incorporate *SDQ count* and *SDQ link* features. While the SDQ count is an integer (stored as a continuous number), the SDQ links are a multi-hot vector with 7,425 dimensions (i.e., these links are categorical features). In total, each node/word receives a vector with 7,428 feature values.

5.2.2 Model Architecture

The GNN adopts a *Graph Convolutional Network* (GCN) (Kipf and Welling, 2017) architecture, as implemented in *PyTorch Geometric* (Fey and Lenssen, 2019). Appendix C visualizes its fairly simple architecture. After adding the node features to the final MAG, the single-layer GCN (a *GCNConv*[6] layer) aggregates the features of each node's neighbors. The results are 7,425 scores per node, one for each SDQ. We normalize these scores with *sigmoid* as a non-linear output activation function. Finally, we apply a threshold, accepting only word-SDQ links with a score ≥ 0.999. The GCNConv layer has 55,160,325 parameters in total.

Modified Identity Matrix Initialization. After initializing the weight matrix and bias vector of our model's GCN layer with small random weights, we overwrite parts of it. Our initialization strategy is similar to an identity initialization, which uses an identity matrix as a weight matrix.

Our weight matrix has the shape 7,428 $\times$ 7,425 (see Section 5.2.1). Of the 7,428 input features, 7,425 are a multi-hot vector that encodes the SDQ links. We modify the identity initialization by overwriting the diagonal of this 7,425 $\times$ 7,425 submatrix with large weights (50.0). We also initialize the entire bias vector with low weights (-5.0). Thus,

[5] fast-align repository: https://github.com/clab/fast_align (visited on 2023-10-20)

[6] PyTorch Geometric documentation: https://pytorch-geometric.readthedocs.io/en/latest/generated/torch_geometric.nn.conv.GCNConv.html (visited on 2023-10-10)

during optimization, the learning process starts at the point that a word can e.g. belong to the SDQ "*What words refer to the sun?*" only if at least one neighbor does.

Soft F_1 Loss. As the loss function, we use the soft F_1 loss[7]. The soft F_1 loss uses continuous ("*soft*") instead of discrete values.

6 Experimental Setup

This section provides details about the environment in which we executed GUIDE and how we evaluated it.

6.1 Configuration

We split our development data with a random 80%/10%/10% node split. We train the model ten times in a range of 30 to 40 epochs on the development dataset with a batch size of 6,000 and a learning rate of 0.05 using *Adam* optimization (Kingma and Ba, 2014). We use early stopping after five epochs with a warm-up time of 30 epochs.

Hardware. We run all experiments on an *ASUS ESC8000 G4* with 500 GB of RAM, two *AMD Intel Xeon Silver 4214 processors* with twelve cores and 2.20 GHz, and eight *NVIDIA Quadro RTX A6000* (each having 48 GB VRAM) GPUs. We train the model on a single GPU. The entire training process takes less than 30 minutes and the inference time is approximately ten milliseconds per word.

6.2 Evaluation Setup

We use two evaluation methods: evaluation on the incomplete semantic domain dictionaries (dataset-based) and manual evaluation (questionnaire-based).

Dataset-based Evaluation. In the calculation of soft F_1 loss as well as precision, recall, and F_1 score, we ignore "empty" SDQs. An empty SDQ is an SDQ that has no assigned words in the dataset in a specific language. Ignoring empty questions allows us to evaluate our model even using incomplete semantic domain dictionaries.

Human Evaluation using Questionnaires. For each language, we built one questionnaire to evaluate 100 – 120 random and shuffled predicted word-SDQ links. We recruited human annotators who speak the respective languages, in part by seeking out language-specific online fora and communities. The human annotators who answered the questionnaires could select only "*yes*" or "*no*" for each pair. We always consider only the first 100 answers in the evaluation.

Appendix D lists the URLs to the 20 completed questionnaires. To clarify the SDQs, we also provided a list of valid English answers for each SDQ (except in the English questionnaire). The 14 languages for which a tokenizer or lemmatizer could change a word's spelling (see Section 5.1.1 and Section 5.1.2) also included this note: *"Please also answer "yes" if there is a typo but you still recognize a matching word."* An example of a preprocessing-related "*typo*" is the German word "*Hüfte*" (hip), which became "*huft*". This word does not exist because the Stanza lemmatizer applied stemming.

7 Evaluation

This section evaluates GUIDE's performance, shows the results of an ablation study, and discusses the findings.

7.1 Results

Table 2 shows the evaluation results. We include a random baseline, as we are not aware of any other approach to automatically link words from low-resource languages to SDQs. For each word-SDQ pair, the random classifier predicts an existing word-SDQ link with a probability of 50%. There are $N = 199,605$ words in the MAG with 81,632 links to SDQs. Therefore, the random classifier predicts 741 million ($N \times 7,425/2$) word-SDQ links, of which 40,816 are correct. This ratio leads to a precision of 0.00006. The recall is 0.5, and the F_1 score is 0.0001.

7.2 Ablation Study

Table 3 shows how GUIDE's (dataset-based) performance changes when components are removed.

Interestingly, four components harm the model's F_1 score: the isolated node removal and all features of the node feature vector, but the SDQ link feature.

7.3 Discussion of the Results

GUIDE predicted 71,094 word-SDQ links in total, of which 19,166 (37%) belong to zero-shot evaluation languages. 31,873 (62%) of the links predicted for the development languages are new. Because the total number of matched words in the MAG is 199,605, the model predicts one word-SDQ link

[7]Our implementation is inspired by this GitHub page: `https://gist.github.com/SuperShinyEyes/dcc68a08ff8b615442e3bc6a9b55a354` (visited on 2023-10-16).

Language	Evaluation with dataset			Manual evaluation	
	Precision	Recall	F_1	Precision	# Predicted links
Random baseline	0.00	**0.500**	0.000	n/a	741,033,563
Development					
Bengali	0.22 ± 0.11	0.002 ± 0.001	0.004 ± 0.003	0.56	2,809 (2,770)
Chinese (simplified)	0.17 ± 0.02	0.014 ± 0.002	0.026 ± 0.004	0.34	5,752 (**5,036**)
English	**0.63** ± 0.02	**0.125** ± 0.006	**0.208** ± 0.009	**0.86**	7,119 (2,314)
French	0.59 ± 0.03	0.097 ± 0.005	0.167 ± 0.008	0.78	6,993 (2,527)
Hindi	0.25 ± 0.02	0.029 ± 0.003	0.051 ± 0.006	0.78	3,914 (2,835)
Indonesian	0.34 ± 0.05	0.035 ± 0.005	0.064 ± 0.009	0.77	1,799 (1,068)
Kupang Malay	0.14 ± 0.05	0.013 ± 0.005	0.024 ± 0.009	0.79	1,440 (1,351)
Malayalam	0.10 ± 0.03	0.015 ± 0.004	0.026 ± 0.007	0.45	2,768 (2,480)
Nepali	0.20 ± 0.01	0.022 ± 0.002	0.039 ± 0.004	0.38	2,641 (2,156)
Portuguese	0.43 ± 0.02	0.088 ± 0.006	0.146 ± 0.009	**0.86**	6,759 (3,737)
Spanish	0.59 ± 0.02	0.090 ± 0.005	0.155 ± 0.008	0.84	**7,614** (3,579)
Swahili	0.33 ± 0.04	0.018 ± 0.003	0.033 ± 0.005	0.75	2,320 (2,020)
Evaluation (zero-shot)					
German	n/a	n/a	n/a	0.67	**5,022**
Hiri Motu	n/a	n/a	n/a	0.62	1,190
Igbo	n/a	n/a	n/a	0.45	1,405
Mina-Gen	n/a	n/a	n/a	**0.80**	3,063
Motu	n/a	n/a	n/a	0.32	2,731
South Azerbaijani	n/a	n/a	n/a	0.58	2,238
Tok Pisin	n/a	n/a	n/a	0.69	880
Yoruba	n/a	n/a	n/a	0.63	2,637
Averages					
Development set	0.33 ± 0.04	0.046 ± 0.004	0.079 ± 0.007	0.68 ± 0.19	4,327 ± 2,338
Zero-shot evaluation set	n/a	n/a	n/a	0.60 ± 0.15	2,396 ± 1,324
Stanza	**0.43** ± 0.02	**0.068** ± 0.005	**0.117** ± 0.008	**0.74** ± 0.17	**5,622** ± 1,975
SentencePiece	0.21 ± 0.05	0.014 ± 0.003	0.026 ± 0.005	0.53 ± 0.13	2,364 ± 524
Punctuation mark split	0.14 ± 0.05	0.013 ± 0.005	0.024 ± 0.009	0.64 ± 0.18	1,990 ± 927
Total	0.33 ± 0.04	0.046 ± 0.004	0.079 ± 0.007	0.65 ± 0.18	3,555 ± 2,180

Table 2: Evaluation results: For each development language, cells with "±" show the average value of ten runs and the standard deviation. In the six bottom rows, "±" shows the average and the respective standard deviation. The six "average" rows show the average values for the development set, zero-shot evaluation set, and the languages tokenized with Stanza, SentencePiece, and punctuation mark splitting, respectively (see Section 5.1.1), as well as the average of all languages. The number of predicted word-SDQ links in the rightmost column is only from the run that we used to create the questionnaires. The number in parentheses is the number of new links. The highest values in each category are bolded.

per 2.8 words. Taking the model's precision of 0.65 into account, it predicts one correct word-SDQ link per 4.4 words. This number demonstrates GUIDE's few-shot learning capabilities.

The human evaluation using questionnaires reveals that GUIDE's precision is in fact almost twice as high as suggested by the dataset-based evaluation (0.65 instead of 0.34). The precision of 0.65 and the (dataset-based) recall of 0.046 show that the model predicts mostly correct word-SDQ links, but it creates only fractions of complete semantic domain dictionaries. Nevertheless, the recall is likely to be higher in practice because the evaluation with the incomplete dataset fails to recognize true positive predictions. While GUIDE cannot replace linguists who compile semantic domain dic-

	Δ Precision	Δ Recall	ΔF_1
GUIDE (reference values)	0.33 ± 0.04	0.046 ± 0.004	0.079 ± 0.007
Preprocessing			
¬ Stanza pipeline	−0.01 ± 0.04	−0.017 ± 0.005	−0.027 ± 0.008
¬ MWT expansion	+0.02 ± 0.03	−0.001 ± 0.003	−0.001 ± 0.006
¬ Lemmatization	+0.00 ± 0.03	−0.016 ± 0.003	−0.025 ± 0.006
¬ SentencePiece tokenization	−0.00 ± 0.04	−0.005 ± 0.003	−0.008 ± 0.006
¬ Lowercasing	+0.01 ± 0.05	−0.001 ± 0.005	−0.002 ± 0.008
¬ Isolated node removal	−0.02 ± 0.03	+0.013 ± 0.006	+0.019 ± 0.009
Node features			
¬ Degree	−0.00 ± 0.04	+0.012 ± 0.005	+0.016 ± 0.007
¬ Weighted degree	+0.01 ± 0.04	+0.007 ± 0.004	+0.010 ± 0.007
¬ SDQ count	+0.02 ± 0.04	+0.001 ± 0.004	+0.002 ± 0.007
¬ SDQ links	−0.33 ± 0.00	−0.045 ± 0.000	−0.077 ± 0.001
Other			
¬ Modified identity matrix initialization	−0.05 ± 0.07	−0.038 ± 0.001	−0.063 ± 0.003

Table 3: Changes in GUIDE's performance for eleven ablations: Cells with "±" show the average value of three runs and the standard deviation. Deactivating the Stanza pipeline and SentencePiece tokenization means that we used tokenization by punctuation mark split instead (see Figure 4).

tionaries, it can provide an initial dictionary with thousands of entries, of which a significant percentage is correct.

8 Conclusion

This paper presents the language-agnostic tool GUIDE, which creates and fills up multiparallel semantic domain dictionaries in 20 languages from seven language families. The model achieves state-of-the-art performance in linking words to their SDQs and supports 833 languages. Although GUIDE has a recall of only 0.046, we show that it has a precision of 0.60 even in languages for which it has no training data, probably due to language similarity and the model's multilingual nature.

We propose 32,000 new word-SDQ links for twelve existing dictionaries and 19,000 word-SDQ links for eight new dictionaries. Ten out of these 20 languages are low-resource languages.

Limitations

We discuss the limitations of our approach across multiple components.

Computational Limitations

The node feature matrix is a memory bottleneck. It is saved as a dense vector of size $N \times 7,428$, where N is the number of nodes/words. The model allocates approximately 3.5 GB of VRAM per language. Therefore, 48 GB of VRAM (see Section 6.1) limit us to loading approximately 13 languages. Therefore, we cannot load the entire MAG of 20 languages at once but load a subgraph of the twelve development languages plus only a single zero-shot evaluation language. This approach does not affect the quality of the results because the evaluation languages do not have labeled data and cannot learn word-SDQ links from each other.

Dataset

The used Bible translations and semantic domain dictionaries cause various limitations that we discuss in the following.

Bible translations. The general challenge of using only the Bible as parallel data is the narrow domain (Ebrahimi and Kann, 2021). The Bible does not include all the words used in today's world, particularly those related to technology, science, and modern culture, such as "*computer*". The language in the Bible is often of a high register and does not reflect the way people talk in everyday life (e.g., with slang and idioms). Although different Bible translations convey the same meaning, they differ in their proximity to the original text (in Hebrew, Aramaic, and Greek). While some are literal translations, others paraphrase a lot to be understandable to a modern audience. These different approaches to Bible translation cause noise in the word alignments.

Semantic domain dictionaries. The semantic domain dictionaries are incomplete. They cover a part of the languages' vocabularies and are also missing SDQ links for the words they cover. This limitation is the nature of language data because living languages are constantly evolving. They receive new words and new meanings for existing words. However, we found only a handful of incorrect SDQ links in our training data, listed in Appendix E.

Preprocessing Pipeline

The preprocessing pipeline produces a MAG that contains misleading edges (leading to false positives) and lacks useful edges and nodes (leading to false negatives). We now discuss three reasons for these limitations.

Ambiguity. Words are often ambiguous (e.g., "*date*") and thus align to different words in another language. The preprocessing pipeline treats them as if they are the same word, which confuses semantic patterns in the MAG, leading to misclassifications.

Noisy alignments. There is a lot of noise in word alignments because we train Eflomal on a small corpus that contains many words only once. We mitigate this noise by aggregating all alignments from all languages.

Collocations. We ignore most word groups (so-called collocations (Smadja et al., 1996), e.g., "*harvest moon*") in the semantic domain dictionaries unless Stanza provides an MWT expansion model for the language.

Node Features

Although three node features turned out to harm the model's performance, it could also ignore other potentially useful node properties.

Ethics Statement

We are not aware of any adverse effects on any individual or group resulting from the study we have conducted. However, we acknowledge that the limitations raised above may lead to dictionaries of inferior quality compared to manual language documentation. Thus, automated techniques cannot be taken as a reason to forgo traditional language documentation.

Acknowledgments

We would like to thank Lukas Ehrig and Jonathan Schneider for their kind and thoughtful feedback, as well as the anonymous SIGTYP reviewers. We also would like to express our sincere gratitude to everyone who completed a language questionnaire.

References

Cosmas Julius Abah, Jane Wong Kong Ling, and Anantha Govindasamy. 2018. Root-Oriented Words Generation: An Easier Way Towards Dictionary Making for the Dusunic Family of Languages. *Malaysian Journal of Social Sciences and Humanities (MJSSH)*, 3(2):95 – 112.

Khalid Alnajjar, Mika Hämäläinen, Niko Tapio Partanen, and Jack Rueter. 2022. Using graph-based methods to augment online dictionaries of endangered languages. In *Proceedings of the Fifth Workshop on the Use of Computational Methods in the Study of Endangered Languages*, pages 139–148, Dublin, Ireland. Association for Computational Linguistics.

Brenda H. Boerger. 2017. Rapid Word Collection, dictionary production, and community well-being. In *International Conference on Language Documentation & Conservation*.

Gerard de Melo and Gerhard Weikum. 2009. Towards a Universal Wordnet by Learning from Combined Evidence. In *Proceedings of the 18th ACM Conference on Information and Knowledge Management (CIKM)*, pages 513–522, New York, NY, USA. ACM Press.

Chi Thang Duong, Thanh Dat Hoang, Haikun Dang, Quoc Viet Hung Nguyen, and K. Aberer. 2019. On Node Features for Graph Neural Networks. *arXiv*.

David M. Eberhard, Gary F. Simons, and Charles D. Fennig. 2023. *Ethnologue: Languages of the World*, twenty-sixth edition. SIL International.

Abteen Ebrahimi and Katharina Kann. 2021. How to adapt your pretrained multilingual model to 1600 languages. In *Proceedings of the 59th Annual Meeting of the Association for Computational Linguistics and the 11th International Joint Conference on Natural Language Processing (Volume 1: Long Papers)*, pages 4555–4567, Online. Association for Computational Linguistics.

Christiane Fellbaum. 2000. WordNet: An Electronic Lexical Database. *Language*, 76:706.

Matthias Fey and Jan E. Lenssen. 2019. Fast Graph Representation Learning with PyTorch Geometric. In *ICLR Workshop on Representation Learning on Graphs and Manifolds*.

Naman Goyal, Cynthia Gao, Vishrav Chaudhary, Peng-Jen Chen, Guillaume Wenzek, Da Ju, Sanjana Krishnan, Marc'Aurelio Ranzato, Francisco Guzmán, and Angela Fan. 2022. The Flores-101 evaluation benchmark for low-resource and multilingual machine translation. *Transactions of the Association for Computational Linguistics*, 10:522–538.

Francisco Guzmán, Peng-Jen Chen, Myle Ott, Juan Pino, Guillaume Lample, Philipp Koehn, Vishrav Chaudhary, and Marc'Aurelio Ranzato. 2019. The FLORES evaluation datasets for low-resource machine translation: Nepali–English and Sinhala–English. In *Proceedings of the 2019 Conference on Empirical Methods in Natural Language Processing and the 9th International Joint Conference on Natural Language Processing (EMNLP-IJCNLP)*, pages 6098–6111, Hong Kong, China. Association for Computational Linguistics.

Ayyoob Imani, Lütfi Kerem Senel, Masoud Jalili Sabet, François Yvon, and Hinrich Schuetze. 2022. Graph neural networks for multiparallel word alignment. In *Findings of the Association for Computational Linguistics: ACL 2022*, pages 1384–1396, Dublin, Ireland. Association for Computational Linguistics.

Ayyoob Imani Googhari, Lütfi Kerem Şenel, Masoud Jalili Sabet, François Yvon, and Hinrich Schütze. 2022. Graph Neural Networks for Multiparallel Word Alignment. In *arXiv*.

Ayyoob ImaniGooghari, Silvia Severini, Masoud Jalili Sabet, François Yvon, and Hinrich Schütze. 2022. Graph-based multilingual label propagation for low-resource part-of-speech tagging. In *Proceedings of the 2022 Conference on Empirical Methods in Natural Language Processing*, pages 1577–1589, Abu Dhabi, United Arab Emirates. Association for Computational Linguistics.

Diederik P. Kingma and Jimmy Ba. 2014. Adam: A Method for Stochastic Optimization. *arXiv*.

Thomas N. Kipf and Max Welling. 2017. Semi-Supervised Classification with Graph Convolutional Networks. *arXiv*, pages 215–223.

Philipp Koehn, Amittai Axelrod, Alexandra Birch Mayne, Chris Callison-Burch, Miles Osborne, and David Talbot. 2005. Edinburgh system description for the 2005 IWSLT speech translation evaluation. In *Proceedings of the Second International Workshop on Spoken Language Translation*, Pittsburgh, Pennsylvania, USA.

Taku Kudo and John Richardson. 2018. SentencePiece: A simple and language independent subword tokenizer and detokenizer for neural text processing. In *Proceedings of the 2018 Conference on Empirical Methods in Natural Language Processing: System Demonstrations*, pages 66–71, Brussels, Belgium. Association for Computational Linguistics.

Ronald Moe. 2010. Compiling Dictionaries Using Semantic Domains. *Lexikos*, 13.

Peng Qi, Yuhao Zhang, Yuhui Zhang, Jason Bolton, and Christopher D. Manning. 2020. Stanza: A python natural language processing toolkit for many human languages. In *Proceedings of the 58th Annual Meeting of the Association for Computational Linguistics: System Demonstrations*, pages 101–108, Online. Association for Computational Linguistics.

Franco Scarselli, Marco Gori, Ah Chung Tsoi, Markus Hagenbuchner, and Gabriele Monfardini. 2009. The Graph Neural Network Model. *IEEE Transactions on Neural Networks and Learning Systems*, 20(1):61–80.

Frank Smadja, Kathleen R. McKeown, and Vasileios Hatzivassiloglou. 1996. Translating collocations for bilingual lexicons: A statistical approach. *Computational Linguistics*, 22(1):1–38.

NLLB Team, Marta R. Costa-jussà, James Cross, Onur Çelebi, Maha Elbayad, Kenneth Heafield, Kevin Heffernan, Elahe Kalbassi, Janice Lam, Daniel Licht, Jean Maillard, Anna Sun, Skyler Wang, Guillaume Wenzek, Al Youngblood, Bapi Akula, Loic Barrault, Gabriel Mejia Gonzalez, Prangthip Hansanti, John Hoffman, Semarley Jarrett, Kaushik Ram Sadagopan, Dirk Rowe, Shannon Spruit, Chau Tran, Pierre Andrews, Necip Fazil Ayan, Shruti Bhosale, Sergey Edunov, Angela Fan, Cynthia Gao, Vedanuj Goswami, Francisco Guzmán, Philipp Koehn, Alexandre Mourachko, Christophe Ropers, Safiyyah Saleem, Holger Schwenk, and Jeff Wang. 2022. No Language Left Behind: Scaling Human-Centered Machine Translation. *arXiv*.

Vesa Åkerman, David Baines, Damien Daspit, Ulf Hermjakob, Taeho Jang, Michael Martin, Joel Mathew, and Marcus Schwarting. 2023. The eBible Corpus: Data and Model Benchmarks for Bible Translation for Low-Resource Languages. *arXiv*.

Robert Östling and Jörg Tiedemann. 2016. Efficient Word Alignment with Markov Chain Monte Carlo. *The Prague Bulletin of Mathematical Linguistics*, 106(1):125–146.

A Appendix A. Semantic Domain Hierarchy

Figure 3 visualizes the semantic domain hierarchy.

B Appendix B. Bible Translation Sources

Table 4 shows the web source of the Bible translations we used.

C Appendix C. Pipeline and Model Visualization

Figure 4 and Figure 5 visualize our preprocessing pipeline. Figure 6 shows the model architecture.

D Appendix D. Questionnaires

Table 5 provides the links to the questionnaires that we used to manually evaluate GUIDE's performance.

E Appendix E. Incorrect Semantic Domain Dictionary Entries

Table 6 shows incorrect entries that we discovered in the development dataset.

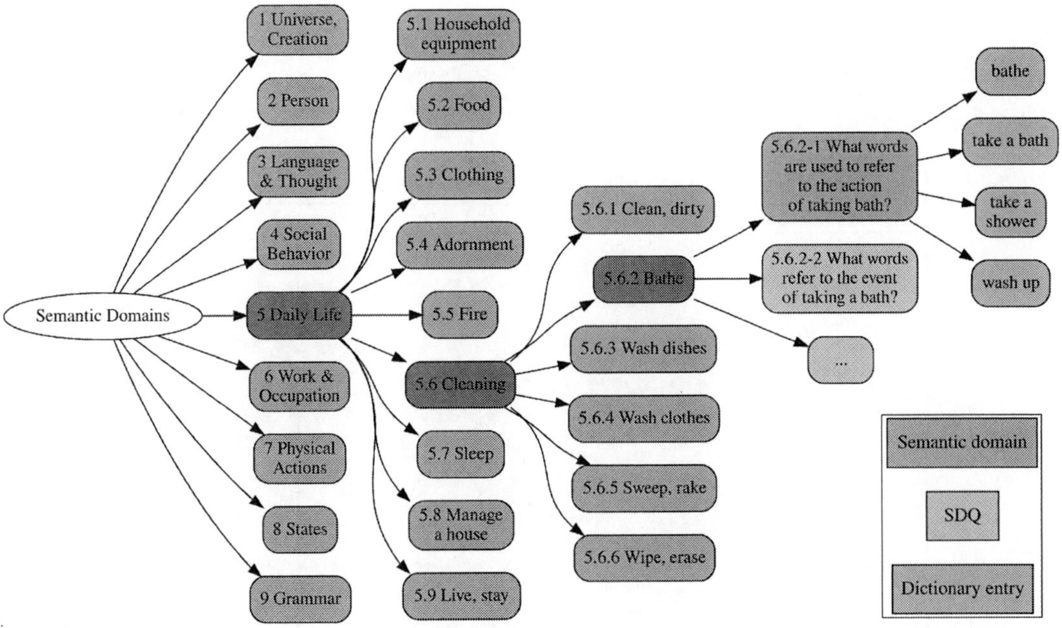

Figure 3: A drill-down into the tree-structured hierarchy of semantic domains: Nodes with expanded children are highlighted.

Language	Bible translation URL
Development	
Bengali	https://github.com/BibleNLP/ebible/blob/main/corpus/ben-ben2017.txt
Chinese	https://github.com/BibleNLP/ebible/blob/main/corpus/cmn-cmn-cu89s.txt
English	https://github.com/BibleNLP/ebible/blob/main/corpus/eng-eng-web.txt
French	https://github.com/BibleNLP/ebible/blob/main/corpus/fra-frasbl.txt
Hindi	https://github.com/BibleNLP/ebible/blob/main/corpus/hin-hin2017.txt
Indonesian	https://github.com/BibleNLP/ebible/blob/main/corpus/ind-ind.txt
Kupang Malay	https://github.com/BibleNLP/ebible/blob/main/corpus/mkn-mkn.txt
Malayalam	https://github.com/BibleNLP/ebible/blob/main/corpus/mal-mal.txt
Nepali	https://github.com/BibleNLP/ebible/blob/main/corpus/npi-npiulb.txt
Portuguese	https://github.com/BibleNLP/ebible/blob/main/corpus/por-porbrbsl.txt
Spanish	https://github.com/BibleNLP/ebible/blob/main/corpus/spa-spablm.txt
Swahili	https://github.com/BibleNLP/ebible/blob/main/corpus/swh-swhulb.txt
Evaluation (zero-shot)	
German	https://github.com/BibleNLP/ebible/blob/main/corpus/deu-deu1951.txt
Hiri Motu	https://github.com/BibleNLP/ebible/blob/main/corpus/hmo-hmo.txt
Igbo	https://ebible.org/details.php?id=ibo
Mina-Gen	https://www.bible.com/sl/versions/2236-gen-gegbe-biblia-2014
Motu	https://github.com/BibleNLP/ebible/blob/main/corpus/meu-meu.txt
South Azerbaijani	https://github.com/BibleNLP/ebible/blob/main/corpus/azb-azb.txt
Tok Pisin	https://github.com/BibleNLP/ebible/blob/main/corpus/tpi-tpi.txt
Yoruba	https://github.com/BibleNLP/ebible/blob/main/corpus/yor-yor.txt

Table 4: The links show the source of the Bible translations: All translations are from ebible.org, except for the Mina-Gen Bible, which was provided by a language expert. We downloaded the Igbo Bible from ebible.org because it is not in the eBible corpus (i.e., on GitHub). All URLs were visited on 2023-10-21.

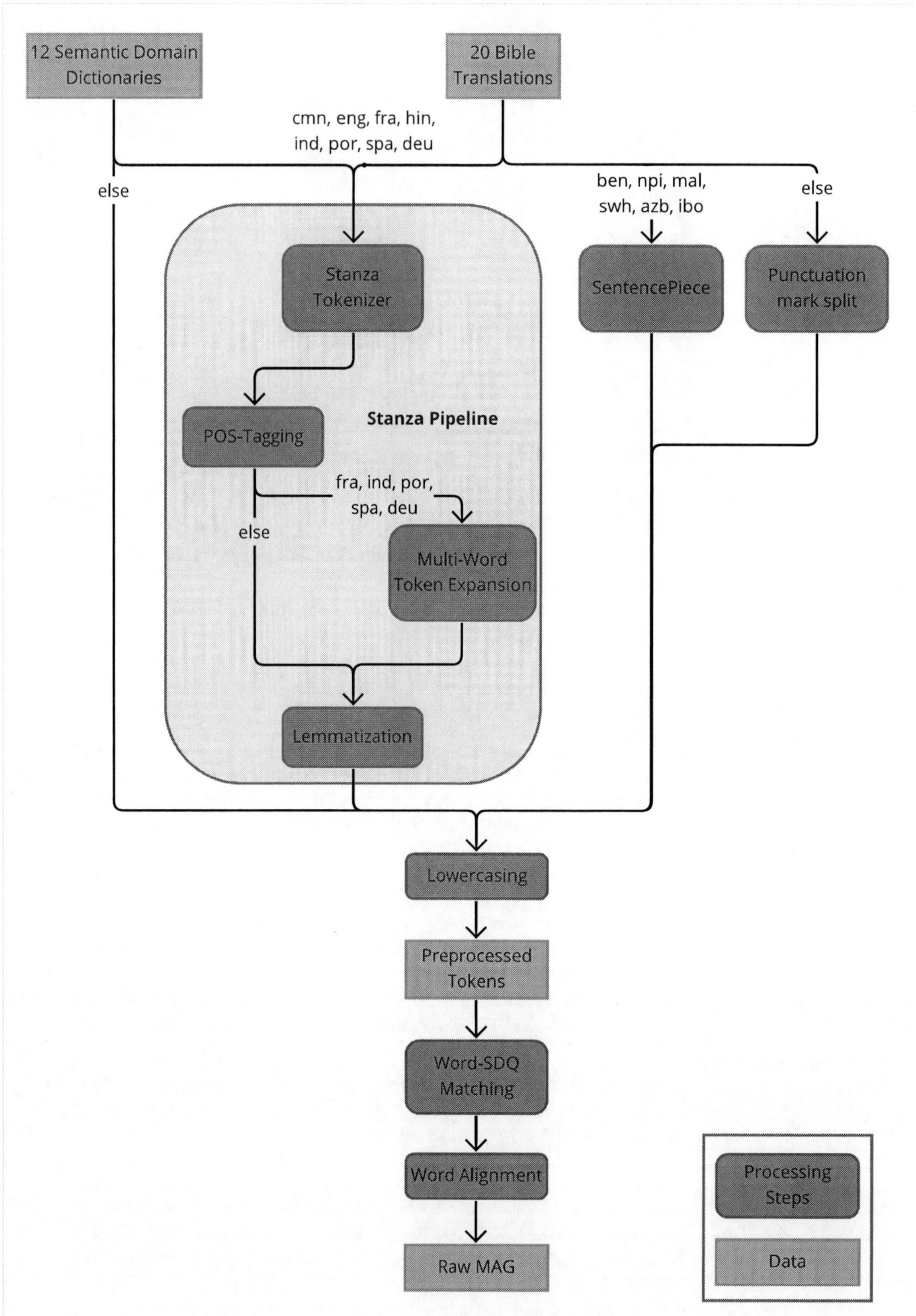

Figure 4: The first part of the preprocessing pipeline (graph creation).

Figure 5: The second part of the preprocessing pipeline (graph refinement).

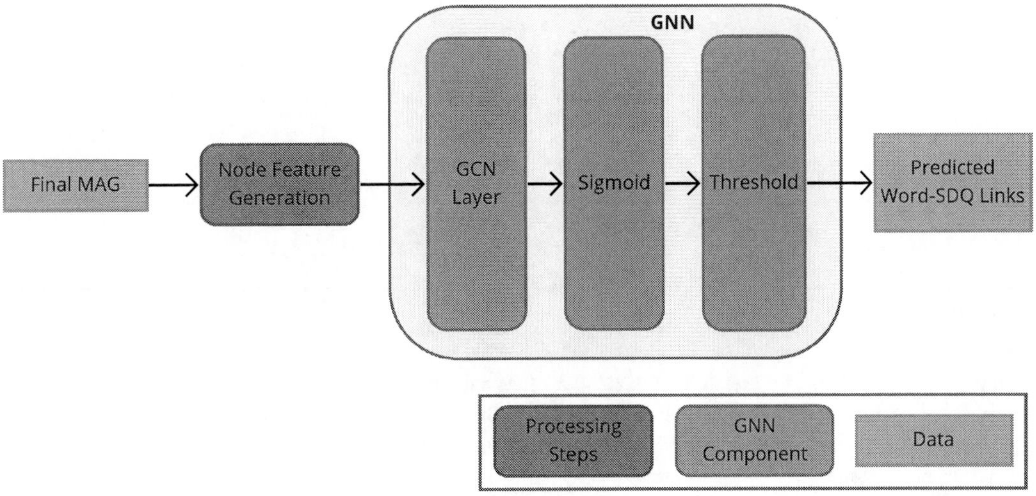

Figure 6: Model architecture: GUIDE takes the MAG with node features and predicts SDQ-links for these nodes.

Language	Questionnaire URL
Development	
Bengali	https://docs.google.com/spreadsheets/d/1_qoYnswufDY0gVZuebcoQ1DD9BLqSVD8NozWzqiGWR8
Chinese (simplified)	https://docs.google.com/spreadsheets/d/1sppwKhC5Ev3frbQ8Mq_MoQGc5ehym6QdQSPcjjdWNPg
English	https://docs.google.com/spreadsheets/d/1zt_3gqNrbSYsIOzjwm3BxewOaulFY1laVXshCZIYGLU
French	https://docs.google.com/spreadsheets/d/1eWkOK5T9ttWx-9ZmETc-fUY1Q7HzihbTr6mK8irZ83g
Hindi	https://docs.google.com/spreadsheets/d/14D6pGKgQtoHG5LWORaU9Ko5XUn_wDh0-x4Hnxj2nHag
Indonesian	https://docs.google.com/spreadsheets/d/13iVFF0xxwpQ_pXf-zKFW2jebA3TZnIiSL9rFpD-dWPY
Malayalam	https://docs.google.com/spreadsheets/d/1-DFjBkS1wjCahowBjg-iGLBV-moZww-J8lKpO0HN44Y
Nepali	https://docs.google.com/spreadsheets/d/1n-f9LbF0vYfO4gtu1YmD6LZB1_Gyo-VxV35WaYBN9_Q
Portuguese	https://docs.google.com/spreadsheets/d/1_WKQmj5KHDE6p8MsCFawvQoxOcLn3MYPWb-4aYpgV6U
Kupang Malay	https://docs.google.com/spreadsheets/d/1EP1ctJ7yl5QYFdY6eV6KYDQg1_mz90j-J8jDGwT9yJY
Spanish	https://docs.google.com/spreadsheets/d/1-2ZwbunnsqOYBW_beI9Rax3XW1Zjpacl5GrrzlPtfF0
Swahili	https://docs.google.com/spreadsheets/d/1H9RVi1mCkL9WmcH2zXYuOwwj73CAMg1My6P-jAAWYgI
Evaluation (zero-shot)	
German	https://docs.google.com/spreadsheets/d/1mPtzuD3_NFWOhLBXUElRNeAGtmiiXcKx_7n7Er3kZsc
Hiri Motu	https://docs.google.com/spreadsheets/d/1gTiNxhvRV9UtUq84Q0E3itJ2nYS8Gv4ElpIp3mEEHAE
Igbo	https://docs.google.com/spreadsheets/d/1yU8FCS19KRIWkbqm1aQBUCBEjVA4zoC60TuM0fTQN8Q
Mina-Gen	https://docs.google.com/spreadsheets/d/1Ib-xD6-1FuBLQ9M3F2UVbocnnbK7NBgv62Lg9h0p_6o
Motu	https://docs.google.com/spreadsheets/d/1e45Hw000K6OrluBQxe-8ifAR3h_Dz725sg3ZBlVnXRM
South Azerbaijani	https://docs.google.com/spreadsheets/d/1q8WfBhZDlOzRsihUbjH-wFyruudA11Chosotgf71rx0
Tok Pisin	https://docs.google.com/spreadsheets/d/1EENt0FJpTdDHpm2P1i-MQ56ZkdQKkBi5GnUDw30gx_o
Yoruba	https://docs.google.com/spreadsheets/d/11LBgUSHSnUFOP3Zp2ikgTp8vjGB6xR8cQkcdZeKNaSQ

Table 5: The completed questionnaires on Google Sheets for each of the 20 languages: We instructed the participants to answer 100 – 120 questions (see Section 6.2).

Language	Word	Translation	SDQ ID	SDQ
English	stock		3.2.5.1-1	What words refer to believing that something is true?
Hindi	राल (*rāl*)	resin	1.2.2.4-2	What types of minerals are there?
Portuguese	estoque	stock	3.2.5.1-1	What words refer to believing that something is true?
Portuguese	rebelião	rebellion	4.5.4.6-10	What do the authorities do to stop a rebellion?
Portuguese	estoque	stock	4.7.7.3-7	What means are used to restrain prisoners?
Portuguese	deter	detain	3.4.2.1.2-1	What words refer to feeling hateful?
Portuguese	carmesim	crimson	8.3.3.3.4-7	What are the shades of blue?
Spanish	rebelión	rebellion	4.5.4.6-10	What do the authorities do to stop a rebellion?
Spanish	sedición	sedition	4.5.4.6-10	What do the authorities do to stop a rebellion?

Table 6: Nine incorrect entries in the semantic domain dictionaries that we discovered, verified by native speakers: The incorrect word-SDQ links in the dataset are rare. The text in parentheses shows a transliteration.

A New Dataset for Tonal and Segmental Dialectometry from the Yue- and Pinghua-Speaking Area

Ho Wang Matthew Sung[1], **Jelena Prokić**[2] and **Yiya Chen**[3]
Leiden University / Leiden, Netherlands
{h.w.m.sung[1], j.prokic[2], yiya.chen[3]}@hum.leidenuniv.nl

Abstract

Traditional dialectology or dialect geography is the study of geographical variation of language. Originated in Europe and pioneered in Germany and France, this field has predominantly been focusing on sounds, more specifically, on segments. Similarly, quantitative approaches to language variation concerned with the phonetic level are in most cases focusing on segments as well. However, more than half of the world's languages include lexical tones (Yip 2002). Despite this, tones are still underexplored in quantitative language comparison, partly due to the low accessibility of the suitable data. This paper aims to introduce a newly digitised dataset which comes from the Yue- and Pinghua-speaking areas in Southern China, with over 100 dialects. This dataset consists of two parts: tones and segments. In this paper, we illustrate how we can computationaly model tones in order to explore linguistic variation. We have applied a tone distance metric on our data, and we have found that 1) dialects also form a continuum on the tonal level and 2) other than tonemic (inventory) and tonetic differences, dialects can also differ in the lexical distribution of tones. The availability of this dataset will hopefully enable further exploration of the role of tones in quantitative typology and NLP research.

1 Introduction

Traditional dialectology or dialect geography (Chambers and Trudgill 1998: 14), is the study of geographical variation of language. This field originated in Europe, pioneered in Germany and France, and has always been focusing on sounds, more specifically, on segments. In the second half of the 20th century, the quantitative turn in dialectology, known as *dialectometry*, is no exception to this. While these methodologies have been widely used in Europe and America, there are only limited regions in the rest of the world which employ these methodologies, although there is a sign of growth in recent years. For instance, Yucatec Mayan (Pfeiler and Skopeteas 2022), Bantu languages (Nerbonne 2010), Japanese (Jeszenszky et al. 2019).

Tonal languages are defined as "[languages] in which an indication of pitch enters into the lexical realisation of at least some morphemes" (Hyman 2006: 229), and more than half of the world' s languages include lexical tones (Yip 2002). Despite this, tones are still gaining little attention in quantitative models of language variation. This lack of attention on tones is not surprising, however, since most European languages mostly do not use pitch to differentiate lexical meaning. One other reason could be the fact that digital data is not accessible and freely available. These factors cause barriers to the development of computational methods for tonal languages. For example, it is unclear whether the existing methods (e.g. Yang and Castro 2008) are suitable and adequate to deal with tones in tonal languages (Sung et al. forthcoming).

Take Chinese dialectology as an example, there are numerous studies on dialects spoken in China, and it has a century-long tradition, but most studies on tonal variation are descriptive. Traditional studies usually report the tonal inventory of a dialect after a fieldwork investigation, and/or tones are analysed in terms of how they correspond to historical tone categories (from the Middle Chinese period, based on the ancient rhyme dictionary descriptions). Although there is a huge amount of dialect data available for Chinese (in the form of IPA transcriptions, including tones), they are mostly printed on paper and are not digitised, ready to be used for quantitative analyses.

Until today, there is generally a very limited number of digital datasets which allows us to quantitatively model variation of tones, which is problematic given that the majority of the world's languages are tonal. Furthermore, although there are tools which allow us to align Southeast Asian tone

Proceedings of the 6th Workshop on Research in Computational Linguistic Typology and Multilingual NLP (SIGTYP 2024), pages 25–36
March 22, 2024 ©2024 Association for Computational Linguistics

languages (Wu et al. 2020), and then visualize the correspondences (both tones and segments) in table form (List 2019), these tools were developed for historical linguistics. In order to understand the synchronic dialect variation on the tonal level, alternative methods are needed in order to investigate how tones vary beyond correspondences.

This paper aims to introduce a newly digitised dataset which comes from the Yue- and Pinghua-speaking areas in Southern China, with over 100 dialects.[1] This dataset consists of two parts: segments (Section 3) and tones (Section 4). The availability of this dataset will hopefully be an invitation to researchers around the world to initiate an exploration of tonal variation, which has long been neglected. In section 5 we present out preliminary research on tonal variation, followed by a conclusion.

2 Data Sources

The data presented in this paper consists of segments and tones. Segments contain impressionistic transcriptions of consonants and vowels of the words. Impressionistic tone transcriptions of pitch contours are represented using Chao's (1930) *tone letters*. The two sets of transcriptions are from the same sources; they were extracted from the same words (see below) and from the same dialects.

There are two main sources for the dataset, namely word lists and homonymic syllabaries, which came from various dialect surveys and individual studies. Both sources are based on impressionistic transcriptions from word elicitation, but they are presented differently. Word lists are word-based, meaning words are organised in a tabular format (Francis 1983: 105-106), where the IPA transcriptions of each word are listed for each dialect all at once. On the other hand, homonymic syllabaries are pronunciation-based, meaning words with the same pronunciation are grouped together under one pronunciation (represented by the IPA transcriptions).

2.1 Sources

Our dataset consists of IPA transcriptions of over 130 words in 104 dialects. These dialects include traditional Yue and (Southern) Pinghua dialects (Chinese Academy of Social Sciences (CASS) 2012), which are Sinitic languages spoken in the Guangdong and Guangxi provinces in Southern China.

The dialect surveys include *Survey of Dialects in the Pearl River Delta* (*SDPRD*, Zhan and Cheung 1987), *Survey of Yue Dialects in Northern Guangdong* (*SYDNG*, Zhan and Cheung 1994), *Survey of Yue Dialects in Western Guangdong* (*SYDWG*, Zhan and Cheung 1998), *The Phonological Study of the Yue Dialects spoken in the Zhan-Mao area in Western Guangdong* (*SYDZM*, Shao 2016), *Chinese Dialect Research in the Guangxi Province* (*CDRGP*, Xie 2007), *Yue, Pinghua and Tuhua Dialect Survey Collection Part 1* (*YPTDSC1*, Chen and Lin 2009). Other (individual) studies include Liu (2015), Zhong (2015), Huang (2006), Chen (2009), Yang (2013), Tan (2017), Shi (2009) and Chen and Weng (2010).

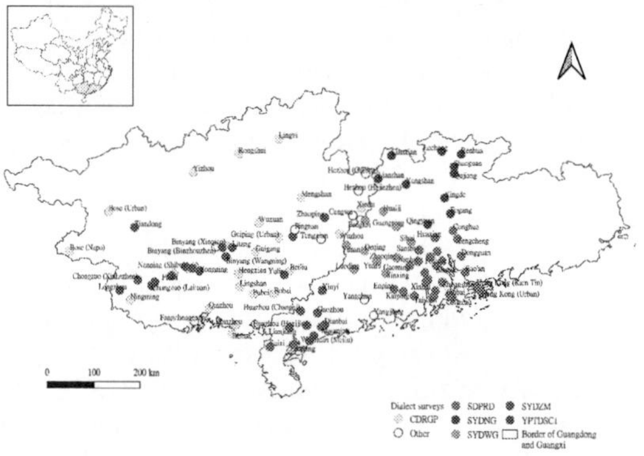

Figure 1: Localities and their respective sources.[2]

2.2 Selection of Words

Out of the 130 words in our Yue dialect dataset, a portion of the items comes from the Swadesh 100-word list (Swadesh 1955), while some additional items come from outside this list. The Swadesh list is chosen because it is a standard word list for language comparison, with the assumption that words on this list represent the basic or core vocabulary – words that are universal, relatively culture free and thus less likely to be replaced compared to other vocabulary (Campbell 2013: 448). In addition, Swadesh's 100 basic-word list has been tested by Wang and Wang (2004) to be the most suitable word list for sub-grouping Chinese dialects.

Not all items from the Swadesh list are, however, suitable for the data extraction process. One

[1]The datasets can be found under **Supplementary Material**.

[2]Map created using *QGIS* (QGIS Development Team 2022).

group of such items are polysyllabic words. The data collected in the Yue and Pinghua dialect surveys are mainly monosyllabic words (or cognate morphemes), because records of polysyllabic words are not available (collected) for a big portion of the dialects in this dataset. Therefore, only a subset of the items in the Swadesh list is used, in order to ensure the commensurability of the dataset for all dialects. Another group of items from the Swadesh list was excluded because they were not included in the dialect survey. An example is 'tongue'. The pronunciation of the written form of this word (舌 *sit3*) is included in the Swadesh list, but the actual spoken form used in Cantonese, 脷 *lei3*, is not included. One other group of words include items which can have two pronunciations, namely *literary* and *colloquial* pronunciations. Colloquial pronunciations of the characters usually reflect the pronunciations inherited by the dialects from their ancestors, while literary pronunciations are borrowings from the koine from different historical periods (Li 2007: 93). Although Yue has relatively fewer characters with literary pronunciations (Lau 2001: 134-135), it is still present in the Swadesh list, like 聽 'listen' (Lit. *ting3*, Col. *teng1*). Therefore, such items are discarded. Lastly, some items are doublets, meaning that both the spoken and written forms can be found. Both variants are included in the dataset.

In total, 54 words in our dataset do not come from the Swadesh list. These words can be considered to be common, although not 'basic' or 'core' as such. The domains of these supplementary words include the rest of the numbers up to 10 (Swadesh list only includes one and two), colour terms, direction, animals, and some words with known phonological variation, like 'flower', 'spring', and 'duck'. This addition is set out to enlarge the range of variation within the Yue dialects which are not present in the Swadesh list already.

The list of items can be found in Appendix A.

3 Modifications to the Original Segmental Transcriptions

Dialect survey data are often found with transcribers' differences (or fieldworker isoglosses, Trudgill 1983; Mathussek 2016) when there are more than one fieldworker documenting dialects in the field. Transcribers' differences are inconsistencies of impressionistic transcriptions due to the different uses of phonetic symbols to represent the same sound by different transcribers. In other words, the differences we see in the data might be due to the habitual difference of the fieldworker instead of 'real' linguistic difference. To reduce the effects from the transcribers' differences, we have made some modifications to the original data.

3.1 Comparison with Existing Recordings

The data sources we have used do not have acoustic data accompanying the transcriptions. One of the ways to find out whether transcribers used different symbols to represent the same sound is to compare these transcriptions with the existing recordings from different projects on the same or nearby dialects. We have used recordings from the Yubao database (中國語言資源保護研究中心 [Research Centre of Linguistic Resource Reservation in China] 2022) for such comparisons. For instance, this task allows us to identify subphonemic contrasts such as Cantonese [ɵ] (International Phonetic Association 2005) before -n and -t, which are often transcribed as <œ> in the transcriptions in varieties such as Guangzhou and Hong Kong (Urban) dialects.

3.2 Maintaining Contrasts

Another approach to reducing transcriber's differences is to collapse contrasts between different notations, i.e. to merge symbols. However, this would potentially lead to a loss of information, with the risk of merging actual contrasts which are present in different dialects. To avoid collapsing unnecessary contrasts, when minimal pairs could be found in the rhyme inventory (provided in the dialect surveys for all localities), contrasts would be kept.

For example, one common difference in transcriptions is the high back vowel symbol before -ŋ, namely [ʊŋ]. The tendency across Yue dialects is that there are two non-low back vowels which commonly pair with -ŋ, namely /ʊ/ and /ɔ/. Based on this tendency, we can derive the phonetic values of the vowels by inspecting the symbols used and the phonemic contrasts in the dialects. The main transcriptions of [ʊŋ] are <oŋ> and <uŋ> cross-dialectally. We have chosen <oŋ> to be the default in representing [ʊŋ]. However, the tendency does not imply all instances of <uŋ> represent a [ʊŋ]. To make the more plausible judgement, we have checked 1) whether the inventory also has <oŋ>, and 2) whether <oŋ> could represent some other sounds, such as [ɔŋ]. This relies on the presence of minimal pairs. In the Hong Kong (Kam Tin) dialect, the original data have <uŋ> and <oŋ>. In addition, the Hong Kong (Kam Tin) dialect also has <ɔŋ>. Because [ɔ] already occupies the vowel in <ɔŋ>, <oŋ> that implies the pronunciation [ʊŋ]. At the same time, it implies that <uŋ> has the value [uŋ], a combination of a sound sequence uncommon across the Yue dialects (as a result of sound change).

In contrast, in the Nanning (Urban) dialect, <uŋ> does not form a minimal pair with <oŋ> (since it does not exist). Furthermore, the absent <oŋ> cannot be [ɔŋ] since <ɔŋ> already exists in the inventory. This implies that <uŋ> represents [ʊŋ]. This is indeed also the case in the recording from the Yubao database (under '南寧白話').

3.3 Removal of Redundant Characters

There are cases where symbols were added to the transcription in the original data, but they do not actually contribute to the actual phonetic realization of the word. The <ɲi-> sequence is an example. In words such as 人 'man/human/people' (which is typically transcribed as <ɲiɐn> in Western Yue dialects), the -i- medial is not really perceptible in the Yubao recordings. The addition of <-i-> is perhaps due to the fact that [ɲ] often appears before an -i- medial, and it is analysed as an allophone of /ŋ/ (Shao 2016: 42) or /n/ (e.g. Zhan and Cheung 1998). For <ɲiɐn>, since [ɐ] is not a high vowel, the medial -i- then could be a convention which indicates the presence of /i/ (but phonetically silent). While this information could be useful in the synchronic phonological analysis of the dialect, it creates inconsistencies for dialect comparison. Therefore, such redundant information (for dialect comparison) was removed.

3.4 Simplification of Overly Detailed Transcriptions

Different transcribers would transcribe sounds in different broadness. Some (usually a minority) are narrower, with all the diacritics included, while some are broader, without diacritics.

The different degrees of transcription broadness cause additional inconsistencies to the data. In order to level the broadness, we have removed diacritics for the vowel backness and height parameters. For example, Hong Kong (Kam Tin) dialect has a non-standard IPA symbol <A>, which stands for [a̠]. This is further simplified to <a>. Superscripted segments, such as ^{u}V, NC (nasal+obstruent, could be ^{N}C or N^{C}), were all treated as full segments. This is because it is difficult to verify the status of the ^{u} in the ^{u}V sequence. For the nasal+obstruent sequence, some descriptions noted that these sequences have variation, like the Guangning dialect (Zhan and Cheung 1998: 14), which were not reflected in the data. We have decided to level these contrasts to full segments.

3.5 Consistency of Onsets

Consistency of onsets mainly concerns word-initial high vowels. In Yue dialectology, it is common to see a zero-onset plus a medial (i.e. starting with i-, u- or y- instead of j- and w-) in the transcription, but not all transcribers do this. To our knowledge, the Zhongshan dialect (Zhan and Cheung 1990: 72) and a few dialects in Guangxi (Xie 2007) do not start with a glide before a high vowel nucleus. For other dialects, it is unclear whether the choice between the vowel-initial vs. glide-initial reflects transcribers' differences. Therefore, the chosen normalised form is an onset with a glide for these syllables, until further reports of the presence (or absence) of an initial glide for the dialects in our dataset.

3.6 Converting Chinese IPA to Standard IPA

There are a few differences between the Chinese IPA and Standard IPA (International Phonetic Association 2005). These non-standard IPA symbols were converted to Standard IPA. For instance, the symbol for aspiration <'> was replaced with <^{h}>; capital vowel symbols <A> and <E> (roughly [a̠] and [e̞]/[ɛ̝] (between [e] and [ɛ]) respectively, Handel 2015; Li 2017: 31) were converted into diacritic-less IPA symbols. One exception is the apical vowel <ɿ>, which remains in the dataset as a contrastive sound to the existing IPA symbols.[3] In terms of consonants, palatal nasals <ȵ> and laminal <ʃ>[4]are replaced by IPA <ɲ> and <s> respectively.

[3]There could actually be more than one phonetic realisation for what is represented as an 'apical vowel'. However, since this information is not available in the dialect survey data, we treat this pool of possible sounds as one homogenous sound value by using the apical vowel symbol.

[4]Chinese IPA uses tongue positions instead of the palate as the places of articulation.

3.7 Phonetic Alignment

We have also modified the kv- and kʋ-, versus the ku- sequence. All the ku- sequences were converted to kw-, so that the medial -u- would be treated as a consonant. In quantitative language comparison, phonetic transcriptions are often aligned using pairwise or multiple sequence alignment algorithms. Introducing the above mentioned modification allows the medial -u- to be aligned with -v- and -ʋ-, instead of a nucleus vowel which does not belong to the onset.

3.8 Descriptive Statistics

In Table 1, we have illustrated how the data look before and after the cleaning process.

Dialect	Item	Raw	Cleaned
Guangzhou	'water'	sœy	sɵy
Guangzhou	'skin1'	p'ei	p^hei

Table 1: Examples of Raw vs. Cleaned transcriptions

A reduction in the contrasts from the raw data can yield information loss. We have calculated the *Normalized Levenshtein distance* (Levenshtein 1966; Heeringa 2004) to see how much our cleaned transcription deviate from the raw transcription. The distribution of the deviation scores per dialect can be found in Figure 2 below.

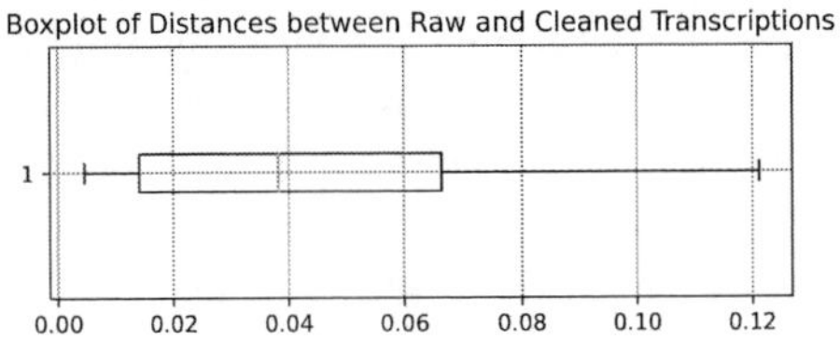

Figure 2: Boxplot of Distances between Raw and Cleaned Transcriptions.

The mean Levenshtein distance is 0.043, and the standard deviation is 0.029. The minimum distance found between the raw and the cleaned transcriptions within a dialect is 0.004 (found in Zengcheng), while the maximum distance is 0.121 (found in Binyang (Binzhouzhen)).

The descriptive statistics of the raw vs. cleaned transcriptions does not suggest a huge deviation from the raw data after we have removed some potential transcribers' differences. On average, we might see 4 changes per 100 segments (mean value 0.04 multiplied by 100).

4 Tone Data

The second half of the dataset consists of the tonal data from the same words and the same dialects. Up to date, there are no large-scale dialectometric studies on tones; the highest number of dialects involved are no more than 20 dialects (see Yang and Castro (2008); Tang (2009)). In some dialectometric studies, tones were neglected (e.g. Wichmann and Ran (2019)), others used a rather simplified method (e.g. Stanford (2012)). In addition, there are studies on the correlation between phonetic distance and the perception of tones (e.g. Yang and Castro (2008)), which do not focus on the application of these measures on dialect classification. Research questions regarding to the variation of tones in larger dialect areas, or if there is a correlation between tonal and segmental variation cannot be researched upon using these datasets.

Our tonal dataset is different from existing digital datasets, since it allows comparisons between tonal and segmental levels. The tones were transcribed in Chao's (1930) tone letters, which is a system for tone transcription consisting of 5 digits, 1, 2, 3, 4, 5, representing different (possible) contour levels in a tone. In this system, 1 represents the lowest contour level and 5 represents the highest. When combined together (with two digits or three digits), they can indicate a change in the contour, which represents the shape of the tone. For example, 53 is a falling tone, whereas 213 is a dipping tone (a falling contour followed by a rising contour).

The tonal transcriptions cannot directly be used for the purpose of dialectometry, though. Sung et al. (forthcoming) have found that directly applying Levenshtein distance on the tone letters and comparing these tones categorically (the 'binary' method, Sung et al. (forthcoming)) do not yield satisfying tone distances for the purpose of dialectometry. Further conversion of these tones to another representation (e.g. Onset-Contour-Offset, Yang and Castro 2008) is required in order to get more meaningful tone distances. The availability of tones as tone letters allows users to apply any conversion of their choice. The question raised in Sung et al. (forthcoming) shows that currently there is no existing satisfying tone distance metric for dialectometry. In the subsections below, we briefly introduce three quantitative models of tone representation, tested in Sung et al. (forthcoming), as well as our modified version of the existing representation proposed by Yang and Castro (2008)[5].

4.1 Chao's representation

The *tone-to-string* method applies the Levenshtein distance algorithm directly to Chao's (1930) tone letters. Levenshtein distance (Levenshtein 1966) is a string distance metric which seeks the least amount of operations, namely *insertions* (addition of element in string), *deletions* (removal of element in string) and *substitutions* (replacement of element in string) in order to transform one string into the other. The degrees of difference in the digits (pitch contours) are not accounted in this method, i.e. a substitution from 2 to 1 costs the same distance as from 4 to 1. This implementation of the tone-to-string method follows Tang (2009), where a two-digit tone aligns with a three-digit tone from the second digit of the three-digit tone, see the example below. Note that short tones are not distinguished from their longer counterpart, since it has not been proposed yet how tones like a short concave tone are represented under this method. Users should remove the '#' (length marker) in their data before applying this method. Take two tones, 15 vs. 325, as an example, we calculate the Levenshtein distance between the tones, which is demonstrated in Table 2. In this example, one substitution and deletion are required to convert 325 to 15, and that yields 2 / 3 = 0.67 difference between the two tones.

Slot 1	Slot 2	Slot 3	Operations	Distance
3	2	5	-	-
-	2	5	Deletion of 3	1
-	1	5	Substitution of 2 > 1	1
Sum				2

Table 2: Calculation of Levenshtein Distance between 325 and 15 with the tone-to-string method

4.2 Onset-Contour-Offset (OCO)

Onset-Contour-Offset (OCO hereafter) is a representation of tones proposed by Yang and Castro (2008). This representation gives a more phonetic representation of tones, instead of an abstract one, as its purpose is to approximate multiple cues of tones in the distance measure in order to generate a more accurate prediction for intelligibility between dialects (the purpose of Yang and Castro's study).

OCO involves a transformation of the tone letters/ 5-level transcription (Chao 1930) into a representation which consists of three components: *Onset*, *Contour* and *Offset*, each represented with one character, except for Contour, which can have up to two characters. Onset and Offset are the starting and ending contour levels of the tone, and the Contour is the shape of the tone. For the contour levels, the original 5-level transcription is converted into three categories, which are *H(igh)*, *M(id)* and *L(ow)*. H represents levels 4 and 5, M represents 3 and L represents 1 and 2. For contours, the basic shapes include *R(ising)*, *F(alling)*, *L(evel)*, and the complex tones are represented by the combination of the basic shapes, hence it has up to two characters. Examples of the Contour representations can be found in Table 3 below.

Representation	Contour	Example
L	Level	11, 33
R	Rising	12, 35
F	Falling	31, 52
RF	Convex	131, 253
FR	Concave	213, 424

Table 3: Contours in OCO representation with examples

As an example, the OCO representation of 221 would be LLFL, and for 24, it would be LRH. To calculate tone distances, Yang and Castro (2008) applied the Levenshtein distance algorithm on the OCO representation. This is illustrated in Table 4 below.

When two tones with different lengths are compared (length of three and four, like in Table 4), the Onset (Slot 1) and Offset (Slot 4) are always aligned together. In this example, we can find two substitutions and one deletion out of four alignment slots, which yields a Levenshtein distance of 0.75 between the tone pair.

Slot 1	Slot 2	Slot 3	Slot 4	Operations	Distance
L	L	F	L	-	-
L	R	F	L	Substitution of L > R	1
L	R	-	L	Deletion of F	1
L	R	-	H	Substitution of L > H	1
Sum					3

Table 4: Calculation of Levenshtein Distance between 221 and 24 with the OCO method

4.3 Modified Onset-Contour-Offset (mOCO)

In Sung et al. (forthcoming), it has been shown that the biggest drawback of the OCO represen-

[5]The scripts for the conversion of the original tone data to each of the representations introduced below are provided in the **supplementary material**. The converted tones can then be processed by existing dialectometric tools online, such as *Gabmap* (Nerbonne et al. 2011; Leinonen et al. 2016).

tation is that it is not able to distinguish enough tones in the Yue dataset (only 43.8%). Therefore, we made some adjustments in order to differentiate more tones present in our data. This representation is largely the same as OCO, and it still operates with a transformed representation of Chao's tone letters into onset-contour-offset.

Firstly, the pitch levels are expanded from originally differentiating three levels (merging 1 and 2 and merging 4 and 5) to distinguishing all five levels found in Chao's (1930) tone letters. Our modification creates a five-level contrast by having HH (5), H (4), M (3), L (2) and LL (1). The double representation 'HH' and 'LL' make their immediate neighbouring pitch levels, i.e. H and L respectively, costing a difference of 1, while all other pitch levels cost a difference of 2. Another modification we have made has to do with tone length. The differences in tone length are usually found between checked syllables and non-checked syllables. We have decided to represent tone length with a superscript ^{h}, which indicates a difference of 0.5.[6]

This representation of the highest and lowest pitch levels maintains the dimensions of 'direction' and 'average pitch', which has been identified in Gandour and Harshman (1978).

With the mOCO representation, when we apply Levenshtein distance between the tones in our dataset, we can differentiate 72 out of 73 tones (98.6%). The tone distances calcualted with the mOCO representation can be found in Figure 3. Since the mOCO representation can differentiate 72 tones, it should also be sufficient for other tonal languages in Southeast Asia, and perhaps in other parts of the world (given the same tone notation is used in the documentation, so that the conversion can be done).

5 Preliminary Results of Tonal Dialectometry of Yue Dialects

In this section, we will present our preliminary analysis of the tonal data, using the mOCO tone representation. The first question that we will try to answer is whether dialects form a dialect continuum, which has previously been observed in different languages on the segmental level. A follow-up question we investigated is in what ways do tones differ gradually from one dialect to another.

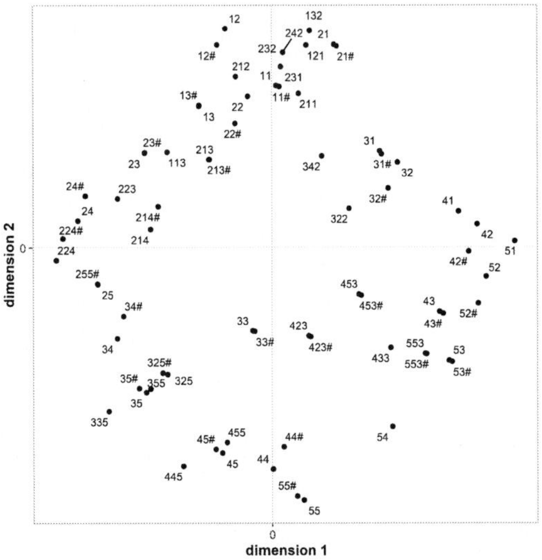

Figure 3: Multidimensional Scaling plot of tone distances calcualted with the mOCO representation.

5.1 Methodology

Firstly, the whole tonal dataset is converted to the mOCO representation. Next, for each pair of dialects, the tone distances for all the lexical items are calculated using normalized Levenshtein distance, summed and then divided by the total number of lexical items compared in the pairwise dialect comparison. These procedures yield a normalised aggregate tonal distance between all pairs of dialects in the data, which we store in a distance matrix. The distance calculation procedures described above were computed with *Gabmap* (Nerbonne et al. 2011; Leinonen et al. 2016).

5.2 Multidimensional Scaling Plot

Since a distance matrix is not interpretable for human eyes, we have employed *multidimensional scaling* to our distance matrix of the dialect tonal distances, in order to gain further insights into the tonal variation in our data. Multidimensional Scaling (MDS hereafter) is a dimensionality reduction method which represents "measurements of similarity (or dissimilarity) among pairs of objects as distances between points" (Borg and Groenen 2005: 3). In our case, an MDS plot would represent the dialects as points, and the further the points are from each other, the more different they

[6] Superscripted characters are counted as a difference of 0.5 in the Levenshtein algorithm implemented in *Gabmap*, if the last character of the *Offset* of both tones (but not the length) are identical. This implies that the tone length is only differentiated if the final character of the offset in the mOCO representation is identical. Please note that LED-A.org does not have the same implementation of the superscript ^{h}.

are. Unlike cluster analysis, the points on an MDS plot are not partitioned into discrete groups. In addition, no geographical information is added to the plot, so the distances projected on the plot is simply based on the distance matrix generated in the distance calculation. This technique is useful to visualize continuum-like dialect relations (existence of transitional dialects), as well as clusters. However, it requires one to interpret the plot themselves, including in what ways dialects differ from each other.

It is also important to check how much the distances represented in an MDS plot correlate to the original distance matrix. This is indicated by the explained variance (r^2) or by the Stress value (Heeringa 2004).

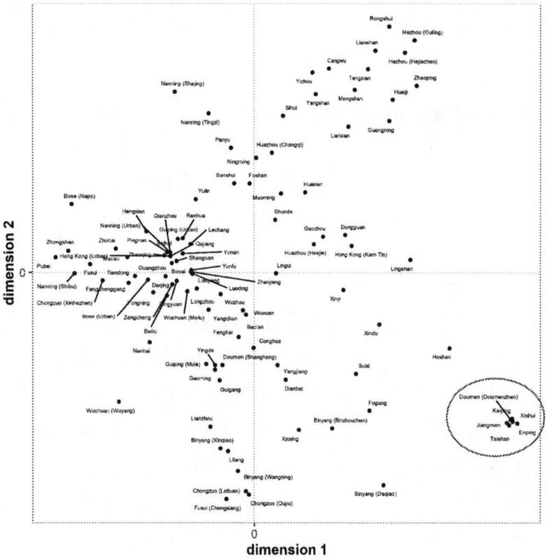

Figure 4: MDS plot of tone distances between Yue dialects (r^2= 0.70).

In Figure 4, we see a continuum-like distribution for the majority of the dialects in our data, with the possible exception of the Siyi dialects. They are marked with a red circle in Figure 4 and are clearly separate from the rest of the dialects. This corresponds to the analysis done on the segmental level (Sung 2023; Sung and Prokic 2023). This dialect group serves as our preliminary investigation into the ways in which tones vary in between dialects.

Figure 5 is a zoomed-in view of the Siyi cluster in Figure 4. We can see that although these dialects are relatively similar to each other in Figure 4, they do not completely overlap, meaning their tones are not completely identical. To gain more

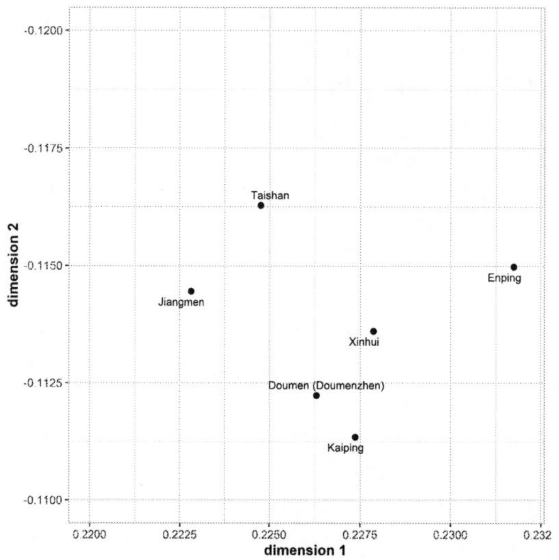

Figure 5: MDS plot of tone distances between Siyi dialects (Figure 4 zoomed in).

insights into how their tones differ from each other, we turn to the tonal inventories of these dialects.

In Table 5, the tonal inventories of the Siyi dialects are listed as the reflexes of the Middle Chinese (MC) tone categories. We can see that Taishan, Doumen and Kaiping dialects share the exact same inventory. Enping dialect has an almost identical inventory as these three dialects, except two MC tone categories share the same reflex, indicated by the merged cell in gray. Another group of dialects consists of Jiangmen and Xinhui. Their tonal inventories only differ from Taishan, Doumen and Kaiping dialects by one tone: the reflex of Yin Shang category is 45 instead of 55. Based on the inventories, we would expect the MDS plot to show overlaps of Taishan-type dialects (with Enping slightly further away), and the Jiangmen-type dialects to be even further away. This is however not the case in Figure 4. If we look at the tone correspondences between the Taishan and Kaiping dialects (see Appendix B), we can see that even though the tones in their inventories are identical, their correspondences are not perfect. This suggests that there are *lexical distribution* (Wells 1982) differences between these dialects occurring in the data.

Our preliminary results suggest that mOCO can detect both tonemic (inventory) and sub-tonemic (phonetic) differences between dialects. In addition, it can also detect lexical distributional differences between dialects with identical tone invento-

<table>
<tr><th>Tone Categories</th><th>Taishan</th><th>Kaiping</th><th>Doumen</th><th>Enping</th><th>Jiangmen</th><th>Xinhui</th></tr>
<tr><td>Yin Ping</td><td>33</td><td>33</td><td>33</td><td>33</td><td>23</td><td>23</td></tr>
<tr><td>Yang Ping</td><td>22</td><td>22</td><td>22</td><td>22</td><td>22</td><td>22</td></tr>
<tr><td>Yin Shang</td><td>55</td><td>55</td><td>55</td><td>55</td><td>45</td><td>45</td></tr>
<tr><td>Yang Shang</td><td>21</td><td>21</td><td>21</td><td rowspan="2">31</td><td>21</td><td>21</td></tr>
<tr><td>Qu</td><td>31</td><td>31</td><td>31</td><td>31</td><td>31</td></tr>
<tr><td>Yin Ru1</td><td>55#</td><td>55#</td><td>55#</td><td>55#</td><td>55#</td><td>55#</td></tr>
<tr><td>Yin Ru2</td><td>33#</td><td>33#</td><td>33#</td><td>33#</td><td>33#</td><td>33#</td></tr>
<tr><td>Yang Ru</td><td>21#</td><td>21#</td><td>21#</td><td>21#</td><td>21#</td><td>21#</td></tr>
</table>

Table 5: Tone inventories of Siyi dialects (based on Middle Chinese tone categories)

ries.

6 Conclusion

Our Yue dataset has provided new possibilities in the study of language variation. It consists of both tonal and segmental data for the same lexical items for over 100 dialects. To our knowledge, this is one of the biggest dialectal dataset for tones within one language area. Our tonal dataset is digitised from dialects surveys which were transcribed in Chao's (1930), which means that it can be converted to any existing tone representations for further dialectometric analyses. In this paper, we have briefly demonstrated how we can use one of these representations to investigate how tones vary across different dialects. By using the mOCO representation, which can differentiate almost 99% of the tones in our data, we have identified a dialect continuum as well as a dialect island, namely the Siyi dialect group. Through a comparison of tone inventories and tone correspondences of Siyi dialects, we have further identified that dialects can differ on the tonal level tonemically, sub-tonemically and in terms of lexical distribution.

Tonal languages have been neglected in the study of linguistic variation for decades, partly due to the lack of available data. We hope this dataset will serve as the first step to remove the barrier for any scholars who are interested in variation of tones.

References

I. Borg and P. J. F. Groenen. 2005. *Modern multidimensional scaling: Theory and applications*. Springer Science and Business Media.

L. Campbell. 2013. *Historical linguistics*. Edinburgh University Press.

J. K. Chambers and P. Trudgill. 1998. *Dialectology*, 2nd edition. Cambridge University Press.

Y.-R. Chao. 1930. A system of tone letters. *Le maître phonétique*, 8(45):24–27.

H. Chen and Y. Lin. 2009. 粵語平話土話方音字彙第 *1* 編: 廣西粵語、桂南平話部分 *[Yue, Pinghua and Tuhua Dialect Survey Collection Part 1]*. Shanghai Educational Publishing House.

X. Chen. 2009. 廣西賀州八步 (桂岭) 本地话音系 [the phonology of the hezhou babu (guiling) dialect in guangxi]. 方言 *[Dialect]*, (1):53–71.

X. Chen and Z. Weng. 2010. 粵語西翼考察–廣西貴港粵語個案研究 *[Investigating Western Yue - A case study on Guigang Yue in Guangxi]*. Jinan University Press.

Chinese Academy of Social Sciences (CASS). 2012. 中國語言地圖集 *[Language Atlas of China]*, 2nd edition. Commercial Press.

W. N. Francis. 1983. *Dialectology: an introduction*. Longman Group Limited.

J. Gandour and R. A. Harshman. 1978. Crosslanguage differences in tone perception: A multidimensional scaling investigation. *Language and Speech*, 21(1):1–33.

Z. Handel. 2015. Non-ipa symbols in ipa transcriptions in china. In R. Sybesma, editor, *Encyclopedia of Chinese Language and Linguistics*. Brill Reference Online.

W. Heeringa. 2004. *Measuring dialect pronunciation using Levenshtein distance*. Ph.D. thesis, University of Groningen.

Q. Huang. 2006. 賀州市賀街本地話同音字匯 [homonymic syllabary of the hezhou hezhoujie local vernacular]. *Journal of Guilin Normal College*, 20(3):6–13.

L. M. Hyman. 2006. Word-prosodic typology. *Phonology*, 23(2):225–257.

International Phonetic Association. 2005. *Handbook of the International Phonetic Association: A guide to the use of the International Phonetic Alphabet*. Cambridge University Press.

P. Jeszenszky, Y. Hikosaka, S. Imamura, and K. Yano. 2019. Japanese lexical variation explained by spatial contact patterns. *ISPRS International Journal of Geo-Information*, 8(9):400.

C. Lau. 2001. 粵客方言文白異讀的比較 [the comparison between literary and colloquial readings in yue and hakka dialects]. In C. Lau, editor, 香港粵客方言比較研究 *[The Comparative Study of Hong Kong Yue and Hakka Dialects]*, pages 134–147. Jinan University Press.

T. Leinonen, Ç. Çöltekin, and J. Nerbonne. 2016. Using gabmap. *Lingua*, 178:71–83.

V. I. Levenshtein. 1966. Binary codes capable of correcting deletions, insertions, and reversals. *Soviet physics doklady*, 10(8):707–710.

R. Li. 2007. 漢語方言學 *[Chinese Dialectology]*, 2nd edition. Higher Education Press.

R. Li. 2017. 漢語方言調查 *[Surveying Chinese Dialects]*. Commercial Press.

Johann-Mattis List. 2019. Automatic inference of sound correspondence patterns across multiple languages. *Computational Linguistics*, 45(1):137–161.

C. Liu. 2015. 廣東兩陽粵語語音研究 *[Research in the Phonetics of Yue in the Guangdong Liangyang Area]*. Ph.D. thesis, Jinan University.

A Mathussek. 2016. On the problem of field worker isoglosses. In M.-H. Côté, R. Knooihuize, and J. Nerbonne, editors, *The future of dialects*, pages 99–116. Language Science Press.

J. Nerbonne. 2010. Measuring the diffusion of linguistic change. *Philosophical Transactions of the Royal Society B: Biological Sciences*, 365(1559):3821–3828.

J. Nerbonne, R. Colen, C. Gooskens, P. Kleiweg, and T. Leinonen. 2011. Gabmap-a web application for dialectology. *Dialectologia: revista electrònica*, pages 65–89.

B. Pfeiler and S. Skopeteas. 2022. Sources of convergence in indigenous languages: Lexical variation in yucatec maya. *PLoS ONE*, 17(5):e0268448.

QGIS Development Team. 2022. *QGIS Geographic Information System*. Open Source Geospatial Foundation Project.

H. Shao. 2016. 粵西湛茂地區粵語語音研究 *[The Phonological Study of the Yue Dialects spoken in the Zhan-Mao area in Western Guangdong]*. Sun Yat-Sen University Press.

R. Shi. 2009. 廣西防城區粵語音系 [the phonology of the fangcheng yue dialect in guangxi]. 百色學院學報 *[Journal of Baise University]*, 22(2):106–116.

J. N. Stanford. 2012. One size fits all? dialectometry in a small clan-based indigenous society. *Language Variation and Change*, 24(2):247–278.

H. W. M. Sung. 2023. Is a typologically, genetically different language similar to european languages? a dialectometrical analysis on yue and pinghua. In *73. Studentischen Tagung Sprachwissenschaft (StuTS), Oral Presentation*, Frankfurt, Germany.

H. W. M. Sung and J. Prokic. 2023. What are guangfu dialects? In *27th International Conference on Yue Dialects*, Ohio State University, Online Presentation.

H. W. M. Sung, J. Prokic, and Y. Chen. forthcoming. Applying the state–of–the–art tonal distance metrics to a large dialectal dataset. In U. Stange-Hundsdörfer S. Wagner, editor, *(Dia)lects in the 21st century: Selected papers from Methods in Dialectology XVII (Mainz, 2022)*. Language Science Press. Forthcoming.

M. Swadesh. 1955. Towards greater accuracy in lexicostatistic dating. *International Journal of American Linguistics*, 21:121–137.

Y. Tan. 2017. 廣西賓陽縣 (賓州鎮) 本地話音系 [the phonology of binzhouzhen in the binyang county in guangxi]. 梧州學院學報 *[Journal of Wuzhou University]*, 27(5):58–71.

C. Tang. 2009. *Mutual intelligibility of Chinese dialects: an experimental approach*. Ph.D. thesis, Leiden University.

P. Trudgill. 1983. *On dialect: Social and geographical perspectives*. New York University Press.

F. Wang and W. S. Y. Wang. 2004. Basic words and language evolution. *Language and linguistics*, 5(3):643–662.

J.C. Wells. 1982. *Accents of English: Introduction*, volume 1. Cambridge University Press.

S. Wichmann and Q. Ran. 2019. Asjp 模式的漢語方言計算分析——以 65 個漢語方言語檔為例 [a phylogenetic study on 65 chinese doculects: with asjp tools]. 現代語文 *[Modern Chinese]*, (5):4–13.

M.-S. Wu, N.E. Schweikhard, T.A. Bodt, N.W. Hill, and J.-M. List. 2020. Computer-assisted language comparison: State of the art. *Journal of Open Humanities Data*, 6(1):2.

J. Xie. 2007. 廣西漢語方言研究 *[Studies on the Chinese dialects in Guangxi]*. People's Publishing House of Guangxi.

C. Yang and A. Castro. 2008. Representing tone in levenshtein distance. *International Journal of Humanities and Arts Computing*, 2(1-2):205–219.

S. Yang. 2013. 廣西藤縣濛江方言音系 [the phonology of the tengxian mengjiang dialect in guangxi]. 方言 *[Dialect]*, (1):71–85.

M. Yip. 2002. *Tone*. Cambridge University Press.

B. Zhan and Y. Cheung. 1987. *A Survey of Dialects in the Pearl River Delta, Vol. 1, Comparative Morpheme-Syllabary*. People's Publishing House of Guangdung.

B. Zhan and Y. Cheung. 1990. *A Survey of Dialects in the Pearl River Delta, Vol. 3, A Synthetic View*. People's Publishing House of Guangdung.

B. Zhan and Y. Cheung. 1994. *A Survey of Yue Dialects in North Guangdong*. Jinan University Press.

B. Zhan and Y. Cheung. 1998. *A Survey of Yue Dialects in West Guangdong*. Jinan University Press.

Z. Zhong. 2015. 廣西蒼梧本地話音系 [the phonology of cangwu local vernacular in guangxi]. 方言 *[Dialect]*, (2):177–192.

中國語言資源保護研究中心 [Research Centre of Linguistic Resource Reservation in China]. 2022. 中國語言資源保護工程採錄展示平台 [platform of linguistic resource reservation].

Supplementary Material

The datasets and the tone conversion scripts can be found in `https://osf.io/m9g2a/`.

Appendix A: List of Items in the Data

Chinese	English	Chinese	English
一	one	二	two
三	three	四	four
五	five	六	six
七	seven	八	eight
九	nine	十	ten
我	I	你	you
全	all	多	many
大	big	長	long
細	small_col	小	small_lit
男	man	女	woman
人	person	魚	fish
鳥	bird_lit	雀	bird_col
狗	dog	虱	lice
樹	tree	葉	leaf
根	root	皮	skin1
膚	skin2	肉	meat
血	blood	骨	bone
脂	fat	角	horn
尾	tail	羽	feather
髮	hair_head	毛	hair_body
頭	head	耳	ear
眼	eye	鼻	nose
口	mouth	牙	tooth1
齒	tooth2	爪	claws
腳	leg	膝	knee
手	hand	肚	abdomen
胸	breast	心	heart
肝	liver	飲	to drink
食	to eat	咬	to bite
看	to see_lit	知	to know
睡	to sleep	死	to die
殺	to kill	游	to swim
飛	to fly	走	to walk
來	to sit	企	to stand
講	to speak_col	日	sun
月	moon	水	water
雨	rain	石	stone
沙	sand	土	soil/earth
地	floor/ground	雲	cloud
煙	smoke	火	fire
灰	ash	燒	to burn
路	road	山	mountain
紅	red	綠	green
黃	yellow	藍	blue
白	white	黑	black
夜	night	熱	hot
凍	cold	滿	full
新	new	好	good
圓	round	乾	dry
史	history	蛇	snake
虎	tiger	鼠	mouse/rat
馬	horse	牛	cow
船	boat	春	Spring
夏	Summer	秋	Autumn
冬	Winter	西	West
北	North	出	out
入	enter	墳	tomb
想	to think	雙	double
見	to see_col	雞	chicken
豬	pig	湖	lake
合	together/to merge	村	village
愛	love	鴨	duck
奇	strange	具	tool
花	flower	光	light
師	teacher	去	to go

Appendix B: Tone Correspondences

Correspondences	No. of Items
11# : 21#	1
21:21	4
21:31	2
21# : 21#	12
21# : 33#	1
22:22	21
22:55	1
31:31	10
33:21	2
33:33	33
33:55	1
33# : 21#	1
33# : 33#	3
35:21	1
55:55	26
55# : 55#	11

Correspondence Table of Tones between Taishan (left) and Kaiping (right) Dialects (irregular correspondences in gray)

A Computational Model for the Assessment of Mutual Intelligibility Among Closely Related Languages

Jessica Nieder
MCL Chair
University of Passau
Passau, Germany
jessica.nieder@uni-passau.de

Johann-Mattis List
MCL Chair / DLCE
University of Passau / MPI-EVA
Passau / Leipzig, Germany
mattis.list@uni-passau.de

Abstract

Closely related languages show linguistic similarities that allow speakers of one language to understand speakers of another language without having actively learned it. Mutual intelligibility varies in degree and is typically tested in psycholinguistic experiments. To study mutual intelligibility computationally, we propose a computer-assisted method using the Linear Discriminative Learner, a computational model developed to approximate the cognitive processes by which humans learn languages, which we expand with multilingual semantic vectors and multilingual sound classes. We test the model on cognate data from German, Dutch, and English, three closely related Germanic languages. We find that our model's comprehension accuracy depends on 1) the automatic trimming of inflections and 2) the language pair for which comprehension is tested. Our multilingual modelling approach does not only offer new methodological findings for automatic testing of mutual intelligibility across languages but also extends the use of Linear Discriminative Learning to multilingual settings.

1 Introduction

Speakers of a given language can often partially comprehend other languages in the same language family. This mutual intelligibility has been demonstrated to be dependent on several linguistic variables, such as phonological, orthographic or lexical similarity, and extralinguistic factors, such as the amount of previous exposure to or the attitude towards the other language (Gooskens and Swarte, 2017; Gooskens et al., 2015; Heeringa et al., 2014). In addition, the phonetic similarity between words expressing similar meanings has been shown to be a major factor driving cross-linguistic mutual intelligibility (Gooskens et al., 2018). Phonetically and semantically similar words are often called *cognates* in studies on mutual intelligibility, foreign language learning, and bilingualism (Squires et al., 2020). Originally, however, the term denotes words inherited from the same ancestral language in genetically related languages (List, 2016). Although cognates in the original sense often exhibit phonetic and semantic similarity across related languages, they do not necessarily do so, and words can also be similar in pronunciation and meaning due to other factors, including – most importantly – intensive borrowing, and – to a much lower degree – different kinds of sound symbolism (see Casad 1987, 87 for more details on the difference between mutual intelligibility and genetic relationship).

Due to a focus on the abilities of language users, research on mutual intelligibility often involves experimental studies with different groups and numbers of participants. Experiments are diverse, usually consisting of certain comprehension tasks. Experimental studies show some general limitations, in so far as uniform methods are rarely used (1), finding participants with a minimum or no exposure to the test language is difficult (2), and comparing several languages simultaneously is a time- and resource-consuming effort (3) (Gooskens and Swarte, 2017; Tang and van Heuven, 2009). Gooskens and Swarte (2017) present a large-scale study on mutual intelligibility of five Germanic languages using a *Cloze Test*, i.e. a written or audibly presented text in the target language with gaps that need to be filled in. However, they report a substantial loss in the number of participants when testing *inherent intelligibility*, the ability to comprehend the target language with no or little previous exposure (Gooskens and Swarte, 2017). In an ideal setting with zero exposure to the target language, inherent intelligibility captures how comprehensible the target language is based on structural similarities only. This, in turn, would offer insights into what linguistic structures give rise to mutual intelligibility without extralinguistic or other language exposure-based interference. In reality, the goal of finding participants with no or

Proceedings of the 6th Workshop on Research in Computational Linguistic Typology and Multilingual NLP (SIGTYP 2024), pages 37–43
March 22, 2024 ©2024 Association for Computational Linguistics

a minimum of exposure to certain languages is an almost impossible requirement to fulfill due to the status of some languages of being a common *lingua franca* (Gooskens and Swarte, 2017; Hongyan, 2017).

In this study we propose a computer-assisted method couched in the discriminative lexicon framework by Baayen et al. (2019) to assess mutual intelligibility in Germanic languages. By focusing on computational methods instead of human subjects we can overcome the mentioned limitations. Our proposed model does not involve the recruitment of participants, there are no extralinguistic factors nor target language exposure involved in training. We offer a uniform method that can be adapted to various language families and lead to new insights into intelligibility based on a careful selection of linguistic factors that are involved in language comprehension.

2 Linear Discriminative Learning

With the discriminative lexicon framework (DL), Baayen et al. (2019) propose a model of language processing that explores the cognitive mapping mechanisms involved in language learning. Language comprehension is understood as a mapping of phonological forms onto meaning (Baayen et al., 2019). Mathematically, it is implemented as multivariate multiple regression in the Linear Discriminative Learner (LDL) model. Given a phonological matrix C and a semantic matrix S, the comprehension matrix F is obtained by post-multiplying C with F: $CF = S$. The F matrix then specifies the associaton weights between all phonological cues and all semantic dimensions (Chuang et al., 2023). Multiplying C with F finally predicts the semantic vector $\hat{S}$ for all input word forms that can be used for evaluating comprehension accuracy of the model. Computationally, the LDL model conceptualizes language comprehension as a simple artificial neural network directly connecting phonological and semantic vectors without any hidden layers (Nieder et al., 2023; Chuang et al., 2023). In this study, we make use of LDL to explore the mutual comprehension of the Germanic languages Dutch, German and English based on a cross-language learning setting (see also Chuang et al., 2018, for another multilingual approach using LDL). As phonological input we use cognate sets from all languages. For the semantic matrix, we opted for the multilingual ConceptNet Numberbatch word embeddings *version 19.08* from Speer et al. (2017) that offer the possibility to directly compare the meaning of cognate concepts.

3 Materials and Methods

3.1 Dataset of German Cognates

We use cognate sets derived from Kluge's etymological dictionary in a rather recent, updated edition (Kluge, 2002). From the etymological dictionary of German, we hand-selected 340 entries that had reflexes in Dutch, German, and English with their proto-forms in Proto-Germanic, added phonetic transcriptions, and provided phonetic alignments by annotating the data with the help of the *EDICTOR* tool (List, 2023).

In order to ease data sharing and reuse, the etymological dataset was shared in the formats recommended by the Cross-Linguistic Data Formats initiative (Forkel et al., 2018) using the workflow developed for the construction of the Lexibank repository (`https://lexibank.clld.org`, List et al. 2022). This means in this specific case that languages are linked to Glottolog (`https://glottolog.org`, Hammarström et al. 2023) and that the individual speech sounds employed in the phonetic transcription we provide follows the Cross-Linguistic Transcription Systems (CLTS, `https://clts.clld.org`, List et al. 2021). CLTS is a reference catalog for speech sounds which provides a standard transcription system that defines a subset of the International Phonetic Alphabet (IPA, 1999) as a standard (Anderson et al., 2018), which has by now been mapped to several datasets providing phoneme inventory data (Anderson et al., 2023) and also underlies most data in Lexibank.

3.2 Multilingual Semantic Vectors

For semantic vectors, we used the multilingual ConceptNet Numberbatch word embeddings *version 19.08* from Speer et al. (2017). The ConceptNet Numberbatch word embeddings did not provide any data for the Dutch word form *beukeboom* 'beech', thus we deleted the German and English counterparts from the data resulting in a set of 339 cognates in total. To ensure that the embeddings capture semantic similarites of the cognate dataset, we computed the cosine similarity for each word triplet across the languages. Figure 1 shows the distribution of cosine similarity values between language pairs. While the peaks for all language pairs are located at around 0.9, indicating an overall

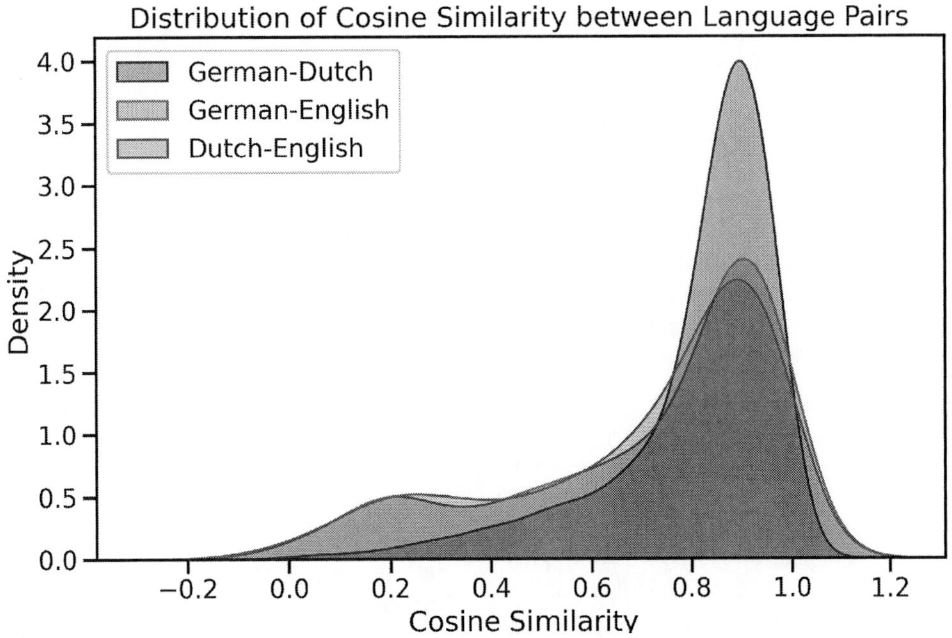

Figure 1: Distribution of cosine similarity scores between language pairs for all cognate triplets. Note that smoothing of the distribution results in values exceeding 1.0.

high semantic similarity of the word embeddings for cognate triplets, some of the German-English data and Dutch-English data is distributed over a lower cosine similarity range (green and red curve). This results in less concentrated peaks for these language pairs. From this we can conclude that German vs. Dutch cognates are semantically more similar than German vs. English or Dutch vs. English cognates.

3.3 Multilingual Sound Classes

Scholars have proposed to test mutual intelligibility by representing word forms in phonetic transcriptions and measuring string similarity for words that express the same meaning (Tang and van Heuven, 2007). This approach to intelligibility has, however, the disadvantage of not being able to test for *asymmetric forms* of intelligibility by which speakers of one language can understand speakers of another language more properly than vice versa. For our model-based approach, we need a more abstract – phonetically broader – representation of speech sounds that allows us to capture broad phonetic similarities in a multilingual setting. Taking inspiration from computational approaches in historical linguistics, we decided to represent word forms with *sound class models*. Sound classes have been first introduced by Dolgopolsky (1986), who proposed 9 broad classes by which all possible consonants can be represented, searching for cognates across distantly related languages. While this is a really crude reduction of phonetic detail, Dolgopolsky sound classes have been shown to work very well for comparative tasks (Turchin et al., 2010). In our approach, we use Dolgopolsky's original consonant classes and represent vowels by an additional symbol.

	English	**German**
Word	drink	trinken
IPA	d ɾ ɪ ŋ k	t ɾ ɪ ŋ k ə n
IPA (trimmed)	d ɾ ɪ ŋ k	t ɾ ɪ ŋ ʁ ə
Sound Classes	T R V N K	T R V N K V N
Sound Cl. (trimmed)	T R V N K	T R V N K V

Table 1: Exemplary data representation for English and German with full forms vs. trimmed forms and sound class representations.

The fact that our original data are provided in CLDF with standardized phonetic transcriptions is a great advantage when it comes to the conversion of phonetic strings to sound classes. Since sound class conversion routines are readily available for phonetic transcriptions that conform to the standard for IPA proposed in CLTS, converting the cognate sets in German, Dutch, and English to sound classes requires very few preprocessing operations.

3.4 Trimming Word Forms

We experiment with two different representations of word forms, full forms and trimmed forms, where we automatically exclude endings. Full forms reflect the word forms as they are typically encountered in dictionaries (with nominative case for nouns in German and infinitive endings for verbs). Bare stems are typically used in historical language comparison in order to show how words were historically related before they were modified in the respective descendant languages by various morphological processes. In order to obtain bare stems from our cognate sets in German, English, and Dutch, we make use of the recently introduced technique for the *trimming* of phonetic alignments (Blum and List, 2023). With this technique, those sites (columns) in a multiple phonetic alignment that show an exceeding amount of gaps (sounds that do not have counterparts across all languages in the sample) are excluded from the alignment. Although not identical with manually prepared word stem representations, we find that applying this technique drastically reduces the amount of gaps in the multiple alignments, while at the same time successfully removing verb endings in our sample. Table 1 displays the representation of our data with full forms vs. bare stems sound class representation.

3.5 Linear Discriminative Learning Model

In a first step, we evaluated the LDL model on the cognate data of each language separately. The model is trained and tested on all 339 word forms. Phonological input cues are 4-gram, 3-gram and 2-gram chunks of sound classes, while multilingual word embeddings are representing the semantic vectors. In a second step, we train the model on a single language, i.e. creating a naive speaker of a language with zero exposure to other languages, and subsequently test the model on the cognate data from the target language. In doing so, we are replicating the setting of psycholinguistic studies but overcome the limitations of previous language exposure to exclusively focus on the predictiveness of historical sound classes as cues to mutual intelligibility.

	4-grams	**3-grams**	**2-grams**
German	0.99	0.93	0.51
Dutch	1.0	0.93	0.52
English	1.0	0.95	0.54

(a) Training data (full words)

	4-grams	**3-grams**	**2-grams**
German	0.99	0.92	0.50
Dutch	1.0	0.89	0.48
English	1.0	0.99	0.57

(b) Training data (trimmed words)

Table 2: Comprehension accuracies on full (a) and trimmed (b) training data. Top-1 candidate is taken into account to compute accuracies.

3.6 Implementation

The experiments are implemented in the form of Python and Julia scripts. For sound class conversion, we used the LingPy Python package (List and Forkel, 2023a). For the extraction of bare word stems through trimming, the LingRex package was used (List and Forkel, 2023b). For the implementation of the LDL models, the Linear Discriminative Learner from the *JudiLing* package (an implementation of DL in the *Julia* programming language) was used (Luo et al., 2021). Data and code needed to replicate the experiments from this study are curated on GitHub (`https://github.com/digling/intelligibility`) and archived with Zenodo (`https://doi.org/10.5281/zenodo.10609356`). Detailed instructions on how to run the code are given in the repository.

4 Evaluation

4.1 Evaluation on Individual Languages

Table 2(a) displays the comprehension accuracies on the training data for full word forms. For the evaluation process only the predicted meaning, the top-1 candidate, was considered. The evaluation results suggest a good comprehension memory of the model when Dolgopolsky sound classes are provided as 4-gram or 3-gram chunks. If sound classes are fed into the model as 2-gram chunks we observe a substantial drop in accuracy, indicating a reduced discriminative power to predict a semantic vector $\hat{S}$ that is similar to the gold standard vector S of the training language. Table 2(b) displays the evaluation results after trimming word forms. Comprehension accuracy remains high for 4-gram and 3-gram chunks. Again, the accuracy drops

Language Pair	(a) Full Word Forms			(b) Trimmed Word Forms		
	4-grams	3-grams	2-grams	4-grams	3-grams	2-grams
GER-DUT	0.57 (0.71)	0.51 (0.68)	0.28 (0.52)	0.81 (0.86)	0.75 (0.86)	0.39 (0.65)
DUT-GER	0.51 (0.67)	0.48 (0.61)	0.25 (0.48)	0.82 (0.83)	0.75 (0.83)	0.40 (0.67)
GER-ENG	0.68 (0.75)	0.62 (0.73)	0.29 (0.53)	0.79 (0.85)	0.75 (0.84)	0.33 (0.59)
ENG-GER	0.48 (0.59)	0.46 (0.55)	0.23 (0.45)	0.60 (0.66)	0.59 (0.64)	0.32 (0.53)
DUT-ENG	0.68 (0.75)	0.6313 (0.72)	0.31 (0.55)	0.77 (0.84)	0.71 (0.81)	0.30 (0.60)
ENG-DUT	0.53 (0.64)	0.50 (0.59)	0.29 (0.49)	0.60 (0.67)	0.59 (0.64)	0.35 (0.54)

Table 3: Comprehension accuracies of multilingual models for comprehension for (a) full word forms and (b) trimmed word forms. Values without brackets indicate results when the top-1 candidate is considered to compute accuracies, values in brackets indidcate results when top-5 candidates are considered.

substantially when 2-gram chunks are taken into account.

4.2 Evaluation Across Languages

Table 3(a) illustrates the result of the multilingual models for full word forms. The first column contains the training-test language pairs. Values without brackets indicate accuracies when the top-1 candidate was taken into account for evaluation, values in brackets indicate accuracies when the correct meaning among top-5 candidates was considered. Allowing the model to evaluate comprehension accuracy based on a set of top-5 candidates accounts for possible confusion of the target word form with similar word forms, giving the model room for multiple answers. The cross-linguistic comprehension results in Table 3(a) unsurprisingly replicate the chunk size effect we have seen in our training models, with 4-gram chunks providing the best comprehension results. We observe the best comprehension results for the language pair Dutch-English with an accuracy of 68% (75% for an evaluation on top-5 candidates), followed by German-English and German-Dutch. The worst comprehension results are given for a training on English and a test on German cognates (see row 4 of Table 3(a)). Gooskens and Swarte (2017) report a similar result for human participants, indicating that our LDL models show a human-like performance when assessing comprehension abilities across languages.

Table 3(b) displays the comprehension accuracies after applying the trimming procedure. Trimming phonetic alignments results in a substantial rise of prediction accuracies with Dutch-German, German-Dutch and German-English providing the best comprehension results. Again, the language pair English-German shows the lowest comprehension accuracy, similar to human results (Gooskens and Swarte, 2017).

5 Discussion and Conclusion

In this study we presented a computer-assisted method to mutual intelligibility based on a model that captures the cognitive processes by which humans comprehend languages. We expanded the model with multilingual semantic vectors and multilingual sound classes. Our multilingual sound classes were predictive when a combination of at least 3 sound classes is given, indicating that knowing the order of sound classes allows the model to comprehend languages from the same language family. However, we observe an effect of the training language, with English being the least advantageous language in our setting and in the data of Gooskens and Swarte (2017) with human participants. We report a higher accuracy for German-English than German-Dutch, again in line with the human data of Gooskens and Swarte (2017). If sound classes are trimmed, we find the opposite effect. The pair Dutch-English shows better comprehension accuracies than Dutch-German, again with the opposite picture for the trimmed version. From a language learning perspective, the change of direction, i.e. the better prediction for German-Dutch and Dutch-German after trimming would imply a certain morphological knowledge of speakers. Speakers of German or Dutch knowing verb endings and ignoring them purposefully have an advantage in comprehending English. Our proposed model does not only offer a new method for automatic testing of mutual intelligibility but shows clear similarities to data obtained from human participants, making it a useful cognitive tool for research on language comprehension.

Supplementary Material

All data and code needed to replicate the experiments discussed in this study are curated on GitHub (https://github.com/digling/intelligibility) and archived with Zenodo (https://doi.org/10.5281/zenodo.10609356). The German cognate dataset is also curated on GitHub (https://github.com/lexibank/germancognates) and archived with Zenodo (https://doi.org/10.5281/zenodo.10609476).

Limitations

While our model offers some fruitful results for further investigation of mutual intelligibility, the dataset we provided contains a limited amount of carefully selected historical cognates. It remains to be seen how the model would deal with a much larger set of random words. Moreover, we cannot account for other language families or other languages than German, Dutch and English. However, we see our modeling procedure as a starting point for assessing mutual intelligibility computationally. For that reason, limiting our data to historical cognates and three languages only is a necessary step. For a complete picture, more languages from the Germanic language family need to be tested and the results need to be compared with comprehension results for other language families.

Ethics Statement

This research does not involve human or animal data. No potential ethical conflict or conflict of interest was reported by the authors.

Acknowledgements

This research was supported by the Max Planck Society Research Grant *CALC³* (JML, https://digling.org) and the ERC Consolidator Grant *ProduSemy* (JML, Grant No. 101044282, see https://doi.org/10.3030/101044282). Views and opinions expressed are however those of the authors only and do not necessarily reflect those of the European Union or the European Research Council Executive Agency (nor any other funding agencies involved). Neither the European Union nor the granting authority can be held responsible for them. We thank Maria Heitmeier and Harald Baayen for their valuable input regarding the computational models used in this study.

References

Cormac Anderson, Tiago Tresoldi, Thiago Costa Chacon, Anne-Maria Fehn, Mary Walworth, Robert Forkel, and Johann-Mattis List. 2018. A Cross-Linguistic Database of Phonetic Transcription Systems. *Yearbook of the Poznań Linguistic Meeting*, 4(1):21–53.

Cormac Anderson, Tiago Tresoldi, Simon J. Greenhill, Robert Forkel, Russell D. Gray, and Johann-Mattis List. 2023. Variation in phoneme inventories: quantifying the problem and improving comparability. *Journal of Language Evolution*, 0(0):1–20.

R. Harald Baayen, Yu-Ying Chuang, Elnaz Shafaei-Bajestan, and James P. Blevins. 2019. The discriminative lexicon: A unified computational model for the lexicon and lexical processing in comprehension and production grounded not in (de)composition but in linear discriminative learning. *Complexity*, 2019.

Frederic Blum and Johann-Mattis List. 2023. Trimming phonetic alignments improves the inference of sound correspondence patterns from multilingual wordlists. In *Proceedings of the 5th Workshop on Computational Typology and Multilingual NLP*, pages 52–64. Association for Computational Linguistics.

Eugene H. Casad. 1987. *Dialect intelligibility testing*. Summer Institute of Linguistics, Dallas.

Yu-Ying Chuang, Melanie J. Bell, Isabelle Banke, and R. Harald Baayen. 2018. Bilingual and multilingual mental lexicon: A modeling study with linear discriminative learning. *Language Learning*, 71(S1):219–292.

Yu-Ying Chuang, Mihi Kang, Luo Xuefeng, and R. Harald Baayen. 2023. Vector space morphology with linear discriminative learning. In Davide Crepaldi, editor, *Linguistic Morphology in the Mind and Brain*, 1st edition, pages 17–248. Routledge, London.

Aharon B. Dolgopolsky. 1986. A probabilistic hypothesis concerning the oldest relationships among the language families of northern Eurasia. In Vitalij V. Shevoroshkin, editor, *Typology, Relationship and Time*, pages 27–50. Karoma Publisher, Ann Arbor.

Robert Forkel, Johann-Mattis List, Simon J. Greenhill, Christoph Rzymski, Sebastian Bank, Michael Cysouw, Harald Hammarström, Martin Haspelmath, Gereon A. Kaiping, and Russell D. Gray. 2018. Cross-Linguistic Data Formats, advancing data sharing and re-use in comparative linguistics. *Scientific Data*, 5(180205):1–10.

Charlotte Gooskens and Femke Swarte. 2017. Linguistic and extra-linguistic predictors of mutual intelligibility between Germanic languages. *Nordic Journal of Linguistics*, 40(2):123–147.

Charlotte Gooskens, Renée van Bezooijen, and Vincent J. van Heuven. 2015. Mutual intelligibility of Dutch-German cognates by children: The devil is in the detail. *Linguistics*, 53(2):255–283.

Charlotte Gooskens, Vincent J. van Heuven, Jelena Golubović, Anja Schüppert, Femke Swarte, and Stefanie Voigt. 2018. Mutual Intelligibility between Closely Related Languages in Europe. *International Journal of Multilingualism*, 15(2):169–193.

Harald Hammarström, Martin Haspelmath, Robert Forkel, and Sebastian Bank. 2023. *Glottolog. Version 4.8.* Max Planck Institute for Evolutionary Anthropology, Leipzig.

Wilbert Heeringa, Femke Swarte, Anja Schüppert, and Charlotte Gooskens. 2014. Modeling Intelligibility of Written Germanic Languages: Do We Need to Distinguish Between Orthographic Stem and Affix Variation? *Journal of Germanic Linguistics*, 26(4):361–394.

Wang Hongyan. 2017. *English as a lingua franca: Mutual intelligibility of Chinese, Dutch and American speakers of English.* Ph.D. thesis, University of Utrecht.

International Phonetic Organisation IPA. 1999. *Handbook of the International Phonetic Association.* Cambridge University Press, Cambridge.

Friedrich Kluge. 2002. *Etymologisches Wörterbuch der deutschen Sprache*, 24 edition. de Gruyter, Berlin.

Johann-Mattis List. 2016. Beyond cognacy: Historical relations between words and their implication for phylogenetic reconstruction. *Journal of Language Evolution*, 1(2):119–136.

Johann-Mattis List. 2023. *EDICTOR. A web-based tool for creating, editing, and publishing etymological datasets [Software Tool, Version 2.1.0].* MCL Chair at the University of Passau, Passau.

Johann-Mattis List, Cormac Anderson, Tiago Tresoldi, and Robert Forkel. 2021. *Cross-Linguistic Transcription Systems. Version 2.1.0.* Max Planck Institute for the Science of Human History, Jena.

Johann-Mattis List and Robert Forkel. 2023a. *LingPy. A Python library for quantitative tasks in historical linguistics [Software Library, Version 2.6.13].* MCL Chair at the University of Passau, Passau.

Johann-Mattis List and Robert Forkel. 2023b. *LingRex: Linguistic reconstruction with LingPy.* Max Planck Institute for Evolutionary Anthropology, Leipzig.

Johann-Mattis List, Robert Forkel, Simon J. Greenhill, Christoph Rzymski, Johannes Englisch, and Russell D. Gray. 2022. Lexibank, a public repository of standardized wordlists with computed phonological and lexical features. *Scientific Data*, 9(316):1–31.

Xuefeng Luo, Yu-Ying Chuang, and R. Harald Baayen. 2021. JudiLing: An implementation in Julia of linear discriminative learning algorithms for language modeling.

Jessica Nieder, Yu-Ying Chuang, Ruben van de Vijver, and R. Harald Baayen. 2023. A discriminative lexicon approach to word comprehension, production, and processing: Maltese plurals. *Language*, 99(2):242–274.

Robyn Speer, Joshua Chin, and Catherine Havasi. 2017. ConceptNet 5.5: An open multilingual graph of general knowledge. In *Proceedings of the AAAI Conference on Artificial Intelligence 2017*, pages 4444–4451.

Lindsey R. Squires, Sara J. Ohlfest, Kristen E. Santoro, and Jennifer L. Roberts. 2020. Factors influencing cognate performance for young multilingual children's vocabulary: A research synthesis. *American Journal of Speech-Language Pathology*, 29(4):2170–2188.

Chaoju Tang and Vincent J. van Heuven. 2007. Mutual intelligibility and similarity of Chinese dialects. Predicting judgments from objective measures. In Bettelou Los and Marjo van Koppen, editors, *Linguistics in the Netherlands 2007*, pages 223–234. John Benjamins Publishing Company.

Chaoju Tang and Vincent J. van Heuven. 2009. Mutual intelligibility of Chinese dialects experimentally tested. *Lingua*, 119(5):709–732.

Peter Turchin, Ilja Peiros, and Murray Gell-Mann. 2010. Analyzing genetic connections between languages by matching consonant classes. *Journal of Language Relationship*, 3:117–126.

Predicting Mandarin and Cantonese Adult Speakers' Eye-Movement Patterns in Natural Reading

Understanding how language knowledge is processed and integrated incrementally has been an important question in language science. The reading of Chinese languages provides an interesting environment for investigating such inquires as its morphosyntactic nature and writing systems require a greater reliance on the lexical context during comprehension (Chen et al., 1992; Jian et al., 2013; Hsu et al., 2023), even in the initial stage of processing (Zhao et al., 2019). Chinese languages encompass varieties in written forms with nuanced visual complexity of words and morpho-syntactic structures. For example, Mandarin and Cantonese differ not only in their grammars and lexicon, but also in their writing systems among different Chinese speaking regions. For instance, Mandarin in Mainland China uses simplified Chinese characters in writing whereas Cantonese in Hong Kong uses traditional Chinese characters. This distinction raises the question of whether the visual complexity of characters influences the processing of characters, despite representing the same meanings (e.g., 书 'book' and 書 'book'). Moreover, simplified characters tend to be more ambiguous than traditional characters, as the former often associates multiple meanings with one character (e.g., 后 means either 'the back' or 'the queen'), while the traditional characters have more one-to-one correspondence between character and meaning (e.g., 后 means 'queen' and 後 means 'back'). Therefore, the contextual influence and predictability of words may differ between writing systems using simplified and traditional characters, in addition to understanding whether each character co-occurs with other characters to form either a word or a phrase. By comparing the processing of Chinese languages, we can gain profound insights into understanding linguistic variations as well as the integration of multilevel linguistic processing.

Eye movement data offer valuable insights into the cognitive processes involved in reading, shedding light on how language is processed across various aspects, such as morphology (Clifton Jr et al., 2007), syntax (Van Schijndel and Schuler, 2015), and semantics (Ehrlich and Rayner, 1981). Many studies have shown that certain characteristics of words can impact language processing, and reading behavior. These features include word position, word length, word frequency, and the number of syllables within the word (Just and Carpenter, 1980). Furthermore, the spillover effect (Rayner et al., 1989) suggests that the cognitive load imposed by a word can affect the processing of subsequent words (Pollatsek et al., 2008). Another important factor that impacts language comprehension is the predictability of a word at the sentence level, based on the preceding context (Kliegl et al., 2004). By measuring and examining eyemovement data, we can gain insights into how these factors influence the cognitive processes during language comprehension.

Therefore, the aim of the current study is twofold. First, adopting a computational approach, and using matched materials read by mature adult native speakers, we introduce a joint benchmark of eye-tracking data that capture natural reading patterns of reading Mainland Mandarin and Hong Kong Cantonese texts. An example fixation heatmap of the two languages is shown in Fig. 1.

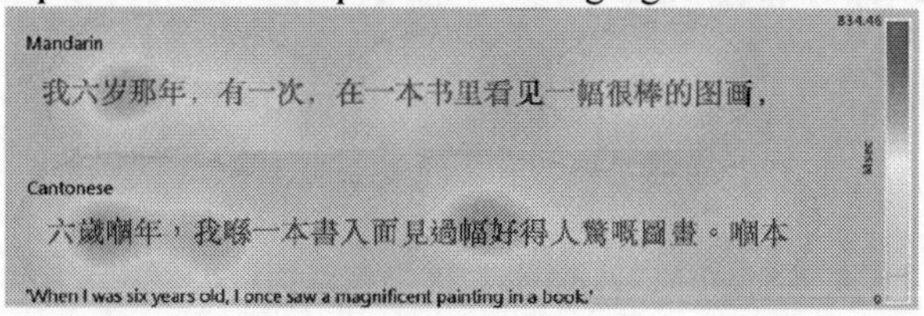

Fig. 1. A fixation heatmap of Mandarin and Cantonese sentences.

This dataset doubles the size of the dataset introduced in Li et al. (2023) and includes several new eye-movement metrics that capture initial lexical processing and later integrated structural processing (e.g., skipping, saccadic landing position, regression out), in addition to the commonly studied measures in eye-movement prediction studies (i.e., first fixation duration, and total reading time). Second, using this dataset, we examine the efficacy and interpretability of recent large language models in predicting early

Proceedings of the 6th Workshop on Research in Computational Linguistic Typology and Multilingual NLP (SIGTYP 2024), pages 44–45
March 22, 2024 ©2024 Association for Computational Linguistics

and late eye-movement metrics during reading Mandarin and Cantonese texts. Fig. 2 shows an example that visualizes the distribution of predicted and ground-truth fixations over a Cantonese sentence (left) and its corresponding Mandarin sentence (right).

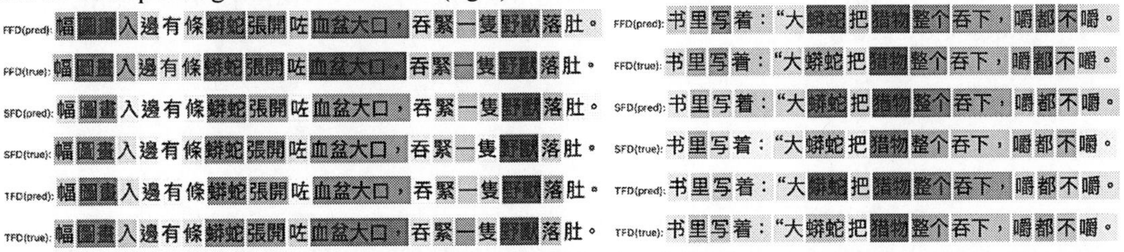

Fig. 2. Distribution of predicted (pred) and ground-true (true) fixations over target sentences. *Note: FFD refers to first fixation duration, SFD refers to second fixation duration, TFD refers to total fixation duration.*

Moreover, it has been shown that language models can be used to generate features capturing human-like behavior in terms of eye-tracking metrics, e.g., surprisal (Hale, 2001; Levy, 2008; Fossum and Levy, 2012; Hao et al., 2020) and token embeddings (Schrimpf et al., 2020; Hollenstein et al., 2021). Therefore, we also focus on whether and to what extent the features generated by language models help to predict various levels of cognitive processing during language comprehension. We conduct a comprehensive evaluation on the prediction of eye-tracking metrics using regression analysis. First, we target at a comparison of features' predictive power on Mandarin and Cantonese reading patterns. Second, we extend the examination to types of language models, specifically, on mono-lingual language model and multilingual language model. For each language, we use both incremental, autoregressive and masked language models, from which we extract features such as token embeddings and surprisals, and we combine them with lexical, orthographic, and syntactic features. In addition to monolingual, pre-trained language models for Chinese (Zhao et al., 2019), we also test multilingual models that have been trained simultaneously for Mandarin and Cantonese (Yang et al., 2022).

Our study presents some highlights on how to account for multilinguality by language models and how they facilitate in-depth investigation of closely related languages in comprehension. Specifically, Mandarin and Cantonese exhibit different advantages in terms of the cognitive effort on word-visual processing (for Mandarin) and sentence contextual processing (for Cantonese). Results of our study will further inform the performance of different types of language models and metrics' usefulness in predicting eye-movement patterns in reading Mandarin and Cantonese texts.

Selected References

Chen, H. C. (1992). Reading comprehension in Chinese: Implications from character reading times. In Advances in psychology (Vol. 90, pp. 175-205). North-Holland.

Jian, Y. C., Chen, M. L., & Ko, H. W. (2013). Context Effects in Processing of Chinese Academic Words: An Eye-Tracking Investigation. Reading Research Quarterly, 48(4), 403-413.

Li, J., Peng, B., Hsu, Y. Y., & Chersoni, E. (2023). Comparing and Predicting Eye-tracking Data of Mandarin and Cantonese. In *Proceedings of the EACL Workshop on NLP for Similar Languages, Varieties and Dialects.*

Zhao, S., Li, L., Chang, M., Xu, Q., Zhang, K., Wang, J., & Paterson, K. B. (2019). Older adults make greater use of word predictability in Chinese reading. Psychology and Aging, 34(6), 780.

Hao, Y., Mendelsohn, S., Sterneck, R., Martinez, R., & Frank, R. (2020). Probabilistic predictions of people perusing: Evaluating metrics of language model performance for psycholinguistic modeling. arXiv preprint arXiv:2009.03954.

Yang, Z., Xu, Z., Cui, Y., Wang, B., Lin, M., Wu, D., & Chen, Z. (2022). CINO: A chinese minority pre-trained language model. Proceedings of COLING.

The Typology of Ellipsis: A Corpus for Linguistic Analysis and Machine Learning Applications

Damir Cavar
Indiana University
dcavar@iu.edu

Ludovic Vetea Mompelat
University of Miami
lvm861@miami.edu

Muhammad Abdo
Indiana University
mabdo@iu.edu

Abstract

Ellipsis constructions are challenging for State-of-the-art (SotA) Natural Language Processing (NLP) technologies. Although theoretically well-documented and understood, there needs to be more sufficient cross-linguistic language resources to document, study, and ultimately engineer NLP solutions that can adequately provide analyses for ellipsis constructions. This article describes the typological data set on ellipsis that we created for currently seventeen languages. We demonstrate how SotA parsers based on a variety of syntactic frameworks fail to parse sentences with ellipsis, and in fact, probabilistic, neural, and Large Language Models (LLM) do so, too. We discuss experiments that focus on detecting sentences with ellipsis, predicting the position of elided elements, and predicting elided surface forms in the appropriate positions. We show that cross-linguistic variation of ellipsis-related phenomena has different consequences for the architecture of NLP systems.

1 Introduction

Ellipsis is a linguistic phenomenon that results in the omission of words in sentences that are usually obligatory in a given syntactic context and that the speaker and hearer can understand and reconstruct without effort. Simple noun phrase (NP) or Forward Conjunct Reduction (FCR), as in example (1), is common cross-linguistically.

(1) a. My sister lives in Utrecht and ___ works in Amsterdam.
b. My sister lives in Utrecht and **she/my sister** works in Amsterdam.

The possibility to elide phrases or words in coordinated constructions has universal and language-specific aspects to it. Common FCR is possible in all languages we are aware of. It is not only possible but the preferred form of presentation in text or spoken language whenever coordination occurs. If ellipsis can be applied in unmarked cases, it is applied. The form in (1b) without ellipsis might be perceived as emphatic or, in a pragmatic or semantic sense, as specific, in contrast to the unmarked default in example (1a).

Other variants of ellipsis include so-called *gapping*, as in (2a) where the verb complex *is reading* is elided. In example (2b), a case of VP-Ellipsis, the entire predicate or Verb Phrase (VP) is elided.

(2) a. Peter is reading a book and Mary ___ a newspaper.
b. She will hi-five Daniel, but I won't ___

Such ellipsis phenomena are context-independent and intra-sentential because no context outside of the sentence boundaries is necessary to license the ellipsis.

Context-dependent forms of ellipsis can be found in responses to questions, as in example (3). In the response (3b), the words *each candidate will talk* are elided.

(3) a. Will each candidate talk about taxes?
b. No, ___ about foreign policy.

While English exhibits limited examples with lexical mismatches of elided word forms, as in example (4a), highly inflecting languages like Hindi or Croatian (4b) show that the elided words do not have to be homophonous. The words in round brackets in (4) are preferably elided in unmarked contexts.

(4) a. John **reads** a book, but Paul and Mary (**read**) a newspaper.
b. Ivan **je čitao** knjigu a Marija i Petar (**su čitali**) novine.
I. be read book but M. and P. be read newspaper

Proceedings of the 6th Workshop on Research in Computational Linguistic Typology and Multilingual NLP (SIGTYP 2024), pages 46–54
March 22, 2024

Elided elements can also be scattered over multiple positions in a clause, as in example (5), where the words *will*, *greet*, and *first* are elided in the respective slots in the second conjunct.

(5) Will Jimmy greet Jill first, or ___ Jill ___ Jimmy ___ ?

As discussed in Testa et al. (2023) and Hardt (2023), ellipsis constructions are very common and often accompanied by specific semantic effects. While various quantifier scope effects[1] can be observed in ellipsis constructions, Common semantic issues involve so-called *zeugma* (Sennet, 2016) effects as in example (6).

(6) a. John stole a book and Peter stole kisses from Mary.

b. John stole a book and Peter ___ kisses from Mary.

The second conjunct in example (6a) includes an idiomatic predicate causing semantic deviation without significantly impacting grammaticality judgments.

We observed that NLP pipelines fail to provide appropriate syntactic structures for such sentences in downstream tasks and for common information extraction from business reports or medical documents. Using ellipsis constructions from our corpus, we tested the most recent versions of Stanza (Qi et al., 2020), spaCy (Honnibal and Johnson, 2015), Benepar (Kitaev and Klein, 2018; Kitaev et al., 2019), and the Xerox Linguistic Environment (XLE) (Crouch et al., 2011). None of the parse trees based on the different grammar formalisms were adequate in our evaluation. Our team of syntacticians judged the adequacy of parse trees. This is true for SotA Dependency parsers, neural Constituency parsers, as well as for rule-based systems like the XLE-based Lexical-functional Grammar (LFG) parser using the English, German, or Polish grammar. LLMs are as challenged with such constructions as these rule-based, statistical, or neural syntactic parsers.

Figure 1 shows an example in which the overt subject of the first conjunct is labeled as the subject. The same element is the syntactic subject and semantic object of the second conjunct. These functional relations are missing in the Dependency tree and cannot be easily resolved in a generic way for any kind of ellipsis construction with multiple conjoined clauses. While this parse tree might be argued to result from the Dependency Grammar framework as such, all parse trees that we have analyzed were definitely useless for subsequent information retrieval or semantic analysis that depend on sentential functional relations of clausal constituents, as for example, the arguments subject and object of the main predicate in the clause.

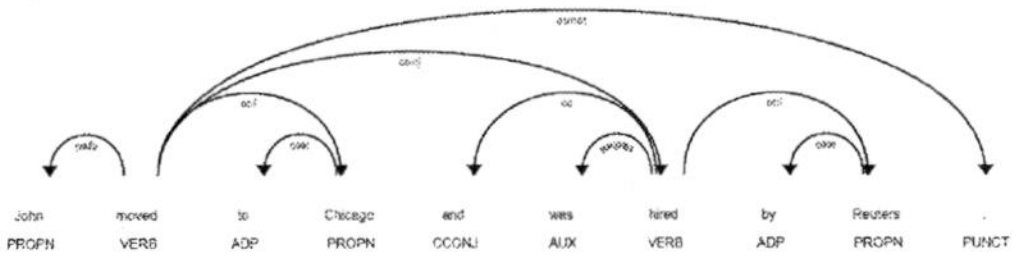

Figure 1: Stanza Dependency Tree.

Additional errors emerge when looking at simple gapping constructions as in Figure 2. While in most cases, the parser would generate a hypothesis that indicates that *bicycle* and *Mary* are coordinated, in this case, the parser coordinates the verb of the first conjunct and the object noun, declaring *Mary* to be the subject of the nominal object *truck*.

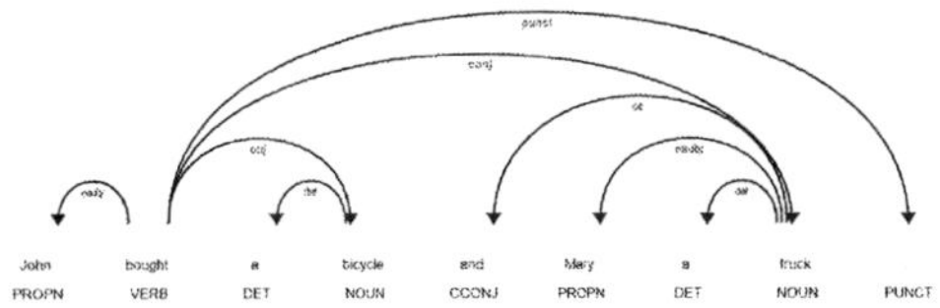

Figure 2: Stanza Dependency Tree.

This does not improve when looking at constituency parser outputs, as in Figure 3. The constituency parser assumes the coordination to be local, rather than clausal, that is, *a bicycle and Mary* is analyzed as the object of *buying*, and the Noun Phrase *a truck* appears to be an orphaned object of the same predicate, too.

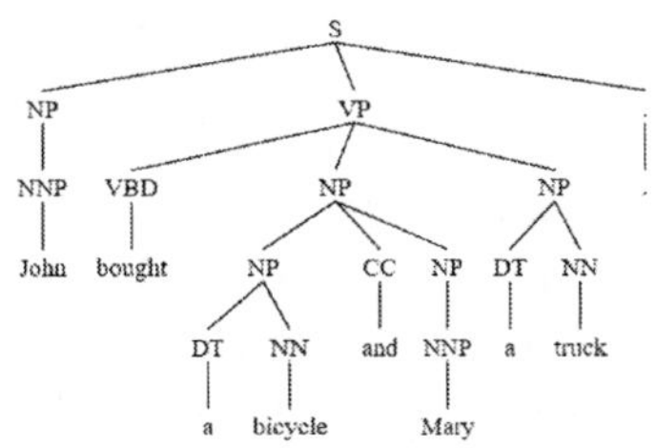

Figure 3: Stanza Constituency tree

For a simple gapping construction XLE using the English grammar generates a C-structure as in

[1] A discussion of semantic changes caused by quantifier scope effects in ellipsis constructions would go beyond the scope of this article.

Figure 4 corresponding to the constituency parse tree in Figure 3.

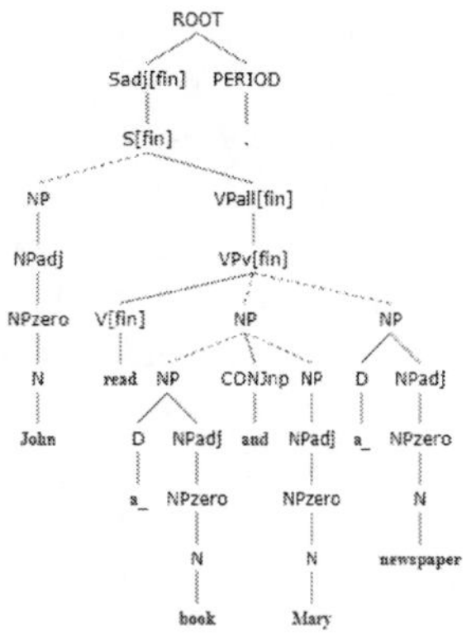

Figure 4: XLE English C-structure

In LFG the F(functional) structure represents morphosyntactic features of c-structure phrases and lexical elements, as well as grammatical functions like subject and object. The corresponding F-structure in Figure 5 provided by XLE shows that the coordination is wrongly assumed to be local, implying that *John* engaged in reading *a book and Mary*.

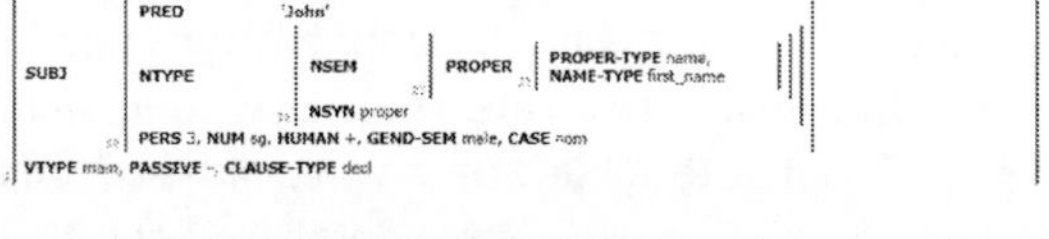

Figure 5: XLE English F-structure

These examples are not rare mistakes that these parsers make in constructions with ellipsis. These are the typical mistakes that we observe in the vast majority of ellipsis constructions.

The following data and corpus creation and experiments were motivated by the fact that document types like business reports, medical or technical documentation, as well as social media content, chat, or spoken language discourse, contain a large number of sentences with ellipses. Given that common SotA NLP pipelines fail to provide adequate syntactic representations as tree structures, higher-level processing of discourse and semantic properties is not possible using their output.

Our motivation to create larger data sets for a larger group of languages was not only driven by this fact but also by a lack of a comparative typological description of ellipses in different languages and across different language groups.

As the example in (4) shows, morphologically rich languages allow lexically matching words to be elided, although the morpho-phonological surface form does not match. This does not seem to be a challenge for native speakers of these languages. However, it is a significant computational challenge to identify the correct morpho-phonological forms that were subject to ellipsis.

Scattered ellipsis, as in example (5), does not appear to be cognitively challenging, either; however, from a Machine Learning (ML) and NLP perspective, we expect to see significant errors and issues in identifying the ellipsis slots and guessing the elided words.

Other typologically interesting aspects of ellipsis and cross-linguistic comparisons are related to the unmarked underlying word order. While VP-ellipsis might manifest itself in different ways in SVO languages, it might result in very different surface phenomena in SOV languages like Hindi or German. In the German example (7) the VP containing the direct object and main verb (*Mutter helfen*) can be elided in the first conjunct.

(7) Karl soll seiner (**Mutter helfen**) und Maria soll ihrer Mutter helfen.

While we have a good understanding of VP-ellipsis in English, it must be made clear whether an elided verb in a transitive predicate construction in Hindi is similar to gapping or, rather, the result of partial VP-ellipsis.

There are numerous research questions that we try to address. On the one hand, syntax internal constraints license sentence-internal ellipsis. In gapping constructions, the gapped verb is not necessarily licensed by discourse conditions and previously mentioned context. On the other hand, the ellipsis of discourse-introduced and -linked words and phrases cannot be assumed to be restricted by purely syntactic constraints. At the same time, complex gapping constructions seem to indicate that ellipsis is not restricted by syntactic phrase boundaries, but rather licensed by phonological correspondence of word sequences. As example 8 shows, the repeated word sequence can be elided, ignoring syntactic phrase structure boundaries.

(8) Jimmy was always dreaming about going to Paris, and Mary ___ to Tokyo?

One interpretation of 8, the default one, implies that *Mary was always dreaming about going to Tokyo*. The elided sequence of words, in this case, does not match with clear-cut syntactic phrase boundaries.

The corpus and research presented in this article are part of the Hoosier Ellipsis Corpus (HEC) project at the NLP-Lab. The goal of the HEC Project is to provide a resource for qualitative and quantitative typological studies of ellipsis over different language types and groups, as well as to provide corpora for the evaluation and development of NLP pipelines that can generate semantically more adequate syntactic structures for ellipsis constructions.

1.1 Previous Work

There is a rich body of literature covering ellipsis in linguistics, as summarized in the Handbook of Ellipsis (van Craenenbroeck and Temmerman, 2018). Summarizing the data discussed and the different theoretical approaches presented in these articles would go beyond the scope of this article. In the following, we focus on the most recent computational approaches and descriptions of ellipsis corpora.

Testa et al. (2023) built a dataset of elliptical constructions, *ELLie*, and evaluated GPT-2 (Radford et al., 2019) and BERT (Devlin et al., 2018), two Transformer-based language models, on their ability to retrieve the omitted verb in elliptical constructions that demonstrate the impact of prototypicality and semantic compatibility between the missing element and its arguments. They found that while the performances of the two language models were influenced by the semantic compatibility of an elided element and its argument, these models had an overall limited mastery of elliptical constructions.

Anand et al. (2021) built the Santa Cruz sluicing dataset. In sluicing constructions as in (9) the elided word list (*John/he can play*) is preceded by an interrogative pronoun (*what*).

(9) John can play something, but I don't know what (**he can play**).

They compiled a corpus of 4,700 instances of sluicing in English, with each instance represented as a short text and annotated for syntactic, semantic, and pragmatic attributes. Most of the data they used comes from the New York Times subcorpus of the English Gigaword corpus. The data set was created by identifying all verb phrases whose final child was a wh-phrase and then manually culling false positives. Each of the instances is marked with five tags, namely, the antecedent, the wh-remnant, the omitted content, the primary predicate of the antecedent clause, and the correlate of the wh-remnant, if available.

Motivated by the assumption that noun ellipsis is more frequent in conversational settings, Khullar et al. (2020) compiled NoEl (An Annotated Corpus for Noun Ellipsis in English), where they annotated the first 100 movies of the Cornell Movie Dialogs dataset for noun ellipsis. Their annotation process involved using the Brat annotation tool to mark ellipsis remnants and their antecedents in the dataset. The dataset was manually annotated by three linguists, and an inter-annotator agreement was measured using Fleiss's Kappa coefficient, which indicated a high level of agreement among annotators. Their results show that a total of 946 cases of noun ellipsis existed in their corpus, corresponding to a rate of 14.08 per 10,000 tokens. The models they used included Naive Bayes, Liner and RBF SVMs, Nearest Neighbors, and Random Forest. They achieved an F1 score of 0.73 in detecting noun ellipsis using linear SVM and 0.74 in noun ellipsis resolution using Random Forest.

Droganova et al. (2018a,b) first created treebanks containing elliptical constructions for English, Czech, and Finnish, using the Universal Dependencies (UD) (Nivre et al., 2016) annotation standard by artificially introducing ellipsis to the sentences. They evaluated several parsers in order to identify typical errors these parsers generate when dealing with elliptical constructions. Note that UD v2 used the *orphan* relation to attach the orphaned arguments to the position of the omitted element. The authors found that the F1-scores of most parsers were below 30%. This highlights how difficult it is for dependency parsers to identify elliptical constructions and warrants data enrichment for ellipsis resolution to improve dependency parsers' performances.

Liu et al. (2016) investigated Verb Phrase Ellipsis (VPE) and conducted three tasks on two datasets. The first dataset consists of the Wall Street

Journal (WSJ) section of the Penn Treenbank with VPE annotation (Bos and Spenader, 2011), and the second dataset was compiled from the sections of the British National Corpus annotated by Nielsen (2005) and converted by Liu et al. (2016) to the format used by Bos and Spenader (2011). The first task consisted of identifying the position of the element, called *target*, that is used to represent the elided verb phrase, called the *antecedent*. This first task only treats cases in which such a *target* is overtly present in the case of VPE, but this is not always the case, as shown in example 2b. The second and third tasks consisted of correctly linking the *target* to its *antecedent* and identifying the exact boundaries of the *antecedent*. Liu et al. (2016) found that the second and third tasks yielded better results when they were treated separately using two different learning paradigms rather than when they were treated jointly. They also found that a logistic regression classification model worked better for the first and third task, but that a ranking-based model yielded better results for the second task.

McShane and Babkin (2016) developed ViPER (VP Ellipsis Resolver), which is a system that uses linguistic principles, and more specifically syntactic features, to detect and resolve VP ellipsis. This system is knowledge-based and does not use empirical data for training. It is not intended to solve all cases of VP-ellipsis, and instead, it first detects the cases of VP ellipsis that are simple enough for the system to treat and then uses string-based resolution strategies. The system identifies the best string to fill and replace the elliptical gap (*sponsor*). The system, evaluated against a GOLD standard dataset generated by the authors, had correctly resolved 61% of the VP ellipsis constructions it identified as simple enough to treat from the Gigaword corpus.

1.2 Summary

The previous work described above was mainly focusing on isolated ellipsis types or specific languages. Our goal was to build on the previous work and expand the data set to more languages and language types, and to broaden the ellipses types documented and studied to the full known set of constructions.

2 The Hoosier Ellipsis Corpus

The Hoosier Ellipsis Corpus V 0.1 consists of data from seventeen languages. Among those languages are low-resourced languages like Navajo, a language of the Athabaskan branch of the Na-Dené language family, and Kumaoni, an Indo-Aryan language spoken in northern India and parts of western Nepal, as well as common Slavic languages (Russian, Ukrainian, Polish), Germanic languages (English, German, Swedish), as well as Hindi, Arabic, Japanese, and Korean.

The corpus includes the following ellipsis types: VP-ellipsis, Sluicing, Gapping, Stripping, Forward (FCR), and Backward Coordinate Reduction (BCR).

The collected data set consists of sentence pairs and possible contexts that precede or follow the target sentence in a text or discourse. The examples in the corpus are collected from linguistic and typological literature. Example sentences from low-resourced languages were collected and validated by native speakers.

We selected a simple Unicode text-based format to encode the data using separator lines and line prefixes to indicate the data entry type. In the encoded data files, the target sentence with an ellipsis is followed by a line of 4 dashes. Within the ellipsis target structure, three underscores indicate each canonical position of the elided word sequence. Complex ellipsis constructions can contain numerous elided slots. The pair of sentences with ellipses and the full form are optionally accompanied by meta information indicated by lines that start with the hash symbol. In the meta-information lines we provide the opportunity to translate the sentence, to provide the original source of the example from publications, and to specify who contributed this example to the data collection. Each example sentence in the data file is followed by at least one empty line. Figure 6 shows a sample entry with the core elements.

```
Wird sie kommen oder ___ er gehen?
----
Wird sie kommen oder wird er gehen?
# TR eng: Will she come or will he go?
# added by: John Smith
# source: Wolfgang Klein (1981)
#         Some Rules of Regular ...
```

Figure 6: Example entry in the Ellipsis Corpus.

This annotation format allows us to indicate and study the distribution of elided elements in the clause. It also provides the 'understood' or 'implied' sequence of words as understood by human native speakers. From a computational perspective, this format allows us to train models that detect the positions of elided elements in sentences. We can also train models that generate the elided word forms. We can use the data set to evaluate existing models and, in particular, LLMs, as discussed in the following section.

The format allows us to convert most of the ellipsis and full-form pairs into the UD 2 format for encoding ellipsis.[2] At the same time, tree structures based on the different grammar formalisms can be encoded as bracketed-notation strings, triple sets for dependencies, or c- and f-structure strings in the meta-information section of each example.

The Ellipsis Corpus is continuously expanded. Many languages in the corpus are expanded using examples from peer-reviewed publications and theoretical or documentary linguistics publications. For low-resourced languages, we rely on contributions from native speakers and their speaker communities. While some of the languages are as of writing this article under-represented, we describe the following experiments and results for a couple of languages that we collected sufficient data on for training models and evaluating their performance, or testing the performance of pre-trained LLMs.

3 NLP Experiments: Methods & Results

We designed three main experimental settings to test the capabilities of current SotA NLP technologies. The tasks are described as follows:

1. Detection of ellipsis in sentences as a general binary classification task.

2. Identification of the positions of elided words or phrases in sentences with ellipsis.

3. Prediction of the correct surface form (morpho-phonological shape) of elided words in sentences with ellipsis.

These tasks we compare across three different NLP-approaches:

1. Logistic Regression classifier

2. Transformer-based classifier and labeler

3. Large Language Models

[2]See for details `https://universaldependencies.org/u/overview/specific-syntax.html`.

We assume that the Logistic Regression approach represents a baseline for the binary classification task but that it is less useful for guessing the positions of elided words or generating the elided word forms.

While we expected transformer-based models to perform well as classifiers, we also expected that they would be less efficient for guessing the position of elided elements.

We expected current SotA LLMs to be most successful in all three tasks, in particular when it comes to the generation of the elided word forms since this is the natural task for Generative AI models.

3.1 Dataset

Using our manually compiled Ellipsis Corpus, we constructed three datasets. For English, we expanded the data with the ELLie corpus Testa et al. (2023). We added some corrections and modifications to the ELLie corpus since some native speakers complained about the naturalness of some sentences. We also used sluicing examples from the Santa Cruz Sluicing dataset (Anand et al., 2018).

The first dataset was aimed at a simple binary classification task to detect and label sentences with 1 if they contain ellipsis and with 0 if not. The binary classification datasets were monolingual and a balanced mixture of target sentences and distractors. We generated a 10-fold randomized rotation of the examples to minimize any kind of sequencing effect when training classifiers or

Our corpus comprises pairs of examples showcasing ellipsis constructions, which specify both the location of the omitted element and the full form.

At this early stage of the Ellipsis Corpus, the languages that were represented with sufficient data were English, Russian, Arabic, and Spanish. The experiments described in the following thus focus on these languages. We limit our description here to English and Arabic, since the format and results are equivalent to the settings for the other languages.

3.1.1 English Data

For English, we used 575 examples from ELLie and 559 examples from our manually compiled English Ellipsis Sub-Corpus. Combining each of the datasets with 658 distractor sentences, we generated a ten-fold randomized rotation of sentences.

For Task 1, the classification of ellipsis, we generated sentence and label tuples using the label 1 for ellipsis and 0 for no ellipsis.

For Task 2, we generated pairs of ellipsis and full-form sentences, leaving the underscore indicators in the ellipsis example sentence to be able to train labeling algorithms that predict the ellipsis position or to evaluate predicted ellipsis positions directly.

3.1.2 Arabic Data

For the experiments on Modern Standard Arabic, we selected 375 target structures that contain ellipses from the manually compiled Arabic Ellipsis Sub-Corpus and combined those sentences with 500 distractor sentences. The distractor sentences were a random selection of examples without ellipses, as well as the full-form sentences from the ellipses corpus. To the best of our knowledge, there is no other such corpus of Ellipsis in Arabic. The Arabic Ellipsis Sub-Corpus covers various types of syntactic ellipsis (e.g., NP ellipsis, VP-ellipsis, gapping, fragment answers, forward and backward coordinate reduction, and sluicing as in example 10).

(10) لا بد من منع مثل هذه الكارثة ولكن كيف ___؟
[We have to stop this crisis but how___?]

3.2 Task 1: Binary Sentence Classification

The goal of task 1 was to evaluate the performance of baseline approaches with transformer models and LLMs. As the baseline approach, we specified a simple Logistic Regression (LR) model that uses a sentence vectorization approach based on ten simple cues using linguistic intuition. For the generation of cue vectors for each sentence, we used the spaCy[3] NLP pipeline with the part-of-speech tagger and Dependency parser. The classification vectors for each English sentence were generated using the following information:

the number of nouns
the number of subject dependency labels
the number of object dependency labels
the number of conjunctions
the number of *do so*
a boolean whether a *wh*-word is sentence-final
the number of verbs
the number of auxiliaries
the number of *acomp* Dependency labels
the number of tokens *too*

[3]See https://spacy.io/ for more details.

We trained a binary LR classifier using these ten-dimensional vectors. The goal was not to optimize the classifier and achieve the best possible result but to develop a simple baseline classifier using just a few linguistic cues for ellipsis constructions.

The transformer-based classifier is based on BERT for English and the language-specific counterparts for the other languages.

3.3 Task 2: Locate of Ellipsis

In this task, we evaluate Language Models and specific transformer models with respect to their ability to predict the precise location of elided words. The complexity in this task varies from one elided word, multiple elided words as in example (8), and scattered multi-slot ellipsis as in example (5).

The data set for this task consists of sentence pairs. One sentence contains the indicators (3 underscores) for the ellipsis positions, while the other one does not contain such indications and is used for testing the models. The models are trained and tested only using examples that contain ellipses.

Ten-fold random rotations of examples are tested on BERT-based sequence labeling and GPT-4.

For GPT-4 we used a prompt with a rich context: "Annotate the following sentence by placing ___ in the position of each ellipsis. Ellipses indicate gapping, pseudogapping, stripping, and sluicing. If there are no ellipses, answer with only the original sentence."

We have not run few-shot experiments for task 2 yet. but will report on those in the near future.

3.4 Task 3: Generate Elided Words

In this task, we evaluate LLMs for their ability to generate the elided word in the correct positions. The data set consists of sentence pairs. One of the sentences contains ellipsis and the other is the "full-form" of the same sentence with the elided words spelled out. Only examples with ellipses were used for training and testing the models.

For the GPT-4-based evaluation, we used a prompt with a rich context: "Insert any missing words implied by ellipses. Ellipses indicate gapping, pseudogapping, stripping, and sluicing. Answer with only the new sentence. If there are no ellipses, answer with only the original sentence."

As for task 2, we have not performed few-shot experiments for task 3 yet, leaving these experiments for future work.

4 Results

In the zero-shot GPT-4 setting, we used the context "You are a linguistic expert." The prompt "Classify the following sentence as containing ellipsis or not and return a 1 for a sentence with ellipsis and a 0 for a sentence without ellipsis" was preceding each sentence.

We tested various LLMs, including GPT-4, GPT-3.5, Falcon, Llama, Zephyr. We decided to focus on GPT-4 only, since none of the other LLMs turned out to be useful in any of the three tasks, given accuracies below 0.5. For task 1 for English the results are given in table 1. The results for languages like Arabic, Russian, or Spanish vary insignificantly.

model	accuracy
LR	0.74
BERT	**0.94**
GPT-4 zero-shot	0.72

Table 1: Task 1 Binary Classifier

It is surprising that the GPT-4 zero-shot classification is worse than the LR-baseline, and significantly worse than the BERT-based classifier. The precise scores from the zero-shot GPT-4 experiment show a Recall of 0.599, a Precision of 0.756, and an F1 Score of 0.668.

In task 1, the zero-shot GPT-4 experiment achieved using the Arabic data resulted in a surprising accuracy of 0.87.

In the default setting, the output from GPT-4 is not discrete for a given example sentence. With the temperature set to the default 0.7 when requesting a label for a sentence in task 1, 2 of 10 responses were the opposite label. When we reduce the temperature to 0, there are no mismatches; the judgments were deterministic. However, with the temperature set to 0, the accuracy was 70%. With the temperature set to 0.7, the accuracy was 75%.

In task 2, we tested an initial BERT-based ellipsis position guesser and achieved first test accuracy of 0.7. The GPT-4-based experiments on task 2 were challenging. The prompt engineering for the zero-shot experiment resulted in an accuracy of only 0.15 for the English data.

For task 3, we exclusively focused on the evaluation of GPT-4. In this task, using the zero-shot strategy, we achieved an accuracy of 0.25 with GPT-4.

5 Conclusion

Ellipsis constructions are obviously still challenging for all the common SotA NLP pipelines, including rule-based systems like the LFG-based XLE. Use of Dependency or Constituency parse trees, or even LFG c- and f-structures for syntactic and semantic processing of real-world data from different genres or registers is limited due to the fact that ellipsis is a common and widespread phenomenon in all languages.

The problem can be partially linked to grammar frameworks like Dependency Grammar or LFG, which do not necessarily foresee opaque linguistic elements (e.g., elided words or phrases) to be active rule elements modeled in grammar rules or descriptive formal annotation frameworks. While UD provides the instruments for annotating or handling ellipses, those instruments need to be more extensive to describe the different intra- and cross-linguistic ellipses types. We also suspect that parsing algorithms and the training of parsers need to include such opaque elements and potentially new learning strategies.

The fact that specific models trained on the prediction of ellipses in sentences outperform LLMs seems to indicate that the lack of explicit data and pure self-supervised machine learning is not sufficient to handle opaque elements in language, either. Training LLMs on purely overt data ignores significant properties of language. Ellipsis phenomena are grammatical and systematic, and it seems problematic for current LLMs to guess covert continuations.

Given that there is too little data on ellipsis in general, and none at all for most languages, it seems necessary to continue our Ellipsis Corpus project and provide not only sufficient data for the different languages, but also a good typological overview of the different manifestations of ellipsis phenomena in different languages and language groups.

Acknowledgements

We are grateful to the NLP-Lab team, in particular Luis Abrego, Billy Dickson, Vance Holthenrichs, Calvin Josenhans, Soyoung Kim, John MacIntosh Phillips, Zoran Tiganj, Khai Willard, Yuchen Yang.

The Ellipsis Corpus and the relevant code for the experiments described in the article are made accessible on GitHub (`https://github.com/dcavar/hoosierellipsiscorpus`).

References

Pranav Anand, Daniel Hardt, and James McCloskey. 2021. The Santa Cruz sluicing data set. *Language*, 97(1):e68–e88.

Pranav Anand, Jim McCloskey, and Dan Hardt. 2018. Santa Cruz Ellipsis Consortium Sluicing Dataset (1.0).

Johan Bos and Jennifer Spenader. 2011. An annotated corpus for the analysis of VP ellipsis. *Language resources and evaluation*, 45:463–494.

Richard Crouch, Mary Dalrymple, Ronald M. Kaplan, Tracy Holloway King, John T. Maxwell, III, and Paula Newman. 2011. *XLE Documentation*. Xerox Palo Alto Research Center, Palo Alto, CA.

Jacob Devlin, Ming-Wei Chang, Kenton Lee, and Kristina Toutanova. 2018. BERT: Pre-training of deep bidirectional transformers for language understanding. *arXiv preprint arXiv:1810.04805*.

Kira Droganova, Filip Ginter, Jenna Kanerva, and Daniel Zeman. 2018a. Mind the gap: Data enrichment in dependency parsing of elliptical constructions. In *Proceedings of the Second Workshop on Universal Dependencies (UDW 2018)*, pages 47–54.

Kira Droganova, Daniel Zeman, Jenna Kanerva, and Filip Ginter. 2018b. Parse me if you can: Artificial treebanks for parsing experiments on elliptical constructions. In *Proceedings of the Eleventh International Conference on Language Resources and Evaluation (LREC 2018)*.

Daniel Hardt. 2023. Ellipsis-dependent reasoning: a new challenge for large language models. In *Proceedings of the 61st Annual Meeting of the Association for Computational Linguistics (Volume 2: Short Papers)*, pages 39–47, Toronto, Canada. Association for Computational Linguistics.

Matthew Honnibal and Mark Johnson. 2015. An improved non-monotonic transition system for dependency parsing. In *Proceedings of the 2015 Conference on Empirical Methods in Natural Language Processing*, pages 1373–1378, Lisbon, Portugal. Association for Computational Linguistics.

Payal Khullar, Kushal Majmundar, and Manish Shrivastava. 2020. NoEl: An annotated corpus for noun ellipsis in English. In *Proceedings of the Twelfth Language Resources and Evaluation Conference*, pages 34–43.

Nikita Kitaev, Steven Cao, and Dan Klein. 2019. Multilingual constituency parsing with self-attention and pre-training. In *Proceedings of the 57th Annual Meeting of the Association for Computational Linguistics*, pages 3499–3505, Florence, Italy. Association for Computational Linguistics.

Nikita Kitaev and Dan Klein. 2018. Constituency parsing with a self-attentive encoder. In *Proceedings of the 56th Annual Meeting of the Association for Computational Linguistics (Volume 1: Long Papers)*, pages 2676–2686, Melbourne, Australia. Association for Computational Linguistics.

Wolfgang Klein. 1981. Some rules of regular ellipsis in German. In W. Klein and W.J.M. Levelt, editors, *Crossing the Boundaries in Linguistics. Studies Presented to Manfred Bierwisch*, pages 51–78. Reidel, Dordrecht.

Zhengzhong Liu, Edgar Gonzàlez, and Dan Gillick. 2016. Exploring the steps of verb phrase ellipsis. In *Proceedings of the Workshop on Coreference Resolution Beyond OntoNotes (CORBON 2016), co-located with NAACL 2016*, pages 32–40, San Diego, California. Association for Computational Linguistics.

Marjorie McShane and Petr Babkin. 2016. Detection and resolution of verb phrase ellipsis. *Linguistic Issues in Language Technology*, 13.

Leif Arda Nielsen. 2005. *A corpus-based study of verb phrase ellipsis identification and resolution*. Ph.D. thesis, Citeseer.

Joakim Nivre, Marie-Catherine De Marneffe, Filip Ginter, Yoav Goldberg, Jan Hajic, Christopher D Manning, Ryan McDonald, Slav Petrov, Sampo Pyysalo, Natalia Silveira, et al. 2016. Universal dependencies v1: A multilingual treebank collection. In *Proceedings of the Tenth International Conference on Language Resources and Evaluation (LREC'16)*, pages 1659–1666.

Peng Qi, Yuhao Zhang, Yuhui Zhang, Jason Bolton, and Christopher D. Manning. 2020. Stanza: A Python natural language processing toolkit for many human languages. In *Proceedings of the 58th Annual Meeting of the Association for Computational Linguistics: System Demonstrations*.

Alec Radford, Jeffrey Wu, Rewon Child, David Luan, Dario Amodei, Ilya Sutskever, et al. 2019. Language models are unsupervised multitask learners. *OpenAI blog*, 1(8):9.

Adam Sennet. 2016. Polysemy. In S. Goldberg, editor, *Oxford Handbooks Online: Philosophy*. Oxford University Press.

Davide Testa, Emmanuele Chersoni, and Alessandro Lenci. 2023. We understand elliptical sentences, and language models should too: A new dataset for studying ellipsis and its interaction with thematic fit. In *Proceedings of the 61st Annual Meeting of the Association for Computational Linguistics Volume 1: Long Papers*, pages 3340–3353. Association for Computational Linguistics.

Jeroen van Craenenbroeck and Tanja Temmerman. 2018. *The Oxford Handbook of Ellipsis*. Oxford University Press.

Language Atlas of Japanese and Ryukyuan (LAJaR): A Linguistic Typology Database for Endangered Japonic Languages

Kanji KATO[*]
jiteng.ganzhi@gmail.com

So MIYAGAWA[†]
runa.uei@gmail

Natsuko NAKAGAWA[†]
nakagawanatuko@gmail.com

Abstract

LAJaR (Language Atlas of Japanese and Ryukyuan) is a linguistic typology database focusing on micro-variation of the Japonic languages. This paper aims to report the design and progress of this ongoing database project. Finally, we also show a case study utilizing its database on zero copulas among the Japonic languages.

1 Introduction

Linguistic typology databases have been created for describing and comparing languages of the world (e.g. World Atlas of Language Structure Online: Dryer and Haspelmath 2013; Grambank: Skirgård et al. 2023) and have been a useful research resource for linguistic typologists. However, due to the large scale of these studies covering the world's languages, they have not been able to capture the fine-grained variations within a single language family.

The Japonic language family is a language family comprising the indigenous languages of the Japanese archipelago (excluding Ainu), i.e. Japanese and Ryukyuan languages, many varieties of which are endangered (Moseley, 2010). Significant differences exist between the Japanese and the Ryukyuan languages and within Japanese dialects. These differences make mutual intelligibility shallow (cf. Shimoji, 2022).

Despite Japan's linguistic diversity, WALS mainly features Tokyo-Japanese, Shuri-Okinawan, and Ainu, largely ignoring other dialects. This overlook suggests a partial portrayal of the diversity of Japanese languages. Although these languages have been studied for decades, such studies remain unincorporated, highlighting a significant gap in the field due to the lack of a comprehensive dataset.

In response to this lacuna, the current research proposes the development of the web platform LAJaR: Language Atlas of Japanese and Ryukyuan. This project aims to contribute to linguistic typology by employing tools such as leaflet.js to visualize Japonic and Ryukyuan grammatical features within a geographic context. We targeted languages from a specific region, in this case, the Japonic language family.

2 Method

In the LAJaR project, we assemble a dataset from grammatical descriptions and fieldwork, adopting the WALS model to chart global languages' traits, like phonemic inventories, geographically. This facilitates empirical research into linguistic diversity's distribution and supports comparative analysis of linguistic features, revealing potential correlations. This methodology aligns with linguistic typology's goals to identify universal language attributes via detailed distribution analysis.

While LAJaR is based on WALS, this project does not intend to add data to WALS, but to create a bespoke dataset. This is to add features that are not in WALS and that are subject to question in the study of Japonic languages (e.g., the presence of dual forms of pronouns). It could also be based on Grambank, but the difference is that WALS treats grammatical features as categorical, whereas Grambank treats almost all features as binary values. Because of this difference, we decided that adapting to Grambank's method was not most appropriate for depicting grammatical features.

Building on the foundation of the WALS model, the proposed LAJaR platform intends to incorporate the methodologies and tools of the Cross-Linguistic Linked Data (CLLD) framework. CLLD is a platform designed to enable the aggregation, comparison, and visualization of linguistic data across different languages. It leverages the Cross-

[*]ROIS-DS Center for Open Data in Humanities
[†]National Institute for Japanese Language and Linguistics

Proceedings of the 6th Workshop on Research in Computational Linguistic Typology and Multilingual NLP (SIGTYP 2024), pages 55–57
March 22, 2024

Linguistic Data Formats (CLDF, Forkel et al., 2018) to standardize data representation, making it more accessible and interoperable.

Incorporating CLLD into LAJaR will offer several advantages. Firstly, it will allow LAJaR to benefit from CLLD's established infrastructure, including its robust data formats and visualization tools. Secondly, by adopting CLLD's standardized data formats, LAJaR can ensure consistency in data representation, facilitating easier comparison and integration with other linguistic databases. Moreover, CLLD supports the inclusion of a diverse range of linguistic data, from phonetics to syntax. This flexibility aligns well with the aim of LAJaR to cover a wide array of grammatical features across the Japonic and Ryukyuan languages.

3 Case study: Zero Copula

We discuss the following as a case study of how LAJaR can promote linguistic research. We annotated whether a language allows zero copula for predicate nominals (120A). We examined 25 languages from 25 sources.

The result shows that some languages of western Japan and Ryukyuans do not have copula for non-past declaratives (1a), whereas other languages do (1b).

(1) a. *wan=ja sinsii*
I=TOP teacher
'I am a teacher.'(Amami, Kato 2022, p.38)

b. *an hita sensee=zjad=do*
that person.TOP teacher=COP=SFP
'That person is a teacher.' (Kagoshima-Japanese, Hiratsuka 2018, p.115)

WALS simply states that Japanese does not allow zero copula, but LAJaR indicates that there is actually variation within the Japonic language family. The result suggests the effectiveness of LAJaR with more finely grained data extraction.

Since WALS speculate that the non-existence of copula correlates with the existence of case markers, we also wanted to examine case markers; however, we encountered some difficulties. First, different sources adopted into LAJaR refer to the region in various granularities. It is necessary to normalize the level of granularity. Second, case markers in many languages of Japan are optional. In such a case, linguists tend to describe only overt case markers and tend not to mention the possibility or impossibility of case marker drops, which makes it challenging to annotate. Third, different sources contradict each other. This might be due to language change or individual differences. It is necessary to decide which source to choose or to invent a way to represent contradicting results. The reliability of the descriptions also varies from one literature to another and must be examined to determine whether they are worthy of adoption.

While we are "digging deeper" into the Japanese data, we are essentially taking the same approach as WALS and are facing the same problems encountered by the WALS authors. On this matter, we are exploring ways to more accurately reflect the variation within languages while referencing the approach of WALS. For instance, we are considering approaches such as allowing multiple values for a specific feature.

4 Conclusion

This paper presented an overview of our ongoing project on the linguistic typology database LAJaR. We have developed a database from existing literature on Japonic languages, which until now has largely been overlooked. Additionally, through our case study, we demonstrated how this database can facilitate new research in linguistic typology.

The LAJaR project marks a significant advance in depicting the Japonic language family's diversity more fully and accurately. Using sources written in Japanese includes a broader array of linguistic data, often overlooked in current databases. Furthermore, the dataset helps members of the endangered language communities know the grammatical diversity of Japonic languages, aiding in understanding their own languages' grammatical features.

Future work will focus on further expanding and refining the database, particularly on endangered Japanese dialects and Ryukyuan languages that have received minimal attention. This expansion will enhance our understanding of the structural complexity and variation within the Japonic languages. Additionally, we aim to utilize the LAJaR database as a platform for international collaboration and exchange among researchers, further advancing the field of linguistic typology. Through this endeavor, we hope to significantly contribute to the field of language typology and raise awareness about the importance of preserving and studying Japonic languages.

References

Matthew S. Dryer and Martin Haspelmath. 2013. Wals online (v2020.3). [last accessed on 2023/12/18].

Robert Forkel, Johann-Mattis List, Simon J. Greenhill, Christoph Rzymski, Sebastian Bank, Michael Cysouw, Harald Hammarström, Martin Haspelmath, Gereon A. Kaiping, and Russell D. Gray. 2018. Cross-linguistic data formats, advancing data sharing and re-use in comparative linguistics. *Scientific Data*, 5(1):180205.

Yusuke Hiratsuka. 2018. Kagoshimaken Kagoshimashi hôgen. In *Zenkoku Hôgen Bumpô Jiten Shiryôshû 4: Katsuyô Taikê 3*, pages 107–116. Hôgen Bumpô Kenkyûkai. [The dialect of Kagoshima-city, Kagoshima Prefecture].

Kanji Kato. 2022. Tokunoshima (Kagoshima, Northern Ryukyuan). In Michinori Shimoji, editor, *An introduction to the Japonic languages : grammatical sketches of Japanese dialects and Ryukyuan languages*, chapter 2, pages 25–57. Brill, Leiden ; Boston.

Christopher Moseley, editor. 2010. *Atlas of the world's languages in danger*. UNESCO.

Michinori Shimoji, editor. 2022. *An introduction to the Japonic languages : grammatical sketches of Japanese dialects and Ryukyuan languages*. Brill, Leiden ; Boston.

Hedvig Skirgård, Hannah J. Haynie, Damián E. Blasi, Harald Hammarström, Jeremy Collins, Jay J. Latarche, Jakob Lesage, Tobias Weber, Alena Witzlack-Makarevich, Sam Passmore, Angela Chira, Luke Maurits, Russell Dinnage, Michael Dunn, Ger Reesink, Ruth Singer, Claire Bowern, Patience Epps, Jane Hill, Outi Vesakoski, Martine Robbeets, Noor Karolin Abbas, Daniel Auer, Nancy A. Bakker, Giulia Barbos, Robert D. Borges, Swintha Danielsen, Luise Dorenbusch, Ella Dorn, John Elliott, Giada Falcone, Jana Fischer, Yustinus Ghanggo Ate, Hannah Gibson, Hans-Philipp Göbel, Jemima A. Goodall, Victoria Gruner, Andrew Harvey, Rebekah Hayes, Leonard Heer, Roberto E. Herrera Miranda, Nataliia Hübler, Biu Huntington-Rainey, Jessica K. Ivani, Marilen Johns, Erika Just, Eri Kashima, Carolina Kipf, Janina V. Klingenberg, Nikita König, Aikaterina Koti, Richard G. A. Kowalik, Olga Krasnoukhova, Nora L.M. Lindvall, Mandy Lorenzen, Hannah Lutzenberger, Tônia R.A. Martins, Celia Mata German, Suzanne van der Meer, Jaime Montoya Samamé, Michael Müller, Saliha Muradoğlu, Kelsey Neely, Johanna Nickel, Miina Norvik, Cheryl Akinyi Oluoch, Jesse Peacock, India O.C. Pearey, Naomi Peck, Stephanie Petit, Sören Pieper, Mariana Poblete, Daniel Prestipino, Linda Raabe, Amna Raja, Janis Reimringer, Sydney C. Rey, Julia Rizaew, Eloisa Ruppert, Kim K. Salmon, Jill Sammet, Rhiannon Schembri, Lars Schlabbach, Frederick W.P. Schmidt, Amalia Skilton, Wikaliler Daniel Smith, Hilário de Sousa, Kristin Sverredal, Daniel Valle, Javier Vera, Judith Voß, Tim Witte, Henry Wu, Stephanie Yam, Jingting Ye, Maisie Yong, Tessa Yuditha, Roberto Zariquiey, Robert Forkel, Nicholas Evans, Stephen C. Levinson, Martin Haspelmath, Simon J. Greenhill, Quentin D. Atkinson, and Russell D. Gray. 2023. Grambank reveals global patterns in the structural diversity of the world's languages. *Science Advances*, 9.

GTNC: A Many-To-One Dataset of Google Translations from NewsCrawl

Damiaan J. W. Reijnaers
University of Amsterdam
info@damiaanreijnaers.nl

Charlotte Pouw
ILLC, University of Amsterdam
c.m.pouw@uva.nl

Abstract

This paper lays the groundwork for initiating research into Source Language Identification; the task of identifying the original language of a machine-translated text. We contribute a carefully-crafted dataset of translations from a typologically diverse spectrum of languages into English and use it to set initial baselines for this novel task. The dataset is publicly available on our GitHub repository: damiaanr/gtnc.

1 Introduction

In an era of globalisation, the world is becoming increasingly reliant on machine translation. But as translation tools find their way into people's daily routines, they spark curiosity about previously unexplored tasks, such as identifying the source language of a machine-translated text. This is an emerging challenge that has been referred to as Source Language Identification (SLI, La Morgia et al. 2023). The task has a relevant application in forensics: knowledge of an individual's native language can offer crucial insights into their identity.

The problem of classifying the original language of a machine-translated text inherently relies on finding markers in the translation that hint at the source (*i.e.*, traces of 'source language interference'). In a first exploration of the field, Reijnaers and Herrewijnen (2023) indicated that such markers can be related to typological differences between the languages involved in the translation process, aligning with theory on human translation (Teich, 2003, pp. 217–20). Typological features contribute to the explainability of SLI models (Kredens et al., 2020, pp. 17–19), a quality essential in forensic contexts (Cheng, 2013, pp. 547–49). However, owing to the novelty of the task, research on SLI is hindered by a lack of sufficiently sized datasets that contain machine translations from a large number of languages into a single language.

This work aims to fill this gap to propel this emerging area of research forward. We introduce **Google Translations from NewsCrawl (GTNC)**: a unique dataset of state-of-the-art machine translations from a diverse set of languages into English, offering a rich typological diversity to facilitate experiments with a wide range of source languages. The dataset spans **50 languages** (listed below), contains **7,500 sentences** per language, and is representative of real-world data given its domain (news articles) and the translation engine used (Google Translate). In addition, we offer initial baselines for future work on SLI and thereby confirm the feasibility of the task.

The next section of this paper will discuss existing datasets that may be used for SLI. In addressing their limitations, we propose a novel dataset in Section 3, which we will then use in a series of experiments in the section that follows. The findings reiterate the value of a typological approach in SLI.

Included languages Amharic, Arabic, Bengali, Bulgarian, Chinese, Croatian, Czech, Dutch, English (untranslated), Estonian, Finnish, French, German, Greek, Gujarati, Hausa, Hindi, Hungarian, Icelandic, Igbo, Indonesian, Italian, Japanese, Kannada, Korean, Kyrgyz, Latvian, Lithuanian, Macedonian, Malayalam, Marathi, Odia, Oromo, Pashto, Persian, Polish, Portuguese, Punjabi, Romanian, Russian, Shona, Spanish, Swahili, Tagalog, Tamil, Telugu, Tigrinya, Turkish, Ukrainian, and Yoruba.

2 Existing datasets

In the realm of *human* translation, several corpora exist that contain translations from multiple languages into a single language, among which the most popular is a collection of proceedings of the European Parliament (Europarl, Koehn 2005). Numerous studies have leveraged this corpus to provide empirical evidence for distinctions between original and translated texts (Koppel and Ordan

Proceedings of the 6th Workshop on Research in Computational Linguistic Typology and Multilingual NLP (SIGTYP 2024), pages 58–65
March 22, 2024 ©2024 Association for Computational Linguistics

2011; Rabinovich and Wintner 2015; Volansky et al. 2013), while some have explicitly aimed to identify the European source language of these documents (Rabinovich et al. 2017; van Halteren 2008). However, *machine* translations are divergent from human translations in a systematic (Fu and Nederhof, 2021) and measurable (van der Werff et al., 2022) way: machine translations often exhibit less morphological and lexical diversity (Vanmassenhove et al., 2021) and adhere more closely to the structure of the source text (Ahrenberg, 2017). Moreover, machine translations are more susceptible to source language interference (Toral, 2019, p. 279), particularly concerning the structural properties of the source language (Bizzoni et al. 2020, p. 288; Popovic et al. 2023). As such, a dataset of purely machine translations is desirable.

A handful of datasets exist that contain machine translations from multiple languages into one. An example is DEMETR (Karpinska et al., 2022), consisting of translations from ten, predominantly Indo-European languages[1] into English. The dataset was constructed to aid models in detecting errors in machine translation output. As a result, a downside is that the authors post-edited the translations to ensure their correctness, thereby potentially eliminating valuable hints that pointed to the source language of these texts. DEMETR is also modest in size, comprising only 100 sentences per language.

Another example is MLQE-PE (Fomicheva et al., 2022), containing the translations of 9,000 sentences for each of five, diverse Indo-European languages[2] into English. Apart from the small number of classes, a drawback of this dataset is that the samples vary widely in length across languages (Figure 2a) and are often noisy (*e.g.*, containing URLs or HTML tags). This could potentially bias SLI models towards relying on spurious features instead of learning linguistic patterns purely governed by typology.

A comparison of the key features mentioned above can be found in Table 1. Notably, all of the above-cited datasets were created to *evaluate* machine translation models. The mentioned limitations thus only come to light when analysing their usefulness for SLI, highlighting the need for a dataset crafted specifically for the task. In the next section, we will introduce such a dataset.

[1]DEMETR includes Chinese, Czech, French, German, Hindi, Italian, Japanese, Polish, Russian, and Spanish.

[2]The relevant languages in MLQE-PE include Estonian, Nepali, Romanian, Russian, and Sinhala.

Table 1: Comparison of dataset size characteristics for usage in a *many-to-one* context.

Dataset	# languages	# sentences/lang.
DEMETR	10	100
MLQE-PE	5	9,000
GTNC	50	7,500

3 A dataset for SLI

In the subsections below, we will describe the steps taken to build GTNC and will provide analyses into its diversity and characteristics. The data and all code used to generate them is available on GitHub.

3.1 Selecting the source texts

To enable a fair comparison of translations across languages, we would ideally obtain a collection of parallel source texts. Yet, while creating a 'one-to-many' corpus is relatively straightforward, building a *many-to-one* variant is practically impossible—it would require the spontaneous utterance of identical content in each language. We therefore aimed to make the data *as parallel as possible*.

On the presumption that the news genre is both universal and relatively consistent worldwide, we selected NewsCrawl (Kocmi et al., 2022) as the repository for the source texts as it contains sentences scraped from news articles in 59 languages and is 'parallel by year'. For GTNC, we sampled from articles that appeared in 2020, '21, and '22, with equal proportions of each year per language.

To enable analyses on the typological level, beyond the prediction of individual language labels, we aimed to include a large number of languages in GTNC. Ultimately, we selected 50 languages.[3] English sentences were naturally left untranslated, allowing for experiments with both translated and original texts. Figure 1 illustrates the data's diversity, based on the World Atlas of Language Structures (WALS, Dryer and Haspelmath 2013). WALS is a resource (wals.info) that contains typological features for over 2,000 languages in tabular format.

3.2 Filtering the samples

The source sentences from NewsCrawl are already shuffled and duplicate-free. We additionally re-

[3]We excluded 9 languages for the following reasons: noise (Kinyarwanda and Somali), similarity to other languages in light of dataset diversity (Bosnian, Serbian, Kazakh), lack of available WALS features to enable effective typological analyses (Afrikaans), lack of data (Tigre and Bambara), and incompatibility with Google Translate (South Ndebele).

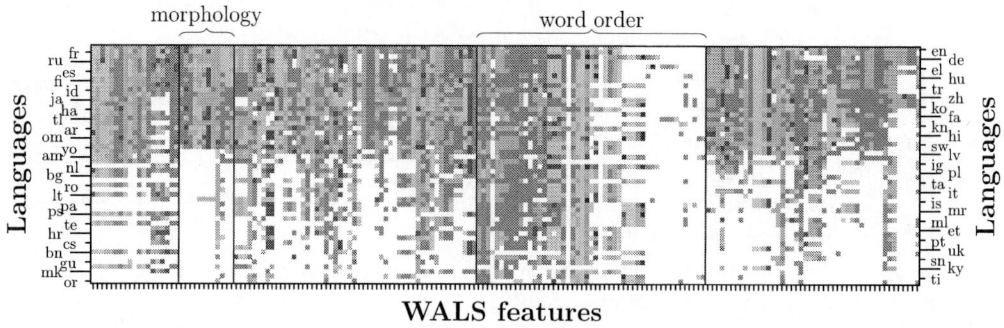

Figure 1: Visualisation of language diversity in GTNC. Columns represent typological features and rows correspond to languages (tagged by ISO 639-1 codes). Hues in columns denote different classes for each feature (overlap in colour thus hints at languages being similar). White boxes indicate unset features. Blue lines act as indicators of feature clusters, of which two are exemplified. Note that each row can intuitively be viewed as a language's unique 'signature', with SLI involving the identification of these signatures through the artifacts they leave in a translation.

moved sentences that contained either of:

- A total of < 30 or > 400 characters.
- Non-alphanumerics, excluding `;:()!?` and equivalences in other languages.
- Characters that directly followed a period (`.`) and were not a white space, a digit, a question mark, another period, or an exclamation mark.
- Four consecutive, identical characters.
- Not `.!?` or equivalences in other languages as the last character of the sentence.
- Latin alphabet characters for non-Latin-script languages and *vice-versa*.
- Russian: Ukrainian-specific characters (as the Russian corpus also contained Ukrainian text).

Furthermore, samples that were deemed 'short' or 'bad' by JusText (Pomikálek, 2011) were also left out.[4] JusText is a tool for removing boilerplate content (*i.e.*, frequently-used and non-unique text).

3.3 Translating and aligning by length

The samples were obtained by using Google Translate.[5] To avoid a spurious correlation between sentence length and language class—which an SLI-model could potentially exploit—we aimed at maintaining a consistent average and median length of 125 characters across all resulting English translations. This was accomplished by selecting sentences of specific lengths, determined by pre-computed, frequentist character-to-character ratios for every translation pair. Ultimately, $42,667,664$ source characters were translated into $46,460,290$ English characters ($\mu \approx 126.42$ characters per sample; not including the original English sentences from NewsCrawl). The data over all languages is normal (Figure 2b). As the resulting ratios might be of interest to other studies in machine translation, we included them as appendix material in Table 2.

Finally, all translated samples were scored by Monocleaner (Sánchez-Cartagena et al., 2018) to denote their 'fluency'. These annotations are essentially language-model scores, calculated as the normalised perplexity of character 7-grams.

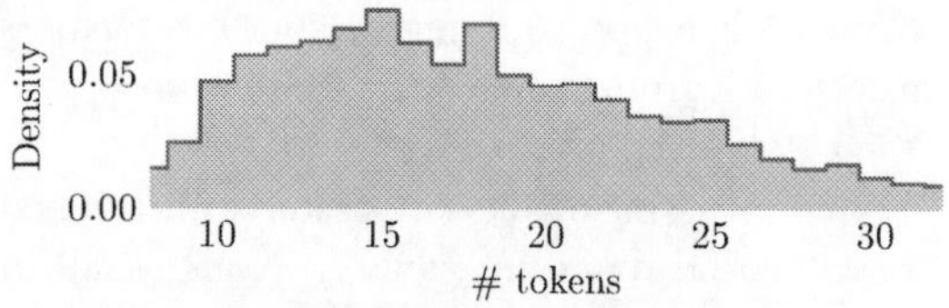

(a) MLQE-PE: Separate length distributions per class.

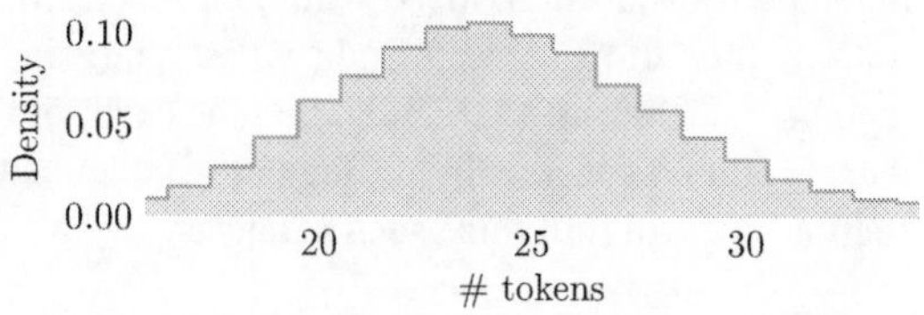

(b) GTNC: Normally distributed length across all classes.

Figure 2: Sample length across many-to-one datasets.

[4]This step was not available for Amharic, Hausa, Japanese, Oromo, Odia, Punjabi, Pashto, Shona, Tigrinya, and Chinese.

[5]The data were translated on June 20th, 2023, using the v3 Translation API. To support the creation of this dataset, Google granted the equivalent of USD $1,000 in API credits.

4 Preliminary Experiments

In this section, we will use the English translations from GTNC to predict the source language of both individual samples and combinations of sentences.

4.1 Input representation

It is through parts of speech that hints about a language's structure—and thereby its typology—may be obtained (Cutting et al., 1992, p. 133). Given the structural nature of source language interference in machine translation, we opted for part of speech (PoS) tags as input features for our models.

When discerning between human-translated and original texts, many studies have achieved good performance by representing input texts as sequences of PoS tags; generally by training an SVM (Hearst et al., 1998) on frequency counts of PoS n-grams (Baroni and Bernardini 2005, p. 268; Rabinovich et al. 2017, p. 534; Pylypenko et al. 2021, p. 8603). In a recent study, Popovic et al. (2023) did so for *machine* translations and likewise indicated the efficacy of PoS tags, affirming their relevance in SLI.

Of the above, the work closest to ours is the paper by Rabinovich et al. (2017). Its authors perform source language identification on human-translated texts and report an accuracy of 75.61% when considering samples from 14 source languages.

4.2 Model architecture and training

To enable the model to capture structural patterns over longer distances, we conducted our experiments using a bidirectional LSTM (Graves and Schmidhuber, 2005) of 64 hidden dimensions. In correspondence with the granularity of the data, the LSTM operates on the sentence level, classifying one sentence at a time. At every timestep, it takes in a 70-dimensional input vector, consisting of a one-hot encoding of a token's PoS tag (fine-grained), concatenated with a multi-hot vector that additionally encodes grammatical number, tense, and person, pronominal type, definiteness, verb form, and whether a word is possessive and/or reflexive. All PoS and morphological tags were assigned by SpaCy (spacy.io) and adhere to the Universal Dependencies standard (Nivre et al., 2017).

The final hidden state of the LSTM is concatenated for every direction and subsequently processed by a single feed-forward layer that directly maps to output classes (*i.e.*, possible source languages). To obtain a prediction for a *group* of sentences, the logits of this layer are averaged over all individually classified samples within the group.

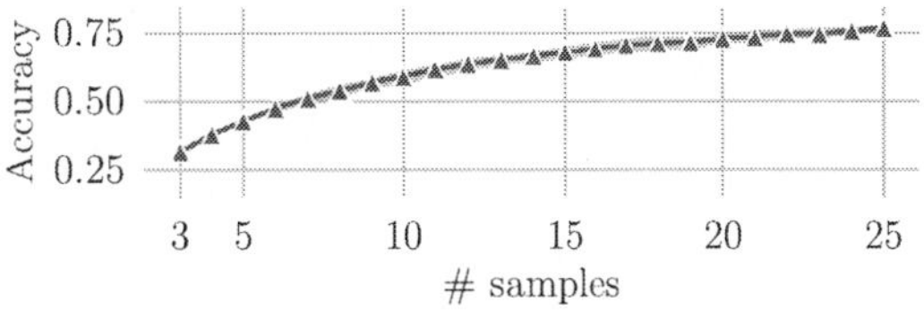

Figure 3: Performance over number of sentences.

We trained all LSTMs for 20 epochs and averaged 'best epoch'-results over three runs. Optimisation was done using Adam (Kingma and Ba, 2017) with a learning rate of 1e-3, a weight decay parameter of 1e-4, and a batch size of 16. Data was split into train and test fractions of 0.9 and 0.1 respectively.

4.3 Initial baseline results for SLI

Figure 3 illustrates the model's accuracy as a function of the number of sentences.[6] Individual samples were classified with an accuracy of 15.68%. Note that we work with samples of only a few tens of tokens in size (Figure 2b), while Rabinovich et al. (2017) use samples of 1,000 tokens. Naturally, the longer the document, the more opportunity the source language has to leave its fingerprints. The positive correlation between document length and accuracy, as shown in Figure 3, provides evidence that supports this tendency.

Inspired by the same work, we reconstructed a phylogenetic tree using hierarchical agglomerative clustering applied to the averaged confusion scores for all Indo-European languages in GTNC. The tree is shown in Figure 4. 'Ward's method' was used as linkage criterion (Ward, 1963). The model was trained only on the 24 Indo-European source languages present in GTNC (excluding English). The tree provides intuitive evidence that the model tends to confuse genetically similar languages, indicating that the model exploits language-specific patterns that align with their typology. This, in turn, implies that the sentences in GTNC do indeed carry typological features of their source counterparts, rendering it a well-suited dataset for SLI. The tree-figure additionally provides insight into the kind of errors that the model makes. For example, when contrasted with the frequently referenced 'gold tree' by Serva, M. and Petroni, F. (2008), Greek is being misclassified as being part of a branch with

[6]Ideally, the samples would have appeared in natural sequence, however, due to lack of data, they were drawn *i.i.d.*

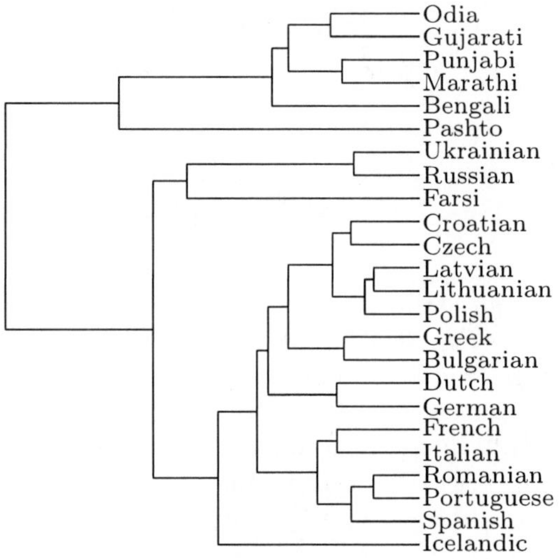

Figure 4: Reconstructed phylogenetic tree.

Bulgarian, among other Slavic languages in higher branches. This suggests that the model mistakenly relies on similar markers to discern between English translations from Greek and those from Slavic languages. A logical next step for future research would therefore involve a detailed analysis of the specific markers employed by such models. Based on the figure, a similar argument could be made for Farsi, or the East Slavic sub-branch.

5 Conclusion and discussion

We showcased GTNC: a thoughtfully designed dataset of Google-Translated news articles from diverse languages into English. Our experiments provide compelling evidence attesting to the feasibility of SLI and emphasise the dataset's suitability for typological approaches—a quality that holds significant promise on the path to *explainable* SLI.

As our goal was to introduce a dataset, we deliberately avoided a lengthy discussion on the underlying phenomena that enable the identification of a source language in the first place; *i.e.*, a more in-depth analysis of how 'artifacts' of the typology of the original language are left behind in a translation. An exploration of the involved scientific concepts, particularly 'translationese' (Nida and Taber, 1969) and 'interlanguage' (Selinker, 1972), and how they relate to machine translation, would demand a thorough examination that is beyond the scope of this short paper.

While GTNC encompasses a wide array of languages, the number of samples per language remains limited. We encourage the community to improve our dataset using the tools that we have made available. Beyond SLI, the data may also help other applications, such as evaluating Google Translate's performance across languages. We hope that GTNC will additionally foster exploration in new directions.

6 Acknowledgements

The authors are grateful for the useful feedback provided by Ella Rabinovich, Wilker Aziz, Willem Zuidema, and the anonymous reviewers. Charlotte Pouw's research is funded by the NWA-ORC grant 'InDeep', no. 1292.19.399, provided by the Netherlands Organisation for Scientific Research.

References

Lars Ahrenberg. 2017. Comparing machine translation and human translation: A case study. In *Proceedings of the Workshop Human-Informed Translation and Interpreting Technology*, pages 21–28, Varna, Bulgaria. Association for Computational Linguistics, Shoumen, Bulgaria.

Marco Baroni and Silvia Bernardini. 2005. A New Approach to the Study of Translationese: Machine-learning the Difference between Original and Translated Text. *Literary and Linguistic Computing*, 21(3):259–274.

Yuri Bizzoni, Tom S Juzek, Cristina España-Bonet, Koel Dutta Chowdhury, Josef van Genabith, and Elke Teich. 2020. How human is machine translationese? comparing human and machine translations of text and speech. In *Proceedings of the 17th International Conference on Spoken Language Translation*, pages 280–290, Online. Association for Computational Linguistics.

Edward K. Cheng. 2013. Being pragmatic about forensic linguistics. *Journal of Law and Policy*, 21(2):541–550.

Doug Cutting, Julian Kupiec, Jan Pedersen, and Penelope Sibun. 1992. A practical part-of-speech tagger. In *Third Conference on Applied Natural Language Processing*, pages 133–140, Trento, Italy. Association for Computational Linguistics.

Matthew S. Dryer and Martin Haspelmath, editors. 2013. *WALS Online (v2020.3)*. Zenodo.

Marina Fomicheva, Shuo Sun, Erick Fonseca, Chrysoula Zerva, Frédéric Blain, Vishrav Chaudhary, Francisco Guzmán, Nina Lopatina, Lucia Specia, and André F. T. Martins. 2022. MLQE-PE: A multilingual quality estimation and post-editing dataset. In *Proceedings of the Thirteenth Language Resources and Evaluation Conference*, pages 4963–4974, Marseille, France. European Language Resources Association.

Yingxue Fu and Mark-Jan Nederhof. 2021. Automatic classification of human translation and machine translation: A study from the perspective of lexical diversity. In *Proceedings for the First Workshop on Modelling Translation: Translatology in the Digital Age*, pages 91–99, online. Association for Computational Linguistics.

Alex Graves and Jürgen Schmidhuber. 2005. Framewise phoneme classification with bidirectional lstm and other neural network architectures. *Neural Networks*, 18(5):602–610. IJCNN 2005.

M.A. Hearst, S.T. Dumais, E. Osuna, J. Platt, and B. Scholkopf. 1998. Support vector machines. *IEEE Intelligent Systems and their Applications*, 13(4):18–28.

Marzena Karpinska, Nishant Raj, Katherine Thai, Yixiao Song, Ankita Gupta, and Mohit Iyyer. 2022. DEMETR: Diagnosing evaluation metrics for translation. In *Proceedings of the 2022 Conference on Empirical Methods in Natural Language Processing*, pages 9540–9561, Abu Dhabi, United Arab Emirates. Association for Computational Linguistics.

Diederik P. Kingma and Jimmy Ba. 2017. Adam: A method for stochastic optimization.

Tom Kocmi, Rachel Bawden, Ondřej Bojar, Anton Dvorkovich, Christian Federmann, Mark Fishel, Thamme Gowda, Yvette Graham, Roman Grundkiewicz, Barry Haddow, Rebecca Knowles, Philipp Koehn, Christof Monz, Makoto Morishita, Masaaki Nagata, Toshiaki Nakazawa, Michal Novák, Martin Popel, and Maja Popović. 2022. Findings of the 2022 conference on machine translation (WMT22). In *Proceedings of the Seventh Conference on Machine Translation (WMT)*, pages 1–45, Abu Dhabi, United Arab Emirates (Hybrid). Association for Computational Linguistics.

Philipp Koehn. 2005. Europarl: A parallel corpus for statistical machine translation. In *Proceedings of Machine Translation Summit X: Papers*, pages 79–86, Phuket, Thailand.

Moshe Koppel and Noam Ordan. 2011. Translationese and its dialects. In *Proceedings of the 49th Annual Meeting of the Association for Computational Linguistics: Human Language Technologies*, pages 1318–1326, Portland, Oregon, USA. Association for Computational Linguistics.

Krzysztof Kredens, Ria Perkins, and Tim Grant. 2020. Developing a framework for the explanation of interlingual features for native and other language infuence detection. *Language and Law/Linguagem e Direito*, 6(2):10–23.

Massimo La Morgia, Alessandro Mei, Eugenio Nerio Nemmi, Luca Sabatini, and Francesco Sassi. 2023. Translated texts under the lens: From machine translation detection to source language identification. In *Advances in Intelligent Data Analysis XXI*, pages 222–235, Cham. Springer Nature Switzerland.

Eugene A. Nida and Charles R. Taber. 1969. *The theory and practice of translation.* Helps for translators. E. J. Brill, Leiden.

Joakim Nivre, Daniel Zeman, Filip Ginter, and Francis Tyers. 2017. Universal Dependencies. In *Proceedings of the 15th Conference of the European Chapter of the Association for Computational Linguistics: Tutorial Abstracts*, Valencia, Spain. Association for Computational Linguistics.

Jan Pomikálek. 2011. *Removing boilerplate and duplicate content from web corpora.* Ph.D. thesis, Masaryk university, Faculty of informatics, Brno, Czech Republic.

Maja Popovic, Ekaterina Lapshinova-Koltunski, and Maarit Koponen. 2023. Computational analysis of different translations: by professionals, students and machines. In *Proceedings of the 24th Annual Conference of the European Association for Machine Translation*, pages 365–374, Tampere, Finland. European Association for Machine Translation.

Daria Pylypenko, Kwabena Amponsah-Kaakyire, Koel Dutta Chowdhury, Josef van Genabith, and Cristina España-Bonet. 2021. Comparing feature-engineering and feature-learning approaches for multilingual translationese classification. In *Proceedings of the 2021 Conference on Empirical Methods in Natural Language Processing*, pages 8596–8611, Online and Punta Cana, Dominican Republic. Association for Computational Linguistics.

Ella Rabinovich, Noam Ordan, and Shuly Wintner. 2017. Found in translation: Reconstructing phylogenetic language trees from translations. In *Proceedings of the 55th Annual Meeting of the Association for Computational Linguistics (Volume 1: Long Papers)*, pages 530–540, Vancouver, Canada. Association for Computational Linguistics.

Ella Rabinovich and Shuly Wintner. 2015. Unsupervised identification of translationese. *Transactions of the Association for Computational Linguistics*, 3:419–432.

Damiaan Reijnaers and Elize Herrewijnen. 2023. Machine-translated texts from English to Polish show a potential for typological explanations in source language identification. In *Proceedings of the 9th Workshop on Slavic Natural Language Processing 2023 (SlavicNLP 2023)*, pages 40–46, Dubrovnik, Croatia. Association for Computational Linguistics.

Víctor M. Sánchez-Cartagena, Marta Bañón, Sergio Ortiz-Rojas, and Gema Ramírez-Sánchez. 2018. Prompsit's submission to wmt 2018 parallel corpus filtering shared task. In *Proceedings of the Third Conference on Machine Translation, Volume 2: Shared Task Papers*, Brussels, Belgium. Association for Computational Linguistics.

Larry Selinker. 1972. Interlanguage. 10(1-4):209–232.

Serva, M. and Petroni, F. 2008. Indo-european languages tree by levenshtein distance. *EPL*, 81(6):68005.

Elke Teich. 2003. *Cross-Linguistic Variation in System and Text*. De Gruyter Mouton, Berlin, Boston.

Antonio Toral. 2019. Post-editese: an exacerbated translationese. In *Proceedings of Machine Translation Summit XVII: Research Track*, pages 273–281, Dublin, Ireland. European Association for Machine Translation.

Tobias van der Werff, Rik van Noord, and Antonio Toral. 2022. Automatic discrimination of human and neural machine translation: A study with multiple pre-trained models and longer context. In *Proceedings of the 23rd Annual Conference of the European Association for Machine Translation*, pages 161–170, Ghent, Belgium. European Association for Machine Translation.

Hans van Halteren. 2008. Source language markers in EUROPARL translations. In *Proceedings of the 22nd International Conference on Computational Linguistics (Coling 2008)*, pages 937–944, Manchester, UK. Coling 2008 Organizing Committee.

Eva Vanmassenhove, Dimitar Shterionov, and Matthew Gwilliam. 2021. Machine translationese: Effects of algorithmic bias on linguistic complexity in machine translation. In *Proceedings of the 16th Conference of the European Chapter of the Association for Computational Linguistics: Main Volume*, pages 2203–2213, Online. Association for Computational Linguistics.

Vered Volansky, Noam Ordan, and Shuly Wintner. 2013. On the features of translationese. *Digital Scholarship in the Humanities*, 30(1):98–118.

Joe H. Ward. 1963. Hierarchical grouping to optimize an objective function. *Journal of the American Statistical Association*, 58(301):236–244.

A Character-to-character ratios

See Table 2 on the next page.

Table 2: Character-to-character ratios of languages in GTNC, relative to English. $n = 100$.

	Source = 100 chrs.				Target = 125 chrs.	
	Length		**Ratio**		**Realised length**	
	μ	σ/μ	$\rightarrow$	$\leftarrow$	μ	σ/μ
Amharic (am)	155.7	.16	1.56	0.64	**124.7**	.15
Arabic (ar)	129.9	.15	1.30	0.77	**128.1**	.15
Bengali (bn)	111.4	.14	1.11	0.90	**127.5**	.14
Bulgarian (bg)	103.5	.12	1.04	0.97	**124.8**	.11
Chinese (zh)	421.7	.16	4.22	0.24	**123.4**	.19
Croatian (hr)	111.1	.12	1.11	0.90	**122.6**	.11
Czech (cs)	112.9	.15	1.13	0.89	**126.3**	.12
Dutch (nl)	94.7	.11	0.95	1.06	**125.7**	.10
English (en)	100.0		1.00	1.00	**125.0**	
Estonian (et)	111.0	.15	1.11	0.90	**123.9**	.12
Finnish (fi)	104.6	.12	1.05	0.96	**125.1**	.12
French (fr)	92.0	.11	0.92	1.09	**125.9**	.10
German (de)	93.6	.11	0.94	1.07	**126.3**	.11
Greek (el)	91.9	.13	0.92	1.09	**126.1**	.11
Gujarati (gu)	108.1	.16	1.08	0.92	**127.5**	.14
Hausa (ha)	100.1	.16	1.00	1.00	**123.4**	.14
Hindi (hi)	117.1	.16	1.17	0.85	**122.2**	.13
Hungarian (hu)	106.8	.12	1.07	0.94	**122.6**	.12
Icelandic (is)	103.1	.12	1.03	0.97	**126.8**	.12
Igbo (ig)	109.3	.14	1.09	0.92	**121.4**	.16
Indonesian (id)	100.0	.14	1.00	1.00	**125.3**	.13
Italian (it)	97.1	.12	0.97	1.03	**125.1**	.10
Japanese (ja)	236.9	.28	2.37	0.42	**142.9**	.23
Kannada (kn)	102.3	.17	1.02	0.98	**126.8**	.15
Korean (ko)	229.0	.24	2.29	0.44	**170.9**	.18
Kyrgyz (ky)	101.9	.15	1.02	0.98	**126.5**	.14
Latvian (lv)	110.1	.11	1.10	0.91	**124.9**	.12
Lithuanian (lt)	107.9	.14	1.08	0.93	**125.3**	.12
Macedonian (mk)	100.2	.11	1.00	1.00	**127.1**	.11
Malayalam (ml)	87.6	.17	0.88	1.14	**129.5**	.14
Marathi (mr)	103.1	.13	1.03	0.97	**122.5**	.14
Odia (or)	106.6	.16	1.07	0.94	**123.6**	.14
Oromo (om)	82.3	.17	0.82	1.22	**121.0**	.17
Pashto (ps)	114.7	.13	1.15	0.87	**127.7**	.13
Persian (fa)	119.5	.13	1.19	0.84	**127.4**	.15
Polish (pl)	102.8	.13	1.03	0.97	**124.5**	.12
Portuguese (pt)	100.6	.11	1.01	0.99	**122.4**	.10
Punjabi (pa)	102.2	.14	1.01	0.99	**125.0**	.13
Romanian (ro)	97.3	.12	0.97	1.03	**124.7**	.11
Russian (ru)	106.7	.14	1.07	0.94	**125.5**	.13
Shona (sn)	100.5	.14	1.01	0.99	**122.7**	.14
Spanish (es)	95.2	.11	0.95	1.05	**125.4**	.10
Swahili (sw)	100.5	.14	1.00	1.00	**124.1**	.13
Tagalog (tl)	90.6	.12	0.91	1.10	**127.0**	.11
Tamil (ta)	89.0	.18	0.89	1.12	**125.8**	.15
Telugu (te)	105.9	.16	1.06	0.94	**123.8**	.14
Tigrinya (ti)	130.9	.20	1.31	0.76	**127.9**	.18
Turkish (tr)	104.7	.17	1.05	0.96	**127.0**	.13
Ukrainian (uk)	111.0	.13	1.11	0.90	**123.3**	.13
Yoruba (yo)	107.8	.16	1.08	0.93	**124.8**	.14

Sociolinguistically Informed Interpretability: A Case Study on Hinglish Emotion Classification

Kushal Tatariya[1] **Heather Lent**[2] **Johannes Bjerva**[2] **Miryam de Lhoneux**[1]
[1] Department of Computer Science, KU Leuven, Belgium
[2] Department of Computer Science, Aalborg University, Denmark
{kushaljayesh.tatariya, miryam.delhoneux}@kuleuven.be
{hcle, jbjerva}@cs.aau.dk

Abstract

Emotion classification is a challenging task in NLP due to the inherent idiosyncratic and subjective nature of linguistic expression, especially with code-mixed data. Pre-trained language models (PLMs) have achieved high performance for many tasks and languages, but it remains to be seen whether these models learn and are robust to the differences in emotional expression across languages. Sociolinguistic studies have shown that Hinglish speakers switch to Hindi when expressing negative emotions and to English when expressing positive emotions. To understand if language models can learn these associations, we study the effect of language on emotion prediction across 3 PLMs on a Hinglish emotion classification dataset. Using LIME (Ribeiro et al., 2016) and token level language ID, we find that models do learn these associations between language choice and emotional expression. Moreover, having code-mixed data present in the pre-training can augment that learning when task-specific data is scarce. We also conclude from the misclassifications that the models may overgeneralise this heuristic to other infrequent examples where this sociolinguistic phenomenon does not apply.

Disclaimer: *This paper contains some examples of language use that readers may find offensive.*

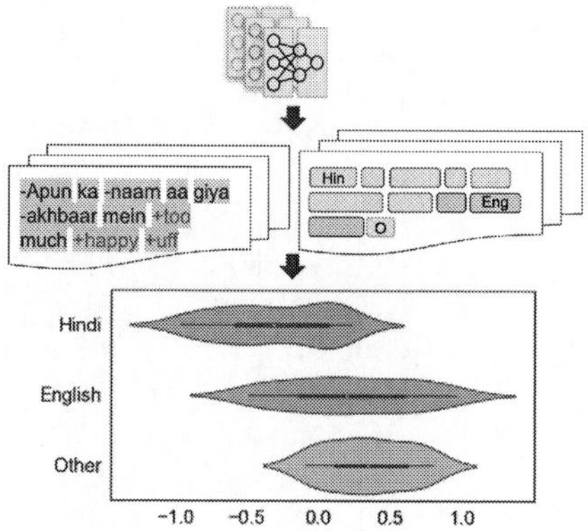

Figure 1: Our workflow. We train 3 emotion classification models, then obtain LIME scores for each token (positive scores in red, negative scores in blue, and zero scores in grey). These same samples are then tagged with token-level language ID, which enables us to examine LIME distributional differences by language.

1 Introduction

An open-ended goal of the NLP community is to develop language technologies robust to the vast and various idiosyncrasies of authentic human communication. Understanding emotion requires knowledge of the subtleties of linguistic expression and inherent human subjectivity, making emotion classification a challenging task. It is further complicated when working with code-mixed utterances. Every language participating in code-mixed communication comes with its own cultural and linguistic baggage that oversees the verbalization of emotion (Kachru, 1978; Hershcovich et al., 2022). The adoption of pre-trained language models (PLMs) has improved performance across the board for this task, but the PLMs still remain black boxes. While research in interpretability aims to address this shortcoming, most analyses remain centered around English (Ruder et al., 2022). In this work, we aim to make explicit what associations are learned when PLMs are trained on code-mixed data, and whether established differences in linguistic expression across languages indeed influence model prediction.

We approach this interpretability problem through the lens of sociolinguistics. In particular, we focus on Hindi-English (Hinglish) code-mixing, prevalent in India and in the Indian diaspora (Orsini, 2015). In a study on Hindi-English bilinguals on Twitter, Rudra et al. (2016) observed that English was the language of choice for expression of a positive emotion and Hindi was more used for negative emotion. Moreover, Hindi was the preferred language for swearing online, a finding also echoed by

Proceedings of the 6th Workshop on Research in Computational Linguistic Typology and Multilingual NLP (SIGTYP 2024), pages 66–74
March 22, 2024

Agarwal et al. (2017). Rudra et al. (2016) explain the reason behind this to be the fact that bilinguals prefer to express strong emotions (Dewaele, 2010) and swear (Dewaele, 2007) in L1, which happens to be Hindi for most Hinglish speakers. Conversely, Rudra et al. (2016) speculate that since English is the language of aspiration in India, it becomes the preferred language for positive emotion.

In this context, we formulate our main questions as: (**RQ1**) Are PLMs likely to associate different emotions with different languages? (**RQ2**) Are English tokens more likely to influence a model to predict a positive emotion? (**RQ3**) Are Hindi tokens more likely to influence a model to predict a negative emotion, and if so, what is the role of Hindi swear words? To this end, we fine-tune 3 different PLMs on a Hinglish emotion classification dataset and leverage LIME and token-level language identification for an interpretability analysis.

2 Related Work

Code-Mixing Previous works in emotion classification and sentiment analysis have demonstrated that processing code-mixed text is more difficult than monolingual text (Sitaram et al., 2019; Zaharia et al., 2020; Yulianti et al., 2021). This is in part due to the complexities of processing emotion from two different languages with varying socio-cultural and grammatical structures at play (Younas et al., 2020; Sasidhar et al., 2020; Ilyas et al., 2023). In this context, Doğruöz et al. (2021) published a survey on the linguistic and social perspectives on code-mixing for language technologies. They emphasized the importance of incorporating the social context of a code-mixed language pair into systems processing code-mixed text.

Interpretability with LIME LIME (Local Interpretable Model-Agnostic Explanations) (Ribeiro et al., 2016) is a popular tool for interpretability that is model agnostic and employable for classification tasks. It learns a linear classifier locally around a model's prediction, leveraging token weights (also learned by the linear classifier) to assign a "LIME score" between 1 and -1 to each token. A positive score indicates that the token influenced the model towards the predicted label, and a negative score indicates that the token influenced the model to *not* predict that label. We leverage LIME due to its availability and easy-to-use implementations, for instance in the Language Interpretability Tool (LIT; Tenney et al., 2020), which we used for this work. Previous work has also indicated the accuracy of its approximation of the models and its ability to provide human-friendly explanations (Madsen et al., 2022; Hajiyan et al., 2023).

3 Methodology

Dataset We utilize a dataset for sentiment analysis of code-mixed tweets by Patwa et al. (2020), later annotated with emotion labels by Ghosh et al. (2023). Each example is annotated with the six basic Ekman emotions (Ekman et al., 1999) - *joy*, *sadness*, *fear*, *surprise*, *disgust* and *anger*. When an example does not fit any of these emotions, or expresses no emotion, it is labelled as *others*. This dataset contains 14,000 examples in the train set, 3,000 in the validation, and 3,000 in the test set. For this work, we randomly sample 1,000 examples from the validation set to enable manual verification of the automatic token tagging described below, maintaining the default distribution across labels (see Appendix B).

Models We fine-tune 3 different PLMs for the task of emotion classification with the Hinglish training data:

- **XLMR** (Conneau et al., 2020), pre-trained on Common Crawl, spanning 100 languages, including English and Hindi, both in the Devanagari script and additional romanized Hindi.
- **IndicBERT v2** (Doddapaneni et al., 2022), pre-trained on data from 24 Indic languages, including Hindi and English that is local to the Indian subcontinent. For Hindi, this model has only seen the Devanagari script, and no romanized Hindi.
- **HingRoBERTa** (Nayak and Joshi, 2022), an XLM-R model that has been further pre-trained on romanized, code-mixed Hindi-English. Thus, in addition to having seen romanized Hindi, this model is specifically intended for code-mixed text.

The full details on model training and performance are given in Appendix A.

Token Tagging For each of the 1,000 samples (20,835 tokens in total) drawn from the validation set, we first obtain LIME scores for each token using LIT (Tenney et al., 2020). We then run the samples through CodeSwitch (Sarkar, 2020), a

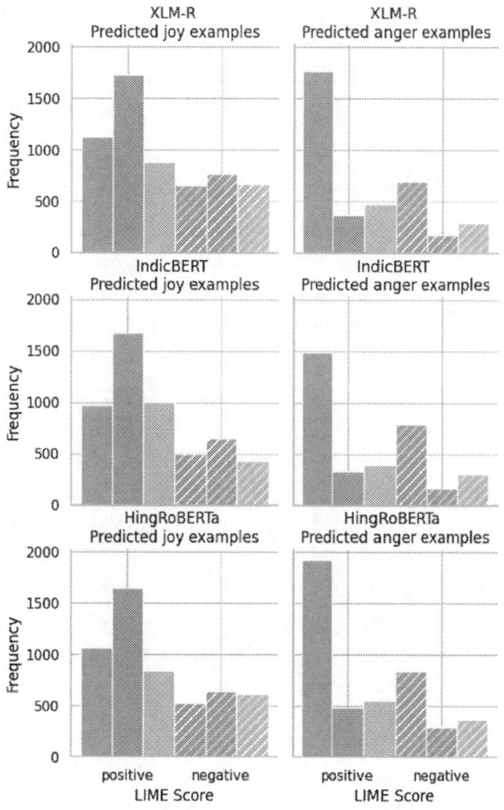

Figure 2: Frequencies of *Hindi* (green), *English* (purple) and *Other* (orange) tokens to be assigned a positive (solid) or a negative (striped) LIME score for examples predicted as *joy* and *anger*, for all models.

Hinglish language identification tool which tags each token as Hindi, English, or Other, to get the language ID tags.[1]

4 Results and Analysis

First, to answer whether the models learn to meaningfully distinguish between languages for emotion prediction (**RQ1**), we examine the distributions of LIME scores across each language ID tag (*English, Hindi, Other*). Concretely, we inspect the frequency with which tokens received a positive or a negative LIME score in our sample, for each language. We then conduct a χ^2 test of independence to determine whether these two variables have some dependency. Table 1 shows the p-values for the entire sample. For all models, we find this dependence to be statistically significant ($p < 0.05$), indicating that there is some influence

[1]Besides the Hindi and English labels, CodeSwitch also tags tokens as "Named-Entity", "Foreign words", and "Other" for punctuation, emojis, and other non-textual tokens. For this work, we combine these 3 additional tags into one category.

	p-values			
Model	**Entire Sample**	**Joy**	**Anger**	**Sadness**
XLM-R	7.06e-12	1.44e-15	6.18e-7	1.78e-3
IndicBERT	1.22e-22	3.28e-4	1.69e-5	3.30e-1
HingRoBERTa	3.30e-7	4.00e-18	1.71e-8	2.18e-5

Table 1: We test the null hypothesis that language ID tags and LIME scores are independent of each other using χ^2. This table contains the p-values for tests done on the entire sample, and also on examples predicted as *joy*, *anger*, and *sadness*.

of language over the LIME scores. We also confirm this with a 1-Way ANOVA test, which can be found in Appendix C, along with our entire statistical analysis.

Next, we examine this dependency on a more granular level to determine whether the presence of English tokens influence the Hinglish emotion classification models to predict more positive emotions (**RQ2**), and whether Hindi tokens influence them to predict negative emotions (**RQ3**). We observe the distribution of language ID across LIME scores for examples that the models predicted as *joy*, *anger*, and *sadness*. These labels were selected in particular as they have the most examples in the dataset (after *others*), and provide the positive (*joy*) and negative (*anger* and *sadness*) polarity discussed in the sociolinguistics literature.

(RQ2) Do English tokens influence models to predict positive emotions? Figure 2 shows which languages tend to have more positive and more negative LIME scores. As observed for *joy*, English tokens have the highest frequency with positive LIME scores. Table 1 shows that there is a significant dependency between language ID and LIME score for all models. Thus, English tokens influence the model significantly more than Hindi and Others when predicting *joy*.

(RQ3) Do Hindi tokens influence models to predict negative emotions? When predicting *anger*, Table 1 again shows that there is dependency between language ID and LIME score for all models. From Figure 2, we can see that Hindi tokens influence the model significantly towards predicting *anger*. When predicting *sadness*, however, we only observe significance with the XLM-R and HingRoBERTa models, but not with IndicBERT. Moreover, for XLM-R, the p-value is not much lower than the threshold. Thus, we cannot make strong conclusions for this label.

Token	Lang_ID	Swear Word?[2]
Fuck	eng	Yes
Chutiye	hin	Yes
Fakeionist	eng	No
Bsdk	hin	Yes
Sadly	eng	No
Bakwas	hin	No
Kutta	hin	Yes
Gaddar	hin	No
Shame	eng	No
Sala	hin	Yes

Table 2: Top 10 tokens with the highest LIME scores when predicting negative emotions, (*anger, sadness, disgust* and*fear*) for all models. They have been mapped to a canonical form and are in descending order of LIME score.

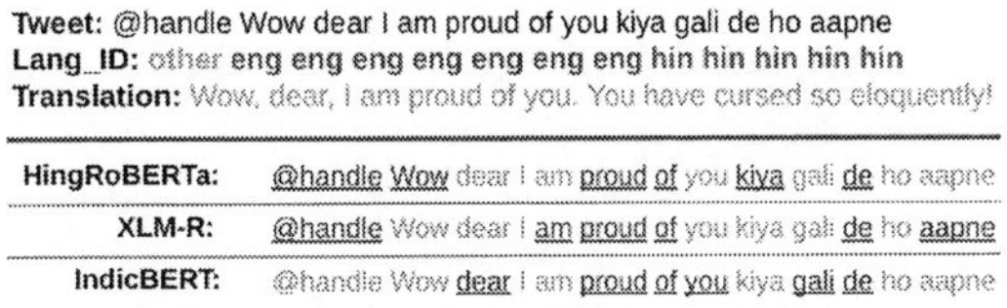

Figure 3: An example from the dataset labelled as *joy*, with the translation and language ID tags. The 3 tokens with the highest LIME scores are marked in blue, and the 3 tokens with the lowest scores are marked in red.

Swear Words Previous works demonstrate that Hinglish speakers prefer to swear in Hindi over English, in a code-mixed setting (Rudra et al., 2016; Agarwal et al., 2017). To check whether this finding is similarly echoed by our fine-tuned models, we examine the top 10 tokens with the highest LIME scores when predicting a negative emotion (*anger*, *sadness*, *disgust*, *fear*), across all models (see Table 2). While the first among these is an English swear word (owing to it being the most used swear word by Hinglish speakers online (Agarwal et al., 2017)) there are 4 Hindi swear words in this list of tokens. As such, we can see that the models not only learn the negative connotation of the Hindi swear words, but also that these Hindi swear words are the *most* negative of all other tokens, regardless of language, thus confirming observations from the sociolinguistics literature.

5 Discussion

From the section above, it can be concluded that the models are able to distinguish patterns of speaker preference detailed by Rudra et al. (2016) when predicting emotion for code-mixed data. English tokens influence the models more towards predicting a positive emotion, and Hindi tokens influence the models more towards predicting a negative emotion. An example of this is provided in Figure 3, where all the models exhibit a strong degree of influence from the English tokens in their prediction of the *joy* label. At the same time, most of the tokens assigned a negative LIME score come from Hindi.

For *sadness*, we surmise that a shortage of training data is responsible for models' failure to learn meaningful differences across the languages. About 10% of the entire dataset consists of examples labelled *sadness*. In contrast, *joy* is 30% and *anger* is about 20% (see Appendix B). Even with less data, however, we still observe a dependency between language and LIME score with HingRoBERTa. It is the only model we examine with code-mixed data present in the pre-training. Thus, when there is less data for a model to learn these associations, it can help to have code-mixed data in the pre-training.

5.1 Do PLMs overgeneralize these learnt associations?

McCoy et al. (2019) found that language models can adapt to heuristics that are valid for frequent cases and fail on the less frequent ones. In a similar vein, we investigate whether these sociolinguistic associations learnt by the models overgeneralise to the less frequent examples where this phenomenon is not seen. We examine instances where the models have misclassified examples labelled as *joy* and *anger*, highlighted in Figure 4.

For both *joy* and *anger*, the models generally either predict another label of the same emotional polarity (for example, *disgust* instead of *anger*), or they predict them as *others*. The dataset is highly imbalanced, and thus we can say that although the models can discern the polarity difference between positive and negative emotion labels (as seen in Figure 4 where the values in the lower left and upper right quadrants are low), they struggle with granular distinctions between them.

We also manually look into the few instances where *joy* examples were assigned a negative emotion label, and *anger* examples were assigned a positive emotion label. Out of the total instances, 15 involve scenarios where either Hindi words with a negative connotation led the model to attribute a negative label to *joy*, or English words with a positive connotation influenced the model to assign a

[2] As decided by a native speaker, and also compared with the lexicon lists of Hindi and English swear words used by Agarwal et al. (2017).

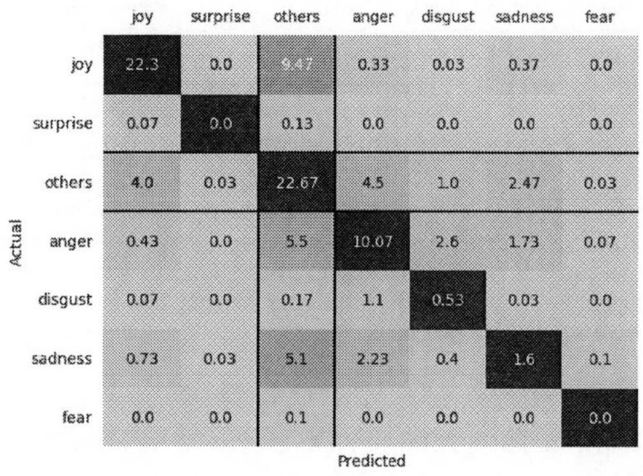

Figure 4: Confusion matrix containing the percentage of correctly and incorrectly classified examples for each label combination. The blue cells represent correct classifications, and the pink cells represent incorrect classifications.

Tweet: @handle Very nice Sir yeh diya sateek jawab Pakistan ab bhi sudhar ja nahi to terey yaha sai jitn ...
Label: Anger **Prediction:** Joy

Figure 5: An example labelled *anger* that was misclassified as *joy* owing to the English phrase (*English* - purple; *Hindi* - green; *Other* - orange) in the sentence having a positive connotation, even though the sentence itself conveys *anger*.

positive emotion label to *anger*. This suggests that examples featuring English words indicating positive emotions on their own can mislead the model into predicting a positive emotion label despite an overall negative tone in the expression (and vice versa for Hindi words), as illustrated in Figure 5.

On a broader scale, we examine the distribution of English, Hindi and Other tokens in the misclassified *joy* and *anger* examples. As seen in Table 3, the normalised frequency of Hindi tokens is higher in the misclassified *joy* examples than the overall distribution. Consequently, more Hindi tokens have a positive LIME score. Thus, McCoy et al. (2019)'s conclusions stated earlier are echoed here as well. While the extreme cases where the models overgeneralise to predict an emotion label of the opposite polarity are few, there is a bias learnt in the models against predicting *joy* for Hindi tokens. For examples labelled *anger*, although there is less difference seen in the frequency of English tokens in the misclassified examples, more English tokens have a positive LIME score. Thus, a similar bias against predicting *anger* for English could be inferred.

Overall, the fact that these associations are learnt by the models, to the extent that they can overgeneralise them, could also be seen as substantiating the sociolinguistic phenomena. If speakers tend to switch to Hindi to express negative emotions, the ability of language models to detect this reinforces the existence of such a tendency. This also encourages deeper engagement between sociolinguistics and interpretability, with both fields offering valuable insights to each other.

	Joy		
	Distribution of tokens in all examples		
	All examples	**Correct**	**Misclassified**
English	0.40	0.44	**0.32**
Hindi	0.34	0.29	**0.44**
Other	0.26	0.27	**0.24**
	Distribution of tokens assigned a positive LIME score		
	All examples	**Correct**	**Misclassified**
English	0.43	0.48	**0.32**
Hindi	0.32	0.28	**0.42**
Other	0.25	0.24	**0.32**
	Anger		
	Distribution of tokens in all examples		
	All examples	**Correct**	**Misclassified**
English	0.15	0.14	**0.17**
Hindi	0.63	0.65	**0.61**
Other	0.22	0.21	**0.22**
	Distribution of tokens assigned a positive LIME score		
	All examples	**Correct**	**Misclassified**
English	0.15	0.13	**0.18**
Hindi	0.64	0.68	**0.60**
Other	0.21	0.19	**0.23**

Table 3: Normalized frequencies of *English*, *Hindi*, and *Other* tokens for instances labeled *joy* and *anger* for correct and incorrect classification. Additionally, the count of tokens in each language category assigned a positive LIME score for all models.

6 Conclusion

In this work, we use sociolinguistics theories to understand what PLMs learn when training emotion classifiers for code-mixed data. We found that the models indeed learn the differences in language use and emotional expression detailed in the sociolinguistics literature. Concretely, these are the associations of English tokens with positive emotions, and Hindi tokens with negative emotions. Adding code-mixed data to the pre-training can help augment this learning when task-specific data is scarce. However, the models can overgeneralise this learning to infrequent examples where it does not apply. In future work, it would be interesting to see if this understanding can be leveraged to help improve systems designed for code-mixed languages.

7 Acknowledgements

The computational resources and services used in this work were provided by the VSC (Flemish Supercomputer Center), funded by the Research Foundation - Flanders (FWO) and the Flemish Government - department EWI (for Kushal Tatariya and Miryam de Lhoneux). Heather Lent and Johannes Bjerva are supported by the Carlsberg Foundation, under the *Semper Ardens: Accelerate* programme (project nr. CF21-0454).

References

Prabhat Agarwal, Ashish Sharma, Jeenu Grover, Mayank Sikka, Koustav Rudra, and Monojit Choudhury. 2017. I may talk in english but gaali toh hindi mein hi denge : A study of english-hindi code-switching and swearing pattern on social networks. In *2017 9th International Conference on Communication Systems and Networks (COMSNETS)*, pages 554–557.

Alexis Conneau, Kartikay Khandelwal, Naman Goyal, Vishrav Chaudhary, Guillaume Wenzek, Francisco Guzmán, Edouard Grave, Myle Ott, Luke Zettlemoyer, and Veselin Stoyanov. 2020. Unsupervised cross-lingual representation learning at scale. In *Proceedings of the 58th Annual Meeting of the Association for Computational Linguistics*, pages 8440–8451, Online. Association for Computational Linguistics.

Jean-Marc Dewaele. 2007. Blistering barnacles! what language do multilinguals swear in?! *Sociolinguistic Studies*, 5.

Jean-Marc Dewaele. 2010. *Emotions in multiple languages*. Palgrave Macmillan, Basingstoke.

Sumanth Doddapaneni, Rahul Aralikatte, Gowtham Ramesh, Shreya Goyal, Mitesh M. Khapra, Anoop Kunchukuttan, and Pratyush Kumar. 2022. Indicxtreme: A multi-task benchmark for evaluating indic languages.

A. Seza Doğruöz, Sunayana Sitaram, Barbara E. Bullock, and Almeida Jacqueline Toribio. 2021. A survey of code-switching: Linguistic and social perspectives for language technologies. In *Proceedings of the 59th Annual Meeting of the Association for Computational Linguistics and the 11th International Joint Conference on Natural Language Processing (Volume 1: Long Papers)*, pages 1654–1666, Online. Association for Computational Linguistics.

Paul Ekman et al. 1999. Basic emotions. *Handbook of cognition and emotion*, 98(45-60):16.

Soumitra Ghosh, Amit Priyankar, Asif Ekbal, and Pushpak Bhattacharyya. 2023. Multitasking of sentiment detection and emotion recognition in code-mixed hinglish data. *Knowledge-Based Systems*, 260:110182.

Hooria Hajiyan, Heidar Davoudi, and Mehran Ebrahimi. 2023. A comparative analysis of local explainability of models for sentiment detection. In *Proceedings of the Future Technologies Conference (FTC) 2022, Volume 3*, pages 593–606, Cham. Springer International Publishing.

Daniel Hershcovich, Stella Frank, Heather Lent, Miryam de Lhoneux, Mostafa Abdou, Stephanie Brandl, Emanuele Bugliarello, Laura Cabello Piqueras, Ilias Chalkidis, Ruixiang Cui, Constanza Fierro, Katerina Margatina, Phillip Rust, and Anders Søgaard. 2022. Challenges and strategies in cross-cultural NLP. In *Proceedings of the 60th Annual Meeting of the Association for Computational Linguistics (Volume 1: Long Papers)*, pages 6997–7013, Dublin, Ireland. Association for Computational Linguistics.

Abdullah Ilyas, Khurram Shahzad, and Muhammad Kamran Malik. 2023. Emotion detection in code-mixed roman urdu - english text.

Braj B. Kachru. 1978. Toward structuring code-mixing: An indian perspective. *International Journal of the Sociology of Language*, 1978(16):27–46.

Andreas Madsen, Siva Reddy, and Sarath Chandar. 2022. Post-hoc interpretability for neural nlp: A survey. *ACM Comput. Surv.*, 55(8).

Tom McCoy, Ellie Pavlick, and Tal Linzen. 2019. Right for the wrong reasons: Diagnosing syntactic heuristics in natural language inference. In *Proceedings of the 57th Annual Meeting of the Association for Computational Linguistics*, pages 3428–3448, Florence, Italy. Association for Computational Linguistics.

Ravindra Nayak and Raviraj Joshi. 2022. L3Cube-HingCorpus and HingBERT: A code mixed Hindi-English dataset and BERT language models. In *Proceedings of the WILDRE-6 Workshop within the 13th Language Resources and Evaluation Conference*, pages 7–12, Marseille, France. European Language Resources Association.

Francesca Orsini. 2015. Dil maange more: Cultural contexts of hinglish in contemporary india. *African Studies*, 74(2):199–220.

Parth Patwa, Gustavo Aguilar, Sudipta Kar, Suraj Pandey, Srinivas PYKL, Björn Gambäck, Tanmoy Chakraborty, Thamar Solorio, and Amitava Das. 2020. SemEval-2020 task 9: Overview of sentiment analysis of code-mixed tweets. In *Proceedings of the Fourteenth Workshop on Semantic Evaluation*, pages 774–790, Barcelona (online). International Committee for Computational Linguistics.

Marco Túlio Ribeiro, Sameer Singh, and Carlos Guestrin. 2016. "why should I trust you?": Explaining the predictions of any classifier. *CoRR*, abs/1602.04938.

Sebastian Ruder, Ivan Vulić, and Anders Søgaard. 2022. Square one bias in NLP: Towards a multi-dimensional exploration of the research manifold. In *Findings of the Association for Computational Linguistics: ACL 2022*, pages 2340–2354, Dublin, Ireland. Association for Computational Linguistics.

Koustav Rudra, Shruti Rijhwani, Rafiya Begum, Kalika Bali, Monojit Choudhury, and Niloy Ganguly. 2016. Understanding language preference for expression of opinion and sentiment: What do Hindi-English speakers do on Twitter? In *Proceedings of the 2016 Conference on Empirical Methods in Natural Language Processing*, pages 1131–1141, Austin, Texas. Association for Computational Linguistics.

Sagor Sarkar. 2020. Code switch.

T Tulasi Sasidhar, Premjith B, and Soman K P. 2020. Emotion detection in hinglish(hindi+english) code-mixed social media text. *Procedia Computer Science*, 171:1346–1352. Third International Conference on Computing and Network Communications (CoCoNet'19).

Sunayana Sitaram, Khyathi Raghavi Chandu, Sai Krishna Rallabandi, and Alan W. Black. 2019. A survey of code-switched speech and language processing. *CoRR*, abs/1904.00784.

Ian Tenney, James Wexler, Jasmijn Bastings, Tolga Bolukbasi, Andy Coenen, Sebastian Gehrmann, Ellen Jiang, Mahima Pushkarna, Carey Radebaugh, Emily Reif, and Ann Yuan. 2020. The language interpretability tool: Extensible, interactive visualizations and analysis for NLP models. In *Proceedings of the 2020 Conference on Empirical Methods in Natural Language Processing: System Demonstrations*, pages 107–118, Online. Association for Computational Linguistics.

Aqsa Younas, Raheela Nasim, Saqib Ali, Guojun Wang, and Fang Qi. 2020. Sentiment analysis of code-mixed roman urdu-english social media text using deep learning approaches. In *2020 IEEE 23rd International Conference on Computational Science and Engineering (CSE)*, pages 66–71.

Evi Yulianti, Ajmal Kurnia, Mirna Adriani, and Yoppy Setyo Duto. 2021. Normalisation of indonesian-english code-mixed text and its effect on emotion classification. *International Journal of Advanced Computer Science and Applications*, 12(11).

George-Eduard Zaharia, George-Alexandru Vlad, Dumitru-Clementin Cercel, Traian Rebedea, and Costin Chiru. 2020. UPB at SemEval-2020 task 9: Identifying sentiment in code-mixed social media texts using transformers and multi-task learning. In *Proceedings of the Fourteenth Workshop on Semantic Evaluation*, pages 1322–1330, Barcelona (online). International Committee for Computational Linguistics.

A Model Details

We used Huggingface to fine-tune the pre-trained language models described in Section 3 on the emotion classification dataset. Our hyperparameters are listed in Table 4 and the performance of our models over the development set are in Table 5, below.

Hyperparameter	Value
Dropout	0.2
Learning Rate	2e-05
Number of Epochs	50
Batch Size	32

Table 4: The hyperparameters used to train all three emotion classification models.

Model	Accuracy
XLM-R	0.57
IndicBERT	0.55
HingRoBERTa	0.58

Table 5: Accuracy scores on the test sets of each pre-trained language model fine-tuned on the Hinglish emotion classification dataset.

B Label Distributions

The sample of 1,000 examples used in the analysis was selected by maintaining the label distribution from the validation set. The distribution is detailed in Table 6.

Label Distributions		
	Our Sample	**Validation Set**
others	347	1048
joy	325	973
anger	204	607
sadness	102	307
disgust	19	55
surprise	2	6
fear	1	4
Total	1,000	3,000

Table 6: Distribution of emotion labels in our random sample versus the original validation set.

C Statistical Analysis

C.1 χ^2

We performed a χ^2 test of independence on the samples for each model to understand the relationship between the two variables - language ID and LIME score. We constructed the contingency tables with the frequencies of how many times each language ID label - *eng*, *hin* and *other* had a positive or a negative LIME score. We did this for the entire sample to confirm a dependency between those variables. We further examined this dependency on a more granular level by conducting the same χ^2 test for examples that were predicted as *joy*, *anger* and *sadness* by the models. The contingency table for the entire sample is in Table 7, and per label is in Table 8.

	Contingency Tables - All Samples					
	XLM-R		IndicBERT		HingRoBERTa	
	Positive	Negative	Positive	Negative	Positive	Negative
English	3658	2264	3840	2082	3728	2194
Hindi	5759	4242	5914	4087	6127	3874
Other	2709	2203	3281	1631	2843	2069

Table 7: χ^2 contingency tables for all samples, across all models

	Contingency Tables - Per Label					
	Joy					
	XLM-R		IndicBERT		HingRoBERTa	
	Positive	Negative	Positive	Negative	Positive	Negative
English	1730	759	1669	643	1643	639
Hindi	1127	648	974	500	1061	527
Other	876	668	1010	429	849	618
	Anger					
	XLM-R		IndicBERT		HingRoBERTa	
	Positive	Negative	Positive	Negative	Positive	Negative
English	365	173	332	165	482	288
Hindi	1760	689	1487	789	1926	840
Other	473	293	393	307	551	370
	Sadness					
	XLM-R		IndicBERT		HingRoBERTa	
	Positive	Negative	Positive	Negative	Positive	Negative
English	248	139	176	80	233	135
Hindi	596	258	389	187	597	272
Other	187	129	135	49	169	143

Table 8: χ^2 contingency tables for examples predicted as *joy*, *anger* and *sadness* by each model

C.2 ANOVA and Tukey HSD

C.2.1 Entire Sample

The p-values from the ANOVA results are in Table 9. They confirm χ^2 results that for the entire sample size, there is dependency between language and LIME score for all models. The key difference between our ANOVA and the χ^2 tests is that, while the χ^2 treats LIME score polarity as a categorical variable (positive versus negative scores), in our ANOVA we directly compute over the numerical values, ranging from -1 to 1.

In order to better understand the relationship between languages (i.e., Hindi versus English; Hindi versus Other; English versus Other), we also performed an additional post-hoc Tukey HSD Test to test which pairs of language ID have means that are significantly different from each other. Results for all samples are in Table 10. For all models, the means for Hindi and English tokens are meaningfully different from each other, and thus we can say that all models are able to distinguish between these two languages. For XLM-R, we cannot reject the null hypothesis that *hin* and *other* have independent distributions, and for IndicBERT, we cannot reject that *eng* and *other* have independent distributions. It is only for HingRoBERTa that we can reject the null hypothesis for all pairs of language ID. Thus, HingRoBERTa, having seen code-mixed data in the pre-training, is the only one that can meaningfully distinguish across *eng*, *hin* and *other*.

ANOVA - All Samples	
Model	p-value
XLM-R	2.09e-31
IndicBERT	3.35e-45
HingRoBERTa	3.97e-20

Table 9: We test the null hypothesis that language ID tags and LIME scores are independent of each other using 1-Way ANOVA. This table contains the p-values for tests done on the entire sample.

Tukey HSD - All Samples						
XLMR						
group1	group2	meandiff	p-adj	lower	upper	reject
en	hin	-0.013	0	-0.0157	-0.0102	True
en	other	-0.0156	0	-0.0188	-0.0124	True
hin	other	-0.0026	0.0854	-0.0055	0.0003	False
p-values: [1.218e-11, 1.218e-11, 8.538e-02]						
IndicBERT						
group1	group2	meandiff	p-adj	lower	upper	reject
en	hin	-0.0144	0	-0.0169	-0.0118	True
en	other	-0.0027	0.095	-0.0057	0.0003	False
hin	other	0.0117	0	0.009	0.0144	True
p-values: [1.22E-11, 9.50E-02, 1.22E-11]						
HingRoBERTa						
group1	group2	meandiff	p-adj	lower	upper	reject
en	hin	-0.0069	0	-0.0096	-0.0042	True
en	other	-0.0126	0	-0.0158	-0.0095	True
hin	other	-0.0057	0	-0.0086	-0.0029	True
p-values: [4.29E-09, 1.22E-11, 8.12E-06]						

Table 10: Results for Tukey HSD for the entire sample size, for all models, along with the adjusted p-values.

C.2.2 Per Label

We also conduct ANOVA tests for one positive label (*joy*) and two negative labels *anger, sadness*, to see whether there is agreement with the χ^2 results. Table 11 shows the p-values for each model.

ANOVA - Per Label			
Model	Joy	Anger	Sadness
XLM-R	2.09e-31	2.86e-10	1.25e-2
IndicBERT	1.53e-19	3.20e-7	5.57e-1
HingRoBERTa	3.74e-37	1.74e-9	2.14e-3

Table 11: p-values for 1-Way ANOVA on examples predicted as *joy*, *anger* and *sadness* by each model.

Both ANOVA and χ^2 find dependency between language and LIME score for the *joy* and *anger* labels. Moreover, for *sadness*, both ANOVA and χ^2 also agree that there is a significant dependency of language and LIME score with HingRoBERTa, and for IndicBERT there is no dependency. Where they differ slightly is with XLM-R, where there is no dependency found with the ANOVA test, but with χ^2, the p-value is slightly below the significance threshold.

A further fine-grained analysis of these conclusions is presented with Tukey HSD in Tables 12, 13 and 14. To summarise the results per label:

1. **Joy** For both XLM-R and IndicBERT, *hin* and *other* have no meaningful difference, but do show significant distinction between *hin* and *eng*. HingRoBERTa, on the other hand, is able to distinguish between all language ID tags.

2. **Anger** We see a significant difference between all language ID pairs and across all models for *anger*.

3. **Sadness** No meaningful difference is observed between *hin* and *eng* for both XLM-R and HingRoBERTa, and for IndicBERT, there is no meaningful difference across any of the language ID pairs.

Tukey HSD - Joy						
XLMR						
group1	**group2**	**meandiff**	**p-adj**	**lower**	**upper**	**reject**
en	hin	-0.0222	0	-0.0281	-0.0164	True
en	other	-0.0284	0	-0.0345	-0.0223	True
hin	other	-0.0062	0.0717	-0.0127	0.0004	False
p-**values:** [0, 0, 0.718]						
IndicBERT						
group1	**group2**	**meandiff**	**p-adj**	**lower**	**upper**	**reject**
en	hin	-0.0218	0	-0.0277	-0.0158	True
en	other	-0.0169	0	-0.0229	-0.011	True
hin	other	0.0048	0.2004	-0.0018	0.0114	False
p-**values:** [0, 8.56E-11, 2.00E-01]						
HingRoBERTa						
group1	**group2**	**meandiff**	**p-adj**	**lower**	**upper**	**reject**
en	hin	-0.0198	0	-0.0257	-0.0139	True
en	other	-0.0326	0	-0.0387	-0.0266	True
hin	other	-0.0129	0	-0.0194	-0.0063	True
p-**values:** [8.54E-13, 8.42E-13, 1.15E-05]						

Table 12: Results for Tukey HSD for examples predicted as *joy* by each model, along with the adjusted p-values.

Tukey HSD - Anger						
XLMR						
group1	**group2**	**meandiff**	**p-adj**	**lower**	**upper**	**reject**
en	hin	0.0076	0.0411	0.0002	0.015	True
en	other	-0.0103	0.0152	-0.019	-0.0016	True
hin	other	-0.0179	0	-0.0243	-0.0115	True
p-**values:** [4.11E-02, 1.52E-02, 1.83E-10]						
IndicBERT						
group1	**group2**	**meandiff**	**p-adj**	**lower**	**upper**	**reject**
en	hin	-0.0129	0.0003	-0.0207	-0.0051	True
en	other	-0.0216	0	-0.0308	-0.0124	True
hin	other	-0.0087	0.0076	-0.0155	-0.0019	True
p-**values:** [3.23E-04, 1.37E-07, 1.37E-07]						
HingRoBERTa						
group1	**group2**	**meandiff**	**p-adj**	**lower**	**upper**	**reject**
en	hin	0.008	0.0184	0.0011	0.0149	True
en	other	-0.0092	0.0258	-0.0175	-0.0009	True
hin	other	-0.0172	0	-0.0236	-0.0107	True
p-**values:** [1.84E-02, 2.58E-02, 1.50E-09]						

Table 13: Results for Tukey HSD for examples predicted as *anger* by each model, along with the adjusted p-values.

Tukey HSD - Sadness						
XLMR						
group1	**group2**	**meandiff**	**p-adj**	**lower**	**upper**	**reject**
en	hin	-0.0003	0.9955	-0.0092	0.0085	False
en	other	-0.0117	0.0323	-0.0227	-0.0008	True
hin	other	-0.0114	0.0139	-0.0209	-0.0019	True
p-**values:** [0.996, 0.032, 0.014]						
IndicBERT						
group1	**group2**	**meandiff**	**p-adj**	**lower**	**upper**	**reject**
en	hin	-0.004	0.5855	-0.0135	0.0055	False
en	other	-0.0008	0.9868	-0.0131	0.0114	False
hin	other	0.0032	0.7648	-0.0075	0.0139	False
p-**values:** [0.585, 0.987, 0.765]						
HingRoBERTa						
group1	**group2**	**meandiff**	**p-adj**	**lower**	**upper**	**reject**
en	hin	-0.0011	0.9558	-0.0104	0.0081	False
en	other	-0.0149	0.0067	-0.0263	-0.0034	True
hin	other	-0.0137	0.003	-0.0236	-0.0039	True
p-**values:** [0.956, 0.007, 0.003]						

Table 14: Results for Tukey HSD for examples predicted as *sadness* by each model, along with the adjusted p-values.

A Call for Consistency in Reporting Typological Diversity

Wessel Poelman[*♣] **Esther Ploeger**[*✿] **Miryam de Lhoneux**[♣] **Johannes Bjerva**[✿]
[♣]Department of Computer Science, KU Leuven, Belgium
[✿]Department of Computer Science, Aalborg University, Denmark
{wessel.poelman,miryam.delhoneux}@kuleuven.be {espl,jbjerva}@cs.aau.dk

1 Introduction

In order to draw generalizable conclusions about the performance of multilingual models across languages, it is important to evaluate on a set of languages that captures linguistic diversity. Linguistic typology is increasingly used to justify language selection, inspired by language sampling in linguistics (e.g., Rijkhoff and Bakker, 1998). In other words, more and more papers suggest generalizability by evaluating on 'typologically diverse languages' (see Figure 1). However, justifications for 'typological diversity' exhibit great variation, as there seems to be no set definition, methodology or consistent link to linguistic typology. In this work, we provide a systematic insight into how previous work in the ACL Anthology uses the term 'typological diversity'. Our two main findings are:

1. What is meant by typologically diverse language selection is not consistent.
2. The actual typological diversity of the language sets in these papers varies greatly.

We argue that, when making claims about 'typological diversity', an operationalization of this should be included. A systematic approach that quantifies this claim, also with respect to the number of languages used, would be even better.

2 Systematic Annotation of Claims

We systematically investigate which papers make claims regarding typological diversity, and which languages they actually use. First, we retrieve[1] all papers in the ACL Anthology that contain the following search string in either the title or abstract:

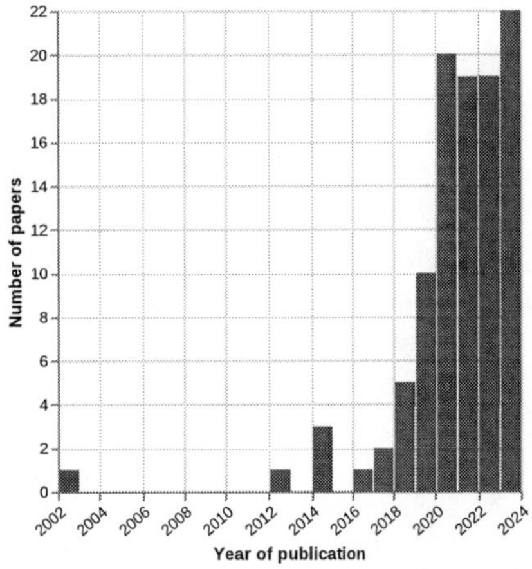

Figure 1: Number of papers in the ACL Anthology claiming a 'typologically diverse' set of languages over the years.

```
typological.+?diverse|
typological.+?diversity|
diverse.+?typological
```

Examples of this are not only *typologically diverse*, but also *typologically maximally diverse language* and *typologically and genetically diverse languages*. In total, this retrieves 140 papers, with the earliest being published in 2002, and the most recent being published in 2023. It contains papers from conferences (e.g., *ACL, EMNLP), journals (e.g., TACL, CL) and workshops (e.g., SIGTYP, SIGMORPHON).

We manually annotate whether these papers contain a claim regarding the typological diversity of their language selection. An example of such a claim is: *"we evaluate on a set of ten typologically diverse languages"* (Pimentel et al., 2020). A paper does not make a claim if it describes related work that claims to use 'a diverse typological test set', for instance. Our annotation is done separately by two annotators (the first two authors). We calculate inter-annotator agreement and retrieve a Cohen's κ of 0.64 ('substantial agreement'). After resolving the disagreements, we are left with 103 papers that

* Equal contribution.
[1]Using the acl-anthology-py package: https://github.com/mbollmann/acl-anthology-py. Papers retrieved on December 11, 2023.

Proceedings of the 6th Workshop on Research in Computational Linguistic Typology and Multilingual NLP (SIGTYP 2024), pages 75–77
March 22, 2024 ©2024 Association for Computational Linguistics

contain a claim, which we use for our analysis. For every such paper, we annotate which languages are actually included in their selection. We normalize these to ISO-639-3 codes.

3 Justifications of Typological Diversity

We find that there is great variation in justifications for typological diversity claims. Some papers explain typological diversity through genealogy. For instance, Xu et al. (2022) *"select 24 typologically different languages covering a reasonable variety of language families"* and Zhang et al. (2023) create a dataset consisting of *"[18] languages that are both typologically close as well as distant from 10 language families and 13 sub-families"*.

Other papers use a selection of typological features, for instance, Mott et al. (2020) mention that *"the nine languages in our corpus cover five primary language families (...), and cover a range of morphological phenomena including suffixation, prefixation, (...)"*. Some papers also mention typological databases in their language selection, for instance, Gutierrez-Vasques et al. (2021) choose *"47 languages [from the] WALS 100-language sample, which aims to maximize both genealogical and areal diversity"*. Similarly, Muradoglu and Hulden (2022) consider *"typological diversity when selecting languages (...) [such as] languages that exhibit varying degrees of complexity for inflection. We also consider morphological characteristics coded in WALS (...)"*. The most systematic approach to typologically diverse language selection we found is done by Jancso et al. (2020). They use a clustering algorithm on vectors with features from two typological databases to find the most distant clusters to sample languages from.

However, there is no consistent typological distance measurement for language selection. Thus, what is commonly meant by typological diverse language selection is not only inconsistent, but also often unsubstantiated.

4 Language Analysis

Next, we investigate the actual languages used in these datasets. Concretely, we aim to answer three questions: 1) how many languages are commonly used? 2) which languages are commonly used? and 3) how typologically diverse are these language selections?

First, we plot the number of languages the papers use in Figure 2. The number of languages

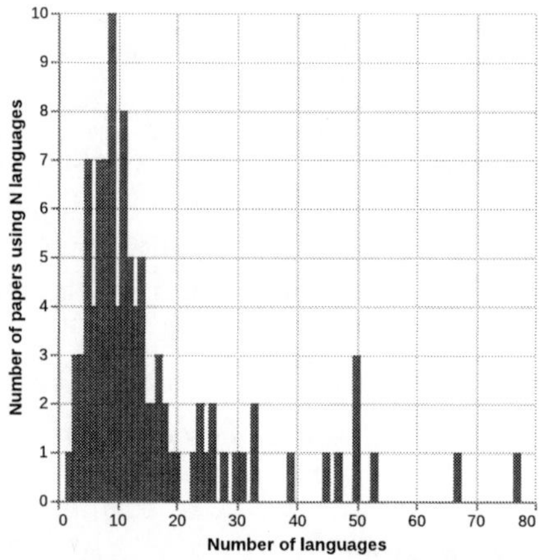

Figure 2: Number of papers using N languages.

used ranges from 2 to 77, with a mean of 16 and a standard deviation of 14. Four of the papers that contain a claim do not mention the languages they use. None the papers in our sample mention whether the number of languages they use relates to or is influenced by their typologically diversity claim. Similarly, only some papers, specifically ones that introduce a dataset, explicitly mention design choices with regard to the number of languages used.

Next, we look at the actual languages involved. The papers use 283 unique languages, of which 147 are used just once. English is the most-used language, followed by German, Finnish, Turkish, Russian and Spanish. Here, we observe a skew towards languages from the Eurasian macroarea.

Figure 3: Mean pairwise syntactic lang2vec distance per paper.

Lastly, we approximate the actual typological diversity across papers by taking the average syntactic lang2vec (Littell et al., 2017) distance of all pairwise combinations in each paper's language set with coverage in lang2vec (97/103)[2]. The measured typological diversity varies across papers, with outliers on either side (Figure 3). The lowest mean pairwise distance (0.42) is found in Goel et al. (2022), who use *"3 typologically diverse languages – English, French and Spanish"*. The highest distance (0.86) is found in (Vania et al., 2019), who evaluate on North Sámi, Galician, and Kazah.

[2]Four papers do not mention the languages they use, two contain languages for which no ISO-693-3 code exists; Kholosi and Pomak.

References

Anmol Goel, Charu Sharma, and Ponnurangam Kumaraguru. 2022. An unsupervised, geometric and syntax-aware quantification of polysemy. In *Proceedings of the 2022 Conference on Empirical Methods in Natural Language Processing*, pages 10565–10574, Abu Dhabi, United Arab Emirates. Association for Computational Linguistics.

Ximena Gutierrez-Vasques, Christian Bentz, Olga Sozinova, and Tanja Samardzic. 2021. From characters to words: the turning point of BPE merges. In *Proceedings of the 16th Conference of the European Chapter of the Association for Computational Linguistics: Main Volume*, pages 3454–3468, Online. Association for Computational Linguistics.

Anna Jancso, Steven Moran, and Sabine Stoll. 2020. The ACQDIV corpus database and aggregation pipeline. In *Proceedings of the Twelfth Language Resources and Evaluation Conference*, pages 156–165, Marseille, France. European Language Resources Association.

Patrick Littell, David R. Mortensen, Ke Lin, Katherine Kairis, Carlisle Turner, and Lori Levin. 2017. URIEL and lang2vec: Representing languages as typological, geographical, and phylogenetic vectors. In *Proceedings of the 15th Conference of the European Chapter of the Association for Computational Linguistics: Volume 2, Short Papers*, pages 8–14, Valencia, Spain. Association for Computational Linguistics.

Justin Mott, Ann Bies, Stephanie Strassel, Jordan Kodner, Caitlin Richter, Hongzhi Xu, and Mitchell Marcus. 2020. Morphological segmentation for low resource languages. In *Proceedings of the Twelfth Language Resources and Evaluation Conference*, pages 3996–4002, Marseille, France. European Language Resources Association.

Saliha Muradoglu and Mans Hulden. 2022. Eeny, meeny, miny, moe. how to choose data for morphological inflection. In *Proceedings of the 2022 Conference on Empirical Methods in Natural Language Processing*, pages 7294–7303, Abu Dhabi, United Arab Emirates. Association for Computational Linguistics.

Tiago Pimentel, Josef Valvoda, Rowan Hall Maudslay, Ran Zmigrod, Adina Williams, and Ryan Cotterell. 2020. Information-theoretic probing for linguistic structure. In *Proceedings of the 58th Annual Meeting of the Association for Computational Linguistics*, pages 4609–4622, Online. Association for Computational Linguistics.

Jan Rijkhoff and Dik Bakker. 1998. Language sampling. *Linguistic Typology*, 2(3):263–314.

Clara Vania, Yova Kementchedjhieva, Anders Søgaard, and Adam Lopez. 2019. A systematic comparison of methods for low-resource dependency parsing on genuinely low-resource languages. In *Proceedings of the 2019 Conference on Empirical Methods in Natural Language Processing and the 9th International Joint Conference on Natural Language Processing (EMNLP-IJCNLP)*, pages 1105–1116, Hong Kong, China. Association for Computational Linguistics.

Ningyu Xu, Tao Gui, Ruotian Ma, Qi Zhang, Jingting Ye, Menghan Zhang, and Xuanjing Huang. 2022. Cross-linguistic syntactic difference in multilingual BERT: How good is it and how does it affect transfer? In *Proceedings of the 2022 Conference on Empirical Methods in Natural Language Processing*, pages 8073–8092, Abu Dhabi, United Arab Emirates. Association for Computational Linguistics.

Xinyu Zhang, Nandan Thakur, Odunayo Ogundepo, Ehsan Kamalloo, David Alfonso-Hermelo, Xiaoguang Li, Qun Liu, Mehdi Rezagholizadeh, and Jimmy Lin. 2023. MIRACL: A multilingual retrieval dataset covering 18 diverse languages. *Transactions of the Association for Computational Linguistics*, 11:1114–1131.

Are Sounds Sound for Phylogenetic Reconstruction?

Luise Häuser
Heidelberg Institute for Theoretical Studies
luise.haeuser@h-its.org

Gerhard Jäger
University of Tübingen
gerhard.jaeger@uni-tuebingen.de

Taraka Rama
Independent Researcher
taraka.kasi@gmail.com

Johann-Mattis List
MPI-EVA / Univ. of Passau
mattis.list@uni-passau.de

Alexandros Stamatakis
Institute of Computer Science
FORTH
stamatak@ics.forth.gr

Abstract

In traditional studies on language evolution, scholars often emphasize the importance of sound laws and sound correspondences for phylogenetic inference of language family trees. However, to date, computational approaches have typically not taken this potential into account. Most computational studies still rely on lexical cognates as major data source for phylogenetic reconstruction in linguistics, although there do exist a few studies in which authors praise the benefits of comparing words at the level of sound sequences. Building on (a) ten diverse datasets from different language families, and (b) state-of-the-art methods for automated cognate and sound correspondence detection, we test, for the first time, the performance of sound-based versus cognate-based approaches to phylogenetic reconstruction. Our results show that phylogenies reconstructed from lexical cognates are topologically closer, by approximately one third with respect to the generalized quartet distance on average, to the gold standard phylogenies than phylogenies reconstructed from sound correspondences.

1 Introduction

Although controversially discussed in the beginning (Holm, 2007), quantitative approaches to phylogenetic reconstruction based on Bayesian phylogenetic inference frameworks have now become broadly accepted and used in the field of comparative linguistics. This is reflected by the increasing number of computer-based phylogenies that have been proposed for the world's largest language families – Dravidian (Kolipakam et al., 2018), Sino-Tibetan (Sagart et al., 2019), and Indo-European (Heggarty et al., 2023) – and even fully automated workflows, in which even cognate words are identified automatically, have shown to be comparatively robust (Rama et al., 2018). While rarely practiced in the pre-computational past of historical linguistics, computing detailed, fully resolved phylogenies with branch lengths and at times even estimated divergence times, has now become a routine tasks in contemporary language evolution studies.

Although traditional scholars have started to accept computational language phylogenies as a new tool deserving its place in the large tool chain of comparative linguistics, scholars still express substantial skepticism against most language phylogenies that have been inferred so far. One of the major arguments typically mentioned in this context is that phylogenetic approaches are usually based on cognate sets (sets of historically related words) that are identified in semantically aligned word lists. Since these *cognate sets* reflect *lexical data* only, many scholars mistrust them, given that lexical data are assumed to be substantially less stable over time than other aspects of languages (Campbell and Poser, 2008). Yet, for being able to infer stable phylogenetic trees a mix of conserved characters and more variable characters might be more beneficial.

In classical historical linguistics, the data used for subgrouping are traditionally composed of small collections of so-called *shared innovations* (Dyen, 1953). What counts as a shared innovation has itself never been clearly defined in the literature, but the largest amount of data used by scholars is traditionally taken from sound correspondences or supposed sound change processes (compare, for example the data in Anttila 1972, 305). Although it is controversially debated in the field (Ringe et al., 2002; Dybo and Starostin, 2008), many classical linguists still emphasize that sound correspondences are largely superior to lexical data to determine subgrouping.

There have only been few attempts to assess how well quantitative approaches to phylogenetic reconstruction perform when using sound correspondences instead of lexical cognates (Chacon and List, 2015). The main reason is that encoding

Proceedings of the 6th Workshop on Research in Computational Linguistic Typology and Multilingual NLP (SIGTYP 2024), pages 78–87

Language	Concept	Form	Cog-Set
English	"big"	big	1
German	"big"	groß	2
Dutch	"big"	groot	2
Norwegian	"big"	stor	3
Danish	"big"	stor	3
Swedish	"big"	stor	3

(A) multi-state matrix

Concept		"big"		
Cog-Set		1	2	3
English	big	0	0	0
German	groß	0	1	0
Dutch	groot	0	1	0
Norweg.	stor	0	0	1
Danish	stor	0	0	1
Swedish	stor	0	0	1

(B) binary-state matrix

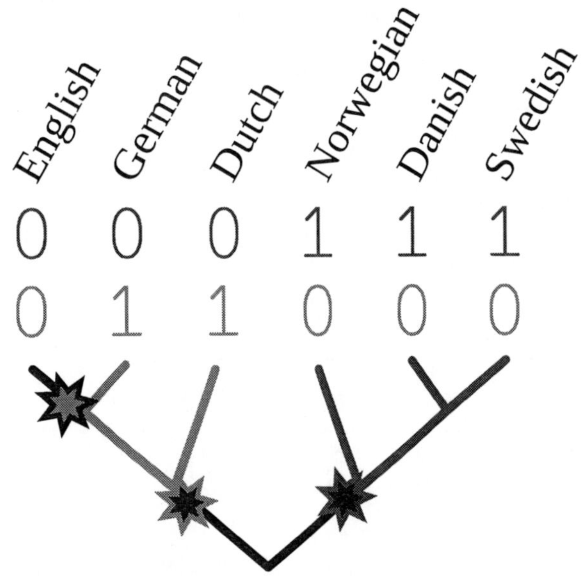

(C) evolutionary scenario (binary-state)

Figure 1: Gain-loss processes derived from binary cognate vectors. A shows a wordlist where cognate words are encoded as multi-state characters. B shows the corresponding binary encoding. C shows how gain and loss processes are modeled on a phylogenetic tree.

data to compute phylogenies from sound change patterns is tedious and labour-intensive even for a dataset comprising only 20 languages. Therefore, there have been but a few attempts to assess how well quantitative approaches to phylogenetic reconstruction perform when using sound correspondences instead of lexical cognates.

Here we build on state-of-the-art methods for automatic cognate detection and phonetic alignment in historical linguistics (List et al., 2016) and combine them with novel approaches for inferring sound correspondence patterns in multilingual datasets (List, 2019). Using this machinery we have devised a new workflow for phylogenetic reconstruction based on sound correspondence patterns. With a new collection of ten gold standard datasets, we test our workflow and compare it with alternative workflows that are exclusively based on lexical data. Our results indicate that sound correspondence patterns are substantially less suitable for the purpose of computer-based phylogenetic reconstruction than postulated.

2 Background

The majority of previous work on phylogenetic reconstruction using Bayesian phylogenetic inference (Kolipakam et al., 2018; Sagart et al., 2019; Rama et al., 2018) is based on cognate sets that are encoded as binary vectors. The presence or absence of a language in a cognate set is thus encoded as **1** or **0**, respectively. Subsequently, phylogenetic trees are inferred by assuming that cognate sets evolve along a phylogenetic tree via a gain and loss processes (see Figure 1).

The binary-state encoding is the most frequently used encoding technique; we deploy it in this study as well. Once such a dataset has been assembled, binary state data evolution can be modeled via a time-reversible binary state Continuous Time Markov Chain model (*binary-CTMC*, Bouckaert et al. 2012), which allows for gain and loss events to occur for an arbitrary number of times. Branch lengths on these trees reflect the mean number of expected substitutions (gain/loss events) per binary character site.

The *major contributions* of this study are: (1) We provide an automated workflow that allows to infer cognates and correspondence patterns and analyze them with the help of Bayesian phylogenetic inference methods, (2) we cross-validate the Bayesian inference results via Maximum Likelihood (ML) tree reconstructions and thereby discover that de-

Dataset	Words	Concepts	Languages	Distances	Sounds	Word Length
ConstenlaChibchan	1214	106	24	0.1	21.71	3.86
CrossAndean	2637	150	19	0.03	28.89	4.32
Dravlex	1341	100	20	0.06	36.85	4.53
FelekeSemitic	2412	150	19	0.05	45.32	4.99
HattoriJaponic	1710	197	10	0.03	34.9	4.47
HouChinese	1816	139	15	0.05	43	6.21
LeeKoreanic	1960	205	14	0.01	36.93	4.31
RobinsonAP	1424	216	13	0.03	24.38	4.51
WalworthPolynesian	6113	207	31	0.05	21.03	4.51
ZhivlovObugrian	1879	110	20	0.04	32.65	3.65

Table 1: Datasets and general aspects of the data. Distances refer to the average pairwise distance between all language pairs in the sample, derived from shared cognate counts (using the LingPy software). Number of sounds refers to the number of distinct sounds per language (on average), and the word length refers to the average length of the words observed in each dataset.

fault Bayesian priors that typically work well on molecular data can induce a prior bias when analyzing language datasets, (3) we show how the quality of phylogenetic reconstruction approaches based on sound correspondences can be compared to phylogenetic reconstruction based on lexical data, and in this way, and (4) we put the debate about the usefulness of sound-based as opposed to cognate-based phylogenies to the test.

As an early example for sound-based approaches to phylogenetic reconstruction, Hruschka et al. (2015) apply a CTMC model that allows for transitions between a fixed number of sounds for detecting the important sound changes in a dataset comprising etymologies across Turkic languages. Hruschka et al. do not infer phylogenies from their data. Instead, they use an established phylogeny (such established phylogenies are not readily available for many language families of the world) to infer branch lengths and transition probabilities between sounds in their data in order to detect sound changes at different time points in a time-calibrated family tree of Turkic.

Wheeler and Whiteley (2015) start from typical word lists (that would otherwise be used in phylogenetic reconstruction based on lexical data) and apply a parsimony-based algorithm that aligns words regardless if they are cognate or not, reconstructs a hypothetical ancestral word from the alignment, and seeks to infer the phylogeny that explains the observed sequences via the minimum amount of changes/mutations (Sankoff, 1975). In a later study, Whiteley et al. (2019) apply the same approach to a dataset of Bantu languages. The method by Wheeler and Whiteley (2015) is linguistically debatable, since words are not assigned to cognate sets prior to aligning them. It is well known that there is a strict difference between regular sound change processes and processes resulting from lexical replacement (Hall and Klein, 2010) and that even words that are cognate are not necessarily fully *alignable* (Schweikhard and List, 2020, 10).

Chacon and List (2015) start from manually extracted sound correspondence patterns for consonants in a dataset of 21 Tukanoan languages, to which proto-forms had also been manually added. Based on these sound correspondence patterns, they apply—in analogy to Wheeler and Whiteley (2015)—an algorithm that searches for the tree that provides the most parsimonious explanation for sound evolution. In contrast to Wheeler and Whiteley (2015), however, they added specific constraints for the transitions from one sound to another sound, which were based on expert judgments for the Tukanoan language family. The approach by Chacon and List (2015), finally, requires an enormous amount of preprocessing that entails the risk of inducing circular results, since proto-forms and major directions of sound change processes are required to be known in advance. While all approaches exhibit individual shortcomings, one of the largest shortcomings lies in the fact that it is very difficult to apply them systematically. This is also supported by the observation that no additional analogous studies have been conducted by other teams, despite the fact that all of the above methods have been proposed years ago.

3 Materials and Methods

3.1 Materials

In order to test whether sound correspondence patterns improve phylogenetic reconstruction or not, we selected ten datasets from the Lexibank repository (`https://lexibank.clld.org`, List et al. 2022) which were previously used to investigate the regularity of correspondence patterns in comparative cognate-coded wordlists (Blum and List, 2023). Lexibank offers published datasets in standardized formats (so-called Cross-Linguistic Data Formats, see Forkel et al. 2018). According to these standards, languages are linked to the Glottolog reference catalog (offering access to expert phylogenies and geolocations, `https://glottolog.org`, Hammarström et al. 2023), concepts are linked to the Concepticon reference catalog (offering fundamental definitions of semantic glosses and further information on concept properties, `https://concepticon.clld.org`, `Concepticon`), and sounds are provided in the phonetic transcription underlying the Cross-Linguistic Transcription Systems initiative (a reference catalog on speech sounds, offering a dynamic system that defines transcriptions for more than 8000 standard speech sounds observed in linguistic datasets, `https://clts.clld.org`, List et al. 2021; Anderson et al. 2018).

Data were preprocessed by first computing the phonetic alignment of all cognate sets in the data using the multiple alignment method proposed by List (2014). In a second step, these alignments were automatically *trimmed*, using the method proposed by Blum and List (2023), which identifies alignment columns with many gaps and ignores them, assuming that these result from morphological variation that would confuse cognate judgments.For phylogenetic inferences on molecular sequence data Tan et al. (2015) suggest that filtering worsens phylogenetic inference accuracy. The study by Blum and List (2023), however, shows that – for linguistic data – the overall regularity among cognates increases substantially, when trimming alignments systematically. Since regular sound correspondences provide the basis for the identification of classical sound laws that linguists typically use for the traditional subgrouping by shared innovations, we therefore consider the use of trimmed data as advantageous over using untrimmed alignments. Using trimmed phylogenies also has the advantage of reducing the noise, as can be seen from a rather drastic drop in the number of divergent sites in phylogenetic datasets that have been trimmed. However, it is beyond doubt that a closer investigation of the effects of trimming should be carried out in follow-up studies. In a third step, the method by List (2019) was used to compute correspondence patterns of the data. Phonetic alignments were conducted with LingPy (2.6.11, List and Forkel 2023a, `https://pypi.org/project/lingpy`). Trimming and correspondence pattern detection were carried out with LingRex (1.4.1, List and Forkel 2023b, `https://pypi.org/project/lingrex`).

Having identified correspondence patterns from the data, both the information on cognate sets and the information on correspondence patterns were converted into binary presence-absence matrices in Nexus format (Maddison et al., 1997), suitable for subsequent phylogenetic analysis.

3.2 Methods

Different methods for phylogenetic reconstruction have been described in the literature and have been controversially discussed among scholars for some time. Here we test two very basic approaches, Bayesian Inference and Maximum Likelihood. Since the data that we use for the inference of phylogenies comes in two flavors, derived as binary presence-absence matrices from cognate sets and from sound correspondence patterns, we test the methods on three different *character matrices*, namely the *cognate matrix*, derived from cognate judgments, the *sound correspondence matrix*, derived from sound correspondence patterns, and a *combined matrix*, in which we combine (concatenate) the cognate and the character matrix within a single new matrix.

In our experiments, we test three basic hypotheses. The first hypothesis assumes that phylogenetic inference on cognate sets is more accurate than phylogenetic inference based on sound correspondence patterns. The second hypothesis assumes that phylogenetic inference based on sound correspondence patterns is more accurate than phylogenetic inference based on cognate sets. The third hypothesis assumes that both character types do not differ substantially regarding their phylogenetic signal.

3.2.1 Bayesian Inference

Phylogenetic inferences were conducted using *MrBayes* (Ronquist and Huelsenbeck, 2003), version 3.2.7. For the final inferences presented here we used the following prior settings for all datasets: (1) Dirichlet$(1.0, 1.0)$ prior for base frequencies, (2) gamma-distributed rates, approximated by 4 discrete categories, with standard exponential prior for the shape of the gamma distribution that models among site rate heterogeneity, (3) uniform prior over tree topologies, and (4) strict clock model of branch lengths.

We initially used an an exponential distribution with a rate of 1.0 as prior for the Γ model of rate heterogeneity. This prior constrains the α shape parameter of the Γ distribution to relatively small values. As a consequence, MrBayes obtains α values below 10 for almost all data sets and posterior samples it draws. This indicates a high to moderate degree of rate heterogeneity. However, our ML analyses (see below) yielded substantially higher ML estimates for α on some datasets. To investigate this discrepancy, we repeated the Bayesian inferences, now using Uniform$(0.01, 100)$ as a prior for the Γ distribution of rate heterogeneity. As a consequence, we obtained a different distribution of the α values that better reflects the corresponding ML estimates.

The more informative default exponential prior in MrBayes has presumably been developed for molecular datasets, which usually exhibit a high degree of rate heterogeneity. In other words, ML estimates of α exhibit a small variance (see, e.g., `https://github.com/angtft/RAxMLGroveScripts/blob/main/figures/test_ALPHA.png` and the corresponding paper by Höhler et al. (2021)). When executing inferences on language datasets, using this default molecular prior can hence bias the results. That is, had we not conducted complimentary ML analyses, this surprising dataset-dependent bi-modal distribution of α values on language datasets (see Table 2) would have gone unnoticed. We thus strongly advocate that all default priors for molecular datasets should be carefully and critically re-assessed when conducting Bayesian inferences on language datasets and that ML analyses should always complement Bayesian Inferences.

Motivated by this observation, the Bayesian analysis was repeated, now using a uniform prior over the interval $[0.01, 100.0]$ for α.

We sampled the state of the Markov chain every 1,000th generation. We stopped MCMC chains when the average standard deviation of split frequencies (ASDSF) was below 0.01 after discarding the first 25% of the samples.[1]

The median posterior value for α are shown in Table 3. From the remaining 75% of the recorded samples from the two cold chains, 1,000 trees were drawn at random and used for further evaluation.

If one of the two individual character types provides the best results, this would be evidence for Hypothesis 1 or Hypothesis 2. If the combined dataset provides the best results, this would be evidence for Hypothesis 3.

To evaluate the quality of the inferred phylogenies, we used the classifications from Glottolog (Hammarström et al., 2023). The topological distance or degree of consistency of an inferred strictly binary (fully bifurcating) phylogeny and a (potentially polytomous/multi-furcating) Glottolog tree was measured as the *generalized quartet distance* (GQD), as proposed in (Pompei et al., 2011).[2]

3.2.2 Maximum Likelihood Tree Inferences

To exclude any potential bias by the selected tree inference method, we also conducted independent Maximum Likelihood (ML) tree inferences. For ML tree inference we used RAxML-NG (Kozlov et al., 2019), version 1.2.0. For each dataset and character matrix type (cognate/sound/concatenated) we executed 20 independent ML tree searches using the default tree search configuration of RAxML-NG (10 searches starting from random trees and 10 searches starting from randomized stepwise addition order parsimony trees) under the BIN+G model of binary character substitution with ML estimated base frequencies. We approximate the Γ model of rate heterogeneity via four discrete rates. Thus, each inference includes the ML estimate of the $\alpha \in [0.0201, 100]$ shape parameter that determines the shape of the Γ distribution. The smaller the estimate of α, the higher the rate heterogeneity in the respective dataset will be (Yang, 1995). For three matrices containing cognate data and for two matrices encoding sound correspondences, we

[1]Note that convergence diagnosis metrics such as ASDSF can only serve to diagnose the failure of an MCMC chain to converge, but can never confirm its convergence.

[2]The GQD is a generalization of the well-known *quartet distance* (Estabrook et al., 1985) that allows to compare fully bifurcating trees with multi-furcating trees. The GQD is defined as the number of quartets that are not shared between the two trees, divided by the number of all possible quartets. The GQD is a number between 0 and 1, where 0 means that the two trees are identical, and 1 means that the two trees are completely different.

Dataset	Cognates	Sound Correspondences	Combined
ConstenlaChibchan	0.592	**99.871**	4.178
CrossAndean	1.243	6.334	1.154
Dravlex	0.702	4.301	2.234
FelekeSemitic	1.062	7.430	2.693
Hattorijaponic	**99.848**	**99.897**	**99.890**
HouChinese	2.357	6.120	4.195
LeeKoreanic	8.316	8.420	3.284
RobinsonAP	**99.869**	15.269	3.486
WalworthPolynesian	1.333	4.233	1.624
ZhivlovObugrian	**99.850**	4.244	3.134

Table 2: ML estimates of the alpha shape value of the Gamma model for among site rate heterogeneity for all languages and all character matrices. Values indicating an extremely low rate heterogeneity (all sites evolve at the same rate) are highlighted in bold.

Dataset	Cognates	Sound Correspondences	Combined
ConstenlaChibchan	1.758	**53.115**	1.138
CrossAndean	1.620	19.558	0.400
Dravlex	0.749	23.613	0.814
FelekeSemitic	0.932	41.669	0.727
HattoriJaponic	**58.012**	**60.602**	0.268
HouChinese	3.011	27.476	0.933
LeeKoreanic	**52.045**	39.354	0.058
RobinsonAP	**56.928**	**51.818**	0.373
WalworthPolynesian	1.480	4.348	0.800
ZhivlovObugrian	**58.652**	**51.280**	0.507

Table 3: Median Bayesian estimates of the alpha shape value of the Gamma model for among site rate heterogeneity for all languages and all character matrices. Values indicating an extremely low rate heterogeneity (all sites evolve at the same rate) are highlighted in bold.

obtain an estimate for $\alpha > 99.8$, which means that all sites evolve at the same rate and that there is essentially no rate heterogeneity. Hence, trees on these datasets could also be inferred without correcting for rate heterogeneity. For the remaining datasets, the ML estimates of α are below 20, indicating a moderate to high degree of rate heterogeneity. This extreme bi-modal distribution of α estimates differs substantially from the distribution we observe on tens of thousands of empirical (i.e., non-simulated) molecular datasets (Höhler et al., 2021) (also see the respective distribution of $alpha$ values plot at `https://github.com/angtft/RAxMLGroveScripts/blob/main/figures/test_ALPHA.png` where $alpha$ values range approximately between 0.01 and 1.5).

We have currently not been able to identify which intrinsic dataset properties cause this surprising and extreme bi-modal distribution of $alpha$ values in language datasets. For the given datasets, we examined the number of concepts and languages under study, the dimensions of the MSAs and the average branch lengths in the trees inferred. We determined the difficulty score using Pythia (Haag et al., 2022) and the number of species using the method for species delimitation implemented in mPTP (Kapli et al., 2017). For none of these properties we were able to find a clear connection to the value estimated for α. One path to explore in analogy to molecular biology is whether some language datasets should be regarded as representing individuals from a population of the same species while others represent distinct species. In fact, for molecular data we have thus far only observed such high estimates of α values (i.e., low or no rate heterogeneity) for population genetic datasets comprising sequences of individuals of the same species or closely related sub-species.

3.3 Implementation

Methods for data handling and preprocessing are implemented in Python (with specific requirements and software packages indicated above), R and Julia. For the phylogenetic analyses, dedicated third party packages are used. All information on how to replicate our study and how to inspect individual analyses are provided in the supplementary material accompanying this study.

4 Results

4.1 Bayesian Inference

We computed the GQD to the goldstandard tree for each of the 1,000 samples from the posterior and computed the median for each dataset and character type. The results of our evaluation are shown in Table 4. As can be seen from the table, phylogenetic inferences based on cognate class data and on concatenated cognate/sound data provide results that are about equally good, with a slight advantage for concatenated data. Phylogenetic inference based on sound correspondences alone yields results that are clearly worse. The concatenated dataset provides the best results for seven out of ten datasets, while in three cases, the cognate class dataset provides the best results. The sound correspondence dataset never yields the best results. These results provide clear evidence in favor of Hypothesis 1 and against Hypothesis 2. The decision about Hypothesis 3 is somewhat equivocal.

4.2 Maximum Likelihood

Table 5 shows the evaluation results for the ML based inferences. Note that we obtain slightly different results when calculate the average distance to all 20 inferred ML trees or when using the BIN model (without accounting for among site rate heterogeneity). The corresponding GQ distances can differ by up to 0.17, although differences of > 0.05 only occur for 7 of the 30 MSAs under study. However, the following observations apply in all cases. First, there is no dataset where the tree inferred on the sound correspondences is substantially closer to the gold standard than the trees inferred on the cognate or concatenated data. On the other hand, there are three datasets (CrossAndean, HouChinese, LeeKoreanic) for which inferences on sound correspondence data yield trees with a substantially higher GQ distance to the gold standard. Inferences on the cognate and combined datasets yield comparable distances to the gold standard. Hence, the results of our ML analyses are consistent with the Bayesian inference results.

5 Discussion and Conclusion

While our results are less conclusive than one might expect, we think that they show clearly enough that sound-correspondence-based phylogenies should be taken with care. As we show, sound-correspondence-based phylogenies do rarely substantially outperform cognate-based phylogenies. Instead, we observe that cognate-based phylogenies are topologically much closer to the gold standard on average. At this point, we cannot say, whether combined approaches significantly outperform phylogenies purely inferred from cognate sets. Future studies that expand the data we used in this study are needed to clarify this question.

Given the prior bias we observed for default parameter priors that work well for Bayesian inference on molecular data, we advocate for a critical re-assessment of all priors that are being routinely used in Bayesian analyses of language data. This reassessment can be conducted by routinely executing analogous ML analyses and carefully inspecting all ML parameter estimates (branch lengths, tree length, base frequencies, α shape parameter) and not only focusing on the resulting tree topology. We also cross-checked the estimates for the base frequencies, but did not observe any discrepancies between ML and Bayesian Inference as a flat default ($\beta(1, 1)$) prior was used. The reasons for the extreme bi-modal distribution of α values we observed remain unclear, despite the fact that we have assessed 30 different dataset characteristics and summary statistics that are, however, all uncorrelated with the α estimate. Using machine learning techniques to predict α values for datasets and thereby potentially understand the dataset properties responsible for this bi-modal distribution is not feasible due to an insufficient amount of available data. Investigating this issue hence remains subject of future work.

Supplementary Material

The supplementary material including data and code necessary to replicate the experiments discussed in this study along with instructions on how to run the code are curated

Dataset	Cognates	Sound Correspondences	Concatenated
ConstenlaChibchan	0.245	0.414	**0.212**
CrossAndean	**0.148**	0.523	0.189
Dravlex	0.336	0.351	**0.320**
FelekeSemitic	**0.083**	0.146	0.113
HattoriJaponic	0.585	0.431	**0.362**
HouChinese	**0.240**	0.494	0.377
LeeKoreanic	0.224	0.358	**0.157**
RobinsonAP	0.424	0.281	**0.259**
WalworthPolynesian	0.179	0.252	**0.146**
ZhivlovObugrian	0.330	0.356	**0.316**
median	0.251	0.358	**0.240**

Table 4: Generalized quartet distances (posterior medians) for Bayesian inference. The best result for each dataset is highlighted in bold.

Dataset	Cognates	Sound Correspondences	Combined
ConstenlaChibchan	0.335	0.360	**0.283**
CrossAndean	0.246	0.470	**0.088**
Dravlex	0.358	0.472	**0.307**
FelekeSemitic	0.126	**0.103**	0.126
HattoriJaponic	**0.532**	0.681	0.559
HouChinese	0.224	0.529	**0.186**
LeeKoreanic	**0.178**	0.386	0.204
RobinsonAP	0.355	**0.321**	0.348
WalworthPolynesian	**0.139**	0.188	0.192
ZhivlovObugrian	**0.322**	0.356	0.360
median	0.284	0.373	**0.243**

Table 5: Generalized quartet distances between the gold standard trees and the the best-scoring ML tree inferred under the **BIN+G** model. The best result for each dataset is highlighted in bold.

on GitHub (`https://github.com/lingpy/are-sounds-sound-paper`) and archived with Zenodo (`https://doi.org/10.5281/zenodo.10610428`).

Limitations

The ongoing debate of what evidence phylogenetic reconstruction should be based on cannot be considered as conclusively solved with this study, although we are confident that our contribution merits the attention of all scholars participating in the debate. One crucial weakness of our approach, which we cannot overcome completely at the moment, is the way we operationalize "sound laws as evidence for phylogenetic reconstruction". Here, we use sound correspondence patterns which we infer automatically from the data sets. One may criticize that this procedure is not identical with the way in which experts do cladistic subgrouping. In response to such criticism, we emphasize, however, that every attempt to arrive at a useful way to compare evidence based on sound correspondence patterns (and sound laws) with evidence based on cognate sets, must start at some point, and that we are convinced that this approach comes quite close to the evidence traditional scholars defending phylogenetic reconstruction by innovation have in mind.

Acknowledgments

This research was supported by the Max Planck Society Research Grant *CALC³* (JML, `https://digling.org`), the ERC Consolidator Grant *ProduSemy* (JML, Grant No. 101044282, see https://doi.org/10.3030/101044282), the ERC Advanced Grant *CrossLingFerence* (GJ, Grant. No. 834050, see https://doi.org/10.3030/834050), the Klaus-Tschira Foundation, and by the European Union (EU) under Grant Agreement No 101087081 (AS, Comp-Biodiv-GR, see https://doi.org/10.3030/101087081). Views and opinions expressed are however those of the authors only and do not necessarily reflect those of the European Union or the European Research Council Executive Agency (nor any other funding agencies involved). Neither the European Union nor the granting authority can be held responsible for them. We thank Maria Heitmeier and Harald Baayen for their valuable input regarding the computational models used in this study.

Funded by the European Union

References

Cormac Anderson, Tiago Tresoldi, Thiago Costa Chacon, Anne-Maria Fehn, Mary Walworth, Robert Forkel, and Johann-Mattis List. 2018. A Cross-Linguistic Database of Phonetic Transcription Systems. *Yearbook of the Poznań Linguistic Meeting*, 4(1):21–53.

Raimo Anttila. 1972. *An introduction to historical and comparative linguistics*. Macmillan, New York.

Frederic Blum and Johann-Mattis List. 2023. Trimming phonetic alignments improves the inference of sound correspondence patterns from multilingual wordlists. In *Proceedings of the 5th Workshop on Computational Typology and Multilingual NLP*, pages 52–64. Association for Computational Linguistics.

Remco Bouckaert, Philippe Lemey, Michael Dunn, Simon J Greenhill, Alexander V Alekseyenko, Alexei J Drummond, Russell D Gray, Marc A Suchard, and Quentin D Atkinson. 2012. Mapping the origins and expansion of the Indo-European language family. *Science*, 337(6097):957–960.

Lyle Campbell and William J. Poser. 2008. *Language Classification: History and Method*. Cambridge University Press.

Thiago Costa Chacon and Johann-Mattis List. 2015. Improved computational models of sound change shed light on the history of the Tukanoan languages. *Journal of Language Relationship*, 13(3):177–204.

Anna Dybo and George S Starostin. 2008. In defense of the comparative method, or the end of the Vovin controversy. In I. S. Smirnov, editor, *Aspekty komparativistiki*, pages 119–258. RGGU, Moscow.

Isidore Dyen. 1953. [Review] Malgache et maanjan: Une comparaison linguistique by Otto Chr. Dahl. *Language*, 29(4):577–590.

George F Estabrook, FR McMorris, and Christopher A Meacham. 1985. Comparison of undirected phylogenetic trees based on subtrees of four evolutionary units. *Systematic Zoology*, 34(2):193–200.

Robert Forkel, Johann-Mattis List, Simon J. Greenhill, Christoph Rzymski, Sebastian Bank, Michael Cysouw, Harald Hammarström, Martin Haspelmath, Gereon A. Kaiping, and Russell D. Gray. 2018. Cross-Linguistic Data Formats, advancing data sharing and re-use in comparative linguistics. *Scientific Data*, 5(180205):1–10.

Julia Haag, Dimitri Höhler, Ben Bettisworth, and Alexandros Stamatakis. 2022. From Easy to Hopeless—Predicting the Difficulty of Phylogenetic Analyses. *Molecular Biology and Evolution*, 39(12):msac254.

David Hall and Dan Klein. 2010. Finding cognate groups using phylogenies. In *Proceedings of the 48th Annual Meeting of the Association for Computational Linguistics*, pages 1030–1039. Association for Computational Linguistics.

Harald Hammarström, Martin Haspelmath, Robert Forkel, and Sebastian Bank. 2023. *Glottolog. Version 4.8*. Max Planck Institute for Evolutionary Anthropology, Leipzig.

Paul Heggarty, Cormac Anderson, Matthew Scarborough, Benedict King, Remco Bouckaert, Lechosław Jocz, Martin Joachim Kümmel, Thomas Jügel, Britta Irslinger, Roland Pooth, Henrik Liljegren, Richard F. Strand, Geoffrey Haig, Martin Macák, Ronald I. Kim, Erik Anonby, Tijmen Pronk, Oleg Belyaev, Tonya Kim Dewey-Findell, Matthew Boutilier, Cassandra Freiberg, Robert Tegethoff, Matilde Serangeli, Nikos Liosis, Krzysztof Stroński, Kim Schulte, Ganesh Kumar Gupta, Wolfgang Haak, Johannes Krause, Quentin D. Atkinson, Simon J. Greenhill, Denise Kühnert, and Russell D. Gray. 2023. Language trees with sampled ancestors support a hybrid model for the origin of indo-european languages. *Science*, 381(6656).

Hans J. Holm. 2007. The new arboretum of Indo-European trees. *Journal of Quantitative Linguistics*, 14(2-3):167–214.

Daniel J Hruschka, Simon Branford, Eric D Smith, Jon Wilkins, Andrew Meade, Mark Pagel, and Tanmoy Bhattacharya. 2015. Detecting regular sound changes in linguistics as events of concerted evolution. *Current Biology*, 25(1):1–9.

Dimitri Höhler, Wayne Pfeiffer, Vassilios Ioannidis, Heinz Stockinger, and Alexandros Stamatakis. 2021. RAxML Grove: an empirical phylogenetic tree database. *Bioinformatics*, 38(6):1741–1742.

P Kapli, S Lutteropp, J Zhang, K Kobert, P Pavlidis, A Stamatakis, and T Flouri. 2017. Multi-rate Poisson tree processes for single-locus species delimitation under maximum likelihood and Markov chain Monte Carlo. *Bioinformatics*, 33(11):1630–1638.

Vishnupriya Kolipakam, Fiona M. Jordan, Michael Dunn, Simon J. Greenhill, Remco Bouckaert, Russell D. Gray, and Annemarie Verkerk. 2018. A Bayesian phylogenetic study of the Dravidian language family. *Royal Society Open Science*, 5(171504):1–17.

Alexey M Kozlov, Diego Darriba, Tomáš Flouri, Benoit Morel, and Alexandros Stamatakis. 2019. RAxML-NG: a fast, scalable and user-friendly tool for maximum likelihood phylogenetic inference. *Bioinformatics*, 35(21):4453–4455.

Johann-Mattis List. 2014. *Sequence comparison in historical linguistics*. Düsseldorf University Press, Düsseldorf.

Johann-Mattis List. 2019. Automatic inference of sound correspondence patterns across multiple languages. *Computational Linguistics*, 1(45):137–161.

Johann-Mattis List, Cormac Anderson, Tiago Tresoldi, and Robert Forkel. 2021. *Cross-Linguistic Transcription Systems. Version 2.1.0*. Max Planck Institute for the Science of Human History, Jena.

Johann-Mattis List and Robert Forkel. 2023a. *LingPy. A Python library for quantitative tasks in historical linguistics [Software Library, Version 2.6.9]*. Max Planck Institute for Evolutionary Anthropology, Leipzig.

Johann-Mattis List and Robert Forkel. 2023b. *LingRex: Linguistic reconstruction with LingPy*. Max Planck Institute for Evolutionary Anthropology, Leipzig.

Johann-Mattis List, Robert Forkel, Simon J. Greenhill, Christoph Rzymski, Johannes Englisch, and Russell D. Gray. 2022. Lexibank, a public repository of standardized wordlists with computed phonological and lexical features. *Scientific Data*, 9(316):1–31.

Johann-Mattis List, Philippe Lopez, and Eric Bapteste. 2016. Using sequence similarity networks to identify partial cognates in multilingual wordlists. In *Proceedings of the Association of Computational Linguistics 2016 (Volume 2: Short Papers)*, pages 599–605, Berlin. Association of Computational Linguistics.

D. R. Maddison, D. L. Swofford, and W. P. Maddison. 1997. NEXUS: an extensible file format for systematic information. *Syst. Biol.*, 46(4):590–621.

Simone Pompei, Vittorio Loreto, and Francesca Tria. 2011. On the accuracy of language trees. *PloS one*, 6(6):e20109.

Taraka Rama, Johann-Mattis List, Johannes Wahle, and Gerhard Jäger. 2018. Are automatic methods for cognate detection good enough for phylogenetic reconstruction in historical linguistics? In *Proceedings of the 2018 Conference of the North American Chapter of the Association for Computational Linguistics: Human Language Technologies, Volume 2 (Short Papers)*, pages 393–400.

Donald Ringe, Tandy Warnow, and Ann Taylor. 2002. Indo-European and computational cladistics. *Transactions of the Philological Society*, 100(1):59–129.

Frederik Ronquist and John P. Huelsenbeck. 2003. MrBayes 3: Bayesian phylogenetic inference under mixed models. *Bioinformatics*, 19(12):1572–1574.

Laurent Sagart, Guillaume Jacques, Yunfan Lai, Robin Ryder, Valentin Thouzeau, Simon J. Greenhill, and Johann-Mattis List. 2019. Dated language phylogenies shed light on the ancestry of sino-tibetan. *Proceedings of the National Academy of Science of the United States of America*, 116:10317–10322.

David Sankoff. 1975. Minimal mutation trees of sequences. *SIAM Journal on Applied Mathematics*, 28(1):35–42.

Nathanael E. Schweikhard and Johann-Mattis List. 2020. Developing an annotation framework for word formation processes in comparative linguistics. *SKASE Journal of Theoretical Linguistics*, 17(1):2–26.

Ge Tan, Matthieu Muffato, Christian Ledergerber, Javier Herrero, Nick Goldman, Manuel Gil, and Christophe Dessimoz. 2015. Current methods for automated filtering of multiple sequence alignments frequently worsen single-gene phylogenetic inference. *Systematic Biology*, 64(5):778–791.

W. C. Wheeler and Peter M. Whiteley. 2015. Historical linguistics as a sequence optimization problem: the evolution and biogeography of uto-aztecan languages. *Cladistics*, 31(2):113–125.

Peter M. Whiteley, Ming Xue, and Ward C. Wheeler. 2019. Revising the bantu tree. *Cladistics*, 35:329–348.

Z Yang. 1995. A space-time process model for the evolution of dna sequences. *Genetics*, 139(2):993–1005.

Compounds in Universal Dependencies: A Survey in Five European Languages

Emil Svoboda, Magda Ševčíková
Charles University, Faculty of Mathematics and Physics
Institute of Formal and Applied Linguistics
{svoboda,sevcikova}@ufal.mff.cuni.cz

Abstract

In Universal Dependencies, compounds, which we understand as words containing two or more roots, are represented according to tokenization, which reflects the orthographic conventions of the language. A closed compound corresponds to a single word in Universal Dependencies (e.g. *waterfall*) while a hyphenated compound (*father-in-law*) and an open compound (*apple pie*) to multiple words. The aim of this paper is to open a discussion on how to move towards a more consistent annotation of compounds. The solution we argue for is to represent the internal structure of all compound types analogously to syntactic phrases, which would not only increase the comparability of compounding within and across languages, but also allow comparisons of compounds and syntactic phrases.

1 Introduction

Compounding, as a word-formation process in which two or more words (bases, roots, or stems) are combined to form a new word (Lieber, 2010, p. 43), is used across languages (Štekauer et al., 2012, pp. 51–100). However, the term compound is not only used to refer to words that result from the combination of two words (cf. *flowerpot*) or are outputs of recursive compounding (e.g. German *Jahresabschlussprüfung* 'end-of-the-year audit'), but also to words that are results of compounding happening in conjunction with derivation or conversion (e.g. the German adjective *blauäugig* 'blue-eyed'),[1] and to words that are both direct and indirect derivatives of these compounds (German *Blauäugigkeit* 'blue-eyedness/naiveté'); cf. Bauer et al. (2013, p. 442).

[1]The compound cannot be traced back to *blau* 'blue' and **äugig* '*eyed', because the latter item does not exist in isolation. It is rather analysed as being formed by combining the adjective *blau* 'blue' and the noun *Auge* 'eye' and simultaneously adding the *-ed* suffix to get the compound adjective.

The criteria for defining compounds (and especially distinguishing them from syntactic phrases) vary from language to language, but features with cross-linguistic validity include, besides the requirement of at least two roots, syntactic and semantic compactness. What is not decisive, on the other hand, is spelling. Compounds are spelled as a single word (closed compounds; e.g. *waterfall*), or as several orthographic words joined by hyphens (hyphenated compounds; e.g. *cyan-magenta-yellow-key*) or separated by spaces (open compounds; e.g. *apple pie*).

The present paper surveys how compounds are treated in Universal Dependencies (UD; version 2.12, Zeman et al. 2023). Five languages, namely English, German, Czech, Latin, and Russian, have been chosen for this pilot survey based on the working criteria that for each of the languages (a) at least one treebank is available in UD, (b) a lexical database exists that contains a non-negligible number of compounds (and can be used to identify compounds in the treebanks), and (c) the authors have a sufficient command of it. We show that the current treatment of compounds in UD, which is determined by the languages' orthographic conventions and by UD's tokenization rules, renders compounds difficult to identify in the data, hindering their comparison within and across languages. However, this paper is not limited to the mere unification of compound annotation according to the existing guidelines. Our proposal is to annotate the relations between the compound's component parts by using the syntactic relations already implemented in UD, making the analogy between compounds and multi-word expressions and syntactic phrases explicit, which has already been pointed out in the literature.

The paper is structured as follows. Section 2 briefly summarizes those aspects of the linguistic discussion on compounding that are necessary for understanding the issues presented. An overview

Proceedings of the 6th Workshop on Research in Computational Linguistic Typology and Multilingual NLP (SIGTYP 2024), pages 88–99
March 22, 2024

of the language data resources that contain compounds and are used in the paper is also provided. In Section 3, we describe how compounds are currently handled in UD, exemplifying the general and language-specific problems of compounds. In Section 4, we discuss steps that can be taken to make the annotation of compounds more coherent and to bring it closer to the way syntactic relations are annotated, but without losing the difference between compounding and syntax. Future directions regarding the automation of compound identification and annotation are outlined to some extent. Section 5 concludes the paper.

2 Background

2.1 Compounds in the linguistic literature

Besides the spelling differences mentioned above, the debate over compounding and compounds has been centered around the following topics:

– boundary between compounding vs. derivation, with a special focus on neo-classical formations (cf. ten Hacken 1994, Bauer 2005, among others), and between compounds vs. syntactic phrases and multi-word expressions in particular (Olsen, 2001; Schlücker, 2019);

– part-of-speech (POS) category of the compound and its components: if the components obtained by splitting the compound do not correspond to independently existing words, the POS of the component is determined according to the closest word; if this applies to the head, the compound's POS is different from its head's POS (cf. the distinctions below; for examples, see Section 2.2);

– headedness: if one of the components plays a prominent role, it is considered the head; left-headed compounds and right-headed compounds are distinguished;

– endocentricity vs. exocentricity: the head determines the POS and meaning in endocentric compounds; an exocentric compound is headless or, as Bauer (2001, p. 70) puts it, it is "a compound which is not a hyponym of its own head element";

– relations between the compound's components: in the literature cited below, the compound's internal structure is indicated by brackets, in analogy to syntactic constituent trees;

– syntactic type of the relation between the compound parts: the crucial distinction is whether the components are independent of each other (coordinate, coordinative, additive or copulative are some of the terms used) or whether one depends on the other (subordinate, determinative, etc.).

These features, assigned varying degrees of importance and priority, have been employed to classify compounds. The classifications proposed by Bloomfield (1933), Bally (1944), Marchand (1969), Spencer (1991), Fabb (1998), Olsen (2001), Haspelmath (2002), Bauer (2001), and Booij (2005) are compared by Bisetto and Scalise (2005), who come up with yet another classification, where the relation between the components is used as the first-level criterion[2] and it is followed by the distinction between endocentric and exocentric compounds. Bisetto and Scalise's classification was implemented in annotation scheme of the MorboComp database, which is one of the resources reported on below.

2.2 Compounds in language data resources

The selective list presented here contains language data sources that include a substantial number of compounds along with annotations reflecting various features discussed in the literature.

MorboComp is a multilingual database of compounds covering 20 languages, including the ones in scope except for Czech (Guevara et al., 2006). In Table 1, the annotation provided in MorboComp is exemplified by three nominal Italian compounds composed of words from different POS categories (cf. 2nd and 3rd column). While the first compound (*madrelingua* 'mother tongue') is endocentric with the right component playing the role of head, the latter two are exocentric (and headless). The components are listed as they occur in the compound (8th and 9th column), they may not be existing words (cf. the third compound in the table). While potentially highly useful for the purposes of this paper, as of 2023 the project seems to have been discontinued and the data are not publicly available.

Compounds are also covered by CELEX2, which is a lexical database of English, German, and Dutch (Baayen et al., 2014). Out of all the linguistic annotations provided in this resource, delimitation of the components (and the linking element, interfix, if present), POS of the components, and annotation of the internal structure using nested brackets (cf. (1) to (3)) were the most important for our survey. In the bracketed structures in German, some

[2]The authors speak of grammatical relations: "The grammatical relations holding between the two constituents of a compound are basically the relations that hold in syntactic constructions: subordination, coordination and attribution".

Compound	POS	Struc	Class	End	Head-C	Head-S	1st-C	2nd-C	Gloss
madrelingua	N	[N+N]	SUB	Tru	right	right	madre	lingua	mother+tongue
mano lesta	N	[N+A]	ATT	Fal	none	none	mano	lesta	quick+hand = thief
dormiveglia	N	[V+V]	CRD	Fal	none	none	dormi	veglia	sleep+be awake = dozing

Table 1: Annotation of Italian compounds in the MorboComp database. The compound's lemma (1st column) is followed by its POS category (2nd column), the POS categories of the components (column Struct[ure]), syntactic relation between the components (Class: subordinate/attributive/coordinate), endocentricity (End[ocentric]: True/False), placement of the semantic head (Head-C), placement of the syntactic head (H-S), the form of the first component (1st-C) and of the second one (2nd-C), and the gloss.

morphs are replaced with a representative form (cf. *gang* substituted by *geh*, which occurs in the infinitive *gehen* 'to go' in (1); but in the English example (3) *woman* is not used instead of *women*). Based on these features, 19,304 compounds were extracted from the German section of CELEX and 6,267 compounds from the resource's English section.

(1) `Umgangssprache ... Umgang+s+Sprache NxN ... ((((um)[V|.V],(geh)[V])[V])[N], (s)[N|N.N],((sprech)[V])[N])[N] ...`

(2) `Grossmachtpolitik ... Grossmacht+Politik NN ... (((gross)[A],(Macht)[N])[N], ((polit)[R],(ik)[N|R.])[N])[N] ...`

(3) `womenfolk ... women+folk NN ((women)[N],(folk)[N])[N] ...`

The GermaNet compound list (Henrich and Hinrichs, 2011) contains more than 120,000 compounds in its 2023 edition. This source lists for each compound the lemmas of two immediate ancestors from which it was composed ((4) to (6)). The ancestors provided are existing words, not just strings occurring in the compound (cf. (5) where the verb *abbiegen* 'to turn' is given, because **Abbiege* is not a separate word in German). Compounds with more than two roots are split in succession; see (6) where the second ancestor is a compound which is analyzed in a separate entry in the resource. For the first component, two possibilities are given, if both are equally relevant (cf. the action noun *Umfrage* 'survey' and the verb *umfragen* 'to survey' in (6)).

(4) `Umgangssprache Umgang Sprache`

(5) `Abbiegeassistent abbiegen Assistent`

(6) `Umfrageteilnehmer Umfrage|umfragen Teilnehmer`

DeriNet is a lexical database of Czech where words that share a common root are arranged into tree-like graphs according to their morphological structure – from the morphologically simplest words (unmotivated words) to the most complex. The database contains over a million entries, of which less than a half are corpus-attested (432 thousand; only this subset is used in this study). While derivatives are linked to a single ancestor, compounds are connected to two or more ancestors. Additional compounds were identified based on heuristics and lexical lists of compound parts. When the compounds both with and without the links to their ancestors are counted (all of them having the explicit Boolean compoundhood flag set to `true`) together with the derivatives of all these compounds, the number totals to 45 thousand corpus-attested compounds available in DeriNet 2.1 (Vidra et al., 2021). The left graph in (7) shows the unmotivated nouns *dům* 'house' and *rod* 'kin' as ancestors of the adjectival compound *domorodý* 'native', from which the noun *domorodec* 'native man' and the adverb *domorodě* 'in a native way' are derived. All of *domorodý*, *domorodec* and *domorodě* are counted as compounds.

(7)

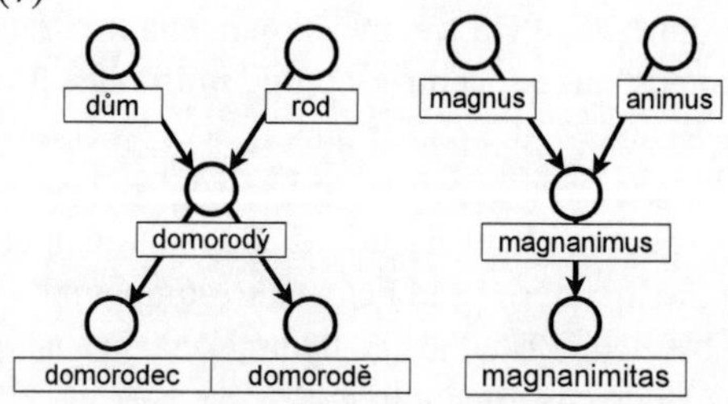

More than 3 thousand Latin compounds and their derivatives are part of the Word Formation Latin database (Litta et al., 2016). The database is organized in a way similar to DeriNet; cf. the right graph in (7) modeling the Latin adjective *magnan-*

Dataset	Language	Compounds	Total entries
CELEX (Baayen et al., 2014)	English	6,267	52,447
CELEX (Baayen et al., 2014)	German	19,304	51,728
GermaNet (Henrich and Hinrichs, 2011)	German	121,655	215,000
Derinet 2.1 (Vidra et al., 2021)	Czech	45,473	431,857
Word Formation Latin (Litta et al., 2016)	Latin	3,198	36,258
Golden Compound Analyses (Vodolazsky and Petrov, 2021)	Russian	1,699	1,699

Table 2: The databases employed in the present survey for identification of compounds in the Universal Dependencies treebanks of the five languages. The last two columns specify the number of lemmas (types).

imus 'high-spirited' as being formed by combining the adjective *magnus* 'high' and the noun *animus* 'spirit', and giving rise to the noun *magnanimitas* 'high-spiritedness'.

Golden Compound Analyses (Vodolazsky and Petrov, 2021) is a database of Russian compounds compiled for training of a compound splitter. It contains 1,699 compounds that a re directly traced back to two or more ancestors. The annotation includes the POS category of each compound, the lemmas and POS of each of the components; cf. полувсерьёз 'half serious' in (8).

(8) полувсерьёз,adv,половина,noun,всерьёз,adv

The sources introduced in this section are, with the exception of MorboComp, further used in this survey to gain preliminary quantitative insights into how many compounds are found in the UD treebanks; cf. Table 2 for a summary.

3 Current annotation of compounds in Universal Dependencies

3.1 The annotation guidelines

We start by introducing how words considered as compounds in the literature are treated according to the UD annotation principles (de Marneffe et al., 2021).[3] The application of these rules to each of the languages under survey is described in the following subsections. Syntactic annotation in UD is based on tokenization, which in turn follows the spelling conventions of individual languages. Since the term compound covers words spelled in several ways, compounds are not annotated uniformly in UD:

– Closed compounds, appearing in the text as continuous orthographic words, are handled as discrete, internally unstructured (= atomic) items which enter into relations with other items of the sentence structure. Although the compound's components are linked by similar relations as the constituents of syntactic phrases, these intra-word relations are not captured in UD because "there is no attempt at segmenting words into morphemes".[4]

– Open compounds, which are spelled as two (or more) separate words, are treated as two (or more) items that are arranged into a subtree with the head component as the root and the less prominent item(s) as dependent node(s). The relation between the head and the other component is labeled with the dedicated syntactic relation `compound`. This relation is assigned to open compounds regardless of the semantic relation between the components (cf. *apple pie* = "pie made from apples" vs. *coffee cup* = "cup for coffee" vs. *water mill* = "mill powered by water", etc.). Besides the bare compound relation, there are 22 subtypes of this relation intended for language-specific phenomena,[5] of which only `compound:prt` is used in some languages under analysis, namely in English and German. The `compound:prt` is used for "[p]article verbs where the particle is realized as a separate word (which may alternate with affixed particles), for example Swedish *byta ut* ('exchange'; cf. *utbytt* 'exchanged')".

– Hyphenated compounds are treated in the same way as in open compounds. The hyphen is attached to the head, with the relation label `punct`.[6]

Annotation of compounds is explored for each language based on all treebanks available in the UD collection (i.e. ten treebanks for English with a total of 46K sentences, four German treebanks containing 208K sentences, six treebanks for Czech with 208K sentences, five Latin treebanks with

[3]See also https://universaldependencies.org/guidelines.html

[4]https://universaldependencies.org/u/overview/tokenization.html

[5]https://universaldependencies.org/ext-dep-index.html

[6]This is the case for the languages in scope, but the claim does not hold for all languages in UD. Swedish hyphenated compounds are for instance handled the same way as closed compounds.

Language	compound relations	Sentences with compound	compound:prt relations	Sentences with compound:prt	Total words	Total sent.
English	22,017 (3,03%)	13,459 (29.27%)	2,485 (0.34%)	2,313 (5.0%)	726K	46K
German	1,787 (0.05%)	1,418 (0.68%)	22,349 (0.59%)	21,897 (10.5%)	3,810K	208K
Czech	2,690 (0.12%)	1,356 (1.06%)	0 (0.00%)	0 (0.0%)	2,222K	128K
Latin	85 (0.01%)	82 (0.1%)	0 (0.00%)	0 (0.0%)	983K	59K
Russian	1,973 (0.11%)	1,812 (1.6%)	0 (0.00%)	0 (0,0%)	1,830K	111K

Table 3: The number of sentences containing a compound relation (assigned to open and hyphenated compounds) and sentences with the compound:prt label (with particle verbs) in the Universal Dependencies treebanks of the five languages. The percentage indicates the proportion of sentences with the labels in all sentences of the language's treebanks.

59K sentences, and five treebanks for Russian with 111K sentences). The number of sentences containing the compound relation in the languages' UD treebanks is listed in Table 3. The compound:prt relation is used only in English and German; it will not be further commented upon.

3.2 The UD treebanks for English

Out of the languages analyzed, English treebanks contain the highest number of compound relations, both in absolute numbers and in percentages, owing to the fact that in this language, NOUN+NOUN sequences are analyzed as compounds. English is also a language where these NOUN+NOUN compounds can alternatively be spelled with a hyphen or even without a space as a single graphical word (cf, Table 4), resulting in different tree structures; cf. the textbook example *flower pot* as an open compound with the hyphenated (*flower-pot*) and closed spelling alternative (*flowerpot*) annotated in line with the UD guidelines in (9).

(9)

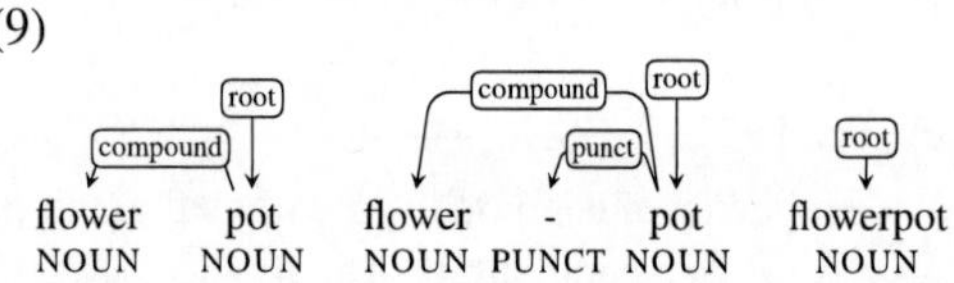

The compound relation is also assigned to NOUN+ADJ phrases (*emerald green*, *labour intensive*), as well as complex open numerals such as *twenty one*.

Even though the relationship between the components of the open compound *stone wall*, which can be paraphrased as "wall of stones", is the same as the relationship between the adjective *wooden* and the noun *wall* ("wall of wood"), the syntactic relations within these sequences are labeled differently, namely compound in the first sequence while amod in the second; cf. (10).

(10)

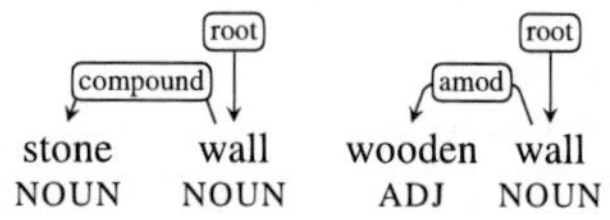

If there were an adjective to the noun *stone* (**stonen*) or if *stone* were considered also as an adjective in English, the annotation would have been no different from *wooden wall*. This is encountered in the phrase *west side*, where *west* is interpreted as an adjective (while the formally identical noun *west* and the formally different adjective *western* exist) and therefore handled as an adjectival modifier (amod) of the nominal governor.

3.3 The UD treebanks for German

German is a language where compounding is widely used, but compounds are typically spelled as compact strings. Nevertheless, both hyphenated compounds (cf. the Anglicism *Trackpad-Click*) and open compounds (NOUN+NOUN sequences, often with proper names; e.g. *Präsident Franjo* 'President Franjo') are documented in the treebanks, both types assigned the compound relation.

In German we also find cases of (here, closed) compounds with the components' relations analogous to those between words in syntactic phrases, but these analogies are not obvious in the current annotation; cf. the compound *altbekannt* 'well-known', which is represented by a single node, and the phrase *älteste bekannt* 'oldest known', which is represented as a tree headed by the second word with the first element linked by the amod relation in (11).

(11)

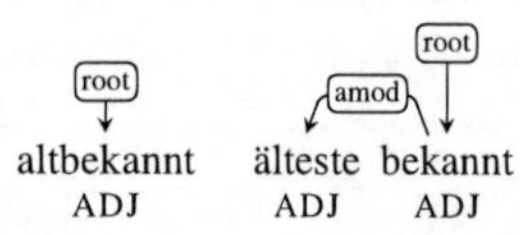

3.4 The UD treebanks for Czech

Also in Czech, compounds are commonly written as continuous strings, still a hyphen may connect the components in coordinate compounds. In the data, however, the `compound` relation appears not only with hyphenated compounds (*indo-australský* 'Indo-Australian'), but also with numeral expressions, which in Czech are separated by spaces.[7] The rightmost component is taken as the head and the other parts are depending on it as modifiers; cf. the right structure in (12). When a numeral construction enters derivation, the output is a closed compound and it is represented by a single node; cf. the adjective *dvacetitisícový* 'twenty-thousand' on the left in (12) which is traced back to the phrase *dvacet tisíc* 'twenty thousand'.

(12)

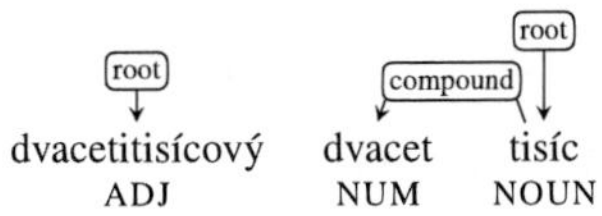

Similarly, nouns modified by adjectival modifiers can give rise to adjectives with two roots and closed spelling. Cf. the noun phrase *pravý úhel* 'right angle' and the adjectival compound *pravoúhlý* 'right-angled' in (13), which is close to the German adjective *blauäugig* 'blue-eyed' mentioned in the introductory section in that the right component does not exist as a separate adjective (**úhlý* 'angled' similar to **äugig* '*eyed').

(13)

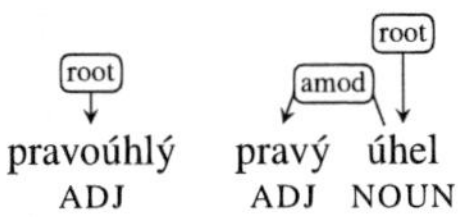

3.5 The UD treebanks for Latin

Latin treebanks contain the lowest number of compound relations, as documented in Table 3. Its current usage is limited to numeral expressions if they are spelled as separate words in a way described above for Czech, with the addendum that sometimes one of the words is *unus* 'one' labeled as a determiner and not a numeral. Example (14) is also analogous to Czech, documenting an adjectival compound (*magnanimus* 'high-spirited') that is based on a noun phrase (here, more specifically, on a phrase with the head noun preceding the adjectival modifier: *animus magnus* lit. 'spirit high' = 'high spirit').

[7] The interpretation of numerals as compounds, though, does not conform to the Czech linguistic tradition.

(14)

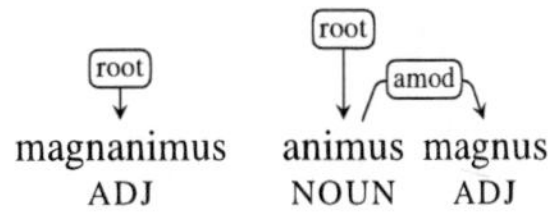

3.6 The UD treebanks for Russian

In the Russian treebanks, the `compound` relation is – unlike in Czech – applied to "noun compounds (e.g., стресс менеджмент 'stress management, Жар птица 'Fire bird'), but also adjective compounds (e.g., бэд блоки 'bad blocks', мини колонка 'mini speaker', Гранд отель 'Grand hotel') and some other types ("+ 1", "№ 1")".[8] Such NOUN+NOUN compounds and ADJ+NOUN compounds are often loanwords or direct translations of foreign expressions.

In addition, now similarly to Czech and also Latin, the `compound` relation appears also with numerals (две тысячи 'two thousand') and hyphenated constructions (город-государство; 'city-state').

Noteworthy are compounds which are analyzed as NOUN+VERB structures in the Golden Compound Analyses database. Since they are closed compounds, they are currently represented by a single node in the treebanks, but the relationship between the components resembles the `obj` relation of the object noun to its governing verb; cf. рукомойник 'washbasin' and the phrase мыть руки 'to wash hands' in (15), or короед 'bark beetle' traced back to есть кору 'to eat bark' and травосеяние 'grass sowing' related to сеять траву 'to sow grass'.

(15)

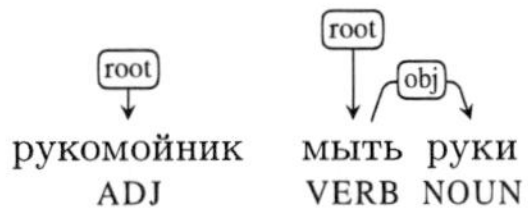

4 A proposal of a syntax-based annotation of compounds

4.1 Covering all types of compounds and annotating their internal structure

As we have tried to show, the current annotation does not allow to get a complex picture of compounds (as multi-root items) either within one language or across languages. On the one hand, the `compound` relation only applies to open and hyphenated compounds while closed compounds are

[8] https://universaldependencies.org/ru/dep/compound.html

not marked in any way. On the other hand, the compound relation is underspecified, without capturing the different relations observed between the components in individual compounds – the exact same label is used for English NOUN+NOUN compounds, which themselves document a variety of internal relationships, and for relations between numerals in Czech, for example.

We now roughly outline a preliminary proposal for a new annotation of compounds in UD that should overcome these issues. Rather than offering an ultimate solution to each individual aspect of compound annotation, we present in our proposal one or more possible solutions based on what we have encountered in the literature or in existing language resources, with our primary goal being to initiate a discussion on this topic.

Compounds with all types of spelling should be approached as complex structures that consist of components which are linked by a relationship that is often similar to syntactic relations between words in syntactic phrases:

(a) Closed compounds should be split into their respective constituents for this purpose, and further handled in the same manner as open and hyphenated compounds. Compounds with three and more components will be divided into individual parts (e.g. the above German example *Umfrageteilnehmer* 'survey participant' into *Umfrage+ Teil+ Nehmer*) and their relationships will be captured by arranging them into a tree structure (see the next points). As illustrated, in closed compounds a "+" sign may be used on the first (or on all non-final) components to indicate the original morphological boundary, so that the information on their orthography is retained. An interfix, if contained in a compound, will be part of the preceding component (cf. *Umgangssprache* 'colloquial language' as *Umgangs+ Sprache*).

(b) Since such an approach would yield strings that do not exist as separate words (cf. **Abbiege* in *Abbiegeassistent*), we propose – in accordance with the fact that the words in syntactic phrases are treated in this way – to assign a lemma to each component. It can be a full word that is identical with the component (i.e. *Umgang* 'dealing' or *umgehen* 'to deal' and *Sprache* 'language' for *Umgangs+ Sprache*) or close to it (*abbiegen* 'to turn' and *Assistent* 'assistant' for *Abbiege+ Assistent*). Derivatives of compounds would share this lemmatization with their ancestors, e.g. *domorodec* 'native man' would be lemmatized as *domo+ rodý* 'native' (i.e. *dům* 'house' and *rod* 'kin').

(c) All types of compounds should be organized into subtrees in a way analogous to syntactic phrases in UD, making a distinction between subordinate compounds (with the compound's head as the governor and its modifier as its dependent; cf. *bohapustý* 'godless' in (16)) and coordinate compounds (with the first component as the root of the subtree and all the other conjuncts depending on it; cf. *černobílý* 'black-and-white' in (17)).

(16)

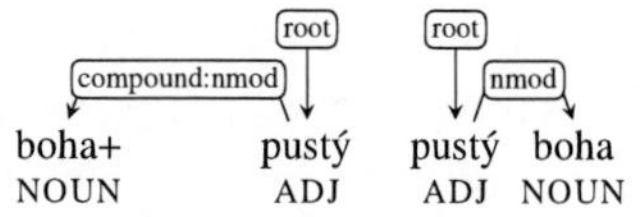

(17)

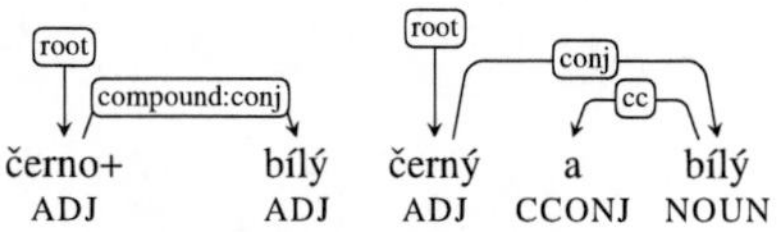

(d) Though the subtree modeling the syntactic structure of a compound's components is proposed to be as close an analogy as possible to the subtrees of syntactic phrases, the relation may retain the compound/phrase distinction. As bare compound relations are not informative, the relations within compounds could be tagged with a `compound:<relation>` label, where `<relation>` is an already-existing UD syntactic relation. This restriction regarding forcing compound subtypes into established relations should pertain solely to a) currently bare compound relations and b) closed compounds currently treated as atomic units, **not** to established, already-subtyped relations such as the `compound:prt` mentioned in Section 3.1. These should not be overwritten, their further usage is neither blocked nor discouraged by our proposal.

How these individual pieces of annotation could be brought into the data is discussed in the next section.

4.2 Steps towards the proposed annotation

Identification of closed compounds. To get a preliminary idea of which part of the treebank data for individual languages would be affected by the proposed annotation, the number of closed compounds in the UD treebanks needs to be estimated in addition to the number of the compound relations (which are in Table 3). In this study, we used the lists of compounds contained in the language resources discussed above in Section 2.2. The figures in Table 4 are heavily conditioned by the size of the resources used. The figures represent a lower

Language	Closed compounds	Total words	Sentences with closed compounds	Total sentences
English	5,934 (0.82%)	726K	5,286 (11.57%)	46K
German	156,629 (4.11%)	3,810K	87,104 (50.14%)	208K
Czech	47,103 (2.11%)	2,222K	34,775 (27.27%)	128K
Latin	26,271 (2.62%)	983K	18,353 (31.27%)	59K
Russian	4,803 (0.27%)	1,830K	4,460 (4.00%)	111K

Table 4: A lower bound estimate of the amount of closed compounds (tokens) in Universal Dependencies, based on searching for the known compounds (and their derivatives) extracted from the data sources listed in Table 2.

bound for the actual amount of closed compounds contained in UD, since none of the data sources list the compounds from their respective languages exhaustively.

With these limitations in mind, Table 4 suggests that the influence of such a change would be substantial, especially in German, where more than 156 thousand closed compounds were identified, which are part of 87 thousand sentences (i.e. 50% of all sentences). The least affected language by our current estimate would be Russian with less than 5 thousand closed compounds distributed over 4 thousand (4%) sentences; this is due to the relatively low coverage of the Golden Compound Analyses database used as the Russian compound data source in this study (see Table 2). The utilization of resources with higher coverage or another more sophisticated approach could render these numbers substantially higher.

For **splitting of compounds and lemmatization of the components**, the language data sources reviewed above can be taken as a starting point, because they contain high-quality, linguistically adequate material. Whereas CELEX both divides the compounds into substrings and assigns representative forms to its individual parts (cf. *geh* for *gang* above), the other resources provide full-fledged ancestors for compounds that would fit our idea of components' lemmas. Even if the resources for some languages are limited, the existing data can – after unifying the annotation according to the proposal – be used for training automatic tools. A prototype of such a tool, *PaReNT* (Svoboda and Ševčíková, 2022), performs both compound splitting and component lemmatization with decent results on Czech.

Specifying the syntactic structure and assigning syntactic relation labels is another important step for which existing sources provide only very limited data (cf. the bracketed structure in CELEX). Since the pilot manual annotation was based around a mostly mechanical process of finding compound-associated phrases, feeding them into UDPipe (Straka et al., 2016), and observing the relation within the phrase, a semi-automatic procedure is being developed that follows this approach. For example, the German compound *Zittergras* 'quaking-grass' encodes the phrase *das Gras zittert*. The syntactic annotation provided for this phrase by UDPipe is then replicated in the compound, cf. the structures of the compound and of the underlying phrase both with *Gras* as `nsubj` in (18). The English example *killjoy* with the `obj` relation follows in (19).

(18)

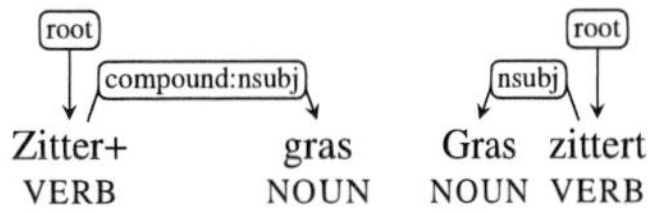

(19)

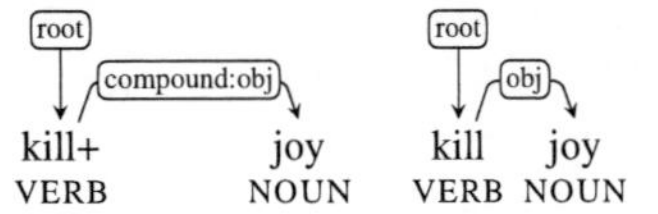

In addition to the examples provided in this section ((16) through (19)), the envisioned annotation scheme is applied to the examples that were presented above in Section 3 – see the Appendix, where the annotation according to the current UD guidelines is shown on the left-hand side and the proposed annotation on the right.

5 Concluding remarks

In this paper, we explored the current treatment of compounds in UD in five languages. We observed that the handling of open and hyphenated compounds varies widely according to the particular language in question, and that closed compounds are taken into account in none of them. Based on these observations and also the long-standing tradition of describing compounds from a syntactic perspective present in the linguistic literature, the objective of the paper was to open a discussion on whether a multilingual annotation scheme for compounds in UD that employs the dependency relations already in use is useful and what features it should have.

The proposed scheme is currently being implemented in the data of the languages under study, and the aim is to extend it to other languages, which will inevitably result in modifications to individual aspects of the scheme.

Acknowledgments

The study was supported by the Charles University, project GA UK No. 128122, and by the Ministry of Education, Youth and Sports of the Czech Republic, Project No. LM2023062 LINDAT/CLARIAH-CZ.

References

RH Baayen, R Piepenbrock, and L Gulikers. 2014. CELEX2 LDC96L14, 1995. *URL https://doi. org/10*, 35111.

Charles Bally. 1944. *Linguistique générale et linguistique francaise*. A. Francke.

Laurie Bauer. 2001. Compounding. In M. Haspelmath, editor, *Language Typology and Language Universals: An International Handbook*, pages 695–707. De Gruyter.

Laurie Bauer. 2005. The Borderline between Derivation and Compounding. In Wolfgang U. Dressler, Dieter Kastovsky, Oskar E. Pfeiffer, and Franz Rainer, editors, *Morphology and its Demarcations*, pages 97–108. John Benjamins.

Laurie Bauer, Rochelle Lieber, and Ingo Plag. 2013. *The Oxford Reference Guide to English Morphology*. Oxford University Press, Oxford.

Antonietta Bisetto and Sergio Scalise. 2005. The classification of compounds. *Lingue and Linguaggio*, 4(2):319–332.

Leonard Bloomfield. 1933. *Language*. A. Francke.

Geert Booij. 2005. Compounding and Derivation: Evidence for Construction Morphology. *Amsterdam Studies in the Theory and History of Linguistic Science Series 4*, 264:109–132.

Marie-Catherine de Marneffe, Christopher D. Manning, Joakim Nivre, and Daniel Zeman. 2021. Universal dependencies. *Computational Linguistics*, 47(2):255–308.

Nigel Fabb. 1998. Compounding. In A. Spencer and A. M. Zwicky, editors, *Handbook of Morphology*, pages 66–83. Blackwell.

Emiliano Guevara, Sergio Scalise, Antonietta Bisetto, and Chiara Melloni. 2006. MORBO/COMP: A Multilingual Database of Compound Words. In *Proceedings of the 5th edition of the International Conference on Language Resources and Evaluation*, pages 2160–2163.

Martin Haspelmath. 2002. *Understanding Morphology*. Arnold.

Verena Henrich and Erhard Hinrichs. 2011. Determining Immediate Constituents of Compounds in GermaNet. In *Proceedings of the International Conference on Recent Advances in Natural Language Processing 2011*, pages 420–426.

Rochelle Lieber. 2010. *Introducing Morphology*. Cambridge University Press, Cambridge.

Eleonora Litta, Marco Passarotti, and Chris Culy. 2016. Formatio formosa est. Building a Word Formation Lexicon for Latin. In *Proceedings of the 3rd Italian Conference on Computational Linguistics*, pages 185–189.

Hans Marchand. 1969. *The Categories and Types of Present Day English Word Formation*. Beck'sche Verlagsbuchhandlung.

Susan Olsen. 2001. Copulative Compounds: A Closer Look at the Interface Between Syntax and Morphology. In *Yearbook of Morphology 2000*, pages 279–320. Springer.

Barbara Schlücker, editor. 2019. *Complex Lexical Units. Compounds and Multi-Word Expressions*. De Gruyter, Berlin.

Andrew Spencer, editor. 1991. *Morphological Theory*. Blackwell, Oxford.

Pavol Štekauer, Salvador Valera, and Lívia Kőrtvélyessy. 2012. *Word-formation in the world's languages: A typological survey*. Cambridge University Press.

Milan Straka, Jan Hajič, and Jana Straková. 2016. UDPipe: trainable pipeline for processing CoNLL-U files performing tokenization, morphological analysis, pos tagging and parsing. In *Proceedings of the Tenth International Conference on Language Resources and Evaluation (LREC'16)*, pages 4290–4297.

Emil Svoboda and Magda Ševčíková. 2022. Word Formation Analyzer for Czech: Automatic Parent Retrieval and Classification of Word Formation Processes. *Prague Bulletin of Mathematical Linguistics*, 118:55–73.

Pius ten Hacken, editor. 1994. *Defining Morphology. A Principled Approach to Determining the Boundaries of Compounding, Derivation and Inflection*. Olms, Hildesheim.

Jonáš Vidra, Zdeněk Žabokrtský, Lukáš Kyjánek, Magda Ševčíková, Šárka Dohnalová, Emil Svoboda, and Jan Bodnár. 2021. DeriNet 2.1. LINDAT/CLARIAH-CZ digital library at the Institute of Formal and Applied Linguistics (ÚFAL), Faculty of Mathematics and Physics, Charles University.

Daniil Vodolazsky and Hermann Petrov. 2021. Compound Splitting and Analysis for Russian. *Resources and Tools for Derivational Morphology (DeriMo 2021)*, pages 145–153.

Daniel Zeman, Joakim Nivre, Mitchell Abrams, Elia Ackermann, Noëmi Aepli, Hamid Aghaei, Željko Agić, Amir Ahmadi, Lars Ahrenberg, Chika Kennedy Ajede, Salih Furkan Akkurt, Gabrielė Aleksandravičiūtė, Ika Alfina, Avner Algom, Khalid Alnajjar, Chiara Alzetta, Erik Andersen, Lene Antonsen, Tatsuya Aoyama, Katya Aplonova, Angelina Aquino, Carolina Aragon, Glyd Aranes, Maria Jesus Aranzabe, Bilge Nas Arıcan, Ĥórunn Arnardóttir, Gashaw Arutie, Jessica Naraiswari Arwidarasti, Masayuki Asahara, Katla Ásgeirsdóttir, Deniz Baran Aslan, Cengiz Asmazoğlu, Luma Ateyah, Furkan Atmaca, Mohammed Attia, Aitziber Atutxa, Liesbeth Augustinus, Mariana Avelãs, Elena Badmaeva, Keerthana Balasubramani, Miguel Ballesteros, Esha Banerjee, Sebastian Bank, Verginica Barbu Mititelu, Starkaður Barkarson, Rodolfo Basile, Victoria Basmov, Colin Batchelor, John Bauer, Seyyit Talha Bedir, Shabnam Behzad, Kepa Bengoetxea, İbrahim Benli, Yifat Ben Moshe, Gözde Berk, Riyaz Ahmad Bhat, Erica Biagetti, Eckhard Bick, Agnė Bielinskienė, Kristín Bjarnadóttir, Rogier Blokland, Victoria Bobicev, Loïc Boizou, Emanuel Borges Völker, Carl Börstell, Cristina Bosco, Gosse Bouma, Sam Bowman, Adriane Boyd, Anouck Braggaar, António Branco, Kristina Brokaitė, Aljoscha Burchardt, Marisa Campos, Marie Candito, Bernard Caron, Gauthier Caron, Catarina Carvalheiro, Rita Carvalho, Lauren Cassidy, Maria Clara Castro, Sérgio Castro, Tatiana Cavalcanti, Gülşen Cebiroğlu Eryiğit, Flavio Massimiliano Cecchini, Giuseppe G. A. Celano, Slavomír Čéplö, Neslihan Cesur, Savas Cetin, Özlem Çetinoğlu, Fabricio Chalub, Liyanage Chamila, Shweta Chauhan, Ethan Chi, Taishi Chika, Yongseok Cho, Jinho Choi, Jayeol Chun, Juyeon Chung, Alessandra T. Cignarella, Silvie Cinková, Aurélie Collomb, Çağrı Çöltekin, Miriam Connor, Daniela Corbetta, Francisco Costa, Marine Courtin, Mihaela Cristescu, Ingerid Løyning Dale, Philemon Daniel, Elizabeth Davidson, Leonel Figueiredo de Alencar, Mathieu Dehouck, Martina de Laurentiis, Marie-Catherine de Marneffe, Valeria de Paiva, Mehmet Oguz Derin, Elvis de Souza, Arantza Diaz de Ilarraza, Carly Dickerson, Arawinda Dinakaramani, Elisa Di Nuovo, Bamba Dione, Peter Dirix, Kaja Dobrovoljc, Adrian Doyle, Timothy Dozat, Kira Droganova, Puneet Dwivedi, Christian Ebert, Hanne Eckhoff, Masaki Eguchi, Sandra Eiche, Marhaba Eli, Ali Elkahky, Binyam Ephrem, Olga Erina, Tomaž Erjavec, Farah Essaidi, Aline Etienne, Wograine Evelyn, Sidney Facundes, Richárd Farkas, Federica Favero, Jannatul Ferdaousi, Marília Fernanda, Hector Fernandez Alcalde, Amal Fethi, Jennifer Foster, Cláudia Freitas, Kazunori Fujita, Katarína Gajdošová, Daniel Galbraith, Federica Gamba, Marcos Garcia, Moa Gärdenfors, Fabrício Ferraz Gerardi, Kim Gerdes, Luke Gessler, Filip Ginter, Gustavo Godoy, Iakes Goenaga, Koldo Gojenola, Memduh Gökırmak, Yoav Goldberg, Xavier Gómez Guinovart, Berta González Saavedra, Bernadeta Griciūtė, Matias Grioni, Loïc Grobol, Normunds Grūzītis, Bruno Guillaume, Céline Guillot-Barbance, Tunga Güngör, Nizar Habash, Hinrik Hafsteinsson, Jan Hajič, Jan Hajič jr., Mika Hämäläinen, Linh Hà Mỹ, Na-Rae Han, Muhammad Yudistira Hanifmuti, Takahiro Harada, Sam Hardwick, Kim Harris, Dag Haug, Johannes Heinecke, Oliver Hellwig, Felix Hennig, Barbora Hladká, Jaroslava Hlaváčová, Florinel Hociung, Petter Hohle, Marivel Huerta Mendez, Jena Hwang, Takumi Ikeda, Anton Karl Ingason, Radu Ion, Elena Irimia, Ọlájídé Ishola, Artan Islamaj, Kaoru Ito, Siratun Jannat, Tomáš Jelínek, Apoorva Jha, Katharine Jiang, Anders Johannsen, Hildur Jónsdóttir, Fredrik Jørgensen, Markus Juutinen, Hüner Kaşıkara, Nadezhda Kabaeva, Sylvain Kahane, Hiroshi Kanayama, Jenna Kanerva, Neslihan Kara, Ritván Karahóǧa, Andre Kåsen, Tolga Kayadelen, Sarveswaran Kengatharaiyer, Václava Kettnerová, Jesse Kirchner, Elena Klementieva, Elena Klyachko, Arne Köhn, Abdullatif Köksal, Kamil Kopacewicz, Timo Korkiakangas, Mehmet Köse, Alexey Koshevoy, Natalia Kotsyba, Jolanta Kovalevskaitė, Simon Krek, Parameswari Krishnamurthy, Sandra Kübler, Adrian Kuqi, Oğuzhan Kuyrukçu, Aslı Kuzgun, Sookyoung Kwak, Kris Kyle, Veronika Laippala, Lorenzo Lambertino, Tatiana Lando, Septina Dian Larasati, Alexei Lavrentiev, John Lee, Phuong Lê Hồng, Alessandro Lenci, Saran Lertpradit, Herman Leung, Maria Levina, Lauren Levine, Cheuk Ying Li, Josie Li, Keying Li, Yixuan Li, Yuan Li, KyungTae Lim, Bruna Lima Padovani, Yi-Ju Jessica Lin, Krister Lindén, Yang Janet Liu, Nikola Ljubešić, Olga Loginova, Stefano Lusito, Andry Luthfi, Mikko Luukko, Olga Lyashevskaya, Teresa Lynn, Vivien Macketanz, Menel Mahamdi, Jean Maillard, Ilya Makarchuk, Aibek Makazhanov, Michael Mandl, Christopher Manning, Ruli Manurung, Büşra Marşan, Cătălina Mărănduc, David Mareček, Katrin Marheinecke, Stella Markantonatou, Héctor Martínez Alonso, Lorena Martín Rodríguez, André Martins, Cláudia Martins, Jan Mašek, Hiroshi Matsuda, Yuji Matsumoto, Alessandro Mazzei, Ryan McDonald, Sarah McGuinness, Gustavo Mendonça, Tatiana Merzhevich, Niko Miekka, Aaron Miller, Karina Mischenkova, Anna Missilä, Cătălin Mititelu, Maria Mitrofan, Yusuke Miyao, AmirHossein Mojiri Foroushani, Judit Molnár, Amirsaeid Moloodi, Simonetta Montemagni, Amir More, Laura Moreno Romero, Giovanni Moretti, Shinsuke Mori, Tomohiko Morioka, Shigeki Moro, Bjartur Mortensen, Bohdan Moskalevskyi, Kadri Muischnek, Robert Munro, Yugo Murawaki, Kaili Müürisep, Pinkey Nainwani, Mariam Nakhlé, Juan Ignacio Navarro Horñiacek, Anna Nedoluzhko, Gunta Nešpore-Bērzkalne, Manuela Nevaci, Luong Nguyễn Thị, Huyền Nguyễn Thị Minh, Yoshihiro Nikaido, Vitaly Nikolaev, Rattima Nitisaroj, Alireza Nourian, Hanna Nurmi, Stina Ojala, Atul Kr. Ojha, Hulda Óladóttir, Adédayọ Olúòkun, Mai Omura, Emeka Onwuegbuzia, Noam Ordan, Petya Osenova, Robert Östling, Lilja Øvrelid, Şaziye Betül Özateş, Merve Özçelik, Arzucan Özgür, Balkız Öztürk Başaran, Teresa Paccosi, Alessio

Palmero Aprosio, Anastasia Panova, Hyunji Hayley Park, Niko Partanen, Elena Pascual, Marco Passarotti, Agnieszka Patejuk, Guilherme Paulino-Passos, Giulia Pedonese, Angelika Peljak-Łapińska, Siyao Peng, Siyao Logan Peng, Rita Pereira, Sílvia Pereira, Cenel-Augusto Perez, Natalia Perkova, Guy Perrier, Slav Petrov, Daria Petrova, Andrea Peverelli, Jason Phelan, Jussi Piitulainen, Yuval Pinter, Clara Pinto, Tommi A Pirinen, Emily Pitler, Magdalena Plamada, Barbara Plank, Thierry Poibeau, Larisa Ponomareva, Martin Popel, Lauma Pretkalniņa, Sophie Prévost, Prokopis Prokopidis, Adam Przepiórkowski, Robert Pugh, Tiina Puolakainen, Sampo Pyysalo, Peng Qi, Andreia Querido, Andriela Rääbis, Alexandre Rademaker, Mizanur Rahoman, Taraka Rama, Loganathan Ramasamy, Joana Ramos, Fam Rashel, Mohammad Sadegh Rasooli, Vinit Ravishankar, Livy Real, Petru Rebeja, Siva Reddy, Mathilde Regnault, Georg Rehm, Arij Riabi, Ivan Riabov, Michael Rießler, Erika Rimkutė, Larissa Rinaldi, Laura Rituma, Putri Rizqiyah, Luisa Rocha, Eiríkur Rögnvaldsson, Ivan Roksandic, Mykhailo Romanenko, Rudolf Rosa, Valentin Roșca, Davide Rovati, Ben Rozonoyer, Olga Rudina, Jack Rueter, Kristján Rúnarsson, Shoval Sadde, Pegah Safari, Aleksi Sahala, Shadi Saleh, Alessio Salomoni, Tanja Samardžić, Stephanie Samson, Manuela Sanguinetti, Ezgi Sanıyar, Dage Särg, Marta Sartor, Mitsuya Sasaki, Baiba Saulīte, Yanin Sawanakunanon, Shefali Saxena, Kevin Scannell, Salvatore Scarlata, Nathan Schneider, Sebastian Schuster, Lane Schwartz, Djamé Seddah, Wolfgang Seeker, Mojgan Seraji, Syeda Shahzadi, Mo Shen, Atsuko Shimada, Hiroyuki Shirasu, Yana Shishkina, Muh Shohibussirri, Maria Shvedova, Janine Siewert, Einar Freyr Sigurðsson, João Silva, Aline Silveira, Natalia Silveira, Sara Silveira, Maria Simi, Radu Simionescu, Katalin Simkó, Mária Šimková, Haukur Barri Símonarson, Kiril Simov, Dmitri Sitchinava, Ted Sither, Maria Skachedubova, Aaron Smith, Isabela Soares-Bastos, Per Erik Solberg, Barbara Sonnenhauser, Shafi Sourov, Rachele Sprugnoli, Vivian Stamou, Steinĥór Steingrímsson, Antonio Stella, Abishek Stephen, Milan Straka, Emmett Strickland, Jana Strnadová, Alane Suhr, Yogi Lesmana Sulestio, Umut Sulubacak, Shingo Suzuki, Daniel Swanson, Zsolt Szántó, Chihiro Taguchi, Dima Taji, Fabio Tamburini, Mary Ann C. Tan, Takaaki Tanaka, Dipta Tanaya, Mirko Tavoni, Samson Tella, Isabelle Tellier, Marinella Testori, Guillaume Thomas, Sara Tonelli, Liisi Torga, Marsida Toska, Trond Trosterud, Anna Trukhina, Reut Tsarfaty, Utku Türk, Francis Tyers, Sveinbjörn Ĥórðarson, Vilhjálmur Ĥorsteinsson, Sumire Uematsu, Roman Untilov, Zdeňka Urešová, Larraitz Uria, Hans Uszkoreit, Andrius Utka, Elena Vagnoni, Sowmya Vajjala, Socrates Vak, Rob van der Goot, Martine Vanhove, Daniel van Niekerk, Gertjan van Noord, Viktor Varga, Uliana Vedenina, Giulia Venturi, Veronika Vincze, Natalia Vlasova, Aya Wakasa, Joel C. Wallenberg, Lars Wallin, Abigail Walsh, Jonathan North Washington, Maximilan Wendt, Paul Widmer, Shira Wigderson, Sri Hartati Wijono, Seyi Williams, Mats Wirén, Christian Wittern, Tsegay Woldemariam, Tak-sum Wong, Alina Wróblewska, Mary Yako, Kayo Yamashita, Naoki Yamazaki, Chunxiao Yan, Koichi Yasuoka, Marat M. Yavrumyan, Arife Betül Yenice, Olcay Taner Yıldız, Zhuoran Yu, Arlisa Yuliawati, Zdeněk Žabokrtský, Shorouq Zahra, Amir Zeldes, He Zhou, Hanzhi Zhu, Yilun Zhu, Anna Zhuravleva, and Rayan Ziane. 2023. Universal dependencies 2.12. LINDAT/CLARIAH-CZ digital library at the Institute of Formal and Applied Linguistics (ÚFAL), Faculty of Mathematics and Physics, Charles University.

Appendix: Compounds annotated according to the current Universal Dependencies guidelines (left) vs. in line with the proposed annotation scheme (right)

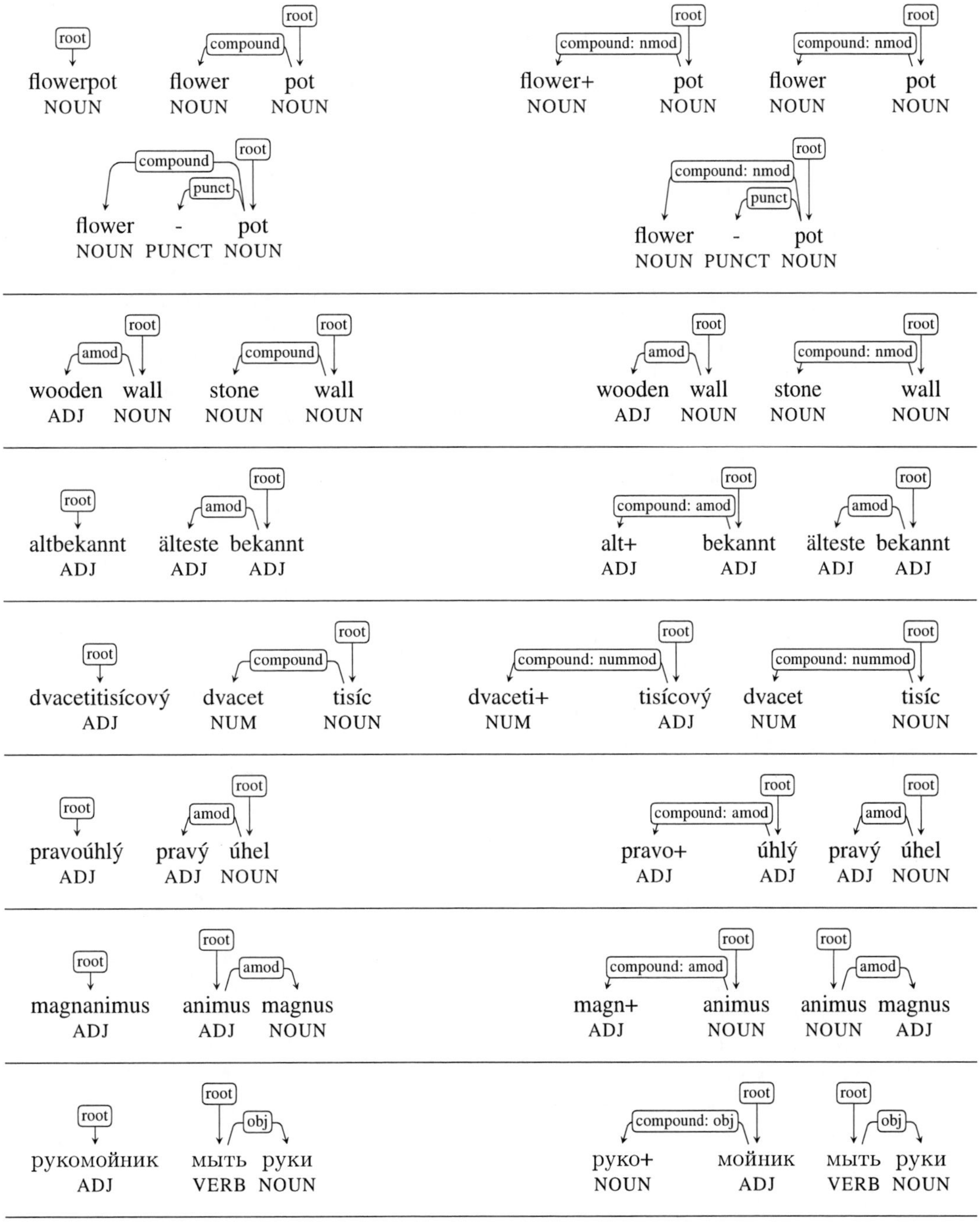

Predicting positive transfer for improved low-resource speech recognition using acoustic pseudo-tokens

Nay San[1], Georgios Paraskevopoulos[2], Aryaman Arora[1], Xiluo He[1], Prabhjot Kaur[3], Oliver Adams[4], Dan Jurafsky[1]
[1]Stanford University; [2]Athena Research Center; [3]Wayne State University; [4]Atos zData
nay.san@stanford.edu

Abstract

While massively multilingual speech models like wav2vec 2.0 XLSR-128 can be directly fine-tuned for automatic speech recognition (ASR), downstream performance can still be relatively poor on languages that are under-represented in the pre-training data. Continued pre-training on 70–200 hours of untranscribed speech in these languages can help — but what about languages without that much recorded data? For such cases, we show that supplementing the target language with data from a similar, higher-resource 'donor' language can help. For example, continued pretraining on only 10 hours of low-resource Punjabi supplemented with 60 hours of donor Hindi is almost as good as continued pretraining on 70 hours of Punjabi. By contrast, sourcing data from less similar donors like Bengali does not improve ASR performance. To inform donor language selection, we propose a novel similarity metric based on the sequence distribution of induced acoustic units: the Acoustic Token Distribution Similarity (ATDS). Across a set of typologically different target languages (Punjabi, Galician, Iban, Setswana), we show that the ATDS between the target language and its candidate donors precisely predicts target language ASR performance.

1 Introduction

For developing automatic speech recognition (ASR), 'low resource' languages are typically classified as such based on the availability of transcribed speech. Untranscribed speech, texts, or reliable metadata about the language are often assumed to be easily obtainable. This assumption may not hold true for under-described languages with little digital representation. For such languages, we are interested in two questions: 1) does leveraging untranscribed speech from a similar, higher-resource 'donor' language for pre-trained model adaptation help improve speech recognition in the target language, and 2) how do we select the best donor?

These questions are of interest as ASR system development with little transcribed speech has become viable with multilingual pre-trained transformer models for speech (e.g. wav2vec 2.0 XLSR-128: Babu et al., 2022). Yet, as most languages are under-represented in the pre-training data, directly fine-tuning these models for ASR in the target language can yield lower performance compared to their well-represented counterparts (Conneau et al., 2023). While recent studies have shown the effectiveness of continued pre-training to adapt these models to the target language (Nowakowski et al., 2023; Paraskevopoulos et al., 2024), they involved using 70–200 hours of target language data. For some languages, it may be quite difficult to source this much speech data — even untranscribed.

Thus, in our first set of experiments, we investigated whether supplementing target language data with data from another language could be a viable approach for model adaptation via continued pre-training (CPT). We selected Punjabi as our target language to establish top-line performance when sufficient data *is* available (70 hours, approximating the setup in Paraskevopoulos et al., 2024), along with a limited data baseline (when only 10 hours of Punjabi is available). We compared this baseline to supplementing the 10 hours of Punjabi with 60 hours of data from 8 other Indic languages (Indo-Aryan: Hindi, Urdu, Gujarati, Marathi, Bengali, Odia; Dravidian: Malayalam, Tamil). We fine-tuned each CPT-adapted model using the same 1 hour of transcribed Punjabi speech.

Results indicated that adding data from unrelated Dravidian languages (Malayalam, Tamil) or dissimilar Indo-Aryan languages (Bengali, Odia) yielded no better than baseline performance, 25% word error rate (WER). By contrast, we observed improved WERs from adding more similar languages (Marathi, Urdu, Gujarati, Hindi), with adding Hindi coming close to the 70-hour Punjabi top-line: 23.2% vs. 22.2%, respectively.

Proceedings of the 6th Workshop on Research in Computational Linguistic Typology and Multilingual NLP (SIGTYP 2024), pages 100–112
March 22, 2024

In our second set of experiments, we investigated how well measures of similarity between the target and donor languages predicted target language ASR performance. We found that commonly used measures based on external typological databases such as lang2vec (Littell et al., 2017) were not sufficiently fine-grained for our use case and, crucially, also varied with the quality/completeness of the available metadata for a given target language.

To sidestep these issues, we propose the **Acoustic Token Distribution Similarity** (ATDS), which measures the degree of similarity for two untranscribed speech corpora based on frequencies of occurrence of recurring acoustic-phonetic sequences. This measure extends Token Distribution Similarity (Gogoulou et al., 2023), shown to correlate with positive transfer in continued pre-training for text-based language models. To account for the text-/token-less nature of untranscribed speech corpora, we induce them in a bottom-up manner using wav2seq (Wu et al., 2023), a method for inducing pseudo-tokens using pre-trained speech embeddings. We compared the ASR performance from the Indic language experiments to various similarity measures and found that ATDS offered the most accurate ranking. Furthermore, ATDS correctly predicted the best donor language between two options for three non-Indic low-resource languages (Galician, Iban, and Setswana).[1]

In sum, the main contributions of this paper are: 1) a systematic study of pairwise transfer between languages in continued pre-training and its effects on target language ASR performance, and 2) the development, analysis, and first validation of ATDS — a fine-grained, bottom-up measure of acoustic-phonetic similarity to predict this ASR performance. To facilitate reproducibility and further research, we make available all our code, model checkpoints, and experimental artefacts.[2]

2 Background: wav2vec 2.0

In this section, we provide a high-level overview of the wav2vec 2.0 model and highlight specific details about its architecture and training objectives that will be relevant to our later discussions. Developed by Baevski et al. (2020), wav2vec 2.0 is a type of *self-supervised pre-trained transformer model*. In machine learning, supervised learning involves the use of human-generated labels (e.g. transcriptions), which can be time- and cost-intensive to create. In self-supervised pre-training, the goal is to first train the model on a proxy task for which it can derive its own labels, before the resulting model is adapted or 'fine-tuned' to the target task (e.g. ASR). Leveraging self-supervised pre-training has shown remarkable success across a variety of tasks when combined with a transformer-based model (Vaswani et al., 2017), which excels at learning how various units in a sequence co-occur (e.g. words in a sentence). Naturally, this has spurred on much experimentation for leveraging such models for low-resource ASR (e.g. Coto-Solano et al., 2022; Guillaume et al., 2022; Macaire et al., 2022; Bartelds et al., 2023).

As illustrated below in Figure 1, the wav2vec 2.0 architecture consists of three parts: 1) a convolutional feature extractor that extracts learnable features from strided frames in the audio input, 2) a quantiser which clusters the audio features into into a set of discrete code vectors (q_1, ..., q_5), and 3) a transformer attention network that learns context-enriched representations (h_1, ..., h_5). For self-supervised pre-training, the model is optimised using a joint contrastive loss and a diversity loss. The contrastive loss requires the model to use the neighbouring context to distinguish each masked frame amongst a set of negative distractors.[3] The diversity loss requires the model to make equal use of all code vectors, preventing the model from relying on a small subset which can lead to trivial/sub-optimal solutions.

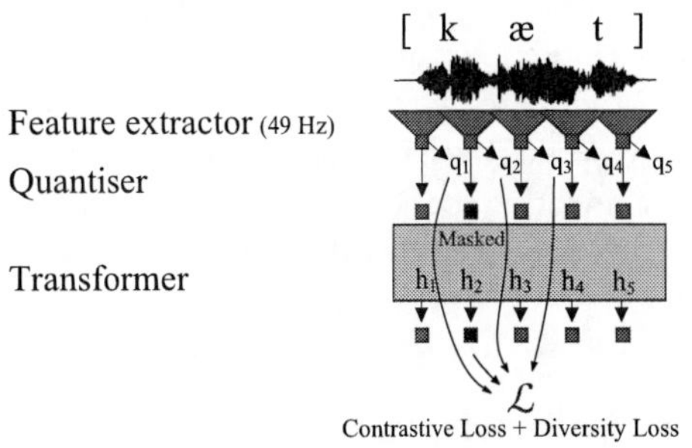

Figure 1: Illustration of the wav2vec 2.0 architecture. Adapted from Baevski et al. (2020).

We highlight here two important details relevant for our later discussions on acoustic tokens. The first is that the representations learned by the trans-

[1] Appendix B provides an overview of the languages.

[2] `https://github.com/fauxneticien/w2v2-cpt-transfer`

[3] A speech variant of a Cloze test: e.g. given "*The big ___ chased the small rat.*", select the correct answer from {*cat, rat, small*}.

former network are particularly useful for speech applications requiring fine-grained comparisons of acoustic-phonetic content, e.g. speech information retrieval (San et al., 2021), second language pronunciation scoring (Bartelds et al., 2022; Richter and Guðnason, 2023), spoken dialect classification (Bartelds and Wieling, 2022; Guillaume et al., 2023) — particularly those learned by the middle layers of the transformer network (e.g. layers 12–16 of a 24-layer network).

The second detail is that these representations are encoded as vectors in a high-dimensional latent space and emitted at a rate of 49 Hz. Combined with the diversity loss that requires exploration of this space, there is a many-to-many relationship between phonetic categories and these vectors — both in the latent space and in time. For example, as illustrated in Figure 1, a single speech sound such as [æ] may last for three time steps (yielding h_2, h_3, h_4). The first two vectors (h_2, h_3) may be very close in the latent space, as they map to the start of [æ] sounds while the third h_4 may map to [æ] sounds preceding [t] and is thus located in a different part of the latent space. Thus to derive phone-like tokens from these representations, we must group them in the latent space (e.g. using k-means clustering) and then again in time according to how the grouped units themselves routinely co-occur (e.g. using subword modelling).

In this way, the goal of tokenisation for both text and speech is driven by the need to derive units of a practical granularity based on the nature of the input: from coarser-grained words to finer-grained sub-words in text and, inversely, finer-grained sub-phones to coarser-grained phones in speech. We return to these two details in our development of the Acoustic Token Distribution Similarity measure for comparing the acoustic-phonetic similarity of two untranscribed speech corpora.

3 A systematic study of pairwise transfer

3.1 Motivation

Since the release of the original English wav2vec 2.0 model pre-trained on the 960 hour LibriSpeech corpus (Panayotov et al., 2015), additional massively multi-lingual variants have also been developed: XLSR-53, pre-trained on 56k hours from 53 languages (Conneau et al., 2021); XLSR-128, pre-trained on 436k hours from 128 languages (Babu et al., 2022); and MMS, pre-trained on 491k hours from 1,406 languages (Pratap et al., 2023). In each case, the vast majority of the pre-training data is drawn from European language sources.

Given the under-represented nature of most languages in these wav2vec 2.0 models, several studies have investigated continued pre-training (CPT) to adapt them for target languages (e.g. Javed et al., 2022; DeHaven and Billa, 2022; Nowakowski et al., 2023; Bartelds et al., 2023; Paraskevopoulos et al., 2024). Nowakowski et al. (2023) adapted the XLSR-53 model using 200 hours of Ainu. Using the same 40 minutes of transcribed Ainu for ASR fine-tuning, they found that the adapted model resulted in a 8.8% absolute word error rate (WER) decrease over the off-the-shelf XLSR-53 model. For many low resource languages, however, obtaining 200 hours of speech data may not be feasible.

In their study of unsupervised domain adaptation for Greek, Paraskevopoulos et al. (2024) found adapting the XLSR-53 model via CPT using a small 12-hour dataset of Greek read speech to be ineffective. However, they found that successful CPT-based adaptation could be achieved with the use of multi-domain data, e.g. 12 hours of read speech mixed with 70 hours of newscasts. Given these findings, we were motivated to investigate whether comparable results could be achieved by supplementing target language data with data from another language.

3.2 Method

3.2.1 Model training

As our primary interest was in examining how downstream ASR performance is affected by the dataset(s) used in continued pre-training (CPT), we carried out nearly identical experiments as those in Nowakowski et al. (2023) by obtaining their configuration file for wav2vec 2.0 pre-training using the official fairseq library.[4] Similarly, we follow the official fine-tuning recipe suitable for 1 hour of transcriptions. For both procedures, we made modifications to suit our hardware configuration and compute budget, as detailed in Appendix A.

3.2.2 Data

For a systematic investigation of how downstream ASR performance in a given target language varies with the choice of donor language added during CPT, we required a dataset with some specific characteristics: a) contains a variety of both similar and dissimilar languages with, b) at least 60 hours

[4] https://github.com/facebookresearch/fairseq

per language, c) and collected in relatively similar acoustic conditions, and d) not have already been used in the original pre-training process. Accordingly, for this set of experiments, we sourced data from IndicSUPERB (Javed et al., 2023), a dataset of 12 Indic languages containing 65–180 hours of read speech per language (Indo-Aryan: Bengali, Gujarati, Hindi, Marathi, Odia, Punjabi, Sanskrit, Urdu; Dravidian: Kannada, Malayalam, Tamil, Telugu).

Amongst these 12 IndicSUPERB languages, we selected Punjabi as our target language as it is relatively low-resourced (cf. Hindi, Tamil), its geographical and typological location (yielding a variety of closer and farther geographic/typological distances to the others), and also native speaker-linguist expertise on our research team for data validation and error analysis.

As illustrated below in Figure 2, we began by selecting for our top-line condition a random 70h subset of Punjabi from the total 136h available in IndicSUPERB, and then from this subset a random 10h selection for our baseline, and again a random 1h subset for fine-tuning. We also selected a random 1h validation and 2h test set both disjoint from each other and any data to be used for pre-training.

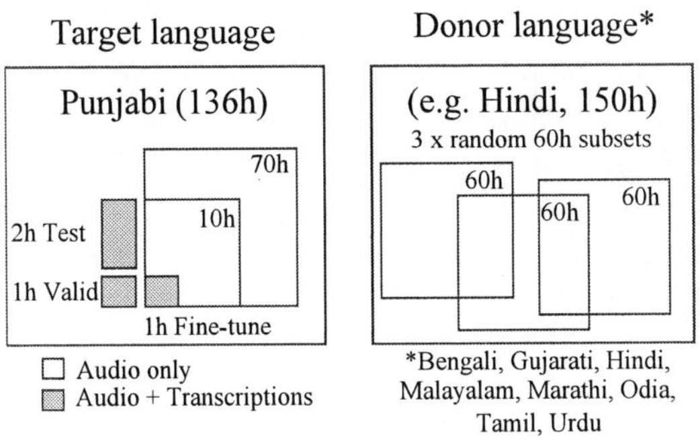

Figure 2: Data selection for transfer experiments

Additionally, for each donor language (Bengali, Gujarati, Hindi, Malayalam, Marathi, Odia, Tamil, Urdu), we created three random 60h subsets. Given the total amounts of data available in IndicSUPERB for each language (e.g. 87h for Urdu but 129h for Gujarati), there is however some unavoidable overlap between these subsets for each language (i.e. they are not disjoint 60h splits). Using each of the 60h subsets, we conducted 3 separate CPT runs per language to obtain estimates for both within- and between-donor language differences on downstream ASR performance.

3.3 Results and discussion

Compared to directly fine-tuning the XLSR-128 model, adapting the model first via continued pre-training (CPT) with 70 hours of Punjabi yields a large improvement in downstream ASR performance (unadapted 30.8% vs. 22.2% CPT-adapted, 70h). This constitutes an absolute WER difference of 8.6% and is consistent with improvements reported in previous CPT experiments (Nowakowski et al., 2023; Paraskevopoulos et al., 2024). We found that model adaptation with only 10 hours of Punjabi still yielded an appreciable improvement over the unadapted model: 5.8% absolute (unadapted 30.8% vs. 25.0% CPT-adapted, 10h).

We now turn to our experiment conditions in which 10h of Punjabi is supplemented with 60h of data from another language. As summarised below in Table 1, the effects of donor language on Punjabi ASR performance can be divided into roughly three strata. In the bottom stratum (E3), we find unrelated Dravidian languages (Tamil, Malayalam) or dissimilar Indo-Aryan languages (Bengali, Odia). When data from these languages are added during CPT, we find no meaningful difference compared to using only 10 hours of Punjabi (WERR: -0.8–0.0%).

In the middle stratum (E2), we find relatively similar Indo-Aryan languages (Marathi, Gujarati, Urdu). When data from these languages are added, we find modest improvements over using only 10 hours of Punjabi (WERR: 1.6–2.4%). In the top stratum (E1), we find Hindi — the most similar Indo-Aryan language amongst our candidate donors. When data from Hindi is added, we find a large improvement over using only 10 hours of Punjabi (WERR: 6.0%). In fact, adding the 60h of Hindi results in ASR performance that is in absolute terms close to the 70h Punjabi topline: 23.5% vs. 22.2%, respectively.

We have established that there are observable differences in target language ASR performance that vary with the donor language added during continued pre-training and that these differences appear to align with qualitative notions of language similarity. In the next section, we investigate quantitative measures of similarity and evaluate their correlations to these observed differences.

4 A bottom-up approach to similarity

4.1 Motivation

A common method for calculating similarities between languages is to use language vectors from the

Condition	Test set WER (WERR)		Data for continued pre-training
	Median	Range	
T. In-domain top-line	22.2 (11.2%)	-	70h Punjabi
E1. Most similar	**23.5 (6.0%)**	23.4–23.8	10h Punjabi + 60h Hindi
E2. Similar	24.4 (2.4%)	24.3–24.5	10h Punjabi + 60h Urdu
	24.4 (2.4%)	24.2–24.4	10h Punjabi + 60h Gujarati
	24.6 (1.6%)	24.5–24.7	10h Punjabi + 60h Marathi
B. Only target data baseline	25.0	-	10h Punjabi
E3. Unrelated/dissimilar	25.0 (0.0%)	25.0–25.2	10h Punjabi + 60h Odia
	25.1 (-0.4%)	25.0–25.4	10h Punjabi + 60h Tamil
	25.1 (-0.4%)	25.0–25.3	10h Punjabi + 60h Malayalam
	25.2 (-0.8%)	25.1–25.2	10h Punjabi + 60h Bengali
U. Unadapted XLSR-128	30.8 (-23.2%)	-	-

Table 1: Automatic speech recognition (ASR) results from fine-tuning wav2vec 2.0 XLSR-128 (Babu et al., 2022) with and without adaptation via continued pre-training (CPT). CPT-adapted models were trained for 10k updates using 70 hours of Punjabi for the topline (T), 10 hours of Punjabi for the baseline (B), and 10 hours of Punjabi combined with 60 hours of data from another language for the experiment conditions (E1, E2, E3). All models were fine-tuned with the same 1 hour of Punjabi data. ASR performance reported in word error rate (WER) and relative word error rates (WERR), relative to the 10 hour CPT baseline (B). For each experiment condition, median and range were obtained from 3 CPT runs per language with different donor data in each run.

lang2vec database (Littell et al., 2017), which itself draws on other databases (e.g. phonological information from WALS: Haspelmath, 2009). Wu et al. (2021) investigated how well measures based on lang2vec and other data sources correlated with successful transfer learning for ASR. Of the lang2vec similarity metrics, they found that genetic and geographic measures correlated highly with better ASR performance but, surprisingly, inventory and phonological measures did not. Acoustic similarities as derived from embeddings of a pre-trained spoken language identification model were also found to correlate strongly with better ASR performance. In the context of continued pre-training, we questioned whether the to-be-adapted model could be used for this purpose.

Investigating an analogous question in the text domain, Gogoulou et al. (2023) evaluated various measures for predicting transfer characteristics for transformer language models initially pre-trained on one language (e.g. English) and subsequently adapted to another (e.g. Icelandic), and how these characteristics varied according to the distributions of data in the respective language corpora. They propose a novel metric: the Token Distribution Similarity (TDS), which correlated with positive transfer. As illustrated below in Figure 3 (a), the TDS is derived by 1) using the pre-trained model's tokeniser to process a sample of data from each language, 2) then generating a token frequency vector for each language, and 3) taking the cosine similarity between these two vectors. Given these promising results for predicting positive cross-lingual transfer for continued pre-training on text, we investigated whether they extended to the speech domain.

4.2 Induction and analysis of acoustic tokens

In order to compute token distribution similarity for two untranscribed speech corpora, we first need to 'tokenise' the corpora. For this purpose, we can leverage speech representations extracted using a middle transformer layer (e.g. Layer 12 of 24) of a pre-trained wav2vec 2.0 model such as XLSR-128. As previously highlighted above (in §2), these representations are useful for fine-grained comparisons of acoustic-phonetic content and, to make use for these representations for inducing phone-like tokens, they must first be grouped in the high-dimensional latent space and then again in time based on their co-occurrences.

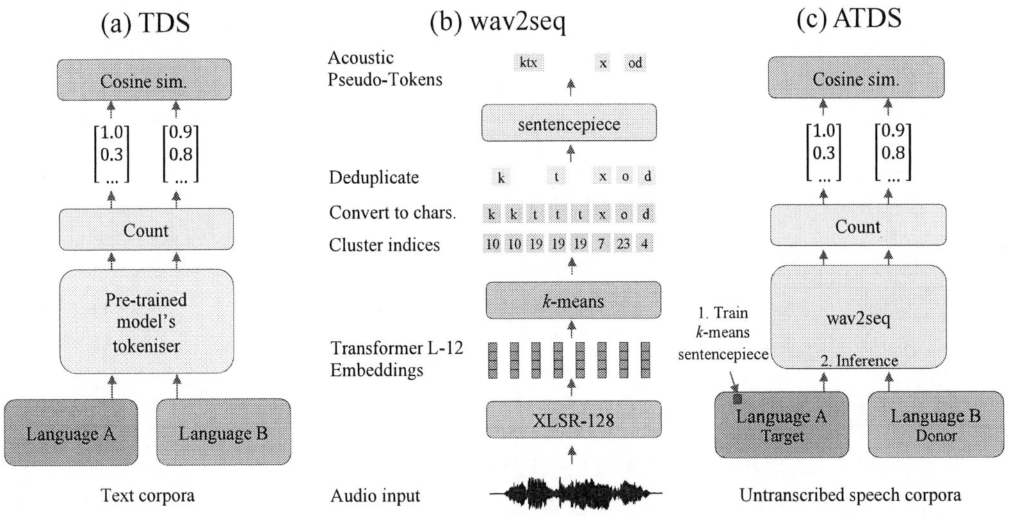

Figure 3: Derivation of the Acoustic Token Distribution Similarity (ATDS) measure for predicting positive transfer between two languages resulting from continued pre-training (CPT) of a pre-trained speech model (e.g. XLSR-128). ATDS extends to the speech domain the concept of Token Distribution Similarity (TDS: Gogoulou et al., 2023), shown to predict positive transfer for CPT in the text domain. To account for the token-less nature of untranscribed speech, pseudo-tokens are derived using the wav2seq process proposed by Wu et al. (2023). As is the case for text tokenisation, the goal is to derive units of practical granularity based on the raw input. While typical text tokenisation sub-divides words into sub-words (e.g. *eating* $\rightarrow$ *eat,ing*), the analogous process for raw speech data involves grouping sub-frames into more phone-like units: first based on featural similarity (e.g. using a k-means model on embeddings) then again based on distributional similarity (e.g. using a sub-word modelling).

Accordingly, we use the wav2seq procedure proposed by Wu et al. (2023).[5] As illustrated below in Figure 3 (b), the first step is using a pre-trained model (e.g. XLSR-128) to extract speech embeddings from a transformer layer. The second step involves training a *k*-means model to cluster these embeddings (i.e. group similar sounds together). The cluster indices are converted to characters (by a simple Unicode table lookup, e.g.10→*k*, 19→*t*, etc.) and then deduplicated. To discover frequently occurring sound sequences, the third step involves using these character strings to train a subword model (e.g. via sentencepiece: Kudo and Richardson, 2018). Once these models are trained on a subset of the corpus, they are used to derive pseudo-tokens for the rest of the corpus and, in our application, also for candidate donor corpora.

To discover whether these pseudo-tokens exhibited both within- and cross-language consistency, we conducted an analysis using the Punjabi and Hindi datasets of the CommonVoice corpus (Ardila et al., 2019), for which forced-aligned phoneme labels are available in the VoxCommunis corpus (Ahn and Chodroff, 2022). For this analysis, we trained the *k*-means and subword models on Punjabi (the target language) and then induced pseudo-tokens for both Punjabi and Hindi.[6]

Results of our analyses revealed that the most frequent pseudo-token in Punjabi, t_1, consistently corresponded to the /ɑ/ label, i.e. $P(/\text{ɑ}/|t_1) = 0.69$. Similarly, we found that t_2 consistently corresponded to high-back vowels: i.e. $P(/\text{o}/|t_2) = 0.56$, $P(/\text{u}/|t_2) = 0.18$, $P(/\text{ʊ}/|t_2) = 0.09$. For Hindi, we found that t_2 also consistently corresponded to the same vowel labels, while t_1 consistently corresponded to /aː/ — also a low vowel. Such minor differences are likely attributable to VoxCommunis labels being automatically derived via grapheme-to-phoneme conversion and thus do not represent narrow phonetic transcriptions. Given their broad categorical consistency, these tokens may be useful for cross-language comparisons.

4.3 Acoustic Token Distribution Similarity

We propose the *Acoustic* Token Distribution Similarity (ATDS) measure, which, as illustrated above in Figure 3 (c), is a straightforward composition of

[5]Originally developed for inducing pseudo-tokens for use in a self-supervised pseudo speech recognition task for jointly pre-training a speech encoder and text decoder.

[6]Appendix A details the analysis procedure.

<table>
<tr><th colspan="11">Punjabi (PAN)</th></tr>
<tr><th rowspan="3"></th><th rowspan="3">Donor Lang.</th><th rowspan="3">Median WERR (of 3 runs)</th><th colspan="8">Similarity Measure</th></tr>
<tr><th rowspan="2">ATDS</th><th rowspan="2">SB</th><th colspan="6">lang2vec</th></tr>
<tr><th>Syn.</th><th>Geo.</th><th>Feat.</th><th>Inv.</th><th>Gen.</th><th>Phon.</th></tr>
<tr><td>E1.</td><td>Hindi</td><td>6.0</td><td>0.96</td><td>0.96</td><td>0.67</td><td rowspan="2">1.0*</td><td rowspan="4">0.6</td><td>0.67</td><td>0.38</td><td>0.41</td></tr>
<tr><td rowspan="3">E2.</td><td>Gujarati</td><td>2.4</td><td>0.93</td><td>0.82</td><td>0.46</td><td>0.72</td><td rowspan="3">0.43</td><td rowspan="3">1.0*</td></tr>
<tr><td>Urdu</td><td>2.4</td><td>0.93</td><td>0.88</td><td>0.51</td><td rowspan="6">0.9</td><td>0.67</td></tr>
<tr><td>Marathi</td><td>1.6</td><td>0.92</td><td>0.89</td><td rowspan="2">0.47</td><td>0.65</td></tr>
<tr><td rowspan="4">E3.</td><td>Bengali</td><td>-0.8</td><td>0.90</td><td>0.81</td><td rowspan="4">0.5</td><td>0.66</td><td>0.38</td><td>0.38</td></tr>
<tr><td>Malayalam</td><td>-0.4</td><td>0.89</td><td>0.83</td><td rowspan="2">0.32</td><td>0.64</td><td>0.00</td><td rowspan="3">1.0*</td></tr>
<tr><td>Odia</td><td>0.0</td><td>0.87</td><td>0.71</td><td>0.65</td><td>0.43</td></tr>
<tr><td>Tamil</td><td>-0.4</td><td>0.86</td><td>0.76</td><td>0.47</td><td>0.59</td><td>0.00</td></tr>
<tr><td colspan="3">Correlation of measure to WERR:</td><td>0.89</td><td>0.78</td><td>0.79</td><td>0.77</td><td>0.83</td><td>0.55</td><td>0.48</td><td>-0.31</td></tr>
</table>

Table 2: Acoustic Token Distribution Similarity (ATDS) measure between Punjabi and donor language predicts downstream speech recognition performance as measured by relative word error rate (WERR) when fine-tuning the wav2vec 2.0 XLSR-128 model adapted using continued pre-training (CPT) on 10 hours of target and 60 hours of donor language speech. Other similarity measures for comparison are derived embeddings of the SpeechBrain language identification model and from the lang2vec database (syntactic, geographic, featural, inventory, genetic, and phonological). * indicate erroneous similarity scores resulting from identical, imputed vectors within the database. Correlations (Pearson's r) calculated using 24 data points (8 donor languages x 3 CPT runs per language with different donor data in each run).

wav2seq (Wu et al., 2023) and Token Distribution Similarity (TDS: Gogoulou et al., 2023). We provide two analyses showing that the ATDS between a target language and its candidate donors precisely predicts downstream ASR performance in the target language resulting from continued pre-training of a speech model on target and donor data.

In our first analysis, we examined how well ATDS can account for the results of the Indic language experiments and how ATDS compares to other measures. Accordingly, for ATDS, we trained the relevant wav2seq models on Punjabi (the target language), induced tokens on Punjabi and all donor languages, then calculated the token frequency vectors and computed the pairwise cosine similarities. Similar to Wu et al. (2021), we also computed similarities using lang2vec and corpus-level means of utterance-level embeddings extracted using a pre-trained spoken language identification model (SpeechBrain: Ravanelli et al., 2021).

Results of this analysis revealed that the two bottom-up acoustic measures provide overall a finer-grained ranking than top-down lang2vec measures. For example, as shown above in Table 2 Feat. (a combination of all lang2vec data sources), the featural similarity, splits the four languages into two groups: similar (0.6: Hindi–Marathi) and dissimilar (0.5: Bengali–Tamil). Additionally, we also found erroneous, perfect similarity values (1.0), resulting from identical language vectors for the category (e.g. Phon.: Marathi-Punjabi), likely an artefact of data imputation. These results demonstrate that while top-down data may be suitable for more noise-tolerant applications (e.g. large-scale typological comparisons), they may not be well suited for helping select donors for a specific under-described target language if the relevant metadata is unavailable or inaccurate.

While both acoustic measures accurately select Hindi as the most suitable donor, ATDS provides a better ranking of the donor languages. As shown in Table 2 (SB), the measure based on SpeechBrain embeddings ranks Gujarati as being as dissimilar to Punjabi as Bengali/Malayalam. We make a similar observation as above that using embeddings from a different pre-trained model than the one to be adapted via CPT risks adding unwanted noise to an inherently hard task. Leveraging the representations of the pre-trained model to be adapted reduces this risk, reflected in ASR improvement being most correlated with ATDS ($r = 0.89$).

In our second analysis, we examined whether the ATDS measure generalised beyond the Indic languages through identical CPT experiments on a typologically varied set of target languages. We selected triplets of languages consisting of 1) a target language, 2) a language more similar to the target as measured by ATDS, and 3) another language

	Galician (GLG)		Iban (IBA)		Setswana (TSN)	
		WER (WERR)		WER (WERR)		WER (WERR)
E1.	SPA (0.96) 10h GLG + 60h SPA	**13.7 (8.7%)**	ZSM (0.91) 7h IBA + 60h ZSM	**15.9 (4.2%)**	SOT (0.96) 10h TSN + 56h SOT	**11.6 (7.9%)**
E2.	POR (0.89) 10h GLG + 60h POR	13.9 (7.3%)	IND (0.88) 7h IBA + 60h IND	16.4 (1.2%)	NSO (0.88) 10h TSN + 56h NSO	12.0 (4.8%)
B.	10h GLG	15.0	7h IBA	16.6	10h TSN	12.6
U.	-	15.4 (-2.7%)	-	21.4 (-28.9%)	-	20.8 (-65.1%)

Table 3: Validation of the Acoustic Token Distribution Similarity (ATDS) measure for predicting target language automatic speech recognition (ASR) performance as a result of continued pre-training (CPT) of the wav2vec 2.0 XLSR-128 model using mix target and donor language data. For each target language (Galician, Iban, Setswana), U. indicates ASR performance from using the unadapted XLSR-128 model, B. indicates performance from CPT adaptation with only target language data (7–10 hours), and E1–E2 using target language data supplemented with 56–60 hours of donor language data. Parentheses next to donor language names indicate ATDS to the target language. Percentages within parentheses indicate relative word error rate (WERR), relative the baseline word error rate (B) within the same column. Donor language codes are: Spanish (SPA), Portuguese (POR), Malay (ZSM), Indonesian (IND), Sesotho (SOT), Sepedi (NSO).

relatively farther. As summarised below in Table 3, the target languages were Galician (West-Iberian), Iban (Malayic), and Setswana (Sotho–Tswana). For Galician, ATDS predicted that Spanish (SPA: 0.96) was more similar than Portuguese (POR: 0.89); for Iban, Malay (ZSM: 0.91) more than Indonesian (IND: 0.88); and for Setswana, Sesotho (SOT: 0.96) more than Sepedi (NSO: 0.88).

Results of these CPT experiments are summarised below in Table 3. We first note the large difference between Galician and the other languages in the improvement yielded by CPT baselines (B) compared to fine-tuning the unadapted XLSR-128 (U). As we sourced Galician data from CommonVoice (on which XLSR-128 was already pre-trained), CPT yields little further gain (U. 15.4% vs. B. 15.0%). By contrast, ASR performance was much improved via CPT adaptation for both Iban (U. 21.4% vs. B. 16.6%) and Setswana (U. 20.8% vs. B. 12.6%). These results constitute further evidence that directly fine-tuning massively multilingual models can yield sub-optimal performance for under-represented languages and that continued pre-training can help close this performance gap.

We found that the ATDS predictions are borne out for all three target languages (even for Galician in spite of relatively reduced benefits). As shown above in Table 3 for each of the target language columns (Galician, Iban, Setswana), larger improvements in target language ASR performance are observed as a result of continued pre-training on target language data supplemented with data from a more similar language as measured by ATDS than a less similar one (respectively, rows E1. vs. E2). Combined with results for Punjabi above, our findings altogether provide strong evidence for the effectiveness of ATDS for predicting positive transfer between target and donor languages for CPT-based model adaptation.

5 Limitations and future directions

We limited the scope of this paper to exploring the transfer between languages and as such used the standard wav2vec 2.0 pre-training recipe for model adaptation. We acknowledge that this requires a large compute budget beyond what is affordable in many low resource scenarios. In future, we hope to investigate whether or to what extent transfer learning can be combined with more compute-efficient adaptation methods.

To conduct a systematic study of pairwise transfer, we used domain-matched, high-quality ASR datasets containing mostly read speech and only examined sourcing data from a single donor language. Questions relating to multi-donor and multi-domain transfer and how such interactions affect downstream performance in the target language will need to be addressed in future research.

6 Conclusion

For developing automatic speech recognition (ASR) systems for languages with very few resources, we demonstrated that massively multilingual pre-trained models for speech can be successfully adapted via continued pre-training using a mix of data from the target language and supplemental data from a similar, higher-resource 'donor' language. Additionally, we motivate and propose the Acoustic Token Distribution Similarity (ATDS) — a novel measure of similarity to predict positive transfer between a donor and target language. Across a set of typologically different target languages (Punjabi, Galician, Iban, Setswana), we show that the ATDS between the target language and its candidate donors precisely predicts target language ASR performance.

We attribute this predictive capability of ATDS to leveraging the knowledge of the pre-trained model to be adapted, its inductive biases and training objectives, and the distributions within the candidate datasets that will be used to adapt it. It is indeed expected that this measure then is able to predict downstream task improvements better than measures based on other models or external information — the latter of which is not always available or reliable for under-described languages. Given the high cost associated with continued pre-training, however, we argue that using a well-calibrated, task-specific measure minimises the chance of costly, unexpected outcomes.

We make a final observation here that various target-donor language pairs where we observed successful transfer exist in linguistic situations with significant, sustained contact. For example, Galician is a minoritised language in Spain and virtually all Galician speakers are bilingual in Spanish (de la Fuente Iglesias and Pérez Castillejo, 2020). Similarly, Macaire et al. (2022) report that fine-tuning a model pre-trained on French was particularly successful for Gwadloupéyen and Morisien, two French-based creole languages. These findings suggest that to develop truly inclusive speech technologies in a resource efficient manner, what will be required is a nuanced understanding of what factors linguistic and non-linguistic yield sufficiently high levels of cross-lingual similarity which in turn permit positive transfer.

Acknowledgements

We thank Karol Nowakowski for helpful correspondence and also making available experiment configuration files. We thank Tolúlọpẹ́ Ògúnrẹ̀mí for assistance with using the Stanford NLP cluster as well as Stanford UIT for providing Google Cloud research credits, both without which extensive continued pre-training experiments would not have been possible. We are very grateful for support from both Alexis Michaud at the Centre National de la Recherche Scientifique (CNRS, France) and the Institut des langues rares (ILARA) at École Pratique des Hautes Études. We are thankful for the continued support from Dr. Weisong Shi from University of Delaware.

References

Emily Ahn and Eleanor Chodroff. 2022. VoxCommunis: A corpus for cross-linguistic phonetic analysis. In *Proceedings of the Thirteenth Language Resources and Evaluation Conference*, pages 5286–5294, Marseille, France. European Language Resources Association.

Rosana Ardila, Megan Branson, Kelly Davis, Michael Henretty, Michael Kohler, Josh Meyer, Reuben Morais, Lindsay Saunders, Francis M Tyers, and Gregor Weber. 2019. Common voice: A massively-multilingual speech corpus. *arXiv preprint arXiv:1912.06670*.

Arun Babu, Changhan Wang, Andros Tjandra, Kushal Lakhotia, Qiantong Xu, Naman Goyal, Kritika Singh, Patrick von Platen, Yatharth Saraf, Juan Pino, Alexei Baevski, Alexis Conneau, and Michael Auli. 2022. XLS-R: Self-supervised Cross-lingual Speech Representation Learning at Scale. In *Proc. Interspeech 2022*, pages 2278–2282.

Alexei Baevski, Yuhao Zhou, Abdelrahman Mohamed, and Michael Auli. 2020. wav2vec 2.0: A framework for self-supervised learning of speech representations. *Advances in neural information processing systems*, 33:12449–12460.

Etienne Barnard, Marelie H Davel, Charl van Heerden, Febe De Wet, and Jaco Badenhorst. 2014. The NCHLT speech corpus of the South African languages. Workshop Spoken Language Technologies for Under-resourced Languages (SLTU).

Martijn Bartelds, Wietse de Vries, Faraz Sanal, Caitlin Richter, Mark Liberman, and Martijn Wieling. 2022. Neural representations for modeling variation in speech. *Journal of Phonetics*, 92:101137.

Martijn Bartelds, Nay San, Bradley McDonnell, Dan Jurafsky, and Martijn Wieling. 2023. Making more of little data: Improving low-resource automatic speech recognition using data augmentation. In *Proceedings of the 61st Annual Meeting of the Association for Computational Linguistics (Volume 1: Long Papers)*, pages 715–729, Toronto, Canada. Association for Computational Linguistics.

Martijn Bartelds and Martijn Wieling. 2022. Quantifying language variation acoustically with few resources. In *Proceedings of the 2022 Conference of the North American Chapter of the Association for Computational Linguistics: Human Language Technologies*, pages 3735–3741, Seattle, United States. Association for Computational Linguistics.

Alexis Conneau, Alexei Baevski, Ronan Collobert, Abdelrahman Mohamed, and Michael Auli. 2021. Unsupervised Cross-Lingual Representation Learning for Speech Recognition. In *Proc. Interspeech 2021*, pages 2426–2430.

Alexis Conneau, Min Ma, Simran Khanuja, Yu Zhang, Vera Axelrod, Siddharth Dalmia, Jason Riesa, Clara Rivera, and Ankur Bapna. 2023. Fleurs: Few-shot learning evaluation of universal representations of speech. In *2022 IEEE Spoken Language Technology Workshop (SLT)*, pages 798–805. IEEE.

Rolando Coto-Solano, Sally Akevai Nicholas, Samiha Datta, Victoria Quint, Piripi Wills, Emma Ngakuravaru Powell, Liam Koka'ua, Syed Tanveer, and Isaac Feldman. 2022. Development of automatic speech recognition for the documentation of Cook Islands Māori. In *Proceedings of the Thirteenth Language Resources and Evaluation Conference*, pages 3872–3882, Marseille, France. European Language Resources Association.

Monica de la Fuente Iglesias and Susana Pérez Castillejo. 2020. Phonetic interactions in the bilingual production of Galician and Spanish /e/ and /o/. *International Journal of Bilingualism*, 24(2):305–318.

Mitchell DeHaven and Jayadev Billa. 2022. Improving low-resource speech recognition with pretrained speech models: Continued pretraining vs. semi-supervised training. *arXiv preprint arXiv:2207.00659*.

John S. Garofolo, Lori F. Lamel, William M. Fisher, Jonathan G. Fiscus, David S. Pallett, Nancy L. Dahlgren, and Victor Zue. 1993. TIMIT Acoustic-Phonetic Continuous Speech Corpus. Web Download.

Evangelia Gogoulou, Timothée Lesort, Magnus Boman, and Joakim Nivre. 2023. A study of continual learning under language shift. *arXiv preprint arXiv:2311.01200*.

Séverine Guillaume, Guillaume Wisniewski, Cécile Macaire, Guillaume Jacques, Alexis Michaud, Benjamin Galliot, Maximin Coavoux, Solange Rossato, Minh-Châu Nguyên, and Maxime Fily. 2022. Fine-tuning pre-trained models for automatic speech recognition, experiments on a fieldwork corpus of Japhug (Trans-Himalayan family). In *Proceedings of the Fifth Workshop on the Use of Computational Methods in the Study of Endangered Languages*, pages 170–178.

Séverine Guillaume, Guillaume Wisniewski, and Alexis Michaud. 2023. From 'Snippet-lects' to Doculects and Dialects: Leveraging Neural Representations of Speech for Placing Audio Signals in a Language Landscape . In *Proc. 2nd Annual Meeting of the ELRA/ISCA SIG on Under-resourced Languages (SIGUL 2023)*, pages 29–33.

Martin Haspelmath. 2009. The typological database of the world atlas of language structures. *The Use of Databases in Cross-Linguistic Studies*, 41:283.

Tahir Javed, Kaushal Bhogale, Abhigyan Raman, Pratyush Kumar, Anoop Kunchukuttan, and Mitesh M. Khapra. 2023. IndicSUPERB: A speech processing universal performance benchmark for Indian languages. In *Proceedings of the Thirty-Seventh AAAI Conference on Artificial Intelligence and Thirty-Fifth Conference on Innovative Applications of Artificial Intelligence and Thirteenth Symposium on Educational Advances in Artificial Intelligence*, AAAI'23/IAAI'23/EAAI'23. AAAI Press.

Tahir Javed, Sumanth Doddapaneni, Abhigyan Raman, Kaushal Santosh Bhogale, Gowtham Ramesh, Anoop Kunchukuttan, Pratyush Kumar, and Mitesh M. Khapra. 2022. Towards building ASR systems for the next billion users. In *Proceedings of the AAAI Conference on Artificial Intelligence*.

Sarah Samson Juan, Laurent Besacier, Benjamin Lecouteux, and Mohamed Dyab. 2015. Using resources from a closely-related language to develop ASR for a very under-resourced language: A case study for Iban. In *Interspeech 2015*.

Taku Kudo and John Richardson. 2018. Sentencepiece: A simple and language independent subword tokenizer and detokenizer for neural text processing. *arXiv preprint arXiv:1808.06226*.

Patrick Littell, David R Mortensen, Ke Lin, Katherine Kairis, Carlisle Turner, and Lori Levin. 2017. Uriel and lang2vec: Representing languages as typological, geographical, and phylogenetic vectors. In *Proceedings of the 15th Conference of the European Chapter of the Association for Computational Linguistics: Volume 2, Short Papers*, pages 8–14.

Cécile Macaire, Didier Schwab, Benjamin Lecouteux, and Emmanuel Schang. 2022. Automatic speech recognition and query by example for creole languages documentation. In *Findings of the Association for Computational Linguistics: ACL 2022*, pages 2512–2520, Dublin, Ireland. Association for Computational Linguistics.

Graham Neubig and Junjie Hu. 2018. Rapid adaptation of neural machine translation to new languages. In *Proceedings of the 2018 Conference on Empirical Methods in Natural Language Processing*, pages 875–880, Brussels, Belgium. Association for Computational Linguistics.

Karol Nowakowski, Michal Ptaszynski, Kyoko Murasaki, and Jagna Nieuważny. 2023. Adapting multilingual speech representation model for a new, underresourced language through multilingual fine-tuning and continued pretraining. *Information Processing & Management*, 60(2):103148.

Vassil Panayotov, Guoguo Chen, Daniel Povey, and Sanjeev Khudanpur. 2015. Librispeech: An ASR corpus based on public domain audio books. In *2015*

IEEE International Conference on Acoustics, Speech and Signal Processing (ICASSP), pages 5206–5210.

Georgios Paraskevopoulos, Theodoros Kouzelis, Georgios Rouvalis, Athanasios Katsamanis, Vassilis Katsouros, and Alexandros Potamianos. 2024. Sample-efficient unsupervised domain adaptation of speech recognition systems: A case study for modern Greek. *IEEE/ACM Transactions on Audio, Speech, and Language Processing*, 32:286–299.

Vineel Pratap, Andros Tjandra, Bowen Shi, Paden Tomasello, Arun Babu, Sayani Kundu, Ali Elkahky, Zhaoheng Ni, Apoorv Vyas, Maryam Fazel-Zarandi, et al. 2023. Scaling speech technology to 1,000+ languages. *arXiv preprint arXiv:2305.13516*.

Mirco Ravanelli, Titouan Parcollet, Peter Plantinga, Aku Rouhe, Samuele Cornell, Loren Lugosch, Cem Subakan, Nauman Dawalatabad, Abdelwahab Heba, Jianyuan Zhong, Ju-Chieh Chou, Sung-Lin Yeh, Szu-Wei Fu, Chien-Feng Liao, Elena Rastorgueva, François Grondin, William Aris, Hwidong Na, Yan Gao, Renato De Mori, and Yoshua Bengio. 2021. SpeechBrain: A general-purpose speech toolkit. ArXiv:2106.04624.

Caitlin Richter and Jón Guðnason. 2023. Relative dynamic time warping comparison for pronunciation errors. In *ICASSP 2023-2023 IEEE International Conference on Acoustics, Speech and Signal Processing (ICASSP)*, pages 1–5. IEEE.

Nay San, Martijn Bartelds, Mitchell Browne, Lily Clifford, Fiona Gibson, John Mansfield, David Nash, Jane Simpson, Myfany Turpin, Maria Vollmer, et al. 2021. Leveraging neural representations for facilitating access to untranscribed speech from endangered languages. In *Proceedings of the Automatic Speech Recognition and Understanding Workshop (ASRU)*.

Tien-Ping Tan, Xiong Xiao, Enya Kong Tang, Eng Siong Chng, and Haizhou Li. 2009. MASS: A Malay language LVCSR corpus resource. In *2009 Oriental COCOSDA International Conference on Speech Database and Assessments*, pages 25–30. IEEE.

Ashish Vaswani, Noam Shazeer, Niki Parmar, Jakob Uszkoreit, Llion Jones, Aidan N Gomez, Łukasz Kaiser, and Illia Polosukhin. 2017. Attention is all you need. *Advances in neural information processing systems*, 30.

Felix Wu, Kwangyoun Kim, Shinji Watanabe, Kyu J. Han, Ryan McDonald, Kilian Q. Weinberger, and Yoav Artzi. 2023. Wav2seq: Pre-training speech-to-text encoder-decoder models using pseudo languages. In *ICASSP 2023 - 2023 IEEE International Conference on Acoustics, Speech and Signal Processing (ICASSP)*, pages 1–5.

Peter Wu, Jiatong Shi, Yifan Zhong, Shinji Watanabe, and Alan W Black. 2021. Cross-lingual transfer for speech processing using acoustic language similarity. In *2021 IEEE Automatic Speech Recognition and Understanding Workshop (ASRU)*, pages 1050–1057.

A Materials and methods

A.1 Data

Galician, Spanish, Portuguese, and Indonesian data were sourced from CommonVoice (Ardila et al., 2019); Setswana, Sesotho, and Sepedi from NCHLT (Barnard et al., 2014); Malay from MASS (Tan et al., 2009); and Iban from Juan et al. (2015). For Iban only 7 hours of target data was available and for Sesotho/Sepedi only 56 hours per language of donor data was available. Experiments were otherwise identical to the Indic experiments.

A.2 Continued pre-training

We carried out nearly identical experiments as the single-language experiments in Nowakowski et al. (2023) for Ainu, as we obtained their configuration file for wav2vec 2.0 pre-training using the fairseq library.[7] We made approriate modifications to suit our hardware configuration (4 x A100 40GB GPUs), setting the batch size to 1.5M samples per GPU and gradient accumulation to 16 steps, yielding an effective batch size of 100 minutes.

As in other wav2vec 2.0 multilingual pre-training configurations (Conneau et al., 2021; Babu et al., 2022; Javed et al., 2023), we form multilingual batches (specifically, *bi*-lingual in our case).[8] We set our sampling alpha to 0.0, which results in data being drawn uniformly from the two languages (i.e. target is over-sampled). We make this modification based on the CPT method in Paraskevopoulos et al. (2024), where in- and out-of-domain Greek data were evenly sampled in each batch. In this way, we consider this method akin to "similar-language regularisation" (Neubig and Hu, 2018), as we are more concerned with preventing over-fitting rather than learning about the donor data.

For each CPT run, we start from the official XLSR-128 model checkpoint and update the model for 10k steps. We determined this value based on our pilot runs. We found that 10k updates were sufficient to observe improved downstream ASR performance comparable to previous results (e.g. Nowakowski et al., 2023). This choice permitted us to maximise the number of languages compared in this paper, as each run required on average 15 hours (for 10k steps). For select runs, we also verified

[7] https://github.com/facebookresearch/fairseq

[8] Specifically, we use the implementation adapted from https://github.com/AI4Bharat/IndicWav2Vec/

that no further improvements could be obtained with additional updates (up to 20k).

A.3 ASR fine-tuning and evaluation

For ASR fine-tuning, we follow the official wav2vec 2.0 fine-tuning recipe suitable for 1 hour of transcriptions, modified for our hardware setup. We use a single A6000 48 GB GPU with a batch size of 5.6M samples per GPU and accumulate gradients for 2 steps, yielding an effective batch size of 11.6 minutes. As standard, the feature extractor is kept frozen across all updates and the transformer is frozen for the first 10k of 13k total updates, optimised using a CTC loss. Each fine-tuning run required on average 3.5 hours. For our findings to be applicable for languages with little external text data, we use Viterbi decoding without a language model to obtain transcriptions from the fine-tuned model for evaluation.

A.4 ATDS analyses

For all analyses, we trained the necessary k-means and sentencepiece models on a random 5-hour subset of target language data (except for CommonVoice Punjabi, which had in total 4 hours available in the latest 15.0 release). We adopted hyperparameters based on previous findings: extracting embeddings from the mid-point layer (12 of 24) of the XLSR-128 model (e.g. San et al., 2021; Bartelds et al., 2022), and k=500 for k-means and V=10k for the subword model which were reported as optimal values in Wu et al. (2023). Using a 12GB 3060 GPU, embedding extraction required about 10 minutes per data subset. The k-means models trained in about 8 minutes and subword models in less than a minute.

For CommonVoice (CV) Punjabi and Hindi, we conducted similar analyses as those reported by Baevski et al. (2020, Appendix D) for analysing correspondences between the wav2vec 2.0 code vectors and hand-aligned phone labels from TIMIT (Garofolo et al., 1993). In our case we used the labels for CV Punjabi and Hindi via grapheme-to-phoneme conversion, forced-aligned to the audio, and released as Praat TextGrids in the VoxCommunis corpus (Ahn and Chodroff, 2022). We then added tiers containing the wav2seq-induced labels. We hand-inspected several TextGrids for data validation then compiled the correspondences between the wav2seq induced tokens and phoneme labels. We make available all TextGrids as well as the aggregated data.

B Languages

B.1 Indo-Aryan and Dravidian

Punjabi (PAN) is a Northwestern Indo-Aryan language spoken by over 100 million people along the five major tributaries of the Indus river, spanning the state of Punjab in India and the province of Punjab in Pakistan. Hindi (HIN) and Urdu (URD) are mutually-intelligible yet sociolinguistically distinct registers of one Central Indo-Aryan language (usually termed Hindi–Urdu), spoken across the Indian subcontinent and by a majority in the northern part. Gujarati (GUJ) is a Central Indo-Aryan language and Marathi (MAR) is a Southern Indo-Aryan language, spoken in the western Indian states of Gujarat and Maharashtra, respectively. Bengali (BEN), spoken in Bangladesh and the Indian state of West Bengal, and Odia (ORI), spoken in the Indian state of Odisha, are both Eastern Indo-Aryan languages. Finally, Tamil (TAM) and Malayalam (MAL) are both Dravidian languages spoken in the Indian states of Tamil Nadu and Kerala, respectively. The Indo-Aryan and Dravidian language families are phylogenetically unrelated but have a long history of contact and cross-family bilingualism.

B.2 Malayo-Polynesian

Iban (IBA) is a Malayo-Polynesian language spoken by over 2 million people in Brunei as well as the Indonesian and Malaysian parts of the island of Borneo. Iban has some use as a medium of education in the Malaysian state of Sarawak but does not possess official status. It is related to Indonesian (IND) and Malay (ZSM), which are the official languages of Indonesia and Malaysia, respectively.

B.3 Sotho-Tswana

Setswana (TSN) is a Bantu language spoken by over 8 million people Botswana, South Africa, and Zimbabwe, where it is an official language. Setswana also possesses minority language status in Namibia. Two other languages of the Sotho-Tswana subgroup of Bantu are Sesotho (SOT, also known as "Southern Sotho") and Sepedi (NSO, "Northern Sotho"). Sesotho is an official language of South Africa, Lesotho, and Zimbabwe, and Sepedi is an official language of South Africa.

B.4 West Iberian

Galician (GLG) is a Romance language spoken in Galicia, an administrative division of northwestern

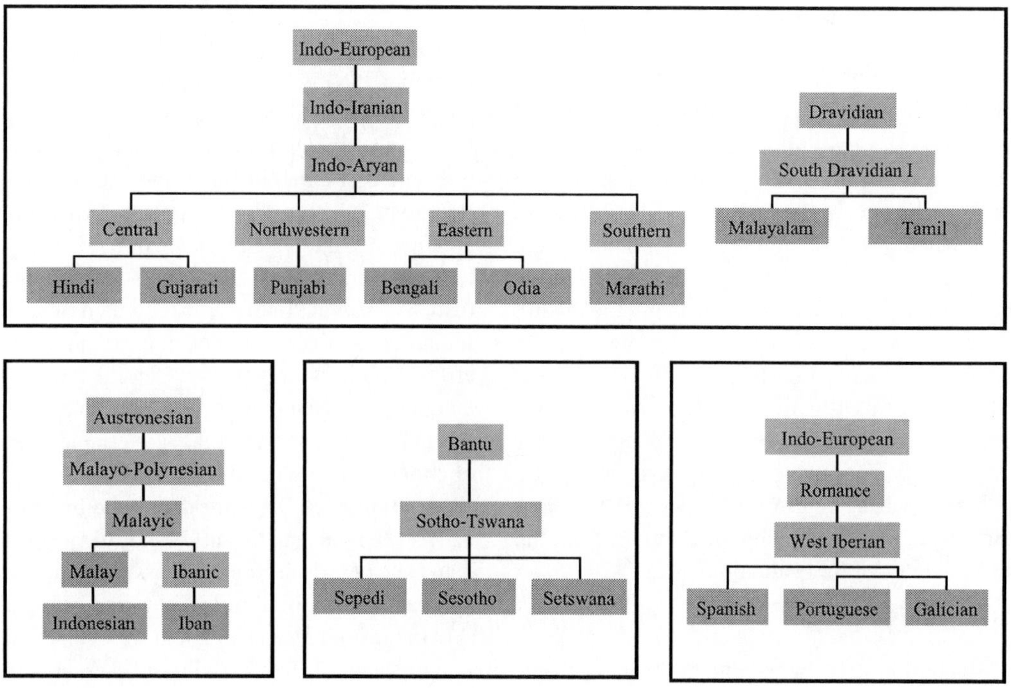

Figure 4: Family trees of the languages studied in this paper. Language families are in red and languages are in blue.

Spain bordering Portugal where it is the official language and spoken by over 2 million people. It is closely related to Spanish (SPA) and Portuguese (POR), and all three are classified under the West Iberian subgroup of Romance languages. Galician and Portuguese split in the late Middle Ages (c. 15th century) and thus are the most closely related pair of the three. Sociolinguistically, Galician speakers use Spanish in literary contexts and thus the two languages have a diglossic relationship.

MODELING: A Novel Dataset for Testing Linguistic Reasoning in Language Models

Nathan A. Chi[1], **Teodor Malchev**[2], **Riley Kong**[3], **Ryan A. Chi**[1],
Lucas Huang[4], **Ethan A. Chi**[1,5], **R. Thomas McCoy**[4,6], **Dragomir Radev**[4]
[1]Stanford University [2]Harvard University [3]MIT [4]Yale University
[5]Hudson River Trading [6]Princeton University
nathanchi@cs.stanford.edu

1 Introduction

Large language models (LLMs) perform well on (at least some) evaluations of both few-shot multilingual adaptation (Lin et al., 2022) and reasoning (Bubeck et al., 2023). However, evaluating the intersection of these two skills—**multilingual few-shot reasoning**—is difficult: even relatively low-resource languages can be found in large training corpora, raising the concern that when we intend to evaluate a model's ability to generalize to a new language, that language may have in fact been present during the model's training. If such **language contamination** (Blevins and Zettlemoyer, 2022) has occurred, apparent cases of few-shot reasoning could actually be due to memorization.

Towards understanding the capability of models to perform multilingual few-shot reasoning, we propose MODELING, a benchmark of *Rosetta stone puzzles* (Bozhanov and Derzhanski, 2013). This type of puzzle, originating from competitions called Linguistics Olympiads, contain a small number of sentences in a target language not previously known to the solver. Each sentence is translated to the solver's language such that the provided sentence pairs uniquely specify a single most reasonable underlying set of rules; solving requires applying these rules to translate new expressions (Figure 1). MODELING's languages are chosen to be extremely low-resource such that the risk of training data contamination is low, and unlike prior datasets (Şahin et al., 2020), it consists entirely of problems written specifically for this work, as a further measure against data leakage. Empirically, we find evidence that popular LLMs do not have data leakage on our benchmark (Section 2.1).

Here are some phrases in Ayutla Mixe:

Ëjts nexp. → *I see.*
Mejts mtunp. → *You work.*
Juan yë'ë yexyejtpy. → *Juan watches him.*
Yë'ë yë' uk yexpy. → *He sees the dog.*
Ëjts yë' maxu'unk nexyejtpy. → *I watch the baby.*

Now, translate the following phrases.

Yë' maxu'unk yexp. → ***The baby sees.***
The baby watches the dog. → **Yë' maxu'unk yë' uk yexyejtpy.**

Figure 1: A representative sample puzzle (based on Ayutla Mixe, which is spoken in Oaxaca, Mexico). Providing the answers (in **bolded red**) requires using the labeled pairs to reason about word meanings, morphology (the *-y* suffix), and word order—all in an extremely low-resource environment (there appear to be fewer than 3 pages in Ayutla Mixe on the Internet, so models are unlikely to have had substantial experience with the language beyond the examples shown here).

2 Dataset

MODELING comprises 48 Rosetta Stone puzzles based on 19 extremely low-resource languages from diverse regions. All problems were written by authors familiar with linguistics problems and were test-solved and rated for difficulty by two International Linguistics Olympiad medalists (Table 2). It includes 272 questions falling into four types, each testing a model's ability to handle a distinct element of linguistic typology:

1. **noun-adjective order** problems, which require determining the relative ordering of nouns and adjectives;
2. **word order** problems, which require determining the relative ordering of subject (S), verb (V), and object (O);
3. **possession** problems, which require reasoning about possessive morphology;
4. **semantics** problems, which require aligning a set of non-English semantic compounds to their English translations (e.g. En. "alcohol" = Wik-Mungkan *ngak way*, lit. "bad water").

Proceedings of the 6th Workshop on Research in Computational Linguistic Typology and Multilingual NLP (SIGTYP 2024), pages 113–119
March 22, 2024 ©2024 Association for Computational Linguistics

2.1 Data leakage

Because all the problems that we designed were newly written, models could not have encountered these puzzles in their training data. Nonetheless, it is possible that they may have encountered the specific words and phrases that we evaluate on.[1] To address this concern, we ran a baseline in which we evaluated all models without any target/reference pairs, prompting them to use "`existing knowledge of the language`" to translate the statements. Answering such questions is impossible without prior knowledge of the target language, so nonzero accuracy would suggest the presence of data leakage (Huang et al., 2022). The performance of all models in this setting is 0%, suggesting that the use of very low-resource languages successfully avoids data leakage.

3 Experiments

We evaluated six GPT models (GPT-3 {Ada, Babbage, Curie, Davinci}; GPT-3.5; and GPT-4) on our dataset on August 13, 2023 (Brown et al., 2020; OpenAI, 2023). We evaluated under the following conditions: **minimal prompt** (a brief, basic prompt specifying the task); **hand-tuned prompt** (a prompt fine-tuned by an International Linguistics Olympiad medalist); **basic chain-of-thought** (Kojima et al., 2022) (which encourages models to think step-by-step); and **full chain-of-thought** (Wei et al., 2022) (which provides an example of reasoning step-by-step). We report exact-match accuracies taken over all individual questions.

We observe strong performance from Davinci, GPT-3.5, and GPT-4 (Table 1). Across prompting approaches, we observe roughly similar accuracies. However, smaller models (Ada, Babbage, Curie) perform much worse, with accuracies near 0. All three of the large, accurate models (GPT-3-Davinci, GPT-3.5, GPT-4) struggle with particular problem categories, with possessive and semantic problems being harder than noun/adjective ordering and basic word order (Figure 2a). Finally, model performance closely follows human difficulty ratings (Figure 3a), suggesting that as large models continue to improve, we can scale our benchmark by producing more challenging problems (even the hardest problems in our benchmark are relatively easy by Linguistics Olympiad standards).

[1] e.g., perhaps their training data included the Ayutla Mixe sentence *Yë' maxu'unk yexp* shown in Figure 1.

Model	Minimal prompt	Hand-tuned prompt	Basic CoT	Full CoT
Ada	.000	.004	.011	.000
Babbage	.011	.011	.004	.018
Curie	.015	.018	.015	.022
Davinci	.496	.485	.490	.514
GPT-3.5	.404	.412	.401	.397
GPT-4	**.588**	**.591**	**.589**	**.607**

Table 1: Accuracy (exact match) of several large language models (LLMs) on **MODELING**. *CoT* stands for *chain of thought.*

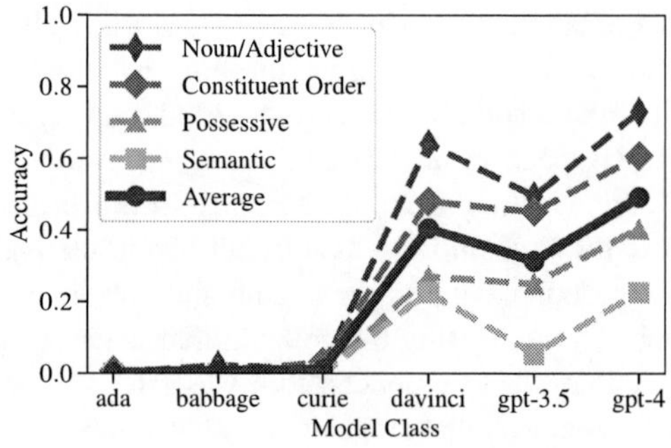

(a) Accuracy across different language models on our dataset, reporting average score across all prompts.

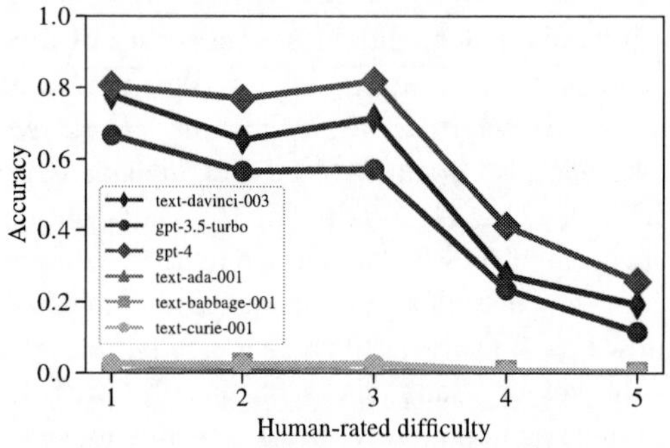

(a) LLM accuracy on our dataset, bucketed by difficulty. The 3 larger models (Davinci, GPT-3.5, GPT-4) display relatively high accuracy, while the smaller models are close to zero.

4 Conclusion

We have introduced **MODELING**, a dataset designed to evaluate LLMs' capacity to reason analytically in unseen languages. We believe that the approach used to develop **MODELING**—given its use of languages that occur very rarely on the Internet and its capacity to be extended to more challenging cases—has a strong potential to serve as a durable approach for evaluating reasoning.

References

Keith Berry, Christine Berry, et al. 1999. *A description of Abun: a West Papuan language of Irian Jaya*. Pacific Linguistics.

Roger Blench and Mallam Dendo. Baŋgi me, a language of unknown affiliation in Northern Mali.

Terra Blevins and Luke Zettlemoyer. 2022. Language contamination helps explains the cross-lingual capabilities of English pretrained models. In *Proceedings of the 2022 Conference on Empirical Methods in Natural Language Processing*, pages 3563–3574, Abu Dhabi, United Arab Emirates. Association for Computational Linguistics.

Bozhidar Bozhanov and Ivan Derzhanski. 2013. Rosetta stone linguistic problems. In *Proceedings of the Fourth Workshop on Teaching NLP and CL*, pages 1–8.

Tom Brown, Benjamin Mann, Nick Ryder, Melanie Subbiah, Jared D Kaplan, Prafulla Dhariwal, Arvind Neelakantan, Pranav Shyam, Girish Sastry, Amanda Askell, Sandhini Agarwal, Ariel Herbert-Voss, Gretchen Krueger, Tom Henighan, Rewon Child, Aditya Ramesh, Daniel Ziegler, Jeffrey Wu, Clemens Winter, Chris Hesse, Mark Chen, Eric Sigler, Mateusz Litwin, Scott Gray, Benjamin Chess, Jack Clark, Christopher Berner, Sam McCandlish, Alec Radford, Ilya Sutskever, and Dario Amodei. 2020. Language models are few-shot learners. In *Advances in Neural Information Processing Systems*, volume 33, pages 1877–1901. Curran Associates, Inc.

Sébastien Bubeck, Varun Chandrasekaran, Ronen Eldan, Johannes Gehrke, Eric Horvitz, Ece Kamar, Peter Lee, Yin Tat Lee, Yuanzhi Li, Scott Lundberg, Harsha Nori, Hamid Palangi, Marco Tulio Ribeiro, and Yi Zhang. 2023. Sparks of artificial general intelligence: Early experiments with GPT-4.

Dmitry V. Bubrikh. 1949. Grammatika literaturnogo komi yazyka (grammar of the Komi literary language).

Anna Bugaeva. 2022. *Handbook of the Ainu Language*, volume 12. Walter de Gruyter GmbH & Co KG.

Matthew S Dryer et al. 1994. The discourse function of the Kutenai inverse. *Voice and Inversion*, pages 65–99.

John B Haviland. 1998. Guugu Yimithirr cardinal directions. *Ethos*, 26(1):25–47.

Jeffrey Heath. 2015. A grammar of Toro Tegu (Dogon), Tabi mountain dialect.

Jie Huang, Hanyin Shao, and Kevin Chen-Chuan Chang. 2022. Are large pre-trained language models leaking your personal information? In *Findings of the Association for Computational Linguistics: EMNLP 2022*, pages 2038–2047, Abu Dhabi, United Arab Emirates. Association for Computational Linguistics.

Eugene S. Hunn, Akesha Baron, Roger Reeck, Meinardo Hernández Pérez, and Hermilo Silva Cruz. A sketch of Mixtepec Zapotec grammar.

Paulus Kievit. 2017. *A grammar of Rapa Nui*. Language Science Press.

Lyle M Knudson. 1975. A natural phonology and morphophonemics of Chimalapa Zoque. *Research on Language & Social Interaction*, 8(3-4):283–346.

Takeshi Kojima, Shixiang Shane Gu, Machel Reid, Yutaka Matsuo, and Yusuke Iwasawa. 2022. Large language models are zero-shot reasoners. In *Advances in Neural Information Processing Systems*.

Jonathan Lane. 2007. *Kalam serial verb constructions*. Pacific Linguistics.

Stephen C Levinson. 1997. Language and cognition: The cognitive consequences of spatial description in Guugu Yimithirr. *Journal of linguistic anthropology*, 7(1):98–131.

Xi Victoria Lin, Todor Mihaylov, Mikel Artetxe, Tianlu Wang, Shuohui Chen, Daniel Simig, Myle Ott, Naman Goyal, Shruti Bhosale, Jingfei Du, et al. 2022. Few-shot learning with multilingual generative language models. In *Proceedings of the 2022 Conference on Empirical Methods in Natural Language Processing*, pages 9019–9052.

Carolyn J MacKay. 1994. A sketch of Misantla Totonac phonology. *International Journal of American Linguistics*, 60(4):369–419.

Teresa Ann McFarland. 2009. *The phonology and morphology of Filomeno Mata Totonac*. University of California, Berkeley.

Mary Beck Moser and Stephen Alan Marlett. 2005. *Comcáac quih yaza quih hant ihíip hac: cmiique iitom, cocsar iitom, maricáana iitom*. Plaza y Valdes.

OpenAI. 2023. Gpt-4 technical report.

Andrew Pawley. 2006. Where have all the verbs gone? Remarks on the organisation of languages with small, closed verb classes. In *11th Binnenial Rice Univerity Linguistics Symposium*, pages 16–18.

Rodrigo Romero-Méndez. 2009. *A reference grammar of Ayutla Mixe (Tukyo'm ayuujk)*. Ph.D. thesis, State University of New York at Buffalo.

Gözde Gül Şahin, Yova Kementchedjhieva, Phillip Rust, and Iryna Gurevych. 2020. PuzzLing Machines: A Challenge on Learning From Small Data. In *Proceedings of the 58th Annual Meeting of the Association for Computational Linguistics*, pages 1241–1254, Online. Association for Computational Linguistics.

Lyle Scholtz. 1967. Kalam verb phrase. *Work Papers of the Summer Institute of Linguistics, University of North Dakota Session*, 11(1):10.

Ineke Smeets. 2008. *A Grammar of Mapuche*. De Gruyter Mouton, Berlin, Boston.

Elaine Thomas. 1969. *A grammatical description of the Engenni language*. University of London, School of Oriental and African Studies (United Kingdom).

Edward Tregear and Stephenson Percy Smith. 1907. *Vocabulary and grammar of the Niue dialect of the Polynesian language*. J. Mackay, Government Printer.

Darrell T Tryon. 1995. *Comparative Austronesian dictionary: An introduction to Austronesian studies*. De Gruyter Mouton.

Jason Wei, Xuezhi Wang, Dale Schuurmans, Maarten Bosma, brian ichter, Fei Xia, Ed H. Chi, Quoc V Le, and Denny Zhou. 2022. Chain of thought prompting elicits reasoning in large language models. In *Advances in Neural Information Processing Systems*.

A Dataset

A.1 Overview

Category	# Problems	# Questions	% Questions
Noun/Adj.	19	112	41%
Order	19	102	37%
Possessive	5	26	10%
Semantics	5	32	12%
Total	**48**	**272**	**100%**

Table 2: Dataset split by problem type (Section 2). We have 48 problems and a total of 272 questions.

A.2 Difficulty

Difficulty	# Problems	# Questions	% Questions
1	2	9	3%
2	16	91	34%
3	12	63	23%
4	6	31	11%
5	12	78	29%
Total	**48**	**272**	**100%**

Table 3: Distribution of difficulty levels over the dataset, as jointly evaluated on a Likert scale by two expert evaluators who have received medals at the International Linguistics Olympiad.

A.3 Orthography

B Prompts

Our four different prompting styles are illustrated inFigures 4 through 7.

C Data sources

Minimal-prompt

Here are some expressions in Language (a never-seen-before foreign language) and their translations in English:

Language: ...
English: ...

Given the above examples, please translate the following statements.

Figure 4: Minimal prompt.

Hand-tuned prompt

This is a translation puzzle. Below are example phrases in Language (a never-seen-before foreign language) as well as their English translations. Some test phrases follow them. Your task is to look closely at the example phrases and use only the information from them to translate the test phrases.

Language: ...
English: ...

Given the above examples, please translate the following statements.

Figure 5: Hand-tuned prompt.

Basic chain-of-thought

This is a translation puzzle. Below are example phrases in Language (a never-seen-before foreign language) as well as their English translations. Some test phrases follow them. Your task is to look closely at the example phrases and use only the information from them to translate the test phrases.

Language: ...
English: ...

Given the above examples, please translate the following statements. Let's think step by step in a logical way, using careful analytical reasoning to get the correct result.

Figure 6: Basic chain-of-thought prompt.

Full chain-of-thought

This is a translation puzzle. In a moment, you will use logic and analytical reasoning to translate from a never-seen-before language (Language) to English. As a training example, here are some expressions in Spanish and their translations in English.

1. Spanish: ventana roja
English: red window

2. Spanish: ventana azul
English: blue window

3. Spanish: manzana azul
English: blue apple

Using the above examples, translate the following.
Spanish: manzana roja

ANSWER: English: red apple
EXPLANATION: The first step we notice is that the word "ventana" must mean window because (1) the word "ventana" appears twice between sentences 1 and 2, and (2) the only word that appears twice in the English translation is "window." Next, we infer that "roja" must be "red" and "azul" must be "blue" by process of elimination. Next, we guess that in Spanish, the noun precedes the adjective because "ventana" comes before "roja" and "azul." Therefore, the noun in sentence 3 ("apple") must correspond to the word preceding the adjective ("manzana") in the Spanish translations. Putting this together, "manzana roja" must mean "red apple" in English.
Do you see how we're using logical and analytical reasoning to understand the grammar of the foreign languages step by step?

Figure 7: Full chain-of-thought prompt.

Language	Original	New
Ayutla Mixe	ë	eu
Bangime	ç	ch
Seri	ö	w
Rapa Nui	ā	aa

Table 4: Sample orthographic conversions.

Language	Family	ISO	#	Type	Source
Abun	West Papuan	kgr	1	POSS	Berry et al. (1999)
Ainu	Ainuic	ain	1	ORDER	Bugaeva (2022)
Ayutla Mixe	Mixe-Zoque	mxp	1	ORDER	Romero-Méndez (2009)
Bangime	Isolate	dba	7	NOUN-ADJ, ORDER	Blench and Dendo
Chimalapa Zoque	Mixe-Zoque	zoh	1	ORDER	Knudson (1975)
Toro-tegu Dogon	Niger–Congo	dtt	2	POSS	Heath (2015)
Engenni	Niger–Congo	enn	5	ORDER	Thomas (1969)
Guugu Yimithirr	Pama-Nyungan	kky	1	SEM	Haviland (1998); Levinson (1997)
Kalam	Kalam	kmh	1	SEM	Pawley (2006); Lane (2007), Scholtz (1967)
Komi-Zyrian	Permic	kpv	1	SEM	Bubrikh (1949)
Kutenai	Isolate	kut	1	SEM	Dryer et al. (1994)
Mapudungan	Araucanian	arn	4	NOUN-ADJ	Smeets (2008)
Misantla Totonac	Totonacan	tlc	1	NOUN-ADJ	MacKay (1994)
Mixtepec Zapotec	Oto-Manguean	zpm	4	NOUN-ADJ	Hunn et al.
Ngadha	Malayo-Polynesian	nxg	2	NOUN-ADJ	Tryon (1995)
Niuean	Malayo-Polynesian	niu	3	NOUN-ADJ	Tregear and Smith (1907)
Rapa Nui	Malayo-Polynesian	rap	7	NOUN-ADJ, ORDER	Kievit (2017)
Seri	Isolate	sei	4	NOUN-ADJ, ORDER, POSS, SEM	Moser and Marlett (2005)
Filomeno Mata Totonac	Totonacan	tlp	1	POSS	McFarland (2009)

Table 5: Problem Data Sources: sentences in MODELINGwere either taken directly from or written according to rules contained within the sources.

Figure 8: The 19 distinct languages included in the **MODELING** benchmark. Note that some languages have more than one problem.

TartuNLP @ SIGTYP 2024 Shared Task: Adapting XLM-RoBERTa for Ancient and Historical Languages

Aleksei Dorkin
Institute of Computer Science
University of Tartu
aleksei.dorkin@ut.ee

Kairit Sirts
Institute of Computer Science
University of Tartu
kairit.sirts@ut.ee

Abstract

We present our submission to the unconstrained subtask of the SIGTYP 2024 Shared Task on Word Embedding Evaluation for Ancient and Historical Languages for morphological annotation, POS-tagging, lemmatization, character- and word-level gap-filling. We developed a simple, uniform, and computationally lightweight approach based on the adapters framework using parameter-efficient fine-tuning. We applied the same adapter-based approach uniformly to all tasks and 16 languages by fine-tuning stacked language- and task-specific adapters. Our submission obtained an overall second place out of three submissions, with the first place in word-level gap-filling. Our results show the feasibility of adapting language models pre-trained on modern languages to historical and ancient languages via adapter training.

1 Introduction

The application of natural language processing techniques and pre-trained language models to analysis of ancient and historical languages is a compelling subject of research that has been so far overlooked. While there exist a number of benchmarks, such as GLUE (Wang et al., 2018), SuperGLUE (Wang et al., 2019), or XGLUE (Liang et al., 2020), for evaluating the quality of embeddings and language models for modern languages, such benchmarks are lacking for ancient and historical languages. Thus, the SIGTYPE 2024 Shared Task on Word Embedding Evaluation for Ancient and Historical Languages contributes to filling this gap.

In the current transformer-based language models paradigm, one of the common approaches to solving the tasks present in such benchmarks is to use the task data to fine-tune an encoder transformer model. The approach was first in introduced in Devlin et al. (2019) and was shown to yield superior results compared to the alternatives on the GLUE benchmark. Additionally, the proposed pre-training method is very similar to the word-level gap-filling problem in the shared task. Consequently, the model can be applied to solving the problem directly. This motivates our choice to use a transformer model in the shared task.

Large pre-trained language models, however, are predominantly trained on corpora of modern languages, with few exceptions such as LatinBERT (Bamman and Burns, 2020). Ancient and historical languages generally lack sufficient data to perform full pre-training of large language models or to continue training from a checkpoint trained on some different language. Full fine-tuning of modern language models on a relatively small amount data in an ancient/historical language might lead to overfitting and catastrophic forgetting. These considerations are also common in context of other low resource tasks or domains.

Several approaches have been proposed to alleviate these issues. For instance, the supplementary training approach proposed by Phang et al. (2018) involves first fine-tuning a pre-trained model on an intermediary labeled task with abundant data, and then on the target task which may have limited data. This approach showed gains over simply fine-tuning on the target task. Pfeiffer et al. (2020b) developed a cross-lingual transfer-learning approach based on the adapters framework for parameter efficient fine-tuning of language models (Houlsby et al., 2019; Bapna and Firat, 2019). Their approach involves fine-tuning a language adapter and a task adapter stacked on top of each other. This adapter-based method is expanded by Pfeiffer et al. (2021) by adopting a custom tokenizer and an embedding layer. Several ways of initializing the new embedding layers are compared on underrepresented modern languages. Since ancient and historical languages are underrepresented, the same techniques should be applicable in this context as well.

A useful feature of both the supplementary train-

Proceedings of the 6th Workshop on Research in Computational Linguistic Typology and Multilingual NLP (SIGTYP 2024), pages 120–130
March 22, 2024 ©2024 Association for Computational Linguistics

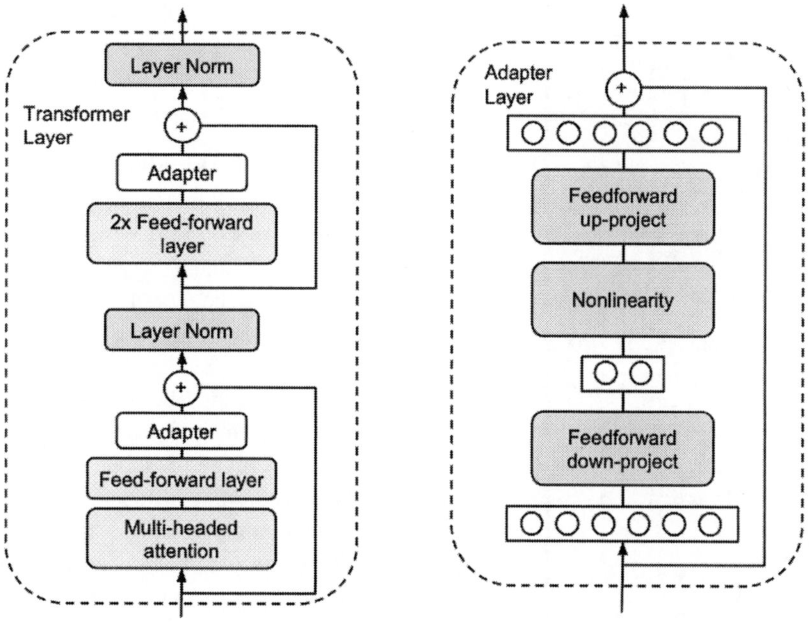

Figure 1: An illustration of the Bottleneck Adapter from (Houlsby et al., 2019). The left side demonstrates how a bottleneck adapter is added to a single transformer layer, while the structure of an individual adapter layer is on the right. Only elements in green are trained, while the rest remains frozen.

ing approach of Phang et al. (2018) and the adapter-based training of Pfeiffer et al. (2020b) is that they provide a uniform framework that can be applied to different languages and tasks in a similar manner. While previous related works mainly focused on modern languages, we aim to assess the feasibility of this unified approach for ancient and historical languages.

Our submission to the SIGTYP 2024 Shared Task on Ancient on Word Embedding Evaluation for Ancient and Historical Languages adopts the methods described by Pfeiffer et al. (2020b, 2021) by stacking fine-tuned language and task adapters, and customizing the tokenizer and the embedding layers. Our system is implemented as a unified framework, where various pre-trained models, languages, and tasks can be plugged in. The system was evaluated on POS tagging, morphological annotation, lemmatization, and filling-in both word-level and character-level gaps for 16 ancient and historical languages. We participated in the unconstrained subtask, which allowed using any additional resources, such as pre-trained language models. Out of 3 participants on the leaderboard we took a close second place, with the first place on the word gap-filling task. Our main contribution is showing that by adopting the parameter-efficient adapter training methodology, the large language models pre-trained on modern languages are applicable also to low-resource ancient and historical languages.

2 Adapters

There exist a number of approaches to parameter efficient fine-tuning. In our submission to the shared task the focus is on adapters exclusively.

Houlsby et al. (2019) propose a parameter efficient fine-tuning strategy that involves injection of a number of additional trainable layers into the original architecture. The architecture of the proposed strategy is illustrated on Figure 1. In each transformer layer an adapter layer is added twice: after the attention sub-layer and after the feedforward sub-layer. To limit the number of trainable parameters, the authors propose a bottleneck architecture of adapter layers: the adapter first projects the input into a smaller dimension, applies non-linearity, then projects back to the original dimension. This is known as the bottleneck adapter.

Pfeiffer et al. (2020b) extend on the strategy in context of cross-lingual transfer learning in two ways. First, the adapter stack technique is introduced (illustrated on Figure 2), which is primarily used to separate language adaptation training and

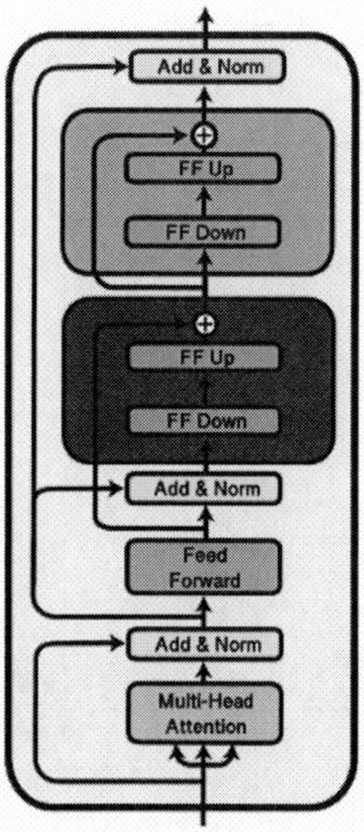

Figure 2: An illustration of an adapter stack as presented on the AdapterHub documentation page[1]. Blue and green blocks represent different adapter layers stacked on top of each other.

task-specific training. In the technique a language adapter is first trained, then a task-specific adapter is stacked on top of it and trained (while the language adapter is frozen). Secondly, the bottleneck adapter is expanded upon to include the embedding layer as well—the invertible adapter is introduced that transforms both input and output token representations to further improve language adaptation.

3 Methodology

Our approach in this work is based on training language adapters and task specific adapters for XLM-RoBERTa (Conneau et al., 2020)—the multilingual variant of RoBERTa (Zhuang et al., 2021) trained on 100 different languages. Since many of the languages in the shared task have related modern languages in the training data of XLM-RoBERTa, or are even included themselves (such as Latin), we expect to benefit from knowledge transfer.

3.1 Data

The dataset provided by the organizers is a compilation of various resources (Bauer et al., 2017; Doyle, 2018; Ó Corráin et al., 1997; HAS Research Institute for Linguistics, 2018; Zeman et al., 2023; Acadamh Ríoga na hÉireann, 2017; Simon, 2014) and comprises 16 languages in total spanning several historical epochs and upper bounded by 1700 CE. The information on the languages in the dataset is presented in Table 1.

3.2 Adapter Training

Full fine-tuning of language models has several difficulties such as the possibility of catastrophic forgetting and the necessity to train and maintain a full copy of the model weights for each individual task. When applying the technique first proposed in (Phang et al., 2018) in a multi-lingual and multi-task setting, the scale of the mentioned disadvantages is magnified. Training and maintaining a separate copy of the model for each combination of language, target task, and intermediate task can become computationally expensive. Meanwhile, each copy of the model is narrowly specialized in a single task, with generalization capabilities being potentially limited. This highlights the practicality of parameter efficient fine-tuning in comparison.

The overall approach is, in general, the same for every language. First, we train a language adapter for every language individually. A language adapter is comprised of a bottleneck adapter and masked language modeling prediction head. Accordingly, the training objective is masked language modeling. This is based on the assumption that a significant portion of the model's parameters is not actually language-specific, and thus does not need changing. We simply need to adapt the model to a new language. The language adapter is trained for 10 epochs regardless of the size of the data. The unmasked part of the training data for the word-filling task is used, while the masked part is not utilized for training. Secondly, we train task-specific adapters for each language. In this setup we use the adapter stack: the language adapter is loaded, but frozen, and we add a task-specific adapter on top of it, and train said adapter. We have two tasks per language: morphological tagging, which combines both POS-tagging and morphological annotation, and lemmatization, which is also implemented as sequence tagging problem. Similarly to language modeling, in both tasks the adapters are trained for 10 epochs.

3.3 Custom tokenizers and embeddings

Some of the languages in the shared task are not covered by the model's tokenizer. In other

[1]https://docs.adapterhub.ml/adapter_composition.html

Language	Code	Train Sentences	Valid Sentences	Test Sentences
Ancient Greek	grc	24,800	3,100	3,101
Ancient Hebrew	hbo	1,263	158	158
Classical Chinese	lzh	68,991	8,624	8,624
Coptic	cop	1,730	216	217
Gothic	got	4,320	540	541
Medieval Icelandic	isl	21,820	2,728	2,728
Classical and Late Latin	lat	16,769	2,096	2,097
Medieval Latin	latm	30,176	3,772	3,773
Old Church Slavonic	chu	18,102	2,263	2,263
Old East Slavic	orv	24,788	3,098	3,099
Old French	fro	3,113	389	390
Vedic Sanskrit	san	3,197	400	400
Old Hungarian	ohu	21,346	2,668	2,669
Old Irish	sga	8,748	1,093	1,094
Middle Irish	mga	14,308	1,789	1,789
Early Modern Irish	ghc	24,440	3,055	3,056

Table 1: Language statistics in the Shared Task.

words, a significant portion of the tokenizer's output includes <unk> tokens. This is possible because XLM-RoBERTa's employs subword tokenization (Sennrich et al., 2016). A subword tokenizer is a trained model that learns a vocabulary of a certain size. The trained model transforms text input into individual tokens by looking for the longest character sequences in the text that are present in its vocabulary. When attempting to tokenize a text that includes symbols that did not appear in the training data (and consequently, are not in the tokenizer's vocabulary), each unrecognized symbol is replaced by the <unk> token.

For each language not covered by the model's tokenizer a new tokenizer is initialized. In addition to that, a new embedding layer is also initialized. The initial weights are copied from the original embeddings for tokens that overlap with the multilingual tokenizer.

To decide whether the model requires a custom tokenizer, two checks are made:

1. The percentage of unknown tokens > 5%

2. <unk> token is in top 10 by frequency

If either of these conditions is true, a custom tokenizer is created. Refer to Table 2 for detailed statistics. Based on these conditions, 5 languages need a separate tokenizer: Old Church Slavonic, Coptic, Classical Chinese, Old Hungarian, and Old East Slavic. When selecting the vocabulary size, the aim was to have as many full words as possible in the vocabulary, but at the same time allow for morphological variation. Thus, the number of items in the vocabulary should be neither too high nor too low. For that reason, we selected the size to be 3000 for all languages, except Classical Chinese. For Classical Chinese the size was insufficient, so it was increased to 10000.

Pfeiffer et al. (2021) suggest several possible options of initializing the weights of the custom embedding layer corresponding to the new tokenizer. These include random initialization, copying the weights of tokens that overlap between multilingual and language-specific tokenizers, as well as a matrix factorization-based approach that aims to identify latent semantic concepts in the original embedding matrix that are useful for transfer. It is noted, however, that the latter approach shows less gains when used with languages with underrepresented scripts. For this reason and for the sake of simplicity, with settled on using the lexical overlap approach for all affected languages.

3.4 Tasks

Filling Word-level Gaps Having trained a masked language modeling adapter for each language, we already have a suitable model to perform word-level gap filling. However, the fact XLM-RoBERTa, as well as most modern language models, is based on subword tokens rather than full words becomes a significant hurdle. The reason is

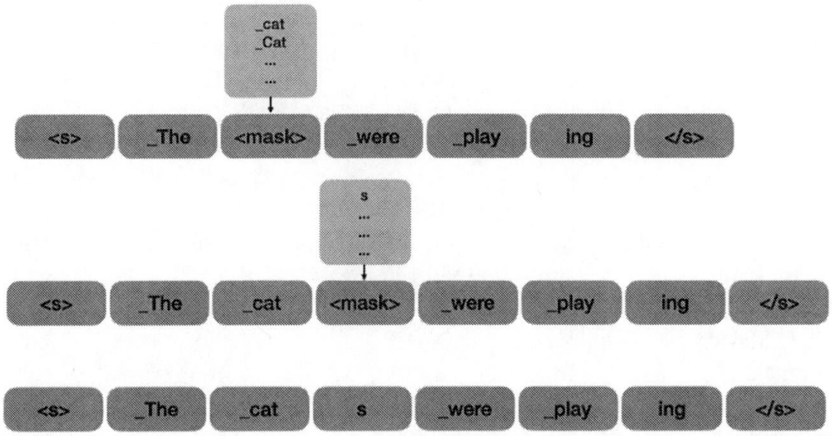

Figure 3: A schematic illustration of the decoding process for word-level mask filling. Blue boxes represent current tokens in the sentence, while orange boxes represent the probability distribution of tokens at the position of the mask token. The upper half represents the first step of decoding. We start with predicting the most likely replacement for the leftmost masked token that starts with _ symbol representing the beginning of a new word. Then, we replace the mask with that token and append a new mask token to the right of it, as represented in the middle part. We predict the most likely replacement for the new mask token. If it starts with _ symbol, we discard the mask token, consider the word predicted, and move to the next masked word if it's present. Conversely, if there's no _ in the predicted token, we append it to the previously predicted token. We repeat this process k times, or until we encounter a token starting with _. k is a hyperparameter that may be tuned, however increasing k increases the decoding time significantly. For this reason we set k to 1 for all languages. At the bottom of the figure the final result with no mask tokens is demonstrated. Note that this description is specific to XLM-RoBERTa tokenizer, other model's tokenizers may have different behaviour.

lang	# tokens	% unknown	<unk> rank
chu	495612	15.31%	1
cop	39771	45.61%	2
fro	55448	0.00%	-
ghc	1282852	0.00%	-
got	98874	1.05%	-
grc	1079457	0.47%	-
hbo	124063	0.36%	-
isl	688580	0.00%	-
lat	296770	0.00%	-
latm	897209	0.00%	-
lzh	408259	1.40%	4
mga	492894	0.00%	-
ohu	352811	5.05%	1
orv	592890	5.00%	2
san	59349	0.01%	-
sga	190711	0.00%	-

Table 2: Tokenizer coverage statistics. <unk> ranks not present in top 10 are not reported.

the we can not know in advance whether the target word we want to predict is comprised of one or more subword units, and that makes the decoding more complicated. To address this issue, for each sentence with masked words in it, we follow the steps (see Figure 3):

1. Locate the first <mask> token
2. Use the model's prediction to determine the most likely token that starts with the whitespace prefix
3. Replace the <mask> token with the prediction, and look ahead up to k steps: does the next token start with the whitespace token? If it does, we break the cycle, and continue processing the remaining <mask> tokens in the sentence, otherwise we append the next predicted token to our previous prediction, and repeat the look ahead.

For Classical Chinese, the process is simplified, and we simply predicted the most likely token.

Filling Character-level Gaps The approach to character-level mask filling is purely algorithmic. We start with building a vocabulary of masked word candidates. We consider a sequence of characters with no whitespaces to be a suitable candidate.

The vocabulary is populated with such candidates. For each masked word a look up among all the words of the same length as the masked word is performed: a regular expression built from the masked word by replacing "[_]" with "." is matched against these words. If there are matches, up to the first 3 matches are returned. For each match character replacements are extracted from each candidate. If there are no matches, and the masked word contains only one "[_]", the masked word is split in two parts, and each part is matched against the dictionary. If there is at least one match, the whitespace is returned as the replacement.

The described algorithmic method could be extended in two ways:

1. Multiple candidates could be reranked using the trained language model
2. If there are no candidates, a suitable word could be generated using the trained model, similarly to the word-level gap-filling task

However, the extensions were not developed for the shared task for the following reasons. Each sentence may contain multiple masked words, and in addition the whitespace symbol may be masked as well. This significantly increases the solution's complexity, yet the magnitude of the benefit is unclear.

Finally, for Classical Chinese the following approach was applied. First, the symbols in the original dataset were decomposed into the lowest possible forms which are mostly strokes and small indivisible units using the Hanzipy library[2], then a masked language model adapter was trained on that decomposed data. The model achieved relatively high masked language modeling evaluation accuracy—about 40%—on the validation set, as measured the by the Trainer class in the transformers library. The trained model was then used to predict the most likely replacement for each masked symbol. The ground truth data provided by the organizers, however, remained in the original composed form. This proved to be a significant problem. An attempt was made to compose the symbols back into their original form algorithmically, since the library used for decomposition doesn't have the option to reconstruct the original symbol from its constituents, to our best knowledge. However, this attempt was unsuccessful given that our submission attained score of 0 on the test set.

[2]https://github.com/Synkied/hanzipy

POS-tagging & Full Morphological Annotation We frame both POS-tagging and full morphological annotation as a single token classification task. For each token we collect all available morphological features and the POS tag from the annotation. Then we concatenate them as a single string, which is then used as the class to predict. Then we employ the adapter stack technique: we load the corresponding language adapter, and create a task specific adapter with token classification prediction head. We only train the task specific adapter. For inference we decompose the predicted class strings back into individual tags. The approach is the same for every language.

Lemmatization Similarly to the previous task, we frame lemmatization as token classification task. To achieve that we generate transformation rules for each lemma/form pair based on the technique first introduced in (Straka, 2018) and expanded upon in (Dorkin and Sirts, 2023). The rules are comprised of individual edits that need to be made to transform the given form into its lemma. The edits are represented as a single string. We use that string as the label to predict. Consequently, inference is done in two steps: first the rule for each token is predicted, then that rule is applied to the form and the resulting lemma is returned. The approach is the same for all language except for Classical Chinese. For Classical Chinese we do not train a model, but rather use a simple dictionary look up which results in nearly 100% accuracy.

3.5 Technical Implementation Details

The implementation is primarily based on the Adapters[3] (Poth et al., 2023) library and the provided training script examples. The most significant change in the training scripts is the addition of custom embedding layer initialization. Some aspects of lemmatization as a token classification task were adopted from our previous work. For languages not utilizing custom tokenizers we employ the invertible bottleneck adapters (Pfeiffer et al., 2020b), while for the languages that do require custom tokenizers we employ the regular bottleneck adapters (Houlsby et al., 2019). The motivation is that when we have a custom embedding layer, there is no need to adapt it additionally. In all experiments we use the base version of XLM-RoBERTa due to time constraints, however we can well expect that the large version would show improved perfor-

[3]https://github.com/adapter-hub/adapters

	Overall results	POS-tagging	Lemmatization	Morphological analysis	Character gap-filling	Word gap-filling
Ancient Greek	0.70	0.96	0.94	0.97	0.61	0.03
Ancient Hebrew	0.61	0.94	0.97	0.95	0.19	0.00
Classical Chinese	0.57	0.83	1.00	0.89	0.00	0.10
Coptic	0.52	0.61	0.75	0.75	0.45	0.02
Gothic	0.70	0.93	0.93	0.92	0.67	0.03
Medieval Icelandic	0.73	0.97	0.98	0.96	0.57	0.17
Classical and Late Latin	0.73	0.96	0.97	0.96	0.66	0.11
Medieval Latin	0.76	0.99	0.99	0.99	0.70	0.14
Old Church Slavonic	0.50	0.66	0.60	0.67	0.54	0.02
Old East Slavic	0.56	0.76	0.69	0.80	0.48	0.06
Old French	0.69	0.95	0.92	0.98	0.52	0.07
Vedic Sanskrit	0.66	0.84	0.88	0.86	0.65	0.05
Old Hungarian	0.52	0.75	0.63	0.76	0.46	0.00
Old Irish	0.19	-	-	-	0.35	0.03
Middle Irish	0.22	-	-	-	0.39	0.04
Early Modern Irish	0.28	-	-	-	0.50	0.06

Table 3: Results of our submission on the leadearboard. For the variants of Irish, training and test data was only provided for gap-filling tasks.

mance. The code and the instructions to reproduce are available on the project's GitHub repository[4].

XLM-RoBERTa uses SentencePiece (Kudo and Richardson, 2018) for tokenization. SentencePiece is a trainable tokenization model limited by a token vocabulary of a specific size. To be able to process languages with scripts which are under-represented by XLM-RoBERTa's tokenizer, we train a new tokenizer for each language in question. The new tokenizer has to remain compatible with original model—it has to retain all the special tokens and their indices. To achieve that we use the `train_new_from_iterator` method of the Tokenizer class instance in HuggingFace transformers associated with model. We supply it with the same data we use for the masked language modeling training.

For training we used a single NVIDIA Tesla V100 GPU on the University's High Performance Cluster (University of Tartu, 2018). The training time for a single task (including masked language modeling) on average was about 10-20 minutes, ranging from 2 to 40 minutes depending on the amount of data, which is notably less than it would take for full fine-tuning.

[4]`https://github.com/slowwavesleep/ancient-lang-adapters/tree/sigtyp2024`

Initially, an error was present in our code that resulted in our models not having trainable language modeling prediction heads. In other words, during the language adaptation stage the models retained the original masked language prediction head of XLM-RoBERTa, rather than training a new language specific prediction head. To our surprise, after fixing the error, the difference turned out to be quite negligible, except for languages that relied on custom embeddings. For these languages, the effect of the fixing the error was most noticeable on the word-level gap-filling task—before that the models were using the prediction head which was mismatched in size with the custom embeddings.

4 Results

According to the results on Table 3, our approach seems to generally underperform on languages that require custom tokenizers and embeddings: Classical Chinese, Coptic, Old Church Slavonic, Old East Slavic, Old Hungarian. This can be explained by the amount of data being too limited to be able to train meaningful input representations, while the lexical overlap technique failed to provide benefit due to significant differences in their scripts. We hypothesize that a more sophisticated approach to embedding initialization and tokenizer training could result in considerable benefits.

We note a surprisingly strong performance of our algorithmic approach to character-level gap-filling with the exception of Classical Chinese where the approach is simply not applicable. We expect the extensions to the approach outlined in Section 3.4 could improve the results further. However, in context of the shared task, we do not believe that the possible improvements would be worth the effort. Due to the whitespaces appearing as masked characters there is no way to know in advance how many individual words in the sentence in total have masked characters in them. In addition to that, a single word may contain several masked characters. The combination of these two factors makes improvements based on language model rescoring quite computationally expensive. For Classical Chinese, however, we hypothesise that the score would be considerably higher if the ground truth was also in the decomposed form, because to the best of our understanding, reconstructing the original characters from individual strokes is not a straightforward task.

Despite taking the first place in the word-level gap filling task, the absolute scores are still very low. This is to be expected, because the difficulty of the task is compounded by the presence of multiple masked words per sentence, as well the reliance on subword tokenization of our approach. Additionally, the implementation may not be suitable at all for certain languages due to differences in the writing systems. Finally, we surmise that due to the amount of training being quite small for the masked language modeling problem, we cannot expect to be able to correctly predict completely new words, however we can, in theory, predict previously unseen word forms due to subword tokenization. This means that experimenting with the k parameter used to limit the number of times the look ahead for word continuation is performed in the word-level gap filling problem could improve the results somewhat.

The pattern-based approach to lemmatization also performs reasonably well in most languages. The approach is restricted by the set of patterns derived based on the training set. If the evaluation set contains many words for which a suitable pattern is missing, the system simply cannot make a correct prediction. However, we believe that this is not the problem here. In particular, we note that those languages which have lower scores on lemmatization, also perform consistently lower on other tasks. Thus, we suggest that the lower performance is rather related to insufficient data for training meaningful representations. In addition to underpeforming on languages with underrepresented writing systems, we observe somewhat low performance on Vedic Sanskrit as well. One explanation could be that the usage of diacritics may negatively affect the character-based transformation rule generation; however this hypothesis requires further investigation.

Finally, our combined approach to POS-tagging and morphological analysis performs quite well on most of the languages. This is somewhat unexpected, because the model is limited in predicting only the combinations of part-of-speech and morphological features that are present in training data.

5 Conclusion

This paper described our solution to the SIGTYP 2024 Shared Task developed based on the adapters framework. The system is simple and uniform, and can be easily extended to other tasks and languages. For each language we trained a language adapter, and two task adapters, one for POS and morphological tagging and one for lemmatization. For languages with scripts underrepresented in the XLM-RoBERTa vocabulary, we additionally created custom tokenizers and embeddings. One notable advantage of the adopted approach is its resource efficiency—adapting the model to a new language and task can be done in less than an hour. As a future work, the system could be improved with more advanced adapter-based techniques such as adapter fusion (Pfeiffer et al., 2020a) to leverage typological relatedness of languages.

References

Acadamh Ríoga na hÉireann. 2017. Corpas Stairiúil na Gaeilge 1600-1926. Retrieved: June 10, 2022.

David Bamman and Patrick J. Burns. 2020. Latin Bert: A Contextual Language Model for Classical Philology.

Ankur Bapna and Orhan Firat. 2019. Simple, Scalable Adaptation for Neural Machine Translation. In *Proceedings of the 2019 Conference on Empirical Methods in Natural Language Processing and the 9th International Joint Conference on Natural Language Processing (EMNLP-IJCNLP)*, pages 1538–1548.

Bernhard Bauer, Rijcklof Hofman, and Pádraic Moran.

2017. St. Gall Priscian Glosses, version 2.0. Accessed: February 14, 2023.

Alexis Conneau, Kartikay Khandelwal, Naman Goyal, Vishrav Chaudhary, Guillaume Wenzek, Francisco Guzmán, Edouard Grave, Myle Ott, Luke Zettlemoyer, and Veselin Stoyanov. 2020. Unsupervised cross-lingual representation learning at scale. In *Proceedings of the 58th Annual Meeting of the Association for Computational Linguistics*, pages 8440–8451, Online. Association for Computational Linguistics.

Jacob Devlin, Ming-Wei Chang, Kenton Lee, and Kristina Toutanova. 2019. BERT: Pre-training of deep bidirectional transformers for language understanding. In *Proceedings of the 2019 Conference of the North American Chapter of the Association for Computational Linguistics: Human Language Technologies, Volume 1 (Long and Short Papers)*, pages 4171–4186, Minneapolis, Minnesota. Association for Computational Linguistics.

Aleksei Dorkin and Kairit Sirts. 2023. Comparison of Current Approaches to Lemmatization: A Case Study in Estonian. In *Proceedings of the 24th Nordic Conference on Computational Linguistics (NoDaLiDa)*, pages 280–285.

Adrian Doyle. 2018. Würzburg Irish Glosses. Accessed: February 14, 2023.

HAS Research Institute for Linguistics. 2018. Old Hungarian Codices.

Neil Houlsby, Andrei Giurgiu, Stanislaw Jastrzebski, Bruna Morrone, Quentin De Laroussilhe, Andrea Gesmundo, Mona Attariyan, and Sylvain Gelly. 2019. Parameter-efficient transfer learning for nlp. In *International Conference on Machine Learning*, pages 2790–2799. PMLR.

Taku Kudo and John Richardson. 2018. SentencePiece: A simple and language independent subword tokenizer and detokenizer for Neural Text Processing. In *Proceedings of the 2018 Conference on Empirical Methods in Natural Language Processing: System Demonstrations*, pages 66–71, Brussels, Belgium. Association for Computational Linguistics.

Yaobo Liang, Nan Duan, Yeyun Gong, Ning Wu, Fenfei Guo, Weizhen Qi, Ming Gong, Linjun Shou, Daxin Jiang, Guihong Cao, Xiaodong Fan, Ruofei Zhang, Rahul Agrawal, Edward Cui, Sining Wei, Taroon Bharti, Ying Qiao, Jiun-Hung Chen, Winnie Wu, Shuguang Liu, Fan Yang, Daniel Campos, Rangan Majumder, and Ming Zhou. 2020. XGLUE: A New Benchmark Dataset for Cross-lingual Pre-training, Understanding and Generation. In *Proceedings of the 2020 Conference on Empirical Methods in Natural Language Processing (EMNLP)*, pages 6008–6018, Online. Association for Computational Linguistics.

Jonas Pfeiffer, Aishwarya Kamath, Andreas Rücklé, Kyunghyun Cho, and Iryna Gurevych. 2020a. AdapterFusion: Non-Destructive Task Composition for Transfer Learning. *CoRR*, abs/2005.00247.

Jonas Pfeiffer, Ivan Vulić, Iryna Gurevych, and Sebastian Ruder. 2020b. MAD-X: An Adapter-Based Framework for Multi-Task Cross-Lingual Transfer. In *Proceedings of the 2020 Conference on Empirical Methods in Natural Language Processing (EMNLP)*, pages 7654–7673, Online. Association for Computational Linguistics.

Jonas Pfeiffer, Ivan Vulić, Iryna Gurevych, and Sebastian Ruder. 2021. UNKs Everywhere: Adapting Multilingual Language Models to New Scripts. In *Proceedings of the 2021 Conference on Empirical Methods in Natural Language Processing*, pages 10186–10203, Online and Punta Cana, Dominican Republic. Association for Computational Linguistics.

Jason Phang, Thibault Févry, and Samuel R Bowman. 2018. Sentence encoders on stilts: Supplementary training on intermediate labeled-data tasks. *arXiv preprint arXiv:1811.01088*.

Clifton Poth, Hannah Sterz, Indraneil Paul, Sukannya Purkayastha, Leon Engländer, Timo Imhof, Ivan Vulić, Sebastian Ruder, Iryna Gurevych, and Jonas Pfeiffer. 2023. Adapters: A Unified Library for Parameter-Efficient and Modular Transfer Learning. In *Proceedings of the 2023 Conference on Empirical Methods in Natural Language Processing: System Demonstrations*, pages 149–160, Singapore. Association for Computational Linguistics.

Rico Sennrich, Barry Haddow, and Alexandra Birch. 2016. Neural machine translation of rare words with subword units. In *Proceedings of the 54th Annual Meeting of the Association for Computational Linguistics (Volume 1: Long Papers)*, pages 1715–1725, Berlin, Germany. Association for Computational Linguistics.

Eszter Simon. 2014. Corpus Building from Old Hungarian Codices. In Katalin É. Kiss, editor, *The Evolution of Functional Left Peripheries in Hungarian Syntax*. Oxford University Press, Oxford.

Milan Straka. 2018. UDPipe 2.0 prototype at CoNLL 2018 UD Shared Task. In *Proceedings of the CoNLL 2018 Shared Task: Multilingual Parsing from Raw Text to Universal Dependencies*, pages 197–207, Brussels, Belgium. Association for Computational Linguistics.

University of Tartu. 2018. UT Rocket.

Alex Wang, Yada Pruksachatkun, Nikita Nangia, Amanpreet Singh, Julian Michael, Felix Hill, Omer Levy, and Samuel Bowman. 2019. Superglue: A stickier benchmark for general-purpose language understanding systems. *Advances in neural information processing systems*, 32.

Alex Wang, Amanpreet Singh, Julian Michael, Felix Hill, Omer Levy, and Samuel Bowman. 2018. GLUE: A Multi-Task Benchmark and Analysis Platform for Natural Language Understanding. In *Proceedings of the 2018 EMNLP Workshop BlackboxNLP: Analyzing and Interpreting Neural Networks for NLP*, pages 353–355, Brussels, Belgium. Association for Computational Linguistics.

Daniel Zeman, Joakim Nivre, Mitchell Abrams, Elia Ackermann, Noëmi Aepli, Hamid Aghaei, Željko Agić, Amir Ahmadi, Lars Ahrenberg, Chika Kennedy Ajede, Salih Furkan Akkurt, Gabrielė Aleksandravičiūtė, Ika Alfina, Avner Algom, Khalid Alnajjar, Chiara Alzetta, Erik Andersen, Lene Antonsen, Tatsuya Aoyama, Katya Aplonova, Angelina Aquino, Carolina Aragon, Glyd Aranes, Maria Jesus Aranzabe, Bilge Nas Arıcan, Hórunn Arnardóttir, Gashaw Arutie, Jessica Naraiswari Arwidarasti, Masayuki Asahara, Katla Ásgeirsdóttir, Deniz Baran Aslan, Cengiz Asmazoğlu, Luma Ateyah, Furkan Atmaca, Mohammed Attia, Aitziber Atutxa, Liesbeth Augustinus, Mariana Avelãs, Elena Badmaeva, Keerthana Balasubramani, Miguel Ballesteros, Esha Banerjee, Sebastian Bank, Verginica Barbu Mititelu, Starkaður Barkarson, Rodolfo Basile, Victoria Basmov, Colin Batchelor, John Bauer, Seyyit Talha Bedir, Shabnam Behzad, Kepa Bengoetxea, İbrahim Benli, Yifat Ben Moshe, Gözde Berk, Riyaz Ahmad Bhat, Erica Biagetti, Eckhard Bick, Agnė Bielinskienė, Kristín Bjarnadóttir, Rogier Blokland, Victoria Bobicev, Loïc Boizou, Emanuel Borges Völker, Carl Börstell, Cristina Bosco, Gosse Bouma, Sam Bowman, Adriane Boyd, Anouck Braggaar, António Branco, Kristina Brokaitė, Aljoscha Burchardt, Marisa Campos, Marie Candito, Bernard Caron, Gauthier Caron, Catarina Carvalheiro, Rita Carvalho, Lauren Cassidy, Maria Clara Castro, Sérgio Castro, Tatiana Cavalcanti, Gülşen Cebiroğlu Eryiğit, Flavio Massimiliano Cecchini, Giuseppe G. A. Celano, Slavomír Čéplö, Neslihan Cesur, Savas Cetin, Özlem Çetinoğlu, Fabricio Chalub, Liyanage Chamila, Shweta Chauhan, Ethan Chi, Taishi Chika, Yongseok Cho, Jinho Choi, Jayeol Chun, Juyeon Chung, Alessandra T. Cignarella, Silvie Cinková, Aurélie Collomb, Çağrı Çöltekin, Miriam Connor, Daniela Corbetta, Francisco Costa, Marine Courtin, Mihaela Cristescu, Ingerid Løyning Dale, Philemon Daniel, Elizabeth Davidson, Leonel Figueiredo de Alencar, Mathieu Dehouck, Martina de Laurentiis, Marie-Catherine de Marneffe, Valeria de Paiva, Mehmet Oguz Derin, Elvis de Souza, Arantza Diaz de Ilarraza, Carly Dickerson, Arawinda Dinakaramani, Elisa Di Nuovo, Bamba Dione, Peter Dirix, Kaja Dobrovoljc, Adrian Doyle, Timothy Dozat, Kira Droganova, Puneet Dwivedi, Christian Ebert, Hanne Eckhoff, Masaki Eguchi, Sandra Eiche, Marhaba Eli, Ali Elkahky, Binyam Ephrem, Olga Erina, Tomaž Erjavec, Farah Essaidi, Aline Etienne, Wograine Evelyn, Sidney Facundes, Richárd Farkas, Federica Favero, Jannatul Ferdaousi, Marília Fernanda, Hector Fernandez Alcalde, Amal Fethi, Jennifer Foster, Cláudia Freitas, Kazunori Fujita, Katarína Gajdošová, Daniel Galbraith, Federica Gamba, Marcos Garcia, Moa Gärdenfors, Fabrício Ferraz Gerardi, Kim Gerdes, Luke Gessler, Filip Ginter, Gustavo Godoy, Iakes Goenaga, Koldo Gojenola, Memduh Gökırmak, Yoav Goldberg, Xavier Gómez Guinovart, Berta González Saavedra, Bernadeta Griciūtė, Matias Grioni, Loïc Grobol, Normunds Grūzītis, Bruno Guillaume, Céline Guillot-Barbance, Tunga Güngör, Nizar Habash, Hinrik Hafsteinsson, Jan Hajič, Jan Hajič jr., Mika Hämäläinen, Linh Hà Mỹ, Na-Rae Han, Muhammad Yudistira Hanifmuti, Takahiro Harada, Sam Hardwick, Kim Harris, Dag Haug, Johannes Heinecke, Oliver Hellwig, Felix Hennig, Barbora Hladká, Jaroslava Hlaváčová, Florinel Hociung, Petter Hohle, Marivel Huerta Mendez, Jena Hwang, Takumi Ikeda, Anton Karl Ingason, Radu Ion, Elena Irimia, Ọlájídé Ishola, Artan Islamaj, Kaoru Ito, Siratun Jannat, Tomáš Jelínek, Apoorva Jha, Katharine Jiang, Anders Johannsen, Hildur Jónsdóttir, Fredrik Jørgensen, Markus Juutinen, Hüner Kaşıkara, Nadezhda Kabaeva, Sylvain Kahane, Hiroshi Kanayama, Jenna Kanerva, Neslihan Kara, Ritván Karahóǧa, Andre Kåsen, Tolga Kayadelen, Sarveswaran Kengatharaiyer, Václava Kettnerová, Jesse Kirchner, Elena Klementieva, Elena Klyachko, Arne Köhn, Abdullatif Köksal, Kamil Kopacewicz, Timo Korkiakangas, Mehmet Köse, Alexey Koshevoy, Natalia Kotsyba, Jolanta Kovalevskaitė, Simon Krek, Parameswari Krishnamurthy, Sandra Kübler, Adrian Kuqi, Oğuzhan Kuyrukçu, Aslı Kuzgun, Sookyoung Kwak, Kris Kyle, Veronika Laippala, Lorenzo Lambertino, Tatiana Lando, Septina Dian Larasati, Alexei Lavrentiev, John Lee, Phuong Lê Hồng, Alessandro Lenci, Saran Lertpradit, Herman Leung, Maria Levina, Lauren Levine, Cheuk Ying Li, Josie Li, Keying Li, Yixuan Li, Yuan Li, KyungTae Lim, Bruna Lima Padovani, Yi-Ju Jessica Lin, Krister Lindén, Yang Janet Liu, Nikola Ljubešić, Olga Loginova, Stefano Lusito, Andry Luthfi, Mikko Luukko, Olga Lyashevskaya, Teresa Lynn, Vivien Macketanz, Menel Mahamdi, Jean Maillard, Ilya Makarchuk, Aibek Makazhanov, Michael Mandl, Christopher Manning, Ruli Manurung, Büşra Marşan, Cătălina Mărănduc, David Mareček, Katrin Marheinecke, Stella Markantonatou, Héctor Martínez Alonso, Lorena Martín Rodríguez, André Martins, Cláudia Martins, Jan Mašek, Hiroshi Matsuda, Yuji Matsumoto, Alessandro Mazzei, Ryan McDonald, Sarah McGuinness, Gustavo Mendonça, Tatiana Merzhevich, Niko Miekka, Aaron Miller, Karina Mischenkova, Anna Missilä, Cătălin Mititelu, Maria Mitrofan, Yusuke Miyao, AmirHossein Mojiri Foroushani, Judit Molnár, Amirsaeid Moloodi, Simonetta Montemagni, Amir More, Laura Moreno Romero, Giovanni Moretti, Shinsuke Mori, Tomohiko Morioka, Shigeki Moro, Bjartur Mortensen, Bohdan Moskalevskyi, Kadri Muischnek, Robert Munro, Yugo Murawaki, Kaili Müürisep, Pinkey Nainwani, Mariam Nakhlé, Juan Ignacio Navarro Horñiacek, Anna Nedoluzhko, Gunta Nešpore-Bērzkalne, Manuela Nevaci, Luong Nguyễn Thị, Huyền Nguyễn Thị Minh, Yoshihiro Nikaido, Vitaly Nikolaev, Rattima Nitisaroj, Alireza Nourian, Hanna Nurmi, Stina Ojala, Atul Kr. Ojha, Hulda Óladóttir, Adédayọ Olúòkun, Mai Omura, Emeka Onwuegbuzia, Noam Ordan, Petya Osenova, Robert Östling, Lilja Øvrelid, Şaziye Betül Özateş, Merve Özçelik, Arzucan Özgür, Balkız Öztürk Başaran, Teresa Paccosi, Alessio Palmero Aprosio, Anastasia Panova, Hyunji Hayley Park, Niko Partanen, Elena Pascual, Marco Passarotti,

Agnieszka Patejuk, Guilherme Paulino-Passos, Giulia Pedonese, Angelika Peljak-Łapińska, Siyao Peng, Siyao Logan Peng, Rita Pereira, Sílvia Pereira, Cenel-Augusto Perez, Natalia Perkova, Guy Perrier, Slav Petrov, Daria Petrova, Andrea Peverelli, Jason Phelan, Jussi Piitulainen, Yuval Pinter, Clara Pinto, Tommi A Pirinen, Emily Pitler, Magdalena Plamada, Barbara Plank, Thierry Poibeau, Larisa Ponomareva, Martin Popel, Lauma Pretkalniņa, Sophie Prévost, Prokopis Prokopidis, Adam Przepiórkowski, Robert Pugh, Tiina Puolakainen, Sampo Pyysalo, Peng Qi, Andreia Querido, Andriela Rääbis, Alexandre Rademaker, Mizanur Rahoman, Taraka Rama, Loganathan Ramasamy, Joana Ramos, Fam Rashel, Mohammad Sadegh Rasooli, Vinit Ravishankar, Livy Real, Petru Rebeja, Siva Reddy, Mathilde Regnault, Georg Rehm, Arij Riabi, Ivan Riabov, Michael Rießler, Erika Rimkutė, Larissa Rinaldi, Laura Rituma, Putri Rizqiyah, Luisa Rocha, Eiríkur Rögnvaldsson, Ivan Roksandic, Mykhailo Romanenko, Rudolf Rosa, Valentin Roșca, Davide Rovati, Ben Rozonoyer, Olga Rudina, Jack Rueter, Kristján Rúnarsson, Shoval Sadde, Pegah Safari, Aleksi Sahala, Shadi Saleh, Alessio Salomoni, Tanja Samardžić, Stephanie Samson, Manuela Sanguinetti, Ezgi Sanıyar, Dage Särg, Marta Sartor, Mitsuya Sasaki, Baiba Saulīte, Yanin Sawanakunanon, Shefali Saxena, Kevin Scannell, Salvatore Scarlata, Nathan Schneider, Sebastian Schuster, Lane Schwartz, Djamé Seddah, Wolfgang Seeker, Mojgan Seraji, Syeda Shahzadi, Mo Shen, Atsuko Shimada, Hiroyuki Shirasu, Yana Shishkina, Muh Shohibussirri, Maria Shvedova, Janine Siewert, Einar Freyr Sigurðsson, João Silva, Aline Silveira, Natalia Silveira, Sara Silveira, Maria Simi, Radu Simionescu, Katalin Simkó, Mária Šimková, Haukur Barri Símonarson, Kiril Simov, Dmitri Sitchinava, Ted Sither, Maria Skachedubova, Aaron Smith, Isabela Soares-Bastos, Per Erik Solberg, Barbara Sonnenhauser, Shafi Sourov, Rachele Sprugnoli, Vivian Stamou, Steinh͡ór Steingrímsson, Antonio Stella, Abishek Stephen, Milan Straka, Emmett Strickland, Jana Strnadová, Alane Suhr, Yogi Lesmana Sulestio, Umut Sulubacak, Shingo Suzuki, Daniel Swanson, Zsolt Szántó, Chihiro Taguchi, Dima Taji, Fabio Tamburini, Mary Ann C. Tan, Takaaki Tanaka, Dipta Tanaya, Mirko Tavoni, Samson Tella, Isabelle Tellier, Marinella Testori, Guillaume Thomas, Sara Tonelli, Liisi Torga, Marsida Toska, Trond Trosterud, Anna Trukhina, Reut Tsarfaty, Utku Türk, Francis Tyers, Sveinbjörn H͡órðarson, Vilhjálmur H͡orsteinsson, Sumire Uematsu, Roman Untilov, Zdeňka Urešová, Larraitz Uria, Hans Uszkoreit, Andrius Utka, Elena Vagnoni, Sowmya Vajjala, Socrates Vak, Rob van der Goot, Martine Vanhove, Daniel van Niekerk, Gertjan van Noord, Viktor Varga, Uliana Vedenina, Giulia Venturi, Veronika Vincze, Natalia Vlasova, Aya Wakasa, Joel C. Wallenberg, Lars Wallin, Abigail Walsh, Jonathan North Washington, Maximilan Wendt, Paul Widmer, Shira Wigderson, Sri Hartati Wijono, Seyi Williams, Mats Wirén, Christian Wittern, Tsegay Woldemariam, Tak-sum Wong, Alina Wróblewska, Mary Yako, Kayo Yamashita, Naoki Yamazaki, Chunxiao Yan, Koichi Yasuoka, Marat M. Yavrumyan, Arife Betül Yenice, Olcay Taner Yıldız, Zhuoran Yu, Arlisa Yuliawati, Zdeněk Žabokrtský, Shorouq Zahra, Amir Zeldes, He Zhou, Hanzhi Zhu, Yilun Zhu, Anna Zhuravleva, and Rayan Ziane. 2023. Universal dependencies 2.12. LINDAT/CLARIAH-CZ digital library at the Institute of Formal and Applied Linguistics (ÚFAL), Faculty of Mathematics and Physics, Charles University.

Liu Zhuang, Lin Wayne, Shi Ya, and Zhao Jun. 2021. A Robustly Optimized BERT Pre-training Approach with Post-training. In *Proceedings of the 20th Chinese National Conference on Computational Linguistics*, pages 1218–1227, Huhhot, China. Chinese Information Processing Society of China.

Donnchadh Ó Corráin, Hiram Morgan, Beatrix Färber, Benjamin Hazard, Emer Purcell, Caoimhín Ó Dónaill, Hilary Lavelle, Julianne Nyhan, and Emma McCarthy. 1997. CELT: Corpus of Electronic Texts. Retrieved: March 15, 2021.

Heidelberg-Boston @ SIGTYP 2024 Shared Task: Enhancing Low-Resource Language Analysis With Character-Aware Hierarchical Transformers

Frederick Riemenschneider*
Dept. of Computational Linguistics
Heidelberg University, Germany
riemenschneider@cl.uni-heidelberg.de

Kevin Krahn*
Dept. of Computer Science
Sattler College, USA
kevin.krahn24@sattler.edu

Abstract

Historical languages present unique challenges to the NLP community, with one prominent hurdle being the limited resources available in their closed corpora. This work describes our submission to the constrained subtask of the SIGTYP 2024 shared task, focusing on PoS tagging, morphological tagging, and lemmatization for 13 historical languages. For PoS and morphological tagging we adapt a hierarchical tokenization method from Sun et al. (2023) and combine it with the advantages of the DeBERTa-V3 architecture, enabling our models to efficiently learn from every character in the training data. We also demonstrate the effectiveness of character-level T5 models on the lemmatization task. Pre-trained from scratch with limited data, our models achieved first place in the constrained subtask, nearly reaching the performance levels of the unconstrained task's winner. Our code is available at `https://github.com/bowphs/SIGTYP-2024-hierarchical-transformers`.

1 Introduction

Unlike modern languages, historical languages come with a notable challenge: their corpora are closed, meaning they cannot grow any further. This situation often puts researchers of historical languages in a low-resource setting, requiring tailored strategies to handle language processing and analysis effectively (Johnson et al., 2021).

In this paper, we focus on identifying the most efficient methods for extracting information from small corpora. In such a scenario, the main hurdle is not computational capacity, but learning to extract the maximal amount of information from our existing data.

To evaluate this, the SIGTYP 2024 shared task offers a targeted platform centering on the evaluation of embeddings and systems for historical languages. This task provides a systematic testbed for researchers, allowing us to assess our methodologies in a controlled evaluation setting for historical language processing.

For the constrained subtask, participants received annotated datasets for 13 historical languages sourced from Universal Dependencies (Zeman et al., 2023), along with data for Old Hungarian that adheres to similar annotation standards (Simon, 2014; HAS Research Institute for Linguistics, 2018). These languages represent four distinct language families and employ six different scripts, which ensures a high level of diversity. The rules imposed in this subtask strictly forbid the use of pre-trained models and limit training exclusively to the data of the specified language. This restriction not only ensures full comparability of the applied methods, it also inhibits any cross-lingual transfer effects.

We demonstrate that, even in these resource-limited settings, it is feasible to achieve high performance using monolingual models. Our models are exclusively pre-trained on very small corpora, leveraging recent advances in pre-training language models. Our submission was recognized as the winner in the constrained task. Notably, it also delivered competitive results in comparison to the submissions in the unconstrained task, where the use of additional data was permitted. This highlights the strength of our approach, even within a more restricted data environment.

2 Pre-trained Language Models for Ancient and Historical Languages

Much of the previous work on Pre-trained Language Models (PLMs) for ancient and historical languages has focused on cross-lingual transfer learning techniques (Krahn et al., 2023; Singh et al., 2021; Yamshchikov et al., 2022; Yousef et al., 2022) or languages with relatively large corpora compared to most historical languages, such as An-

*Equal contribution.

Proceedings of the 6th Workshop on Research in Computational Linguistic Typology and Multilingual NLP (SIGTYP 2024), pages 131–141
March 22, 2024

Language:	chu	cop	fro	got	grc	hbo	isl	lat	latm	lzh	ohu	orv	san
Vocab Size:	196	82	106	87	242	94	150	188	111	5714	166	222	62

Table 1: Character vocabulary sizes (including special tokens). See Appendix C for language identifiers.

cient Greek and Latin (Riemenschneider and Frank, 2023; Bamman and Burns, 2020). In this work, we are interested in maximizing performance in more resource-limited environments while training exclusively on monolingual data.

2.1 Representing Words and Characters

Low-resource historical languages present several challenges for subword tokenizers which are typically used by PLMs. Given that our downstream tasks require predictions at the world level, it is important that the model learns good word representations in training. At the same time, it is important to obtain good character representations because characters carry important morphological information. In small-scale training corpora, subword tokenizers are ineffective at capturing information at both the word and character levels, as shown in prior work (Clark et al., 2022; Kann et al., 2018). As a result, it is difficult for a model to learn meaningful representations for rare tokens, which can be completely opaque to the model with respect to the characters they contain.

Adopting a character-based tokenizer would solve many of these problems, but as a downside would result in a much higher number of input tokens. Critically, the computational requirements of self-attention grow quadratically with sequence length, making training and inference time prohibitive or requiring truncated input sequences.

For these reasons, we adopt a solution for our encoder-only models that combines the advantages of word- and character-level representations. We base our architecture on the Hierarchical Pretrained Language Model (HLM) architecture recently proposed by Sun et al. (2023), which solves many of our problems. HLM is a hierarchical two-level model which uses a shallow intra-word transformer encoder to learn word representations from characters and a deep inter-word encoder that attends to the entire word sequence. As a result, (1) it gives direct access to characters without requiring long sequence lengths, (2) it preserves explicit word boundaries, and (3) it allows for an open vocabulary.

For the intra-word encoder, we use a sequence length of 16 which is long enough to cover the vast majority of words in our training data. While Sun et al. (2023) truncate words that exceed the maximum sequence length of the intra-word encoder, we instead split them into multiple subwords to avoid any loss of information. For the inter-word encoder we use a maximum sequence length of 512. Because the intra-word encoder is limited to characters within the same word and the inter-word encoder operates on word sequences, this approach is computationally more efficient than a vanilla character model, and even approaches the performance of subword-based models (Sun et al., 2023).

The input to the intra-word encoder is produced by encoding each word into a sequence of character tokens, with a special `[WORD_CLS]` token inserted at the beginning of each word. The contextualized `[WORD_CLS]` embeddings from the intra-word encoder are then used as the word representations for the inter-word encoder.

We create a character tokenizer for each language using a character vocabulary consisting of all the unique characters found in the training data for that language. Any unseen characters encountered in the validation or test data are replaced with a special `[UNK]` token. Table 1 shows the vocabulary sizes for each language, including special tokens. The character vocabularies are typically quite small, with the notable exception of Classical Chinese (lzh), where most of the tokens in the training data are single characters. We experimented with several decomposition methods, inspired by the work of Si et al. (2023) on sub-character tokenization for Chinese. However, we were unable to improve performance on our downstream tasks, so we opted to use the same character tokenization method for all languages.

2.2 Hierarchical Encoder-only Models

To conduct PoS and morphological tagging, we rely on an encoder that generates the necessary word embeddings for classification. Our encoder models build on a modified implementation of DeBERTa-V3 (He et al., 2023), combining the advantages of HLM with the DeBERTa architecture. The intra-

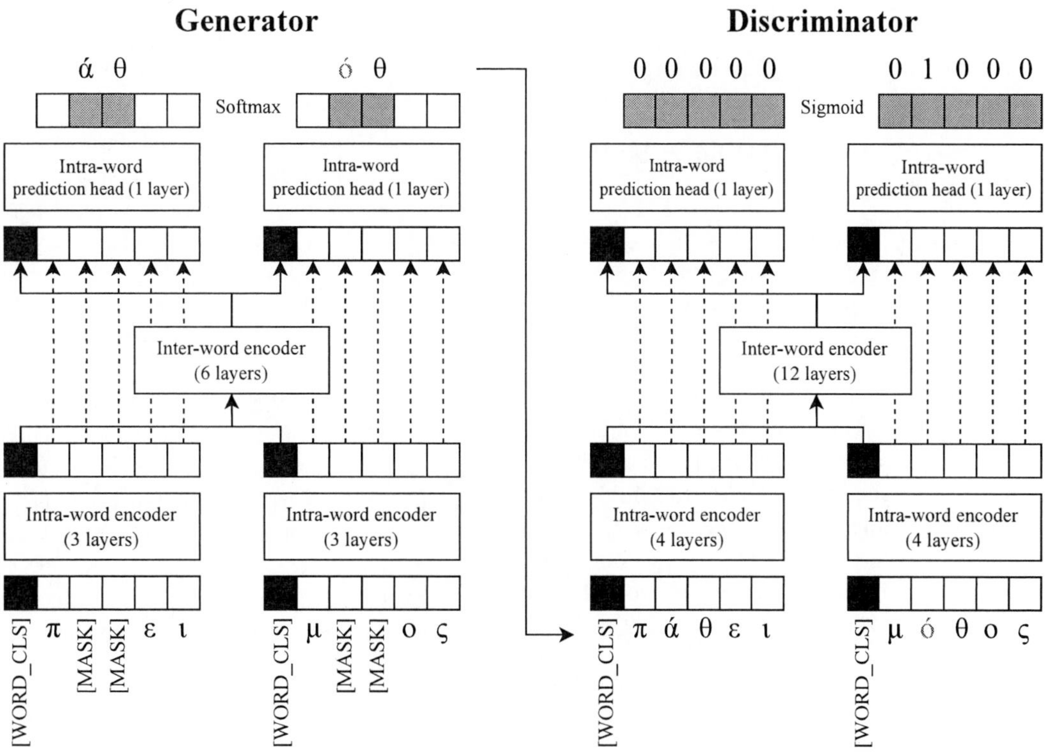

Figure 1: HLM-DeBERTa architecture with RTD pre-training. Input text is "πάθει μάθος".

and inter-word modules are implemented as two separate DeBERTa encoders, utilizing disentangled attention (He et al., 2021) and relative position encoding.

Replaced Token Detection. For the pre-training task we use replaced token detection (RTD), originally proposed by Clark et al. (2020). RTD uses a generator model to generate corrupted input sequences and a discriminator to distinguish between the original and corrupted tokens. After training, the generator is discarded and the discriminator is fine-tuned for downstream tasks. In our experiments, when applying RTD pre-training, we achieve slightly better performance on our downstream tasks compared to masked language modeling (MLM) as the pre-training task. Following previous work (He et al., 2023; Clark et al., 2020), we use a generator with roughly half the model parameters compared to the discriminator. We train a monolingual model for each language for 30 epochs. Further pre-training does not improve performance on downstream tasks.

We utilize DeBERTa-V3's gradient-disentangled embedding sharing (GDES), which allows the embedding gradients from the generator to flow directly to the discriminator, but not vice versa. This results in more stable training compared to the vanilla embedding sharing (ES) used by ELECTRA (Clark et al., 2020), which allows the gradients to flow in both directions.

Masking Strategy. We use character-level masking to allow for open-vocabulary language modeling. The character token sequence is restored by concatenating the character representations from the intra-word module with the word representations from the inter-word module, replacing the initial `[WORD_CLS]` with the contextualized representation. We follow the original HLM approach for the language modeling prediction head: an additional single-layer intra-word transformer module followed by a simple feed-forward network. A softmax layer is used for the generator's output distribution and a sigmoid layer is used for the discriminator. The relative position embedding matrix is shared between the initial intra-word encoder and the intra-word language modeling head. Figure 1 shows an overview of our architecture for RTD pre-training.

We compare the following masking strategies:

- Whole-word masking: mask the characters in 15% of the words (original HLM approach),
- Character masking: randomly mask 15% of the characters,
- Character n-gram masking: mask random spans of 1-4 characters until 15% of the characters are masked.

Through experimentation we found that character n-gram masking performed best for our downstream tasks, by a small margin. Random character masking performed similarly to whole-word-masking. We hypothesize that it is too difficult for the model to learn to predict whole words from the small training corpora. Conversely, random character masking is too easy, as MLM pre-training accuracy reaches high levels very quickly.

2.3 Character-level Encoder-decoder Models

While encoder-only models are very effective for classification tasks, lemmatization is most naturally treated as a sequence-to-sequence problem, where the inflected form is "translated" to its lemma. We therefore choose to train an encoder-decoder model that handles sequence-to-sequence tasks naturally. Specifically, we train a T5 model for each language (Raffel et al., 2020) using the nanoT5 library (Nawrot, 2023) and the t5-v1_1-base configuration. In lemmatization, our aim is to prioritize the characters within a word, rather than focusing on a detailed understanding of contextualized words (see Section 3.3 for our approach). Moreover, extending a hierarchical structure to (encoder-)decoder models like T5 is not straightforward. Therefore, we employ character tokenization in the T5 models for lemmatization.

3 Using our PLMs for Downstream Tasks

Many systems focusing on Universal Dependencies, often introduced in shared tasks, utilize cross-lingual transfer and multi-task learning. For instance, UDPipe (Straka et al., 2019), which employs multilingual BERT, is fine-tuned on specific treebanks for PoS tagging, morphological tagging, lemmatization, and dependency parsing. UDify (Kondratyuk and Straka, 2019) learns these tasks for 75 languages in one model.

Given that in our setting cross-lingual transfer is excluded, we investigate multi-task learning as a remaining option to leverage additional training signals for resource-poor languages.

3.1 Morphological Tagging

Following Riemenschneider and Frank (2023), we treat morphological tagging as a multi-task-classification problem, where every token is processed through k classification heads, corresponding to each possible morphological feature in a dataset. Whenever a feature is missing in a token, the model is trained to predict a class indicating the feature's absence.

To represent a token, the HLM architecture yields two kinds of embeddings: those derived from the intra-word encoder, informed by a word's characters but not by other sentence words, and those that are contextualized by surrounding tokens. In line with Sun et al. (2023) as well as earlier work (Clark et al., 2022; Plank et al., 2016), we concatenate these embeddings to create a unified final word representation.

We use a simple feed-forward network followed by a softmax function on top of the last hidden state of this word representation. The final loss is computed as:

$$\mathcal{L}_{\text{morph}} = \frac{1}{k} \sum_{m=0}^{k-1} \mathcal{L}_m$$

where k is the number of morphological features.

We further extended the multi-task framework to include additional related tasks, hypothesizing that obtaining training signals from auxiliary tasks could improve the model's capabilities, particularly under our low-resource conditions. To this end, we incorporated tasks such as dependency parsing and PoS tagging. Contrary to our expectations, this approach led to slower convergence and did not provide any performance benefits, occasionally even producing marginally inferior results. We discuss these findings in Section 5.

3.2 PoS Tagging

Analogous to our approach in morphological tagging, we represent each token by concatenating its intra- and inter-word embeddings, followed by a classification head. However, in contrast to morphological tagging, we notice slight improvements when the model is also tasked with predicting morphological features. Thus, we determine the loss as $\mathcal{L}_{\text{UPoS}} + \mathcal{L}_{\text{morph}}$, disregarding the morphological tagging predictions during inference.

3.3 Lemmatization

As outlined in Section 2.3, lemmatization is most naturally treated as a sequence-to-sequence problem, where the form to be lemmatized is transduced into its lemma, which is why we propose using a T5 model for this task. Ideally, our model should receive the word to be lemmatized in its original context, while marking the word to be lemmatized, similar to the approach used by Riemenschneider and Frank (2023). For instance, given the input sequence ξύνοιδα [SEP] ἐμαυτῷ [SEP] οὐδὲν ἐπισταμένῳ, the model would be expected to predict the lemma of ἐμαυτῷ, which is ἐμαυτοῦ. This approach would enable us to train the model in an end-to-end fashion, allowing it to autonomously learn the relevant information directly from the word within its contextual surroundings.

However, this training method is prohibitively expensive, requiring repeated passes through the model, once for each token in the sentence. Moreover, we noted that the models exhibited exceptionally slow convergence. Allowing the model to predict lemmata for all words in a sentence in a single forward pass mitigates the computational challenges, as it requires only one pass per sentence per epoch. Yet, this strategy still encounters problems with very slow, and at times nonexistent, convergence, while also introducing new challenges for the model, particularly in assigning exactly one lemma to each token accurately.

Therefore, we adopt a pipeline approach, following Wróbel and Nowak (2022), by providing the model with the inflected form and its corresponding UPoS tag. For training purposes, we use the gold UPoS tag, whereas for inference we rely on the UPoS tag as predicted by our HLM-DeBERTa model. We predict lemmata using beam search with a beam width of 20, restricting the maximum sequence length to 30.

4 Results

Our results are computed using the SIGTYP 2024 official evaluation script.[1] The script computes PoS tagging scores as the unweighted average of the accuracy and the F_1 score. For morphological tagging, it computes the averaged accuracy across each token, with deductions for any feature categories predicted by the model but absent in the label. The lemmatization scores are the unweighted average of the accuracy@1 and the accuracy@3.

We report our results in Table 2 and provide dataset statistics in Appendix C. In **PoS** and **morphological tagging**, our system emerges as the winner of the constrained task. Its performance is consistently almost on-par with that of the unconstrained task winner, being only 0.69 percentage points lower on average. A notable outlier is seen in Old French (fro) PoS tagging, where our system falls short by 3 percentage points. This performance difference might be linked to the small size of the Old French corpus in the treebank, although our model generally shows strong performance in learning from small datasets, as demonstrated by its robust performance in other datasets of similar size, such as Ancient Hebrew (hbo), Gothic (got), and Vedic Sanskrit (san).

Results in **lemmatization** display greater diversity, likely due to the differing architectures in participants' approaches. Our model achieves 99.18% in Classical Chinese (lzh), a language where distinct lemmata do not really exist, usually turning the task into mere form replication. This score, though precise, is somewhat lower than the near-perfect range of 99.81 to 99.96% achieved by the other methods in the shared task.

5 Negative Results

Multi-task Learning. We hypothesized that a model simultaneously doing PoS tagging, morphological tagging and dependency parsing could benefit from the training signals of related tasks.[2] However, this approach did not significantly improve morphological analysis and resulted in longer training times due to slower convergence. On the other hand, jointly performing morphological and PoS tagging in a multi-task learning setup yielded minor improvements in PoS tagging. We believe that including PoS information offers little extra insight to the model for morphological tagging and simultaneously pressures it to form representations apt for PoS tagging. Conversely, enriching the coarser PoS tagging task with morphological labels provides the model with useful additional insights. Furthermore, our dependency parsing technique differs from the more direct classification approach used in PoS and morphological tagging, potentially leading to instabilities during training.

[1] https://github.com/sigtyp/ST2024/blob/main/scoring_program_constrained.zip.

[2] For dependency parsing, we adopt the head selection method as described by Zhang et al. (2017).

	Language:	chu	cop	fro	got	grc	hbo	isl	lat	latm	lzh	ohu	orv	san
Morphological Tagging														
Constrained	Ours	**96.04**	**98.60**	**97.87**	**95.32**	**97.46**	**97.46**	**95.29**	**95.17**	**98.68**	**95.52**	**96.30**	**95.00**	**91.58**
	Team 21a	94.06	80.47	94.08	93.96	96.50	71.20	94.79	93.31	97.98	85.98	94.64	92.16	90.00
	Baseline	85.07	47.41	28.27	18.95	25.10	42.78	35.83	18.17	30.94	43.58	23.20	25.55	08.34
Unconstrained	UDParse	**96.49**	**98.88**	**98.33**	**96.23**	**97.78**	**97.05**	**95.92**	**96.66**	**98.83**	**96.24**	**96.62**	**95.16**	**92.60**
	TartuNLP	67.14	74.86	98.01	92.40	97.33	95.14	95.53	95.91	**98.83**	88.75	75.62	80.00	86.33
PoS Tagging														
Constrained	Ours	**96.57**	**96.92**	**93.10**	**95.41**	**96.39**	**96.68**	**96.08**	**95.54**	**98.43**	**92.92**	**95.98**	**94.46**	**89.71**
	Team 21a	94.62	42.65	85.14	93.48	93.49	27.26	93.85	92.43	94.41	81.79	94.42	91.23	87.32
	Baseline	93.36	94.98	91.57	93.73	90.33	94.07	94.00	92.39	97.22	90.91	93.59	90.33	89.37
Unconstrained	UDParse	**97.00**	**97.33**	**96.01**	**96.47**	**96.49**	**97.84**	**96.88**	**96.83**	**98.79**	**93.76**	**96.71**	**94.99**	**90.02**
	TartuNLP	66.35	60.99	94.51	92.72	95.72	94.15	96.67	95.86	**98.79**	83.28	75.14	75.67	83.83
Lemmatization														
Constrained	Ours	**94.49**	95.07	**92.63**	**93.31**	**94.08**	**97.29**	**96.63**	**96.00**	**98.46**	99.18	85.92	**90.09**	**84.59**
	Team 21a	79.59	46.32	83.32	90.79	88.30	61.75	94.58	92.35	97.22	**99.84**	69.97	78.44	83.21
	Baseline	89.60	**95.74**	91.93	91.95	91.06	95.28	93.78	92.08	97.03	98.81	**89.43**	84.44	84.24
Unconstrained	UDParse	59.56	74.78	92.47	92.81	**94.02**	96.85	**97.96**	**96.74**	**98.91**	**99.96**	63.43	68.55	88.10
	TartuNLP	**92.70**	**98.28**	**95.11**	**95.41**	93.39	**98.15**	97.23	**96.99**	98.69	99.91	**86.91**	**89.23**	**91.48**

Table 2: Results on *SIGTYP 2024 Shared Task on Word Embedding Evaluation for Ancient and Historical Languages*. We mark the winner of each subtask in **bold** and underline the overall winner. See Appendix C for language identifiers.

Tall Models. Xue et al. (2023) found that transformers with a narrower and deeper architecture might surpass the performance of similarly sized models in masked language modeling tasks. Inspired by this finding, we experimented with doubling the number of layers to 24 while reducing the hidden size from 768 to 512 and the number of attention heads from 12 to 8. However, although this adjustment seemed to yield a marginal improvement in pre-training with MLM, it did not result in any performance changes when training with RTD.

6 Conclusion

We present our approach for the SIGTYP 2024 shared task on historical language analysis. Our method employs a hierarchical transformer that first focuses on a word's characters, applying self-attention to generate initial word embeddings. These embeddings are then further developed by integrating the contextual information from surrounding words. We pre-train HLM-DeBERTa-V3 and T5 models with small datasets of historical texts. The character-based methodology of our architecture yielded promising results, effectively leveraging the available data. Contrary to our expectations, the implementation of multi-task learning had only a negligible effect on enhancing our models' performance.

Acknowledgements

We thank Anette Frank for her helpful suggestions and her constructive feedback on our paper. We are deeply grateful to Fabian Strobel for his support and the valuable pointers he provided.

References

David Bamman and Patrick J. Burns. 2020. Latin BERT: A contextual language model for classical philology.

Jonathan H. Clark, Dan Garrette, Iulia Turc, and John Wieting. 2022. Canine: Pre-training an efficient tokenization-free encoder for language representation. *Transactions of the Association for Computational Linguistics*, 10:73–91.

Kevin Clark, Minh-Thang Luong, Quoc V. Le, and Christopher D. Manning. 2020. ELECTRA: Pre-training text encoders as discriminators rather than generators. In *ICLR*.

HAS Research Institute for Linguistics. 2018. Old Hungarian Codices.

Pengcheng He, Jianfeng Gao, and Weizhu Chen. 2023. DeBERTav3: Improving DeBERTa using ELECTRA-style pre-training with gradient-disentangled embedding sharing. In *The Eleventh International Conference on Learning Representations*.

Pengcheng He, Xiaodong Liu, Jianfeng Gao, and Weizhu Chen. 2021. DeBERTa: Decoding-enhanced BERT with disentangled attention. In *International Conference on Learning Representations*.

Kyle P. Johnson, Patrick J. Burns, John Stewart, Todd Cook, Clément Besnier, and William J. B. Mattingly. 2021. The Classical Language Toolkit: An NLP framework for pre-modern languages. In *Proceedings of the 59th Annual Meeting of the Association for Computational Linguistics and the 11th International Joint Conference on Natural Language Processing: System Demonstrations*, pages 20–29, Online. Association for Computational Linguistics.

Katharina Kann, Johannes Bjerva, Isabelle Augenstein, Barbara Plank, and Anders Søgaard. 2018. Character-level supervision for low-resource POS tagging. In *Proceedings of the Workshop on Deep Learning Approaches for Low-Resource NLP*, pages 1–11, Melbourne. Association for Computational Linguistics.

Dan Kondratyuk and Milan Straka. 2019. 75 languages, 1 model: Parsing Universal Dependencies universally. In *Proceedings of the 2019 Conference on Empirical Methods in Natural Language Processing and the 9th International Joint Conference on Natural Language Processing (EMNLP-IJCNLP)*, pages 2779–2795, Hong Kong, China. Association for Computational Linguistics.

Kevin Krahn, Derrick Tate, and Andrew C. Lamicela. 2023. Sentence embedding models for Ancient Greek using multilingual knowledge distillation. In *Proceedings of the Ancient Language Processing Workshop*, pages 13–22, Varna, Bulgaria. INCOMA Ltd., Shoumen, Bulgaria.

Piotr Nawrot. 2023. nanoT5: Fast & simple pre-training and fine-tuning of t5 models with limited resources. In *Proceedings of the 3rd Workshop for Natural Language Processing Open Source Software (NLP-OSS 2023)*, pages 95–101, Singapore. Association for Computational Linguistics.

Barbara Plank, Anders Søgaard, and Yoav Goldberg. 2016. Multilingual part-of-speech tagging with bidirectional long short-term memory models and auxiliary loss. In *Proceedings of the 54th Annual Meeting of the Association for Computational Linguistics (Volume 2: Short Papers)*, pages 412–418, Berlin, Germany. Association for Computational Linguistics.

Colin Raffel, Noam Shazeer, Adam Roberts, Katherine Lee, Sharan Narang, Michael Matena, Yanqi Zhou, Wei Li, and Peter J. Liu. 2020. Exploring the limits of transfer learning with a unified text-to-text transformer. *Journal of Machine Learning Research*, 21(140):1–67.

Frederick Riemenschneider and Anette Frank. 2023. Exploring large language models for classical philology. In *Proceedings of the 61st Annual Meeting of the Association for Computational Linguistics (Volume 1: Long Papers)*, pages 15181–15199, Toronto, Canada. Association for Computational Linguistics.

Chenglei Si, Zhengyan Zhang, Yingfa Chen, Fanchao Qi, Xiaozhi Wang, Zhiyuan Liu, Yasheng Wang, Qun Liu, and Maosong Sun. 2023. Sub-character tokenization for Chinese pretrained language models. *Transactions of the Association for Computational Linguistics*, 11:469–487.

Eszter Simon. 2014. Corpus Building from Old Hungarian Codices. In Katalin É. Kiss, editor, *The Evolution of Functional Left Peripheries in Hungarian Syntax*. Oxford University Press, Oxford.

Pranaydeep Singh, Gorik Rutten, and Els Lefever. 2021. A pilot study for BERT language modelling and morphological analysis for ancient and medieval Greek. In *Proceedings of the 5th Joint SIGHUM Workshop on Computational Linguistics for Cultural Heritage, Social Sciences, Humanities and Literature*, pages 128–137, Punta Cana, Dominican Republic (online). Association for Computational Linguistics.

Milan Straka, Jana Straková, and Jan Hajič. 2019. Evaluating contextualized embeddings on 54 languages in POS tagging, lemmatization and dependency parsing. *arXiv preprint arXiv:1908.07448*.

Li Sun, Florian Luisier, Kayhan Batmanghelich, Dinei Florencio, and Cha Zhang. 2023. From characters to words: Hierarchical pre-trained language model for open-vocabulary language understanding. In *Proceedings of the 61st Annual Meeting of the Association for Computational Linguistics (Volume 1: Long Papers)*, pages 3605–3620, Toronto, Canada. Association for Computational Linguistics.

Krzysztof Wróbel and Krzysztof Nowak. 2022. Transformer-based part-of-speech tagging and lemmatization for Latin. In *Proceedings of the*

Second Workshop on Language Technologies for Historical and Ancient Languages, pages 193–197, Marseille, France. European Language Resources Association.

Fuzhao Xue, Jianghai Chen, Aixin Sun, Xiaozhe Ren, Zangwei Zheng, Xiaoxin He, Yongming Chen, Xin Jiang, and Yang You. 2023. A study on transformer configuration and training objective. In *Proceedings of the 40th International Conference on Machine Learning*, ICML'23. JMLR.org.

Ivan Yamshchikov, Alexey Tikhonov, Yorgos Pantis, Charlotte Schubert, and Jürgen Jost. 2022. BERT in plutarch's shadows. In *Proceedings of the 2022 Conference on Empirical Methods in Natural Language Processing*, pages 6071–6080, Abu Dhabi, United Arab Emirates. Association for Computational Linguistics.

Tariq Yousef, Chiara Palladino, Farnoosh Shamsian, Anise d'Orange Ferreira, and Michel Ferreira dos Reis. 2022. An automatic model and gold standard for translation alignment of Ancient Greek. In *Proceedings of the Thirteenth Language Resources and Evaluation Conference*, pages 5894–5905, Marseille, France. European Language Resources Association.

Daniel Zeman, Joakim Nivre, Mitchell Abrams, Elia Ackermann, Noëmi Aepli, Hamid Aghaei, Željko Agić, Amir Ahmadi, Lars Ahrenberg, Chika Kennedy Ajede, Salih Furkan Akkurt, Gabrielė Aleksandravičiūtė, Ika Alfina, Avner Algom, Khalid Alnajjar, Chiara Alzetta, Erik Andersen, Lene Antonsen, Tatsuya Aoyama, Katya Aplonova, Angelina Aquino, Carolina Aragon, Glyd Aranes, Maria Jesus Aranzabe, Bilge Nas Arıcan, Hórunn Arnardóttir, Gashaw Arutie, Jessica Naraiswari Arwidarasti, Masayuki Asahara, Katla Ásgeirsdóttir, Deniz Baran Aslan, Cengiz Asmazoğlu, Luma Ateyah, Furkan Atmaca, Mohammed Attia, Aitziber Atutxa, Liesbeth Augustinus, Mariana Avelãs, Elena Badmaeva, Keerthana Balasubramani, Miguel Ballesteros, Esha Banerjee, Sebastian Bank, Verginica Barbu Mititelu, Starkaður Barkarson, Rodolfo Basile, Victoria Basmov, Colin Batchelor, John Bauer, Seyyit Talha Bedir, Shabnam Behzad, Kepa Bengoetxea, İbrahim Benli, Yifat Ben Moshe, Gözde Berk, Riyaz Ahmad Bhat, Erica Biagetti, Eckhard Bick, Agnė Bielinskienė, Kristín Bjarnadóttir, Rogier Blokland, Victoria Bobicev, Loïc Boizou, Emanuel Borges Völker, Carl Börstell, Cristina Bosco, Gosse Bouma, Sam Bowman, Adriane Boyd, Anouck Braggaar, António Branco, Kristina Brokaitė, Aljoscha Burchardt, Marisa Campos, Marie Candito, Bernard Caron, Gauthier Caron, Catarina Carvalheiro, Rita Carvalho, Lauren Cassidy, Maria Clara Castro, Sérgio Castro, Tatiana Cavalcanti, Gülşen Cebiroğlu Eryiğit, Flavio Massimiliano Cecchini, Giuseppe G. A. Celano, Slavomír Čéplö, Neslihan Cesur, Savas Cetin, Özlem Çetinoğlu, Fabricio Chalub, Liyanage Chamila, Shweta Chauhan, Ethan Chi, Taishi Chika, Yongseok Cho, Jinho Choi, Jayeol Chun, Juyeon Chung, Alessandra T. Cignarella, Silvie Cinková, Aurélie Collomb, Çağrı Çöltekin, Miriam Connor, Daniela Corbetta, Francisco Costa, Marine Courtin, Mihaela Cristescu, Ingerid Løyning Dale, Philemon Daniel, Elizabeth Davidson, Leonel Figueiredo de Alencar, Mathieu Dehouck, Martina de Laurentiis, Marie-Catherine de Marneffe, Valeria de Paiva, Mehmet Oguz Derin, Elvis de Souza, Arantza Diaz de Ilarraza, Carly Dickerson, Arawinda Dinakaramani, Elisa Di Nuovo, Bamba Dione, Peter Dirix, Kaja Dobrovoljc, Adrian Doyle, Timothy Dozat, Kira Droganova, Puneet Dwivedi, Christian Ebert, Hanne Eckhoff, Masaki Eguchi, Sandra Eiche, Marhaba Eli, Ali Elkahky, Binyam Ephrem, Olga Erina, Tomaž Erjavec, Farah Essaidi, Aline Etienne, Wograine Evelyn, Sidney Facundes, Richárd Farkas, Federica Favero, Jannatul Ferdaousi, Marília Fernanda, Hector Fernandez Alcalde, Amal Fethi, Jennifer Foster, Cláudia Freitas, Kazunori Fujita, Katarína Gajdošová, Daniel Galbraith, Federica Gamba, Marcos Garcia, Moa Gärdenfors, Fabrício Ferraz Gerardi, Kim Gerdes, Luke Gessler, Filip Ginter, Gustavo Godoy, Iakes Goenaga, Koldo Gojenola, Memduh Gökırmak, Yoav Goldberg, Xavier Gómez Guinovart, Berta González Saavedra, Bernadeta Griciūtė, Matias Grioni, Loïc Grobol, Normunds Grūzītis, Bruno Guillaume, Céline Guillot-Barbance, Tunga Güngör, Nizar Habash, Hinrik Hafsteinsson, Jan Hajič, Jan Hajič jr., Mika Hämäläinen, Linh Hà Mỹ, Na-Rae Han, Muhammad Yudistira Hanifmuti, Takahiro Harada, Sam Hardwick, Kim Harris, Dag Haug, Johannes Heinecke, Oliver Hellwig, Felix Hennig, Barbora Hladká, Jaroslava Hlaváčová, Florinel Hociung, Petter Hohle, Marivel Huerta Mendez, Jena Hwang, Takumi Ikeda, Anton Karl Ingason, Radu Ion, Elena Irimia, Ọlájídé Ishola, Artan Islamaj, Kaoru Ito, Siratun Jannat, Tomáš Jelínek, Apoorva Jha, Katharine Jiang, Anders Johannsen, Hildur Jónsdóttir, Fredrik Jørgensen, Markus Juutinen, Hüner Kaşıkara, Nadezhda Kabaeva, Sylvain Kahane, Hiroshi Kanayama, Jenna Kanerva, Neslihan Kara, Ritván Karahóğa, Andre Kåsen, Tolga Kayadelen, Sarveswaran Kengatharaiyer, Václava Kettnerová, Jesse Kirchner, Elena Klementieva, Elena Klyachko, Arne Köhn, Abdullatif Köksal, Kamil Kopacewicz, Timo Korkiakangas, Mehmet Köse, Alexey Koshevoy, Natalia Kotsyba, Jolanta Kovalevskaitė, Simon Krek, Parameswari Krishnamurthy, Sandra Kübler, Adrian Kuqi, Oğuzhan Kuyrukçu, Aslı Kuzgun, Sookyoung Kwak, Kris Kyle, Veronika Laippala, Lorenzo Lambertino, Tatiana Lando, Septina Dian Larasati, Alexei Lavrentiev, John Lee, Phương Lê Hồng, Alessandro Lenci, Saran Lertpradit, Herman Leung, Maria Levina, Lauren Levine, Cheuk Ying Li, Josie Li, Keying Li, Yixuan Li, Yuan Li, KyungTae Lim, Bruna Lima Padovani, Yi-Ju Jessica Lin, Krister Lindén, Yang Janet Liu, Nikola Ljubešić, Olga Loginova, Stefano Lusito, Andry Luthfi, Mikko Luukko, Olga Lyashevskaya, Teresa Lynn, Vivien Macketanz, Menel Mahamdi, Jean Maillard, Ilya Makarchuk, Aibek Makazhanov, Michael Mandl, Christopher Manning, Ruli Manurung, Büşra Marşan, Cătălina Mărănduc, David Mareček, Katrin Marheinecke, Stella Markantonatou, Héctor Martínez Alonso, Lorena

Martín Rodríguez, André Martins, Cláudia Martins, Jan Mašek, Hiroshi Matsuda, Yuji Matsumoto, Alessandro Mazzei, Ryan McDonald, Sarah McGuinness, Gustavo Mendonça, Tatiana Merzhevich, Niko Miekka, Aaron Miller, Karina Mischenkova, Anna Missilä, Cătălin Mititelu, Maria Mitrofan, Yusuke Miyao, AmirHossein Mojiri Foroushani, Judit Molnár, Amirsaeid Moloodi, Simonetta Montemagni, Amir More, Laura Moreno Romero, Giovanni Moretti, Shinsuke Mori, Tomohiko Morioka, Shigeki Moro, Bjartur Mortensen, Bohdan Moskalevskyi, Kadri Muischnek, Robert Munro, Yugo Murawaki, Kaili Müürisep, Pinkey Nainwani, Mariam Nakhlé, Juan Ignacio Navarro Horñiacek, Anna Nedoluzhko, Gunta Nešpore-Bērzkalne, Manuela Nevaci, Lương Nguyễn Thị, Huyền Nguyễn Thị Minh, Yoshihiro Nikaido, Vitaly Nikolaev, Rattima Nitisaroj, Alireza Nourian, Hanna Nurmi, Stina Ojala, Atul Kr. Ojha, Hulda Óladóttir, Adédayọ̀ Olúòkun, Mai Omura, Emeka Onwuegbuzia, Noam Ordan, Petya Osenova, Robert Östling, Lilja Øvrelid, Şaziye Betül Özateş, Merve Özçelik, Arzucan Özgür, Balkız Öztürk Başaran, Teresa Paccosi, Alessio Palmero Aprosio, Anastasia Panova, Hyunji Hayley Park, Niko Partanen, Elena Pascual, Marco Passarotti, Agnieszka Patejuk, Guilherme Paulino-Passos, Giulia Pedonese, Angelika Peljak-Łapińska, Siyao Peng, Siyao Logan Peng, Rita Pereira, Sílvia Pereira, Cenel-Augusto Perez, Natalia Perkova, Guy Perrier, Slav Petrov, Daria Petrova, Andrea Peverelli, Jason Phelan, Jussi Piitulainen, Yuval Pinter, Clara Pinto, Tommi A Pirinen, Emily Pitler, Magdalena Plamada, Barbara Plank, Thierry Poibeau, Larisa Ponomareva, Martin Popel, Lauma Pretkalniņa, Sophie Prévost, Prokopis Prokopidis, Adam Przepiórkowski, Robert Pugh, Tiina Puolakainen, Sampo Pyysalo, Peng Qi, Andreia Querido, Andriela Rääbis, Alexandre Rademaker, Mizanur Rahoman, Taraka Rama, Loganathan Ramasamy, Joana Ramos, Fam Rashel, Mohammad Sadegh Rasooli, Vinit Ravishankar, Livy Real, Petru Rebeja, Siva Reddy, Mathilde Regnault, Georg Rehm, Arij Riabi, Ivan Riabov, Michael Rießler, Erika Rimkutė, Larissa Rinaldi, Laura Rituma, Putri Rizqiyah, Luisa Rocha, Eiríkur Rögnvaldsson, Ivan Roksandic, Mykhailo Romanenko, Rudolf Rosa, Valentin Roșca, Davide Rovati, Ben Rozonoyer, Olga Rudina, Jack Rueter, Kristján Rúnarsson, Shoval Sadde, Pegah Safari, Aleksi Sahala, Shadi Saleh, Alessio Salomoni, Tanja Samardžić, Stephanie Samson, Manuela Sanguinetti, Ezgi Sanıyar, Dage Särg, Marta Sartor, Mitsuya Sasaki, Baiba Saulīte, Yanin Sawanakunanon, Shefali Saxena, Kevin Scannell, Salvatore Scarlata, Nathan Schneider, Sebastian Schuster, Lane Schwartz, Djamé Seddah, Wolfgang Seeker, Mojgan Seraji, Syeda Shahzadi, Mo Shen, Atsuko Shimada, Hiroyuki Shirasu, Yana Shishkina, Muh Shohibussirri, Maria Shvedova, Janine Siewert, Einar Freyr Sigurðsson, João Silva, Aline Silveira, Natalia Silveira, Sara Silveira, Maria Simi, Radu Simionescu, Katalin Simkó, Mária Šimková, Haukur Barri Símonarson, Kiril Simov, Dmitri Sitchinava, Ted Sither, Maria Skachedubova, Aaron Smith, Isabela Soares-Bastos, Per Erik Solberg, Barbara Sonnenhauser, Shafi Sourov, Rachele Sprugnoli, Vivian Stamou, Steinh͡ór Steingrímsson, Antonio Stella, Abishek Stephen, Milan Straka, Emmett Strickland, Jana Strnadová, Alane Suhr, Yogi Lesmana Sulestio, Umut Sulubacak, Shingo Suzuki, Daniel Swanson, Zsolt Szántó, Chihiro Taguchi, Dima Taji, Fabio Tamburini, Mary Ann C. Tan, Takaaki Tanaka, Dipta Tanaya, Mirko Tavoni, Samson Tella, Isabelle Tellier, Marinella Testori, Guillaume Thomas, Sara Tonelli, Liisi Torga, Marsida Toska, Trond Trosterud, Anna Trukhina, Reut Tsarfaty, Utku Türk, Francis Tyers, Sveinbjörn H͡órðarson, Vilhjálmur H͡orsteinsson, Sumire Uematsu, Roman Untilov, Zdeňka Urešová, Larraitz Uria, Hans Uszkoreit, Andrius Utka, Elena Vagnoni, Sowmya Vajjala, Socrates Vak, Rob van der Goot, Martine Vanhove, Daniel van Niekerk, Gertjan van Noord, Viktor Varga, Uliana Vedenina, Giulia Venturi, Veronika Vincze, Natalia Vlasova, Aya Wakasa, Joel C. Wallenberg, Lars Wallin, Abigail Walsh, Jonathan North Washington, Maximilan Wendt, Paul Widmer, Shira Wigderson, Sri Hartati Wijono, Seyi Williams, Mats Wirén, Christian Wittern, Tsegay Woldemariam, Tak-sum Wong, Alina Wróblewska, Mary Yako, Kayo Yamashita, Naoki Yamazaki, Chunxiao Yan, Koichi Yasuoka, Marat M. Yavrumyan, Arife Betül Yenice, Olcay Taner Yıldız, Zhuoran Yu, Arlisa Yuliawati, Zdeněk Žabokrtský, Shorouq Zahra, Amir Zeldes, He Zhou, Hanzhi Zhu, Yilun Zhu, Anna Zhuravleva, and Rayan Ziane. 2023. Universal dependencies 2.12. LINDAT/CLARIAH-CZ digital library at the Institute of Formal and Applied Linguistics (ÚFAL), Faculty of Mathematics and Physics, Charles University.

Xingxing Zhang, Jianpeng Cheng, and Mirella Lapata. 2017. Dependency parsing as head selection. In *Proceedings of the 15th Conference of the European Chapter of the Association for Computational Linguistics: Volume 1, Long Papers*, pages 665–676, Valencia, Spain. Association for Computational Linguistics.

A Pre-Training Details

Parameter	Generator	Discriminator
Activation	GELU	GELU
Hidden Dropout	0.1	0.1
Initializer Range	0.02	0.02
Intra-word encoder		
Layers	3	4
Hidden Size	768	768
Intermediate Size	1536	1536
Attention Heads	12	12
Inter-word encoder		
Layers	6	12
Hidden Size	768	768
Intermediate Size	3072	3072
Attention Heads	12	12

Table 3: HLM-DeBERTa hyperparameters.

Parameter	Value
Optimizer	Adam
Weight Decay	0.01
Batch Size	16
Learning Rate	1e-5
Learning Rate Scheduler	constant
Epochs	30
Warmup Proportion	0.1
Mask Percentage	15%
Max Sequence Length (words)	512
Max Word Length (chars)	16

Table 4: HLM-DeBERTa pre-training hyperparameters.

Parameter	Value
Optimizer	AdamWScale*
Weight Decay	0.0
Batch Size	16
Learning Rate	1e-5
Learning Rate Scheduler	cosine
Epochs	100
Warmup Steps	1000
Mask Percentage	15%
Max Sequence Length	512
Mean Noise Span Length	3

Table 6: T5 pre-training hyperparameters.

* We use the customized AdamW implementation of nanoT5 (Nawrot, 2023) that is augmented by RMS scaling.

Parameter	Encoder	Decoder
Activation	GEGLU	GEGLU
Hidden Dropout	0.0	0.0
Layers	12	12
Hidden Size	768	768
Intermediate Size	2048	2048
Attention Heads	12	12

Table 5: T5 hyperparameters.

B Fine-tuning Details

Parameter	Value
Optimizer	AdamW
Weight Decay	0.01
Batch Size	16
Learning Rate	2e-5
Learning Rate Scheduler	linear
Early Stopping Patience	10

Table 7: HLM-DeBERTa fine-tuning hyperparameters.

Parameter	Value
Optimizer	AdamW
Weight Decay	0.01
Batch Size	16
Learning Rate	1e-3
Learning Rate Scheduler	linear
Early Stopping Patience	10

Table 8: T5 fine-tuning hyperparameters.

C Dataset Statistics

Language	Code	Family	Script	Train Tok.	Valid Tok.	Test Tok.	Train Sent.	Valid Sent.	Test Sent.
Ancient Greek	grc	Indo-European	Greek	334 043	41 905	41 046	24 800	3100	3101
Ancient Hebrew	hbo	Afro-Asiatic	Hebrew	40 244	4862	4801	1263	158	158
Classical Chinese	lzh	Sino-Tibetan	Hanzi	346 778	43 067	43 323	68 991	8624	8624
Coptic	cop	Afro-Asiatic	Egyptian	57 493	7272	7558	1730	216	217
Gothic	got	Indo-European	Latin	44 044	5724	5568	4320	540	541
Medieval Icelandic	isl	Indo-European	Latin	473 478	59 002	58 242	21 820	2728	2728
Classical & Late Latin	lat	Indo-European	Latin	188 149	23 279	23 344	16 769	2096	2097
Medieval Latin	latm	Indo-European	Latin	599 255	75 079	74 351	30 176	3772	3773
Old Church Slavonic	chu	Indo-European	Cyrillic	159 368	19 779	19 696	18 102	2263	2263
Old East Slavic	orv	Indo-European	Cyrillic	250 833	31 078	32 318	24 788	3098	3099
Old French	fro	Indo-European	Latin	38 460	4764	4870	3113	389	390
Vedic Sanskrit	san	Indo-European	Latin (transcr.)	21 786	2729	2602	3197	400	400
Old Hungarian	ohu	Finno-Ugric	Latin	129 454	16 138	16 116	21 346	2668	2669

Table 9: Dataset statistics.

UDParse @ SIGTYP 2024 Shared Task: Modern Language Models for Historical Languages

Johannes Heinecke
Orange Innovation
2 avenue Pierre Marzin
22300 Lannion, France
johannes.heinecke@orange.com

Abstract

SIGTYP's Shared Task on Word Embedding Evaluation for Ancient and Historical Languages was proposed in two variants, constrained or unconstrained. Whereas the constrained variant disallowed any other data to train embeddings or models than the data provided, the unconstrained variant did not have these limits. We participated in the five tasks of the unconstrained variant and came out first. The tasks were the prediction of part-of-speech, lemmas and morphological features and filling masked words and masked characters on 16 historical languages. We decided to use a dependency parser and train the data using an underlying pretrained transformer model to predict part-of-speech tags, lemmas, and morphological features. For predicting masked words, we used multilingual distilBERT (with rather bad results). In order to predict masked characters, our language model is extremely small: it is a model of 5-gram frequencies, obtained by reading the available training data.

1 Introduction

Since word embeddings and the transformer architecture (Vaswani et al., 2017) found their way into natural language processing (NLP), results for all NLP tasks improved to unseen levels. Multilingual pretrained language models like multilingual BERT (Devlin et al., 2019) and XLM-RoBERTa (Conneau et al., 2020) include word embeddings for up to 100 languages. However, historical languages are most unlikely to be covered by these models. Since corpora of historical languages are limited in size and will most likely not grow anymore (unless an archaeological miracle unearths corpora yet unheard of) it will be difficult to include these languages to existing or new language models. In the SIGTYP Shared Task on Word Embedding Evaluation for Ancient and Historical Languages 2024 (ST 2024)[1], it is proposed to present word embeddings/models for 16 historical languages (cf. Table 1) for which part of speech (POS) (task 1), lemmas (task 2), morphological features (task 3) must be predicted. A fourth task asks to unmask masked words (task 4a) or characters (including spaces and punctuation, task 4b). Both masked words and masked characters can appear in an adjacent position. 10% of words and 5% of characters are masked. The shared task comes in two variants, constrained and unconstrained. In the first variant, only the data provided by the organizers can be used to train models, the unconstrained task allows any additional data to be used for training and inference.

The data used for the Shared Task (Dereza et al., 2024) has been compiled from various sources. Old, Middle, and Early Modern Irish is taken from Bauer et al. (2017), Doyle (2018), Ó Corráin et al. (1997), Acadamh Ríoga na hÉireann (2017); the Old Hungarian corpus origins from Simon (2014) and HAS Research Institute for Linguistics (2018), all other corpora have been published in version 2.12 of the Universal Dependencies project (UD) (Zeman et al., 2023)[2].

Both the training and the test data for the tasks 1, 2, and 3 is in CoNLL-U[3] format, i.e. the documents are segmented into tokenised sentences. The values for POS and the morphological features in tasks 1 and 3 are the UPOS and UFeats sets of the UD project. However not all languages use all possible features, e.g., the Old French data does not use the features `Number` or `Person`.

The Evaluation of the shared task is carried out by the CodaLab platform (Pavao et al., 2023) and uses the metrics shown in Table 2. In case of multiple metrics per task an unweighted average of the metrics was used.

We participated in all five tasks of the uncon-

[1] https://sigtyp.github.io/st2024.html

[2] https://universaldependencies.org, (Nivre et al., 2020)

[3] https://universaldependencies.org/format.html

Proceedings of the 6th Workshop on Research in Computational Linguistic Typology and Multilingual NLP (SIGTYP 2024), pages 142–150
March 22, 2024

Language	Code	Script	Dating	corpus size in tokens			corpus size in sentences		
				Train	Valid	Test	Train	Valid	Test
Ancient Greek	grc	Greek	VIII c. BCE – 110 CE	334,043	41,905	41,046	24,800	3,100	3,101
Ancient Hebrew[†]	hbo	Hebrew	X c. CE	40,244	4,862	4,801	1,263	158	158
Classical Chinese[‡]	lzh	Hanzi	47 – 220 CE	346,778	43,067	43,323	68,991	8,624	8,624
Coptic[†]	cop	Coptic	I – II c. CE	57,493	7,282	7,558	1,730	216	217
Gothic	got	Latin	V – VIII c. CE	44,044	5,724	5,568	4,320	540	541
Medieval Icelandic	isl	Latin	1150 – 1680 CE	473,478	59,002	58,242	21,820	2,728	2,728
Classical and Late Latin	lat	Latin	I c. BCE – IV c. CE	188,149	23,279	23,344	16,769	2,096	2,097
Medieval Latin	latm	Latin	774 – early XIV c. CE	599,255	75,079	74,351	30,176	3,772	3,773
Old Church Slavonic	chu	Cyrillic	X – XI c. CE	159,368	19,779	19,696	18,102	2,263	2,263
Old East Slavic	orv	Cyrillic	1025 – 1700 CE	250,833	31,078	32,318	24,788	3,098	3,099
Old French	fro	Latin	1180 CE	38,460	4,764	4,870	3,113	389	390
Vedic Sanskrit	san	Latin (transcr.)	1500 – 600 BCE	21,786	2,729	2,602	3,197	400	400
Old Hungarian[*]	ohu	Latin	1440 – 1521 CE	129,454	16,138	16,116	21,346	2,668	2,669
Old Irish	sga	Latin	600 – 900 CE	88,774	11,093	11,048	8,748	1,093	1,094
Middle Irish	mga	Latin	900 – 1200 CE	251,684	31,748	31,292	14,308	1,789	1,789
Early Modern Irish	ghc	Latin	1200 – 1700 CE	673,449	115,163	79,600	24,440	3,055	3,056

Table 1: Data ([†]Afro-Asiatic language family, [‡]Sino-Tibetan, [*]Finno-Ugric; all other languages are from the Indo-European language family)

Task		Metrics
1	POS-tagging	Accuracy @1, F1
2	Morph/ annotation of Acc. @1 per tag	Macro-average
3	Lemmatisation	Acc. @1, Acc. @3
4a	Filling masked words	Acc. @1, Acc. @3
4b	Filling masked chars.	Acc. @1, Acc. @3

Table 2: Evaluation metrics

strained variant of the shared task, even though our approach for filling mask characters does not use any other data than the data provided by the organizers. Apart from task 4 (filling masked words) we got the best results of all participants.

2 Related Work

Even though this shared task is not about dependency parsing, POS tagging and lemmatisation are often present in dependency parsing. The shared task in dependency parsing 2018 (Zeman et al., 2018) processed three historical languages, Ancient Greek, Latin, and Old Church Slavonic, for which annotated data was present in the Universal Dependencies project at the time. In many of the approaches word embeddings were used (calculated on corpora of these languages using word2vec (Mikolov et al., 2013), GloVe (Pennington et al., 2014), or fastText (Grave et al., 2018), the latter already provides word embeddings for Latin. The best results of the participants of the 2018 shared tasks for historical languages are above 98% for Latin, above 97% for Ancient Greek, and above 96% for Old church Slavonic for POS tagging. Lemmatisation for these languages also performs similarly well as modern languages. Sprugnoli et al. (2021) also studied the creation and evaluation word embeddings on Latin for the analysis of language change. More recently, several large language models for Classical Greek and Latin have been provided by (Riemenschneider and Frank, 2023) who evaluated this models on POS-tagging and lemmatisation (as this shared task), and dependency parsing. Brigada Villa and Giarda (2023) exploited models trained on Modern English to parse Old English, similar to our approach.

Evidently, word embeddings can be used for other tasks as well. E.g., Hamilton et al. (2016) use word embeddings of earlier version of English (but not going beyond the 1800s) to detect semantic shifts in English.

3 Approaches

3.1 Tasks 1 – 3: Inference of POS, Lemmas, and morphological features

Tasks 1, 2 and three consists of predicting the POS, the lemma, and morphological features of 13 historical languages (Table 1, exluding Old, Midlle and Early Modern Irish).

In order to infer POS, lemmas, and morphological features we used our syntactic dependency parser UDParse[4]. This parser is an evolution of UDpipe (Straka, 2018), which won the CoNLL

[4] https://github.com/Orange-OpenSource/udparse

2018 Shared Task on dependency parsing (Zeman et al., 2018). UDpipe is a graph parser using pretrained word embeddings and embeddings of POS and characters to take the context into account. Word embeddings are loaded before the training, POS and characters embeddings are calculated from the training data. In contrast to UDPipe, UDParse uses word embeddings created by a pretrained transformer instead of contextless word embeddings produced by fastText[5]. This configuration proved to be very successful (Heinecke, 2020; Akermi et al., 2020), so we tried training models for the 13 languages for which the dependency syntax training data was available using different pretrained transformer models: bert-base-multilingual-uncased (Devlin et al., 2019), XLM-RoBERTa, GPT2 (Radford et al., 2019) and language specific models like slavicBERT (Arkhipov et al., 2019) for Old Church Slavonic and Old East Slavic or heBERT[6] for Ancient Hebrew. For the training we used 60 epochs with an initial learning rate of 10^{-3}, which decreased to 10^{-4} after 40 epochs[7], batch size was 32. We then chose for each language and each of task (1: POS, 2: lemmas, 3: morphological features) the best underlying pretrained transformer model (cf. Table 3). In nearly all cases XLM-RoBERTa produced the best results on the validation dataset (even though the difference, notably to multilingual BERT, was very small). For some languages we used different transformer models for tasks 1 to 3 to obtain the best results (on validation data).

Note that the test-data provided by the organizers was already tokenized. This simplifies enormously the tasks of assigning a POS, a lemma, or morphological features, especially for (historical) languages, which do not always come with standardized orthographies.

Even though the challenging fact was that most of these languages are not covered by any of the underlying pretrained language models, the results (Table 5, columns 2, 3, and 4) for POS, lemmas, and features, are well above 90% (except the lemmas for Old Hungarian and Old East Slavic). Partly this can be explained by the fact that the modern descendants of these languages are covered by XLM-RoBERTa etc., and at least some of the words of the historical languages still exist in the contemporary languages. Thus, the modern languages might have helped their ancestors. For comparison, UDParse on modern languages, covered by XLM-RoBERTa or mBERT has results[8] only slightly above the results obtained on historical language (Table 4).

Language code	POS	Lemma	Morphological features
chu	XLMR	XLMR	XLMR
cop	XLMR	GPT2	XLMR
fro	XLMR	mBERT	XLMR
got	XLMR	mBERT	mBERT
grc	XLMR	XLMR	XLMR
hbo	heBERT	XLMR	heBERT
isl	XLMR	XLMR	XLMR
lat	XLMR	XLMR	XLMR
latm	XLMR	XLMR	XLMR
lzh	mBERT	mBERT	mBERT
ohu	XLMR	XLMR	mBERT
orv	XLMR	XLMR	XLMR
san	mBERT	mBERT	XLMR

Table 3: Best underlying pretrained transformer models per language and task 1, 2, and 3. For language codes please refer to Table 1.

Code	UPOS	Lemma	Code	UPOS	Lemma
fr	97.93	98.41	fro	96.01	95.11
he	97.81	97.60	hbo	97.84	98.15
hu	97.07	95.51	ohu	96.71	86.91
ru	99.35	98.90	orv	94.99	89.23

Table 4: UDParse results for some modern languages (left) compared to historical languages (right, results copied from Table 5)

However, this does not explain the worse than average results for Old Hungarian and Old East Slavic whose descendants are also covered by XLM-RoBERTa. Old East Slavic contains some characters absent in its modern successors (Russian, Ukrainian and Belorussian). Similarly, the Old Hungarian corpus contains diacritics and characters not used in Modern Hungarian. This could have played a role. For the above average results for Coptic (not covered by XLM-RoBERTa and written in an alphabet totally absent in the vocabulary of XLM-RoBERTa), UDParse seems to exploit the word and character vectors produced during training to perform well in the lemmatisation.

[5]http://github.com/facebookresearch/fastText/blob/master/pretrained-vectors.md

[6]https://huggingface.co/avichr/heBERT

[7]Decreasing the learning rate after 40 epochs is a result of experimenting with UDParse at an earlier stage.

[8]For the results for other languages cf. https://github.com/Orange-OpenSource/UDParse/blob/master/doc/results.md

Code	UPOS	Lemma	Morph. feat.	Word fill	Char fill	Avg.
chu	97.00	92.70	96.49	2.80	66.77	71.15
cop	97.33	98.28	98.88	0.00	0.00	58.90
fro	96.01	95.11	98.33	3.28	62.77	71.10
got	96.47	95.41	96.23	2.67	74.59	73.07
grc	96.49	93.39	97.78	3.07	68.46	71.84
hbo	97.84	98.15	97.05	5.39	36.85	67.05
isl	96.88	97.23	95.92	3.42	66.45	71.98
lat	96.83	96.99	96.66	3.51	67.91	72.38
latm	98.79	98.69	98.83	4.73	72.93	74.79
lzh	93.76	99.91	96.24	6.10	0.00	59.20
ohu	96.71	86.91	96.62	6.31	66.52	70.61
orv	94.99	89.23	95.16	5.03	61.34	69.15
san	90.02	91.48	92.60	3.86	70.10	69.61
ghc	—	—	—	3.29	58.09	30.69
mga	—	—	—	4.03	53.38	28.71
sga	—	—	—	2.79	58.38	30.59

Table 5: Results (Word filling failed for Coptic (cop) and character filling missing for Coptic and Classical Chinese (lzh). For Old Irish (sga) Middle Irish (mga), and Early Modern Irish (hgc), only data for the word and character filling tasks was available)

All results for tasks 1, 2, and 3 are well above the baseline provide by the shared task's organisers (Table 6) with the exception of the lemmatisation of Old Hungarian (ohu).

Code	UPOS	Lemma	Morph. feat
chu	3.64	3.09	11.42
cop	2.35	2.54	51.47
fro	4.44	3.18	70.06
got	2.74	3.46	77.28
grc	6.16	2.33	72.68
hbo	3.77	2.86	54.26
isl	2.88	3.45	60.09
lat	4.44	4.90	78.49
latm	1.56	1.65	67.89
lzh	2.85	1.10	52.66
ohu	3.12	–2.53	73.42
orv	4.66	4.79	69.60
san	0.65	7.24	84.26

Table 6: Difference with respect to the baseline

3.2 Task 4a: Filling masked words

The task of filling one or several single words in a sentence was the most challenging task for historical languages. Consequently, our results are extremely low (Table 5, column 5). This is probably more due to the chosen approaches than to the fact that the pretrained transformers have been trained little or not at all on these languages. We tried two classical approaches, an encoder (distilbert-base-multilingual-cased, Sanh et al. (2019)) and an encoder/decoder (facebook/mbart-large-50, Tang et al. (2020)). In the first case we used Huggingface's `AutoModelForMaskedLM`, the `AdamW` (Loshchilov and Hutter, 2019) optimiser with a learning rate of $5 * 10^{-5}$, a batch size of 8 and early stopping, which stopped the training after 4 to 6 epochs depending on the language. For the training process, we did not use the masks provided in the training corpus, but masked words randomly with a probability of 15%. In the second case (with mBART) we used Huggingface's `MBartForConditionalGeneration` (other hyperparameters were identical).

The difference between distilBERT and mBART was marginal, possibly linked to a problem not identified before the shared task's deadline. We submitted the results of the first approach. However since this approach only predicts a single token (in the sense of distilBERT's vocabulary) for each masked word instead of a word (in most cases two or more tokens) our prediction was wrong for all masked words which are represented by more than one distilBERT token. In other words, masked words which are not in distilBERT's vocabulary, could not be predicted with this approach. The second approach, based on `MBartForConditionalGeneration`, did indeed return most times a word (or more) for a masked word, but we had cases where only a space was obtained.

3.3 Task 4b: Filling masked characters

For this subtask we chose a very old idea: a simple n-gram count and applying the most frequent n-gram which matches the masked character and its context. We trained our model by counting all n-grams in the unmasked part of the training corpus. We then looked for every masked character in test sentences and tried to find the frequency of all n-grams which include the masked character (we experimented with 3-grams and 5-grams, the latter proved to work much better): for instance, forthe following string "Ne␣voloi?␣aler␣nule part."[9] which includes a masked character, we take the frequencies of all the 5 character windows around the masked characters, including spaces ("␣") from the training

[9]Taken from the Old French training corpus. The shared task data used "[_]" as placeholder for masked characters. We replaced it with a single character not occurring anywhere in the data. For a better readability we use "?" here.

corpus. "?" is the masked character. The letter in inverted colors is the candidate letter:

1. "oloi?" →
   - "oloie" which has frequency of 6 in the training corpus,
   - "oloil" (frequency of 3),
   - "oloir" (8),
   - "oloit" (15, at this stage, this 5-gram is the best match. It is therefore kept while the other 5-grams are discarded)
2. "loi?␣" →
   - "loie␣" (2),
   - "loil␣" (2),
   - "loir␣" (6),
   - "lois␣" (1),
   - "loit␣" (22, new best match so far)
3. "oi?␣a" →
   - "oia␣a" (1),
   - "oie␣a" (17),
   - "oif␣a" (1),
   - "oil␣a" (3),
   - "oir␣a" (3),
   - "ois␣a" (14),
   - "oit␣a" (57, retained),
   - "oiz␣a" (8)
4. "i?␣al" →
   - "it␣al" (3); discarded since with "oit␣a" above we have found a more frequent match already
5. "?␣ale" →
   - "␣␣ale" (3),
   - "a␣ale" (1),
   - "e␣ale" (3),
   - "i␣ale" (2),
   - "l␣ale" (1),
   - "n␣ale" (2),
   - "r␣ale" (6),
   - "s␣ale" (2),
   - "t␣ale" (17),
   - "z␣ale" (1),
   - "«␣ale" (1); all discarded

In this example "oit␣a" is the most frequent replacement for one the 5-grams which contain the masked character ("oi?␣a"). So, we can replace the masked character by "t" to obtain "Ne␣voloit␣aler␣nule part.". Note that at least in this example for each of the five 5-ngrams the best match is the one where the masked character is the same ("t"), but this was not always the case.

The results of this approach can be found in Table 5, column 6. For time reason we could not implement the needed post processing for Classical Chinese (lzh) to rebuild the Hanzi characters from the decomposed characters in the train/validation and test data. Apparently we did not submit the Coptic data to the evaluation server, but a run after the deadline resulted in an accuracy of 62.26%. Interestingly, the score for Ancient Hebrew (hbo) is only half as good as for the other languages. Since the number of different characters of Ancient Hebrew is rather low (cf. Table 7), the reason of this bad result must be found elsewhere. Surprisingly the evaluation of the validation corpus, resulted in around 60% accuracy.

lang. code	characters	lang. code	characters
san	37	ghc	92
cop	41	lat	116
got	50	isl	118
fro	64	ohu	120
hbo	67	chu	124
latm	77	orv	156
mga	77	grc	176
sga	78	lzh	318

Table 7: Number of different characters in the fill masked characters test data. Many languages contain accentuated characters, digits, Classical Latin (lat) contains citations in Greek which account for the unexpected high number of different characters.

We think a more word-context-aware approach could have improved the results, even a simple word based bi- or trigram. For instance in the Old French validation corpus is the following masked character "se je ai dite [_]ne response". Our approach finds for the 5-gram "␣?ne␣" the 5-gram "␣␣ne␣" (the most frequent) instead of the correct "␣une␣". Due to the approaching deadline, we did not have the time to implement and test this.

4 Conclusion

We successfully used rather old and well-established techniques to provide a solution to the five tasks of this year's SIGTYP shared task. Putting aside the failed results for filling-masked-words task, we got very good results for POS tagging, lemmatization, and morphological feature assignment, which are as good as for modern languages and well above the baseline. We are not aware of any state-of-the-art values for filling masked characters, however, even though our results are first placed in the shared task, they are probably perfectible. For modern languages, word embedding or transformer-based methods, e.g. such as CharacterBERT, (El Boukkouri et al., 2020) will probably yield much better results.

References

Acadamh Ríoga na hÉireann. 2017. Corpas Stairiúil na Gaeilge 1600-1926. Retrieved: June 10, 2022.

Imen Akermi, Johannes Heinecke, and Frédéric Herledan. 2020. Transformer based natural language generation for question-answering. In *Proceedings of the 13th International Conference on Natural Language Generation*, pages 349–359, Dublin, Ireland. Association for Computational Linguistics.

Mikhail Arkhipov, Maria Trofimova, Yuri Kuratov, and Alexey Sorokin. 2019. Tuning multilingual transformers for language-specific named entity recognition. In *Proceedings of the 7th Workshop on Balto-Slavic Natural Language Processing*, pages 89–93, Florence, Italy. Association for Computational Linguistics.

Bernhard Bauer, Rijcklof Hofman, and Pádraic Moran. 2017. St. Gall Priscian Glosses, version 2.0. Accessed: February 14, 2023.

Luca Brigada Villa and Martina Giarda. 2023. Using modern languages to parse ancient ones: a test on Old English. In *Proceedings of the 5th Workshop on Research in Computational Linguistic Typology and Multilingual NLP*, pages 30–41, Dubrovnik, Croatia. Association for Computational Linguistics.

Alexis Conneau, Kartikay Khandelwal, Naman Goyal, Vishrav Chaudhary, Guillaume Wenzek, Francisco Guzmán, Edouard Grave, Myle Ott, Luke Zettlemoyer, and Veselin Stoyanov. 2020. Unsupervised cross-lingual representation learning at scale. In *Proceedings of the 58th Annual Meeting of the Association for Computational Linguistics*, pages 8440–8451, Online. Association for Computational Linguistics.

Oksana Dereza, Adrian Doyle, Priya Rani, Atul Kr. Ojha, Pádraic Moran, and John P. McCrae. 2024. Findings of the SIGTYP 2024 shared task on word embedding evaluation for ancient and historical languages. In *Proceedings of the 6th Workshop on Research in Computational Linguistic Typology and Multilingual NLP (SIGTYP 2024)*, St. Julians, Malta. Association for Computational Linguistics.

Jacob Devlin, Ming-Wei Chang, Kenton Lee, and Kristina Toutanova. 2019. BERT: Pre-training of deep bidirectional transformers for language understanding. In *Proceedings of the 2019 Conference of the North American Chapter of the Association for Computational Linguistics: Human Language Technologies, Volume 1 (Long and Short Papers)*, pages 4171–4186, Minneapolis, Minnesota. Association for Computational Linguistics.

Adrian Doyle. 2018. Würzburg Irish Glosses. Accessed: February 14, 2023.

Hicham El Boukkouri, Olivier Ferret, Thomas Lavergne, Hiroshi Noji, Pierre Zweigenbaum, and Jun'ichi Tsujii. 2020. CharacterBERT: Reconciling ELMo and BERT for word-level open-vocabulary representations from characters. In *Proceedings of the 28th International Conference on Computational Linguistics*, pages 6903–6915, Barcelona, Spain (Online). International Committee on Computational Linguistics.

Edouard Grave, Piotr Bojanowski, Prakhar Gupta, Armand Joulin, and Tomas Mikolov. 2018. Learning word vectors for 157 languages. In *Proceedings of the Eleventh International Conference on Language Resources and Evaluation (LREC 2018)*, Miyazaki, Japan. European Language Resources Association (ELRA).

William L. Hamilton, Jure Leskovec, and Dan Jurafsky. 2016. Diachronic word embeddings reveal statistical laws of semantic change. In *Proceedings of the 54th Annual Meeting of the Association for Computational Linguistics (Volume 1: Long Papers)*, pages 1489–1501, Berlin, Germany. Association for Computational Linguistics.

HAS Research Institute for Linguistics. 2018. Old Hungarian Codices. Accessed: October 22, 2023.

Johannes Heinecke. 2020. Hybrid enhanced Universal Dependencies parsing. In *Proceedings of the 16th International Conference on Parsing Technologies and the IWPT 2020 Shared Task on Parsing into Enhanced Universal Dependencies*, pages 174–180, Online. Association for Computational Linguistics.

Ilya Loshchilov and Frank Hutter. 2019. Decoupled weight decay regularization. In *7th International Conference on Learning Representations, ICLR 2019, New Orleans, LA, USA, May 6-9, 2019*. OpenReview.net.

Tomas Mikolov, Kai Chen, Greg Corrado, and Jeffrey Dean. 2013. Efficient estimation of word representations in vector space. *CoRR*, abs/1301.3781.

Joakim Nivre, Marie-Catherine de Marneffe, Filip Ginter, Jan Hajič, Christopher Manning, Sampo Pyysalo, Sebastian Schuster, Tyers Francis, and Daniel Zeman. 2020. Universal Dependencies v2: An Evergrowing Multilingual Treebank Collection. In *LREC 2020*, Marseille. ELRA.

Donnchadh Ó Corráin, Hiram Morgan, Beatrix Färber, Benjamin Hazard, Emer Purcell, Caoimhín Ó Dónaill, Hilary Lavelle, Julianne Nyhan, and Emma McCarthy. 1997. CELT: Corpus of Electronic Texts. Retrieved: March 15, 2021.

Adrien Pavao, Isabelle Guyon, Anne-Catherine Letournel, Dinh-Tuan Tran, Xavier Baro, Hugo Jair Escalante, Sergio Escalera, Tyler Thomas, and Zhen Xu. 2023. Codalab competitions: An open source platform to organize scientific challenges. *Journal of Machine Learning Research*, 24(198):1–6.

Jeffrey Pennington, Richard Socher, and Christopher Manning. 2014. GloVe: Global vectors for word representation. In *Proceedings of the 2014 Conference on Empirical Methods in Natural Language Processing (EMNLP)*, pages 1532–1543, Doha, Qatar. Association for Computational Linguistics.

Alec Radford, Jeffrey Wu, Rewon Child, David Luan, Dario Amodei, and Ilya Sutskever. 2019. Language Models are Unsupervised Multitask Learners. https://openai.com/blog/better-language-models/.

Frederick Riemenschneider and Anette Frank. 2023. Exploring large language models for classical philology. In *Proceedings of the 61st Annual Meeting of the Association for Computational Linguistics (Volume 1: Long Papers)*, pages 15181–15199, Toronto, Canada. Association for Computational Linguistics.

Victor Sanh, Lysandre Debut, Julien Chaumond, and Thomas Wolf. 2019. Distilbert, a distilled version of BERT: smaller, faster, cheaper and lighter.

Eszter Simon. 2014. Corpus Building from Old Hungarian Codices. In Katalin Kiss, editor, *The Evolution of Functional Left Peripheries in Hungarian Syntax*. Oxford University Press, Oxford.

Rachele Sprugnoli, Giovanni Moretti, and Marco Passarotti. 2021. Building and Comparing Lemma Embeddings for Latin. Classical Latin versus Thomas Aquinas. *Italian Journal of Computational Linguistics*, 6(1).

Milan Straka. 2018. UDPipe 2.0 prototype at CoNLL 2018 UD shared task. In *Proceedings of the CoNLL 2018 Shared Task: Multilingual Parsing from Raw Text to Universal Dependencies*, pages 197–207, Brussels, Belgium. Association for Computational Linguistics.

Yuqing Tang, Chau Tran, Xian Li, Peng-Jen Chen, Naman Goyal, Vishrav Chaudhary, Jiatao Gu, and Angela Fan. 2020. Multilingual translation with extensible multilingual pretraining and finetuning.

Ashish Vaswani, Noam Shazeer, Niki Parmar, Jakob Uszkoreit, Llion Jones, Aidan N. Gomez, Łukasz Kaiser, and Illia Polosukhin. 2017. Attention is all you need. In *Advances in Neural Information Processing Systems*, volume 30. Curran Associates, Inc.

Daniel Zeman, Jan Hajič, Martin Popel, Martin Potthast, Milan Straka, Filip Ginter, Joakim Nivre, and Slav Petrov. 2018. CoNLL 2018 shared task: Multilingual parsing from raw text to Universal Dependencies. In *Proceedings of the CoNLL 2018 Shared Task: Multilingual Parsing from Raw Text to Universal Dependencies*, pages 1–21, Brussels, Belgium. Association for Computational Linguistics.

Daniel Zeman, Joakim Nivre, Mitchell Abrams, Elia Ackermann, Noëmi Aepli, Hamid Aghaei, Željko Agić, Amir Ahmadi, Lars Ahrenberg, Chika Kennedy Ajede, Salih Furkan Akkurt, Gabrielė Aleksandravičiūtė, Ika Alfina, Avner Algom, Khalid Alnajjar, Chiara Alzetta, Erik Andersen, Lene Antonsen, Tatsuya Aoyama, Katya Aplonova, Angelina Aquino, Carolina Aragon, Glyd Aranes, Maria Jesus Aranzabe, Bilge Nas Arıcan, Þórunn Arnardóttir, Gashaw Arutie, Jessica Naraiswari Arwidarasti, Masayuki Asahara, Katla Ásgeirsdóttir, Deniz Baran Aslan, Cengiz Asmazoğlu, Luma Ateyah, Furkan Atmaca, Mohammed Attia, Aitziber Atutxa, Liesbeth Augustinus, Mariana Avelãs, Elena Badmaeva, Keerthana Balasubramani, Miguel Ballesteros, Esha Banerjee, Sebastian Bank, Verginica Barbu Mititelu, Starkaður Barkarson, Rodolfo Basile, Victoria Basmov, Colin Batchelor, John Bauer, Seyyit Talha Bedir, Shabnam Behzad, Kepa Bengoetxea, İbrahim Benli, Yifat Ben Moshe, Gözde Berk, Riyaz Ahmad Bhat, Erica Biagetti, Eckhard Bick, Agnė Bielinskienė, Kristín Bjarnadóttir, Rogier Blokland, Victoria Bobicev, Loïc Boizou, Emanuel Borges Völker, Carl Börstell, Cristina Bosco, Gosse Bouma, Sam Bowman, Adriane Boyd, Anouck Braggaar, António Branco, Kristina Brokaitė, Aljoscha Burchardt, Marisa Campos, Marie Candito, Bernard Caron, Gauthier Caron, Catarina Carvalheiro, Rita Carvalho, Lauren Cassidy, Maria Clara Castro, Sérgio Castro, Tatiana Cavalcanti, Gülşen Cebiroğlu Eryiğit, Flavio Massimiliano Cecchini, Giuseppe G. A. Celano, Slavomír Čéplö, Neslihan Cesur, Savas Cetin, Özlem Çetinoğlu, Fabricio Chalub, Liyanage Chamila, Shweta Chauhan, Ethan Chi, Taishi Chika, Yongseok Cho, Jinho Choi, Jayeol Chun, Juyeon Chung, Alessandra T. Cignarella, Silvie Cinková, Aurélie Collomb, Çağrı Çöltekin, Miriam Connor, Daniela Corbetta, Francisco Costa, Marine Courtin, Mihaela Cristescu, Ingerid Løyning Dale, Philemon Daniel, Elizabeth Davidson, Leonel Figueiredo de Alencar, Mathieu Dehouck, Martina de Laurentiis, Marie-Catherine de Marneffe, Valeria de Paiva, Mehmet Oguz Derin, Elvis de Souza, Arantza Diaz de Ilarraza, Carly Dickerson, Arawinda Dinakaramani, Elisa Di Nuovo, Bamba Dione, Peter Dirix, Kaja Dobrovoljc, Adrian Doyle, Timothy Dozat, Kira Droganova, Puneet Dwivedi, Christian Ebert, Hanne Eckhoff, Masaki Eguchi, Sandra Eiche, Marhaba Eli, Ali Elkahky, Binyam Ephrem, Olga Erina, Tomaž Erjavec, Farah

Essaidi, Aline Etienne, Wograine Evelyn, Sidney Facundes, Richárd Farkas, Federica Favero, Jannatul Ferdaousi, Marília Fernanda, Hector Fernandez Alcalde, Amal Fethi, Jennifer Foster, Cláudia Freitas, Kazunori Fujita, Katarína Gajdošová, Daniel Galbraith, Federica Gamba, Marcos Garcia, Moa Gärdenfors, Fabrício Ferraz Gerardi, Kim Gerdes, Luke Gessler, Filip Ginter, Gustavo Godoy, Iakes Goenaga, Koldo Gojenola, Memduh Gökırmak, Yoav Goldberg, Xavier Gómez Guinovart, Berta González Saavedra, Bernadeta Griciūtė, Matias Grioni, Loïc Grobol, Normunds Grūzītis, Bruno Guillaume, Céline Guillot-Barbance, Tunga Güngör, Nizar Habash, Hinrik Hafsteinsson, Jan Hajič, Jan Hajič jr., Mika Hämäläinen, Linh Hà Mỹ, Na-Rae Han, Muhammad Yudistira Hanifmuti, Takahiro Harada, Sam Hardwick, Kim Harris, Dag Haug, Johannes Heinecke, Oliver Hellwig, Felix Hennig, Barbora Hladká, Jaroslava Hlaváčová, Florinel Hociung, Petter Hohle, Marivel Huerta Mendez, Jena Hwang, Takumi Ikeda, Anton Karl Ingason, Radu Ion, Elena Irimia, Ọlájídé Ishola, Artan Islamaj, Kaoru Ito, Siratun Jannat, Tomáš Jelínek, Apoorva Jha, Katharine Jiang, Anders Johannsen, Hildur Jónsdóttir, Fredrik Jørgensen, Markus Juutinen, Hüner Kaşıkara, Nadezhda Kabaeva, Sylvain Kahane, Hiroshi Kanayama, Jenna Kanerva, Neslihan Kara, Ritván Karahóğa, Andre Kåsen, Tolga Kayadelen, Sarveswaran Kengatharaiyer, Václava Kettnerová, Jesse Kirchner, Elena Klementieva, Elena Klyachko, Arne Köhn, Abdullatif Köksal, Kamil Kopacewicz, Timo Korkiakangas, Mehmet Köse, Alexey Koshevoy, Natalia Kotsyba, Jolanta Kovalevskaitė, Simon Krek, Parameswari Krishnamurthy, Sandra Kübler, Adrian Kuqi, Oğuzhan Kuyrukçu, Aslı Kuzgun, Sookyoung Kwak, Kris Kyle, Veronika Laippala, Lorenzo Lambertino, Tatiana Lando, Septina Dian Larasati, Alexei Lavrentiev, John Lee, Phuong Lê Hồng, Alessandro Lenci, Saran Lertpradit, Herman Leung, Maria Levina, Lauren Levine, Cheuk Ying Li, Josie Li, Keying Li, Yixuan Li, Yuan Li, KyungTae Lim, Bruna Lima Padovani, Yi-Ju Jessica Lin, Krister Lindén, Yang Janet Liu, Nikola Ljubešić, Olga Loginova, Stefano Lusito, Andry Luthfi, Mikko Luukko, Olga Lyashevskaya, Teresa Lynn, Vivien Macketanz, Menel Mahamdi, Jean Maillard, Ilya Makarchuk, Aibek Makazhanov, Michael Mandl, Christopher Manning, Ruli Manurung, Büşra Marşan, Cătălina Mărănduc, David Mareček, Katrin Marheinecke, Stella Markantonatou, Héctor Martínez Alonso, Lorena Martín Rodríguez, André Martins, Cláudia Martins, Jan Mašek, Hiroshi Matsuda, Yuji Matsumoto, Alessandro Mazzei, Ryan McDonald, Sarah McGuinness, Gustavo Mendonça, Tatiana Merzhevich, Niko Miekka, Aaron Miller, Karina Mischenkova, Anna Missilä, Cătălin Mititelu, Maria Mitrofan, Yusuke Miyao, AmirHossein Mojiri Foroushani, Judit Molnár, Amirsaeid Moloodi, Simonetta Montemagni, Amir More, Laura Moreno Romero, Giovanni Moretti, Shinsuke Mori, Tomohiko Morioka, Shigeki Moro, Bjartur Mortensen, Bohdan Moskalevskyi, Kadri Muischnek, Robert Munro, Yugo Murawaki, Kaili Müürisep, Pinkey Nainwani, Mariam Nakhlé, Juan Ignacio Navarro Horñiacek, Anna Nedoluzhko, Gunta Nešpore-Bērzkalne, Manuela Nevaci, Luong Nguyễn Thị, Huyền Nguyễn Thị Minh, Yoshihiro Nikaido, Vitaly Nikolaev, Rattima Nitisaroj, Alireza Nourian, Hanna Nurmi, Stina Ojala, Atul Kr. Ojha, Hulda Óladóttir, Adédayọ̀ Olúòkun, Mai Omura, Emeka Onwuegbuzia, Noam Ordan, Petya Osenova, Robert Östling, Lilja Øvrelid, Şaziye Betül Özateş, Merve Özçelik, Arzucan Özgür, Balkız Öztürk Başaran, Teresa Paccosi, Alessio Palmero Aprosio, Anastasia Panova, Hyunji Hayley Park, Niko Partanen, Elena Pascual, Marco Passarotti, Agnieszka Patejuk, Guilherme Paulino-Passos, Giulia Pedonese, Angelika Peljak-Łapińska, Siyao Peng, Siyao Logan Peng, Rita Pereira, Sílvia Pereira, Cenel-Augusto Perez, Natalia Perkova, Guy Perrier, Slav Petrov, Daria Petrova, Andrea Peverelli, Jason Phelan, Jussi Piitulainen, Yuval Pinter, Clara Pinto, Tommi A. Pirinen, Emily Pitler, Magdalena Plamada, Barbara Plank, Thierry Poibeau, Larisa Ponomareva, Martin Popel, Lauma Pretkalniņa, Sophie Prévost, Prokopis Prokopidis, Adam Przepiórkowski, Robert Pugh, Tiina Puolakainen, Sampo Pyysalo, Peng Qi, Andreia Querido, Andriela Rääbis, Alexandre Rademaker, Mizanur Rahoman, Taraka Rama, Loganathan Ramasamy, Joana Ramos, Fam Rashel, Mohammad Sadegh Rasooli, Vinit Ravishankar, Livy Real, Petru Rebeja, Siva Reddy, Mathilde Regnault, Georg Rehm, Arij Riabi, Ivan Riabov, Michael Rießler, Erika Rimkutė, Larissa Rinaldi, Laura Rituma, Putri Rizqiyah, Luisa Rocha, Eiríkur Rögnvaldsson, Ivan Roksandic, Mykhailo Romanenko, Rudolf Rosa, Valentin Roșca, Davide Rovati, Ben Rozonoyer, Olga Rudina, Jack Rueter, Kristján Rúnarsson, Shoval Sadde, Pegah Safari, Aleksi Sahala, Shadi Saleh, Alessio Salomoni, Tanja Samardžić, Stephanie Samson, Manuela Sanguinetti, Ezgi Sanıyar, Dage Särg, Marta Sartor, Mitsuya Sasaki, Baiba Saulīte, Yanin Sawanakunanon, Shefali Saxena, Kevin Scannell, Salvatore Scarlata, Nathan Schneider, Sebastian Schuster, Lane Schwartz, Djamé Seddah, Wolfgang Seeker, Mojgan Seraji, Syeda Shahzadi, Mo Shen, Atsuko Shimada, Hiroyuki Shirasu, Yana Shishkina, Muh Shohibussirri, Maria Shvedova, Janine Siewert, Einar Freyr Sigurðsson, João Silva, Aline Silveira, Natalia Silveira, Sara Silveira, Maria Simi, Radu Simionescu, Katalin Simkó, Mária Šimková, Haukur Barri Símonarson, Kiril Simov, Dmitri Sitchinava, Ted Sither, Maria Skachedubova, Aaron Smith, Isabela Soares-Bastos, Per Erik Solberg, Barbara Sonnenhauser, Shafi Sourov, Rachele Sprugnoli, Vivian Stamou, Steinþór Steingrímsson, Antonio Stella, Abishek Stephen, Milan Straka, Emmett Strickland, Jana Strnadová, Alane Suhr, Yogi Lesmana Sulestio, Umut Sulubacak, Shingo Suzuki, Daniel Swanson, Zsolt Szántó, Chihiro Taguchi, Dima Taji, Fabio Tamburini, Mary Ann C. Tan, Takaaki Tanaka, Dipta Tanaya, Mirko Tavoni, Samson Tella, Isabelle Tellier, Marinella Testori, Guillaume Thomas, Sara Tonelli, Liisi Torga, Marsida Toska, Trond Trosterud, Anna Trukhina, Reut Tsarfaty, Utku Türk, Francis Tyers, Sveinbjörn Þórðarson, Vilhjálmur Þorsteinsson, Sumire Uematsu, Roman Untilov, Zdeňka Urešová, Larraitz Uria, Hans Uszkoreit, Andrius Utka, Elena Vagnoni, Sowmya Vajjala, Socrates Vak, Rob van der Goot, Martine Vanhove, Daniel van Niekerk, Gertjan van Noord, Viktor Varga, Uliana Vedenina, Giulia Venturi, Veronika Vincze, Natalia Vlasova, Aya Wakasa, Joel C. Wallenberg, Lars Wallin, Abigail Walsh, Jonathan North Washington, Maximilan Wendt, Paul Widmer, Shira Wigderson, Sri Hartati Wijono, Seyi Williams, Mats Wirén, Christian Wittern, Tsegay Woldemariam, Tak-sum Wong, Alina Wróblewska, Mary Yako, Kayo Yamashita, Naoki Yamazaki, Chunxiao Yan, Koichi Yasuoka, Marat M. Yavrumyan, Arife Betül Yenice, Olcay Taner Yıldız, Zhuoran Yu, Arlisa Yuliawati, Zdeněk Žabokrtský, Shorouq Zahra, Amir Zeldes, He Zhou, Hanzhi Zhu, Yilun Zhu, Anna Zhuravleva, and Rayan Ziane. 2023. Universal dependencies 2.12. LINDAT/CLARIAH-CZ digital library at the Institute of Formal and Applied Linguistics (ÚFAL), Faculty of Mathematics and Physics, Charles University.

Allen Institute for AI @ SIGTYP 2024 Shared Task on Word Embedding Evaluation for Ancient and Historical Languages

Lester James V. Miranda
Allen Institute for Artificial Intelligence
ljm@allenai.org

Abstract

In this paper, we describe Allen AI's submission to the constrained track of the SIGTYP 2024 Shared Task. Using only the data provided by the organizers, we pretrained a transformer-based multilingual model, then finetuned it on the Universal Dependencies (UD) annotations of a given language for a downstream task. Our systems achieved decent performance on the test set, beating the baseline in most language-task pairs, yet struggles with subtoken tags in multiword expressions as seen in Coptic and Ancient Hebrew. On the validation set, we obtained $\geq$70% F1-score on most language-task pairs. In addition, we also explored the cross-lingual capability of our trained models. This paper highlights our pretraining and finetuning process, and our findings from our internal evaluations.

1 Introduction

This paper describes Allen AI's submission to the *constrained* track of the SIGTYP 2024 Shared Task on Word Embedding Evaluation for Ancient and Historical Languages. The constrained track requires participants to build a system for three linguistic tasks—parts-of-speech (POS) tagging, morphological annotation, and lemmatisation—using only the corpora provided by the organizers (Dereza et al., 2024).

The dataset contains Universal Dependencies v2.12 data (Zeman et al., 2023) in eleven languages with five Old Hungarian codices (HAS Research Institute for Linguistics, 2018). The texts were from before 1700 CE, containing four language families (Indo-European, Afro-Asiatic, Sino-Tibetan, and Finno-Ugric), and six scripts (Greek, Hebrew, Hanzi, Coptic, Latin, Cyrillic). Finally, the dataset has over 2.6M tokens for training, and around 330k tokens for validation and testing. Table 1 shows all languages for the subtask with their equivalent language code.

Code	Language
CHU	Old Church Slavonic
COP	Coptic
FRO	Old French
GOT	Gothic
GRC	Ancient Greek
HBO	Ancient Hebrew
ISL	Medieval Icelandic
LAT	Classical and Late Latin
LATM	Medieval Latin
LZH	Classical Chinese
OHU	Old Hungarian
ORV	Old East Slavic
SAN	Vedic Sanskrit

Table 1: Language codes for all thirteen languages in the constrained track of the shared task. We will refer to the language code in the succeeding tables and figures.

Our general approach involves pretraining a transformer-based multilingual language model (LM) on the shared task dataset, and then finetuning the pretrained model using the Universal Dependencies (UD) annotations of each language. Throughout this paper, we will refer to the pretrained model as LIBERTUS. We also explored data sampling and augmentation techniques during the pretraining step to ensure better generalization performance.

On the validation set, we obtained $\geq$70% F1-score for the majority of language-task pairs. Moreover, our systems achieved decent performance on the test set, yet struggled with subtoken tags in multiword expressions as seen in Coptic (COP) and Ancient Hebrew (HBO). Table 2 shows our performance on the shared task test set. Our system achieved better than baseline performance in most language-task pairs, especially in morphological annotation, but underperformed in lemmatisation.

We detail our resource creation, model pretrain-

Proceedings of the 6th Workshop on Research in Computational Linguistic Typology and Multilingual NLP (SIGTYP 2024), pages 151–159
March 22, 2024 ©2024 Association for Computational Linguistics

Lang.	POS tag.	Morph. annot.	Lemma.
CHU	0.946	0.941	0.796
COP	0.426	0.805	0.463
FRO	0.851	0.941	0.833
GOT	0.934	0.940	0.908
GRC	0.935	0.965	0.883
HBO	0.273	0.712	0.618
ISL	0.939	0.948	0.946
LAT	0.924	0.933	0.923
LATM	0.944	0.980	0.972
LZH	0.818	0.860	1.000
OHU	0.944	0.946	0.700
ORV	0.912	0.922	0.784
SAN	0.873	0.900	0.832

Table 2: SIGTYP 2024 Shared Task final leaderboard results as evaluated on the test set. Cells in green indicate scores that are greater than the baseline. The mapping of language codes to languages can be found in Table 1.

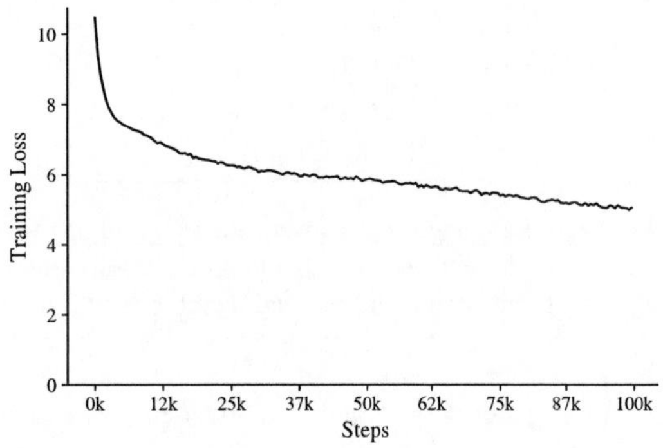

Figure 1: Training loss curve for the 126M-parameter model after 100k steps.

ing, and finetuning methodologies in this paper. The source code for all experiments can be found on GitHub: `https://github.com/ljvmiranda921/LiBERTus`.

2 Methodology

2.1 Model Pretraining

The main purpose of pretraining is to obtain context-sensitive word embeddings that we will finetune further for each downstream task. We approach this by training a multilingual language model akin to the XLM-RoBERTa (Conneau et al., 2020) and multilingual BERT (Devlin et al., 2019) architectures.

Hyperparameters	Value
Hidden size	768
Intermediate size	3072
Max position embed.	512
Num. attention heads	12
Hidden layers	12
Dropout	0.1

Table 3: Hyperparameter configuration for the LIBERTUS pretrained model.

Preparing the pretraining corpora. We constructed the pretraining corpora using the annotated tokens of the shared task dataset. Initially, we explored several data augmentation techniques to ensure that each language is properly represented based on the number of unique tokens. However, we found pretraining to be unstable when we upsampled tokens to achieve the same count as Medieval Latin (LATM), the language with the highest token count. In the end, we found that leaving the token distribution as-is leads to more stable pretraining and lower validation scores. More information about our sampling experiments can be found in Section A.1 of the appendix.

Pretraining the base model. Using the pretraining corpora, we trained a model with 126M parameters that will serve as a base for finetuning downstream tasks. LIBERTUS follows RoBERTa's pretraining architecture (Liu et al., 2019) and takes inspiration from Conneau et al. (2020)'s work on scaling BERT models to multiple languages.

Our hyperparameter choices closely resemble that of the original RoBERTa implementation as seen in Table 3. We also trained the same BPE tokenizer (Sennrich et al., 2016) using the constructed corpora. During model pretraining, we used the AdamW optimizer with β_2=0.98 and a weight decay of 0.01. The base model underwent training for 100k steps with a learning rate of 2e-4. We used a learning rate scheduler that linearly warms up during the first 12k steps of the training process, then linearly decays for the rest. Figure 1 shows the training curve.

2.2 Model Finetuning

For each language, we finetuned a multitask model using spaCy (Honnibal et al., 2020). We used spaCy's tokenization rules for the majority of languages except for Classical Chinese (LZH), where we segmented on characters. The final system consists of a parts-of-speech (POS) tagger, morphological analyzer, and lemmatizer.

Parts-of-speech (POS) tagger. We employed a standard classifier that predicts a vector of tag probabilities for each token. Each POS tag is a unique class that we assign exclusively to a token. We trained a model by taking the context-sensitive vectors from our pretrained embeddings, and passing them to a linear layer with a softmax activation. The network is then optimized using a categorical cross-entropy loss. For languages with subtokens such as Coptic (COP) and Ancient Hebrew (HBO), we merged each subtoken and used the full multi-word expression (MWE) during training.

Morphological analyzer. Similar to the POS tagger, we treat morphological annotation as a token classification task. Instead of directly modeling each feature, we made every unique combination of morphological features as a class. The limitation of this approach is that it can only predict combinations that were present in the training corpora. Similar to the POS tagger, we merged each subtoken for every multi-word expression (MWE) during training.

Lemmatizer. We trained a neural-based edit tree lemmatizer (Müller et al., 2015) by first extracting an edit tree for each token-lemma pair. Because this process can result in hundreds of edit trees, we treat the problem of picking the correct tree as a classification task. Here, each unique tree serves as a class and we compute a probability distribution over all trees for a given token. To obtain the most probable tree, we passed the context-sensitive embeddings from our pretrained model to a softmax layer and trained the network with a cross-entropy loss objective. We set the minimum frequency of an edit tree to 3, and used the surface form of the token as a backoff when no applicable edit tree is found. Finally, we ensured that the lemmatizer checks at least a single tree before resorting to backoff.

Finetuning the pipelines. We trained each component of the system in parallel, although the final "pipeline" assembles them together using the spaCy framework. For all components, the pretrained embeddings are passed on to a linear layer with softmax activation. Sometimes, the tokenization from the multilingual model does not align one-to-one with spaCy's tokenization. In such case, we use a pooling layer that computes the average of each feature to obtain a single vector per spaCy token.

Lang.	POS tag.	Morph. annot.	Lemma.
CHU	0.947	0.876	0.803
COP	0.924	0.846	0.776
FRO	0.890	0.912	0.844
GOT	0.951	0.886	0.914
GRC	0.956	0.915	0.873
HBO	0.624	0.561	0.219
ISL	0.963	0.901	0.949
LAT	0.949	0.882	0.922
LATM	0.984	0.951	0.968
LZH	0.795	0.824	0.942
OHU	0.953	0.919	0.697
ORV	0.933	0.859	0.787
SAN	0.888	0.811	0.817

Table 4: F1-score results on the validation set. The mapping of language codes to languages can be found in Table 1.

During finetuning, we used the Adam optimizer with β_1=0.9, β_2=0.999 and a learning rate of 0.001. The learning rate warms up linearly for the first 250 steps, and then decays afterwards.

3 Results

Table 2 shows the test scores for the shared task using the official shared task metrics:

- **POS-tagging:** Accuracy@1, F1-score
- **Detailed morphological annotation:** Macro-average of Accuracy@1 per tag
- **Lemmatisation:** Accuracy@1, Accuracy@3

Our systems obtained decent performance and beat the baseline for the majority of language-task pairs. In addition, our submission obtained 2nd place against three other submissions.

In the following sections, we will outline our internal evaluations and benchmarking experiments.

3.1 Performance on the validation set

Table 4 shows the validation scores of our finetuned models. We achieved $\geq$70% performance in most language-task pairs. The top performers, calculated by taking the average across all tasks, are Medieval Latin (0.968), Medieval Icelandic (0.938), and Classical and Late Latin (0.918), whereas the

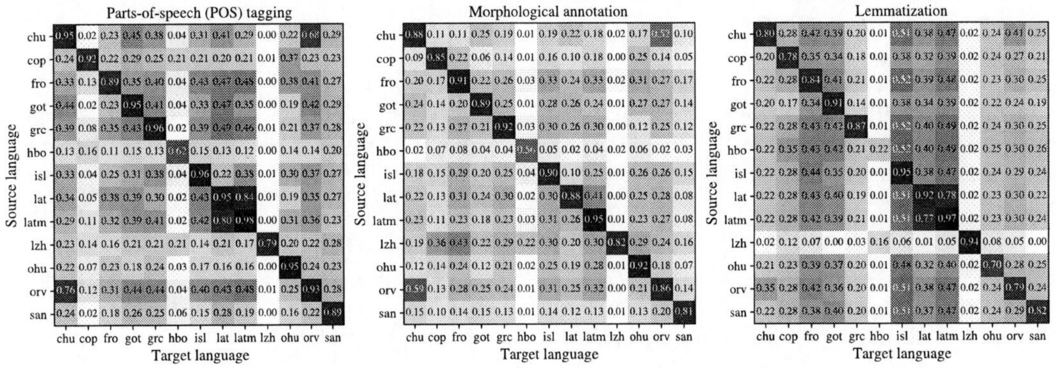

Figure 2: Cross-lingual evaluation, as measured by the F1-score, given a monolingual model from one language and a validation set in another. The mapping of language codes to languages can be found in Table 1.

bottom performers are Coptic (0.849), Vedic Sanskrit (0.839), and Ancient Hebrew (0.468).

Compared to our validation scores, our leaderboard scores on Coptic (COP) and Ancient Hebrew (HBO) are poor. This performance is due to our models being unable to accurately predict subtoken information as it has only seen the full MWE during training. In order to align our tokenization with the shared task's validation script in Codalab (Pavao et al., 2023), we substituted each MWE with its subtokens resulting in potentially incomprehensible text. Finally, for empty tokens such as previously found in Old East Slavic (ORV), we added a rule in our system to produce empty predictions.[1]

3.2 Evaluating cross-lingual capabilities

To test the cross-lingual capability of a language, we evaluated its finetuned model according to the validation set of another. Figure 2 shows the results.

We found that it is practical to adapt a language onto another for parts-of-speech (POS) tagging and lemmatization, especially in cases where the target language lacks sufficient data to train a supervised model. However, this does not extend to its morphology, as the validation set performs best only in the language it was trained on.

Some target languages tend to be cross-lingually receptive on lemmatization, i.e., many source languages can perform decently when applied to them. This pattern is apparent especially between Classical and Late Latin (LAT) and Medieval Latin (LATM) due to the latter being a direct continuation of the former. Finally, we also observed that Old Church Slavonic (CHU) and Old East Slavic (ORV) are also cross-lingually compatible as they came from the same family (i.e., Indo-European).

4 Related Work

Multilingual language modeling. Several efforts in the field of NLP involve pretraining a transformer network (Vaswani et al., 2017) using a corpus of multiple languages such as XLM-RoBERTa (Liu et al., 2019) and multilingual BERT (Conneau et al., 2020). The main advantage of multilingual language modeling is that it can harness the cross-lingual representations of the languages in its corpora to solve several downstream tasks (Chang et al., 2022). However, these models harness modern data sources, not ancient and historical text. The only exemplar that we found for a historical and multilingual LM is hmBERT (Schweter et al., 2022), where they pretrained on English, German, French, Finnish, Swedish, and Dutch languages from 1800 onwards. LIBERTUS aims to extend this literature by providing another multilingual language model focusing on ancient and historical texts from diverse scripts and language families before 1700 CE.

5 Conclusion

This paper describes Team Allen AI's system: a pretrained multilingual model (LIBERTUS) finetuned on different languages for each downstream task. Our system obtained decent performance for the majority of language-task pairs. However, due to our training paradigm, it struggles annotating subtokens of multiword expressions. Nevertheless,

[1]This problem was initially caused by missing brackets in the reference annotations. We used the correct tokens for ORV in the final submission.

our validation scores are high (≥70% F1-score) for the majority of language-task pairs.

We also evaluated each language's cross-lingual capability and showed that transfer learning is possible especially on lemmatization. This approach can be a viable alternative on limited corpora.

Our training and benchmarking source code is on GitHub: `https://github.com/ljvmiranda921/LiBERTus`. The pretrained multilingual model and finetuned pipelines are also available on HuggingFace.[2]

Limitations

Pretrained LM size. Due to constraints in compute, we were only able to pretrain a model akin to the size of $\text{RoBERTa}_{\text{base}}$. We highly recommend pretraining a large LIBERTUS model to obtain performance gains if the resource allows.

Pretraining data mix. In the end, we didn't employ any sampling strategy to balance the token distribution of different languages during pretraining. We only tested simple up-/downsampling strategies and our experiments are limited to repeating available data.

Label combination as individual classes. When training the morphologizer and POS tagger, we treated each feature and parts-of-speech combination as its own class instead of modeling them individually. This limits our text classifier to only predicting combinations it has seen during the training process.

Subtoken performance for multiword expressions. Our systems performed poorly on COP and HBO in the leaderboard due to how we trained our model. Instead of showing subtokens, we used the full multi-word expression during training.

References

Burton H. Bloom. 1970. Space/time trade-offs in hash coding with allowable errors. *Commun. ACM*, 13(7):422–426.

Tyler Chang, Zhuowen Tu, and Benjamin Bergen. 2022. The geometry of multilingual language model representations. In *Proceedings of the 2022 Conference on Empirical Methods in Natural Language Processing*, pages 119–136, Abu Dhabi, United Arab Emirates. Association for Computational Linguistics.

Alexis Conneau, Kartikay Khandelwal, Naman Goyal, Vishrav Chaudhary, Guillaume Wenzek, Francisco Guzmán, Edouard Grave, Myle Ott, Luke Zettlemoyer, and Veselin Stoyanov. 2020. Unsupervised Cross-lingual Representation Learning at Scale. In *Proceedings of the 58th Annual Meeting of the Association for Computational Linguistics*, pages 8440–8451, Online. Association for Computational Linguistics.

Oksana Dereza, Adrian Doyle, Priya Rani, Atul Kr. Ojha, Pádraic Moran, and John P. McCrae. 2024. Findings of the SIGTYP 2024 shared task on word embedding evaluation for ancient and historical languages. In *Proceedings of the 6th Workshop on Research in Computational Linguistic Typology and Multilingual NLP (SIGTYP 2024)*, St. Julians, Malta. Association for Computational Linguistics.

Jacob Devlin, Ming-Wei Chang, Kenton Lee, and Kristina Toutanova. 2019. BERT: Pre-training of Deep Bidirectional Transformers for Language Understanding. In *Proceedings of the 2019 Conference of the North American Chapter of the Association for Computational Linguistics: Human Language Technologies, Volume 1 (Long and Short Papers)*, pages 4171–4186, Minneapolis, Minnesota. Association for Computational Linguistics.

HAS Research Institute for Linguistics. 2018. Old Hungarian Codices. *Hungarian Generative Diachronic Syntax*. Accessed: October 22, 2023.

Matthew Honnibal, Ines Montani, Sofie Van Landeghem, and Adriane Boyd. 2020. spaCy: Industrial-strength Natural Language Processing in Python.

Yinhan Liu, Myle Ott, Naman Goyal, Jingfei Du, Mandar Joshi, Danqi Chen, Omer Levy, Mike Lewis, Luke Zettlemoyer, and Veselin Stoyanov. 2019. RoBERTa: A robustly optimized BERT pretraining approach. *arXiv preprint arXiv:1907.11692*.

Lester James Miranda, Ákos Kádár, Adriane Boyd, Sofie Van Landeghem, Anders Søgaard, and Matthew Honnibal. 2022. Multi hash embeddings in spaCy.

Thomas Müller, Ryan Cotterell, Alexander Fraser, and Hinrich Schütze. 2015. Joint lemmatization and morphological tagging with lemming. In *Proceedings of the 2015 Conference on Empirical Methods in Natural Language Processing*, pages 2268–2274, Lisbon, Portugal. Association for Computational Linguistics.

Adrien Pavao, Isabelle Guyon, Anne-Catherine Letournel, Dinh-Tuan Tran, Xavier Baro, Hugo Jair Escalante, Sergio Escalera, Tyler Thomas, and Zhen Xu. 2023. Codalab competitions: An open source platform to organize scientific challenges. *Journal of Machine Learning Research*, 24(198):1–6.

Stefan Schweter, Luisa März, Katharina Schmid, and Erion cCano. 2022. hmbert: Historical multilingual

[2]`https://huggingface.co/collections/ljvmiranda921/sigtyp2024-shared-task-models-65629ea0462e5ebcbf1a2133`

language models for named entity recognition. In *Conference and Labs of the Evaluation Forum*.

Rico Sennrich, Barry Haddow, and Alexandra Birch. 2016. Neural machine translation of rare words with subword units. In *Proceedings of the 54th Annual Meeting of the Association for Computational Linguistics (Volume 1: Long Papers)*, pages 1715–1725, Berlin, Germany. Association for Computational Linguistics.

Ashish Vaswani, Noam Shazeer, Niki Parmar, Jakob Uszkoreit, Llion Jones, Aidan N Gomez, Ł ukasz Kaiser, and Illia Polosukhin. 2017. Attention is all you need. In *Advances in Neural Information Processing Systems*, volume 30. Curran Associates, Inc.

Thomas Wolf, Lysandre Debut, Victor Sanh, Julien Chaumond, Clement Delangue, Anthony Moi, Pierric Cistac, Tim Rault, Remi Louf, Morgan Funtowicz, Joe Davison, Sam Shleifer, Patrick von Platen, Clara Ma, Yacine Jernite, Julien Plu, Canwen Xu, Teven Le Scao, Sylvain Gugger, Mariama Drame, Quentin Lhoest, and Alexander Rush. 2020. Transformers: State-of-the-art natural language processing. In *Proceedings of the 2020 Conference on Empirical Methods in Natural Language Processing: System Demonstrations*, pages 38–45, Online. Association for Computational Linguistics.

Daniel Zeman, Joakim Nivre, Mitchell Abrams, Elia Ackermann, Noëmi Aepli, Hamid Aghaei, Željko Agić, Amir Ahmadi, Lars Ahrenberg, Chika Kennedy Ajede, Salih Furkan Akkurt, Gabrielė Aleksandravičiūtė, Ika Alfina, Avner Algom, Khalid Alnajjar, Chiara Alzetta, Erik Andersen, Lene Antonsen, Tatsuya Aoyama, Katya Aplonova, Angelina Aquino, Carolina Aragon, Glyd Aranes, Maria Jesus Aranzabe, Bilge Nas Arıcan, Ĥórunn Arnardóttir, Gashaw Arutie, Jessica Naraiswari Arwidarasti, Masayuki Asahara, Katla Ásgeirsdóttir, Deniz Baran Aslan, Cengiz Asmazoğlu, Luma Ateyah, Furkan Atmaca, Mohammed Attia, Aitziber Atutxa, Liesbeth Augustinus, Mariana Avelãs, Elena Badmaeva, Keerthana Balasubramani, Miguel Ballesteros, Esha Banerjee, Sebastian Bank, Verginica Barbu Mititelu, Starkaður Barkarson, Rodolfo Basile, Victoria Basmov, Colin Batchelor, John Bauer, Seyyit Talha Bedir, Shabnam Behzad, Kepa Bengoetxea, İbrahim Benli, Yifat Ben Moshe, Gözde Berk, Riyaz Ahmad Bhat, Erica Biagetti, Eckhard Bick, Agnė Bielinskienė, Kristín Bjarnadóttir, Rogier Blokland, Victoria Bobicev, Loïc Boizou, Emanuel Borges Völker, Carl Börstell, Cristina Bosco, Gosse Bouma, Sam Bowman, Adriane Boyd, Anouck Braggaar, António Branco, Kristina Brokaitė, Aljoscha Burchardt, Marisa Campos, Marie Candito, Bernard Caron, Gauthier Caron, Catarina Carvalheiro, Rita Carvalho, Lauren Cassidy, Maria Clara Castro, Sérgio Castro, Tatiana Cavalcanti, Gülşen Cebiroğlu Eryiğit, Flavio Massimiliano Cecchini, Giuseppe G. A. Celano, Slavomír Čéplö, Neslihan Cesur, Savas Cetin, Özlem Çetinoğlu, Fabricio Chalub, Liyanage Chamila, Shweta Chauhan, Ethan Chi, Taishi Chika, Yongseok Cho, Jinho Choi, Jayeol Chun, Juyeon Chung, Alessandra T. Cignarella, Silvie Cinková, Aurélie Collomb, Çağrı Çöltekin, Miriam Connor, Daniela Corbetta, Francisco Costa, Marine Courtin, Mihaela Cristescu, Ingerid Løyning Dale, Philemon Daniel, Elizabeth Davidson, Leonel Figueiredo de Alencar, Mathieu Dehouck, Martina de Laurentiis, Marie-Catherine de Marneffe, Valeria de Paiva, Mehmet Oguz Derin, Elvis de Souza, Arantza Diaz de Ilarraza, Carly Dickerson, Arawinda Dinakaramani, Elisa Di Nuovo, Bamba Dione, Peter Dirix, Kaja Dobrovoljc, Adrian Doyle, Timothy Dozat, Kira Droganova, Puneet Dwivedi, Christian Ebert, Hanne Eckhoff, Masaki Eguchi, Sandra Eiche, Marhaba Eli, Ali Elkahky, Binyam Ephrem, Olga Erina, Tomaž Erjavec, Farah Essaidi, Aline Etienne, Wograine Evelyn, Sidney Facundes, Richárd Farkas, Federica Favero, Jannatul Ferdaousi, Marília Fernanda, Hector Fernandez Alcalde, Amal Fethi, Jennifer Foster, Cláudia Freitas, Kazunori Fujita, Katarína Gajdošová, Daniel Galbraith, Federica Gamba, Marcos Garcia, Moa Gärdenfors, Fabrício Ferraz Gerardi, Kim Gerdes, Luke Gessler, Filip Ginter, Gustavo Godoy, Iakes Goenaga, Koldo Gojenola, Memduh Gökırmak, Yoav Goldberg, Xavier Gómez Guinovart, Berta González Saavedra, Bernadeta Griciūtė, Matias Grioni, Loïc Grobol, Normunds Grūzītis, Bruno Guillaume, Céline Guillot-Barbance, Tunga Güngör, Nizar Habash, Hinrik Hafsteinsson, Jan Hajič, Jan Hajič jr., Mika Hämäläinen, Linh Hà Mỹ, Na-Rae Han, Muhammad Yudistira Hanifmuti, Takahiro Harada, Sam Hardwick, Kim Harris, Dag Haug, Johannes Heinecke, Oliver Hellwig, Felix Hennig, Barbora Hladká, Jaroslava Hlaváčová, Florinel Hociung, Petter Hohle, Marivel Huerta Mendez, Jena Hwang, Takumi Ikeda, Anton Karl Ingason, Radu Ion, Elena Irimia, Ọlájídé Ishola, Artan Islamaj, Kaoru Ito, Siratun Jannat, Tomáš Jelínek, Apoorva Jha, Katharine Jiang, Anders Johannsen, Hildur Jónsdóttir, Fredrik Jørgensen, Markus Juutinen, Hüner Kaşıkara, Nadezhda Kabaeva, Sylvain Kahane, Hiroshi Kanayama, Jenna Kanerva, Neslihan Kara, Ritván Karahóǧa, Andre Kåsen, Tolga Kayadelen, Sarveswaran Kengatharaiyer, Václava Kettnerová, Jesse Kirchner, Elena Klementieva, Elena Klyachko, Arne Köhn, Abdullatif Köksal, Kamil Kopacewicz, Timo Korkiakangas, Mehmet Köse, Alexey Koshevoy, Natalia Kotsyba, Jolanta Kovalevskaitė, Simon Krek, Parameswari Krishnamurthy, Sandra Kübler, Adrian Kuqi, Oğuzhan Kuyrukçu, Aslı Kuzgun, Sookyoung Kwak, Kris Kyle, Veronika Laippala, Lorenzo Lambertino, Tatiana Lando, Septina Dian Larasati, Alexei Lavrentiev, John Lee, Phuong Lê Hồng, Alessandro Lenci, Saran Lertpradit, Herman Leung, Maria Levina, Lauren Levine, Cheuk Ying Li, Josie Li, Keying Li, Yixuan Li, Yuan Li, KyungTae Lim, Bruna Lima Padovani, Yi-Ju Jessica Lin, Krister Lindén, Yang Janet Liu, Nikola Ljubešić, Olga Loginova, Stefano Lusito, Andry Luthfi, Mikko Luukko, Olga Lyashevskaya, Teresa Lynn, Vivien Macketanz, Menel Mahamdi, Jean Maillard, Ilya Makarchuk,

Aibek Makazhanov, Michael Mandl, Christopher Manning, Ruli Manurung, Büşra Marşan, Cătălina Mărănduc, David Mareček, Katrin Marheinecke, Stella Markantonatou, Héctor Martínez Alonso, Lorena Martín Rodríguez, André Martins, Cláudia Martins, Jan Mašek, Hiroshi Matsuda, Yuji Matsumoto, Alessandro Mazzei, Ryan McDonald, Sarah McGuinness, Gustavo Mendonça, Tatiana Merzhevich, Niko Miekka, Aaron Miller, Karina Mischenkova, Anna Missilä, Cătălin Mititelu, Maria Mitrofan, Yusuke Miyao, AmirHossein Mojiri Foroushani, Judit Molnár, Amirsaeid Moloodi, Simonetta Montemagni, Amir More, Laura Moreno Romero, Giovanni Moretti, Shinsuke Mori, Tomohiko Morioka, Shigeki Moro, Bjartur Mortensen, Bohdan Moskalevskyi, Kadri Muischnek, Robert Munro, Yugo Murawaki, Kaili Müürisep, Pinkey Nainwani, Mariam Nakhlé, Juan Ignacio Navarro Horñiacek, Anna Nedoluzhko, Gunta Nešpore-Bērzkalne, Manuela Nevaci, Luong Nguyễn Thị, Huyền Nguyễn Thị Minh, Yoshihiro Nikaido, Vitaly Nikolaev, Rattima Nitisaroj, Alireza Nourian, Hanna Nurmi, Stina Ojala, Atul Kr. Ojha, Hulda Óladóttir, Adédayọ Olúòkun, Mai Omura, Emeka Onwuegbuzia, Noam Ordan, Petya Osenova, Robert Östling, Lilja Øvrelid, Şaziye Betül Özateş, Merve Özçelik, Arzucan Özgür, Balkız Öztürk Başaran, Teresa Paccosi, Alessio Palmero Aprosio, Anastasia Panova, Hyunji Hayley Park, Niko Partanen, Elena Pascual, Marco Passarotti, Agnieszka Patejuk, Guilherme Paulino-Passos, Giulia Pedonese, Angelika Peljak-Łapińska, Siyao Peng, Siyao Logan Peng, Rita Pereira, Sílvia Pereira, Cenel-Augusto Perez, Natalia Perkova, Guy Perrier, Slav Petrov, Daria Petrova, Andrea Peverelli, Jason Phelan, Jussi Piitulainen, Yuval Pinter, Clara Pinto, Tommi A Pirinen, Emily Pitler, Magdalena Plamada, Barbara Plank, Thierry Poibeau, Larisa Ponomareva, Martin Popel, Lauma Pretkalniņa, Sophie Prévost, Prokopis Prokopidis, Adam Przepiórkowski, Robert Pugh, Tiina Puolakainen, Sampo Pyysalo, Peng Qi, Andreia Querido, Andriela Rääbis, Alexandre Rademaker, Mizanur Rahoman, Taraka Rama, Loganathan Ramasamy, Joana Ramos, Fam Rashel, Mohammad Sadegh Rasooli, Vinit Ravishankar, Livy Real, Petru Rebeja, Siva Reddy, Mathilde Regnault, Georg Rehm, Arij Riabi, Ivan Riabov, Michael Rießler, Erika Rimkutė, Larissa Rinaldi, Laura Rituma, Putri Rizqiyah, Luisa Rocha, Eiríkur Rögnvaldsson, Ivan Roksandic, Mykhailo Romanenko, Rudolf Rosa, Valentin Roșca, Davide Rovati, Ben Rozonoyer, Olga Rudina, Jack Rueter, Kristján Rúnarsson, Shoval Sadde, Pegah Safari, Aleksi Sahala, Shadi Saleh, Alessio Salomoni, Tanja Samardžić, Stephanie Samson, Manuela Sanguinetti, Ezgi Sanıyar, Dage Särg, Marta Sartor, Mitsuya Sasaki, Baiba Saulīte, Yanin Sawanakunanon, Shefali Saxena, Kevin Scannell, Salvatore Scarlata, Nathan Schneider, Sebastian Schuster, Lane Schwartz, Djamé Seddah, Wolfgang Seeker, Mojgan Seraji, Syeda Shahzadi, Mo Shen, Atsuko Shimada, Hiroyuki Shirasu, Yana Shishkina, Muh Shohibussirri, Maria Shvedova, Janine Siewert, Einar Freyr Sigurðsson, João Silva, Aline Silveira, Natalia Silveira, Sara Silveira, Maria Simi, Radu Simionescu, Katalin Simkó, Mária Šimková, Haukur Barri Símonarson, Kiril Simov, Dmitri Sitchinava, Ted Sither, Maria Skachedubova, Aaron Smith, Isabela Soares-Bastos, Per Erik Solberg, Barbara Sonnenhauser, Shafi Sourov, Rachele Sprugnoli, Vivian Stamou, Steinh͡ór Steingrímsson, Antonio Stella, Abishek Stephen, Milan Straka, Emmett Strickland, Jana Strnadová, Alane Suhr, Yogi Lesmana Sulestio, Umut Sulubacak, Shingo Suzuki, Daniel Swanson, Zsolt Szántó, Chihiro Taguchi, Dima Taji, Fabio Tamburini, Mary Ann C. Tan, Takaaki Tanaka, Dipta Tanaya, Mirko Tavoni, Samson Tella, Isabelle Tellier, Marinella Testori, Guillaume Thomas, Sara Tonelli, Liisi Torga, Marsida Toska, Trond Trosterud, Anna Trukhina, Reut Tsarfaty, Utku Türk, Francis Tyers, Sveinbjörn H͡órðarson, Vilhjálmur H͡orsteinsson, Sumire Uematsu, Roman Untilov, Zdeňka Urešová, Larraitz Uria, Hans Uszkoreit, Andrius Utka, Elena Vagnoni, Sowmya Vajjala, Socrates Vak, Rob van der Goot, Martine Vanhove, Daniel van Niekerk, Gertjan van Noord, Viktor Varga, Uliana Vedenina, Giulia Venturi, Veronika Vincze, Natalia Vlasova, Aya Wakasa, Joel C. Wallenberg, Lars Wallin, Abigail Walsh, Jonathan North Washington, Maximilan Wendt, Paul Widmer, Shira Wigderson, Sri Hartati Wijono, Seyi Williams, Mats Wirén, Christian Wittern, Tsegay Woldemariam, Tak-sum Wong, Alina Wróblewska, Mary Yako, Kayo Yamashita, Naoki Yamazaki, Chunxiao Yan, Koichi Yasuoka, Marat M. Yavrumyan, Arife Betül Yenice, Olcay Taner Yıldız, Zhuoran Yu, Arlisa Yuliawati, Zdeněk Žabokrtský, Shorouq Zahra, Amir Zeldes, He Zhou, Hanzhi Zhu, Yilun Zhu, Anna Zhuravleva, and Rayan Ziane. 2023. Universal dependencies 2.12. LINDAT/CLARIAH-CZ digital library at the Institute of Formal and Applied Linguistics (ÚFAL), Faculty of Mathematics and Physics, Charles University.

A Appendix

A.1 Different sampling strategies on pretraining validation performance

We explored different sampling strategies and their effect on the pretraining validation loss curve as shown in Figure 3. We ran the pretraining pipeline for 20k steps (one-fifths of the final hyperparameter value) and measured the validation loss. The evaluation corpus was built from the validation set of the shared task, and we kept it the same throughout the experiment. We tested the following sampling strategies:

- **None:** we used the original dataset without any data sampling or augmentation.

- **Upsampling:** we upsampled each language

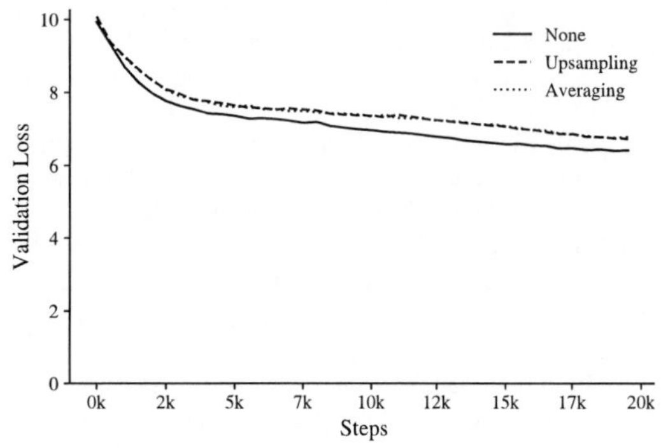

Figure 3: Validation loss curve for different sampling strategies in 20k steps.

to ensure that the number of their unique tokens is greater than or equal to the most dominant language.

- **Averaging:** we took the average number of unique tokens in the whole set and up-/downsampled each language based on this value.

Because any form of sampling resulted to unstable pretraining and higher validation loss, we decided to stick with the dataset's original data distribution. We highly recommend exploring alternative data mixes to ensure that all languages will be represented while keeping the training process stable.

A.2 Finetuning a model per language vs. monolithic system

We investigated if finetuning a model per language is more effective against a monolithic system, i.e., training on the full multilingual annotated corpora. Here, we combined the training corpora for all languages, then shuffled them before batching. The merged dataset has 194,281 documents for training and 26,954 documents for validation. This means that the downstream model sees a language mix per training epoch.

As shown in Figure 4, finetuning a model per language still yields the best results. One advantage of language-specific models is that we were able to set a different tokenizer per language—enabling us to get decent scores on Classical Chinese (LZH). Training the monolithic model is also sensitive to the training data distribution, as shown by the disparity in performance between majority languages (Classical and Late Latin, Medieval Latin) and minority ones (Old Hungarian, Old East Slavic, Vedic Sanskrit). Due to these findings, we decided to train multiple models for our final system.

A.3 Alternative approach—multi-hash embeddings

We considered using multi-hash embeddings (Miranda et al., 2022) as an alternative approach. Instead of pretraining, these embeddings use orthographic features (e.g., prefix, suffix, norm, shape) to create a word vector table. This approach also applies the hashing trick, inspired by Bloom filters (Bloom, 1970), to decrease the vector table's memory footprint.

Figure 5 shows the results in comparison to our final system. It is notable that simple orthographic features are competitive with our transformer-based model. However, we chose to submit the transformer-based pipeline as our final system because it still outperforms the multi-hash embed method in the majority of our language-task pairs. We still recommend investigating this approach further because the hash-embed method has noticeable efficiency gains in terms of model size.

A.4 Open-access models

Finetuned spaCy models. The finetuned models follow spaCy's naming convention and are available on HuggingFace (`https://huggingface.co/ljvmiranda921/{model_name}`, where `model_name` is found on Table 5). Table 5 also lists the size (in MB) for each language. Each model is multi-task in nature and can perform all downstream tasks (i.e., POS tagging, morphological annotation, lemmatisation) in a single call using the spaCy framework.[3]

Pretrained multilingual LM. In addition, the pretrained multilingual language model is also on HuggingFace (`https://huggingface.co/ljvmiranda921/LiBERTus-base`) and can be accessed using the `transformers` library (Wolf et al., 2020).

[3] `https://spacy.io`

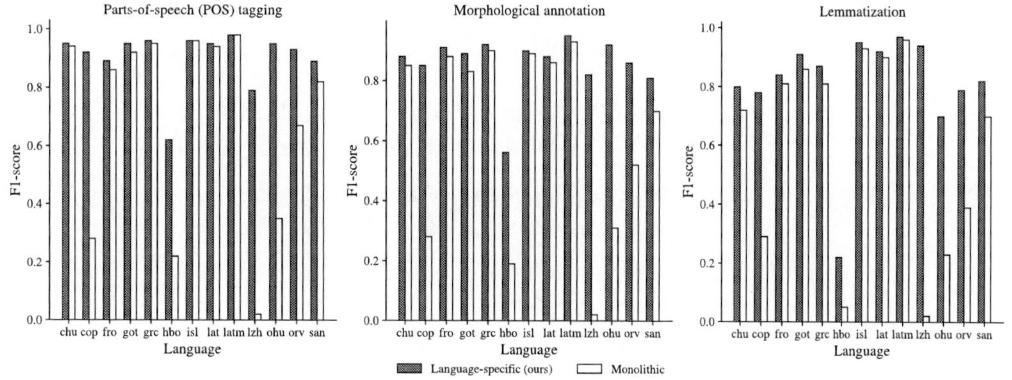

Figure 4: Comparison between training language-specific models versus a single monolithic model as evaluated on the validation set.

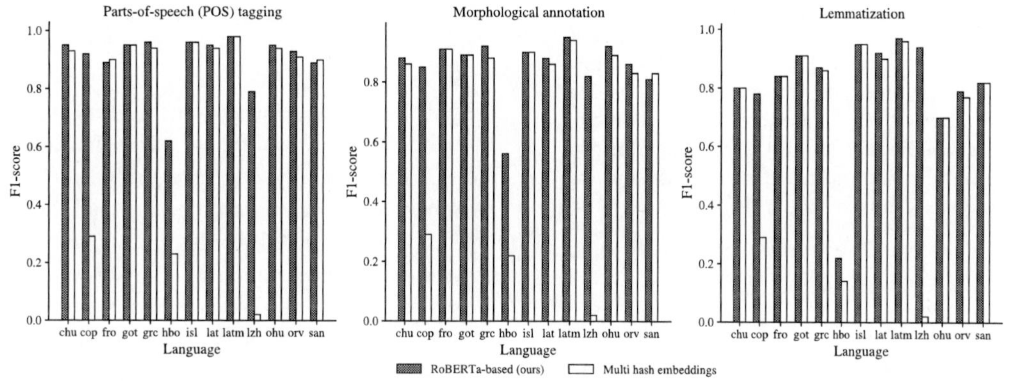

Figure 5: Comparison between a RoBERTa-based pretrained model and multi-hash embeddings (Miranda et al., 2022) as evaluated on the validation set.

Language	spaCy Model Name	Model Size
Old Church Slavonic	xx_chu_sigtyp_trf	491 MB
Coptic	el_cop_sigtyp_trf	477 MB
Old French	xx_fro_sigtyp_trf	471 MB
Gothic	xx_got_sigtyp_trf	474 MB
Ancient Greek	xx_grc_sigtyp_trf	501 MB
Ancient Hebrew	he_hbo_sigtyp_trf	475 MB
Medieval Icelandic	xx_isl_sigtyp_trf	496 MB
Classical and Late Latin	xx_lat_sigtyp_trf	486 MB
Medieval Latin	xx_latm_sigtyp_trf	510 MB
Classical Chinese	zh_lzh_sigtyp_trf	469 MB
Old Hungarian	xx_ohu_sigtyp_trf	488 MB
Old East Slavic	xx_orv_sigtyp_trf	503 MB
Vedic Sanskrit	xx_san_sigtyp_trf	473 MB

Table 5: The finetuned model for each language is available on HuggingFace.

Findings of the SIGTYP 2024 Shared Task on Word Embedding Evaluation for Ancient and Historical Languages

Oksana Dereza[1]★, Adrian Doyle[1]★, Priya Rani[1]★, Atul Kr. Ojha[1], Pádraic Moran[2], John P. McCrae[1]

[1] Insight SFI Centre for Data Analytics, Data Science Institute, University of Galway, Ireland
[2] Classics, University of Galway, Ireland

★firstname.lastname@insight-centre.org,
atulkumar.ojha@insight-centre.org,
padraic.moran@universityofgalway.ie,
john.mccrae@insight-centre.org

Abstract

This paper discusses the organisation and findings of the SIGTYP 2024 Shared Task on Word Embedding Evaluation for Ancient and Historical Languages. The shared task was split into the constrained and unconstrained tracks and involved solving either three or five problems for 12+ ancient and historical languages belonging to four language families and making use of six different scripts.

There were 14 registrations in total, of which three teams participated in each track. Out of these six submissions, two systems were successful in the constrained setting and another two in the unconstrained setting, and four system description papers were submitted by different teams.

The best average results for POS-tagging, lemmatisation and morphological feature prediction were 96.09%, 94.88% and 96.68% respectively. In the mask filling problem, the winning team could not achieve a higher average score across all 16 languages than 5.95% at the word level, which demonstrates the difficulty of this problem. At the character level, the best average result over 16 languages was 55.62%.

1 Introduction

The importance of NLP for studies in the classics is growing, as can be seen by the variety of technologies, digital text resources, and applications being developed to support research tasks in this field in recent years (Hawk et al., 2018; Neidorf et al., 2019; Stifter et al., 2021; Johnson et al., 2021). As the value of machine learning for historical linguistics is becoming more apparent, academic interest in word embedding models for use in these contexts is also increasing (Bamman and Burns, 2020; Singh et al., 2021; Hu et al., 2021; Riemenschneider and Frank, 2023; Dereza et al., 2023b).

Since the rise of word embeddings, their evaluation has been considered a challenging task that sparked considerable debate regarding the optimal approach. The two major strategies that researchers have developed over the years are intrinsic and extrinsic evaluation. The first amounts to solving specially designed problems like semantic proportions, or comparing the similarity of machine-generated words or sentences against human-generated examples. The second one focuses on solving downstream NLP tasks, such as sentiment analysis or question answering, probing word or sentence representations in real-world applications.

In recent years, sets of downstream tasks called benchmarks have become a very popular, if not default, method to evaluate general-purpose word and sentence embeddings. Despite the general trend towards multilinguality and ever-growing attention to under-resourced languages, ancient and historical languages remain under-served by embedding evaluation benchmarks, and the goal of this shared task is to bridge this gap. We argue that there is a need for a universal multilingual evaluation benchmark for embeddings learned from ancient and historical language data and view this shared task as a proving ground for it.

2 Related work

Starting with decaNLP (McCann et al., 2018) and SentEval (Conneau and Kiela, 2018), general-purpose multitask benchmarks for Natural Language Understanding (NLU) have become increasingly common in the literature, and new ones are reported regularly (Wang et al., 2019, 2020;

Proceedings of the 6th Workshop on Research in Computational Linguistic Typology and Multilingual NLP (SIGTYP 2024), pages 160–172
March 22, 2024

Shavrina et al., 2020; Xu et al., 2020; Kurihara et al., 2022; Urbizu et al., 2022; Berdicevskis et al., 2023). However, even the largest multilingual benchmarks, such as XGLUE, XTREME, XTREME-R or XTREME-UP (Hu et al., 2020; Liang et al., 2020; Ruder et al., 2021, 2023), only include modern languages.

The EvaLatin evaluation campaign (Sprugnoli et al., 2020, 2022) attracted some embedding-based solutions for POS-tagging, lemmatisation, and morphological feature prediction challenges (Wróbel and Nowak, 2022; Mercelis and Keersmaekers, 2022), but it did not specifically focus on embedding evaluation. Moreover, it was confined to Latin, which is the English of the ancient world in terms of language resources and technologies available. Individual scholars focusing on Latin and Ancient Greek mostly adopt Large Language Models (LLMs) together with their evaluation techniques through downstream tasks (Bamman and Burns, 2020; Singh et al., 2021; Yamshchikov et al., 2022; Riemenschneider and Frank, 2023; Krahn et al., 2023), while those working with less-resourced languages tend to translate intrinsic evaluation datasets from modern languages or create their own diagnostic tests (Tian et al., 2021; Hu et al., 2021; Dereza et al., 2023a). However, this is not a universal rule: the latest paper on distributional semantic models of Ancient Greek proposes a new dataset for intrinsic evaluation, AGREE (Stopponi et al., 2024), while some recent papers featuring medieval French and Spanish adopt transformer models and test them on Named Entity Recognition (Grobol et al., 2022; Torres Aguilar, 2022).

3 Setup and Schedule

For the purposes of our evaluation, languages are distinguished in accordance with ISO 639-3 codes[1] except for Latin, which was manually separated as discussed in Section 4. As a result, different historical stages of Irish and Latin are treated as distinct 'languages' in this paper. Such a distinction may be linguistically arbitrary, at least in the case of certain texts. However, as Universal Dependencies (UD) (Zeman et al., 2023) corpora are separated in accordance with ISO 639 codes, and the majority of data used in this evaluation was drawn from this resource, the same system for distinguishing languages was utilised here.

[1]https://iso639-3.sil.org

The Shared Task involved three problems (hereafter also referred as 'challenges' and 'downstream tasks') for 13 languages in the constrained setting and five problems for 16 languages in the unconstrained setting. These languages belong to four language families and use six different scripts (see Table 1 for detailed information).

3.1 Subtasks

A. Constrained
   1. POS-tagging
   2. Lemmatisation
   3. Morphological feature prediction

B. Unconstrained
   1. POS-tagging
   2. Lemmatisation
   3. Morphological feature prediction
   4. Filling the gaps (mask filling)
      a. Word-level
      b. Character-level

3.2 Timeline

The final timeline of the shared task is as follows.

05 Nov 2023: Release of training & validation data
02 Jan 2024: Release of test data
15 Jan 2024: System submission
22 Jan 2024: Paper submission
29 Jan 2024: Notification of acceptance
05 Feb 2024: Camera-ready submission

A tokenisation error was identified in the test data for problem 4a and in the Classical Chinese test data for problem 4b after the test data had been released. It was promptly corrected on 12 Jan 2024.

4 Data

For problems 1-3, data from Universal Dependencies v.2.12 (Zeman et al., 2023) was used for 11 ancient and historical languages, omitting corpora which contained fewer than 1,000 tokens or for which only a test set was available. Old Hungarian texts, annotated to the same standard as UD corpora, were added to the dataset from the MGTSZ website[2] (HAS Research Institute for Linguistics, 2018; Simon, 2014). Old Hungarian data was edited to simplify complex punctuation marks

[2]http://oldhungariancorpus.nytud.hu/en-codices.html

Language	Code	Script	Dating	Train-T	Valid-T	Test-T	Train-S	Valid-S	Test-S
Ancient Greek ♣	grc	Greek	800 BCE – 110 CE	334,043	41,905	41,046	24,800	3,100	3,101
Ancient Hebrew ♢	hbo	Hebrew	900 – 999 CE	40,244	4,862	4,801	1,263	158	158
Classical Chinese ♠	lzh	Hanzi	47 – 220 CE	346,778	43,067	43,323	68,991	8,624	8,624
Coptic ♢	cop	Coptic	0 – 199 CE	57,493	7,282	7,558	1,730	216	217
Gothic ♣	got	Latin	400 – 799 CE	44,044	5,724	5,568	4,320	540	541
Medieval Icelandic ♣	isl	Latin	1150 – 1680 CE	473,478	59,002	58,242	21,820	2,728	2,728
Classical & Late Latin ♣	lat	Latin	100 BCE – 399 CE	188,149	23,279	23,344	16,769	2,096	2,097
Medieval Latin ♣	latm	Latin	774 – early 1300s CE	599,255	75,079	74,351	30,176	3,772	3,773
Old Church Slavonic ♣	chu	Cyrillic	900 – 1099 CE	159,368	19,779	19,696	18,102	2,263	2,263
Old East Slavic ♣	orv	Cyrillic	1025 – 1700 CE	250,833	31,078	32,318	24,788	3,098	3,099
Old French ♣	fro	Latin	1180 CE	38,460	4,764	4,870	3,113	389	390
Vedic Sanskrit ♣	san	Latin (transcr.)	1500 – 600 BCE	21,786	2,729	2,602	3,197	400	400
Old Hungarian ♡	ohu	Latin	1440 – 1521 CE	129,454	16,138	16,116	21,346	2,668	2,669
Old Irish ♣	sga	Latin	600 – 900 CE	88,774	11,093	11,048	8,748	1,093	1,094
Middle Irish ♣	mga	Latin	900 – 1200 CE	251,684	31,748	31,292	14,308	1,789	1,789
Early Modern Irish ♣	ghc	Latin	1200 – 1700 CE	673,449	115,163	79,600	24,440	3,055	3,056

Table 1: Language families: ♣ – Indo-European, ♢ – Afro-Asiatic, ♠ – Sino-Tibetan, ♡ – Finno-Ugric. The 'Code' column refers to an ISO 639-3 code with the exception of Medieval Latin. The 'Script' column refers to the scripts used in the dataset rather than the script(s) typical for a particular language. The 'Dating' column describes the period when texts in the dataset were created, not when a particular language existed, cited according to the electronic editions/corpora these texts come from. Finally, we provide the size of each subset in sentences (S) and tokens (T).

masked	src
Cé [MASK] secht [MASK] im gin sóee suilgind, co bráth, mó cech delmaimm, issed ma do-ruirminn.	Cé betis secht tengtha im gin sóee suilgind, co bráth, mó cech delmaimm, issed ma do-ruirminn.

Table 2: An example of training data for word-level gap filling (problem 4a).

masked	src
Cé betis se[_]ht te[_]gtha im gin s[_]ee suilgind, co bráth, mó cech[_]delmaimm, isse[_] ma do-ruirminn.	Cé betis secht tengtha im gin sóee suilgind, co bráth, mó cech delmaimm, issed ma do-ruirminn.

Table 3: An example of training data for character-level gap filling (problem 4b).

used to approximate manuscript symbols. Tokens which were POS-tagged PUNCT were altered so that the form matched the lemma. Otherwise, no characters intended to approximate orthographic manuscript features were changed.

As the ISO 639-3 standard does not distinguish between historical stages of Latin, as it does between other languages like Irish, but it was desirable to approximate this distinction for Latin, we further split Latin data. This resulted in two Latin datasets; Classical and Late Latin, and Medieval Latin. This split was dictated by the composition of the Perseus (Celano et al., 2014) and PROIEL (Haug and Jøhndal, 2008) treebanks. As the Late Latin *Vulgata* is mixed with the work of Classical Latin authors in these treebanks, it was unfeasible to separate Classical Latin from Late Latin, though this may have been preferable. For the purposes of this evaluation we use the ISO 639-3 code `lat` for the Classical and Late Latin dataset, and we apply the faux-code, `latm`, to Medieval Latin.

Historical forms of Irish were only included in mask filling challenges, as the quantity of historical Irish text data which has been tokenised and annotated to a single standard to date is insufficient for the purpose of training models to perform morphological analysis tasks. The Irish texts for problem 4 were drawn from CELT[3] (Ó Corráin et al., 1997), Corpas Stairiúil na Gaeilge[4] (Acadamh Ríoga na hÉireann, 2017), and digital editions of the St. Gall glosses[5] (Bauer et al., 2017) and the Würzburg glosses[6] (Doyle, 2018). This provides a good case study of how performance may vary across different historical stages of the same language. Each Irish text taken from CELT is labelled 'Old', 'Middle' or 'Early Modern' in accordance with the language labels provided in CELT metadata. Because CELT metadata relating to language stages and text dating is reliant on information provided by a variety of different editors of earlier print editions, this metadata can be inconsistent across the corpus and on occasion inaccurate. To mitigate complications arising from this, texts drawn from CELT were included in the dataset only if they had a single Irish language label and if the dates provided in CELT metadata for the text match the expected dates for the given period in the history of the Irish language.

The upper temporal boundary was set at 1700 CE, and texts created later than this date were not included in the dataset. The choice of this date is driven by the fact that most of the historical language data used in word embedding research dates back to the 18th century CE or later, and we would like to focus on the more challenging and yet unaddressed data. A detailed list of text sources for each language in the dataset is provided on our GitHub.[7]

The resulting datasets for each language were then shuffled at the sentence level and split into training, validation and test subsets at the ratio of $0.8 : 0.1 : 0.1$. Table 1 provides an overview of the data: language family, script, dating, and the size of each subset in sentences and tokens.

For word-level mask filling (problem 4a), 10% of tokens in each sentence were randomly replaced with a `[MASK]` token. Masked Language Models (MLMs) conventionally mask 15% of tokens, and Wettig et al. (2023) showed that an even higher masking rate could be beneficial for models the size of BERT-large.[8] However, our dataset is substantially smaller; moreover, sentences from historical texts are often much shorter than in modern language due to their genre or purpose (e.g. glosses, annals, charters etc.) For these reasons, it was unfeasible to set the masking rate higher than 10% for the benchmark presented in this paper, particularly for the smallest datasets.

For character-level gap filling (problem 4b), sentences were split into individual characters for languages with alphabetical writing systems. For Classical Chinese, each Hanzi character was decomposed into individual strokes with the help of `hanzipy`[9] package with the deepest decomposition level available, 'graphical'. Then, 5% of characters in each sentence were randomly replaced with a `[_]` token.

There were no restrictions on masked word/character position, and they could also be consecutive. Some sentences could have more than one masked word or character, and some (shorter) ones could have none.

For problems 1-3, participants received the data in CONLL-U format.[10] The data for tasks 4a and 4b was released in `tsv` format, as shown in Tables 2 and 3.

After the end of the competition an updated version of the dataset, including test labels, was published on Zenodo[11] (Dereza, 2024).

5 Evaluation

The shared task was hosted on CodaLab[12] and will remain available for post-competition submissions for anyone who would be interested in testing their approach on our data.

Our evaluation script calculates a score for each problem in the task (POS-tagging, lemmatisation etc.) per language with the metrics listed in Table 4. Following the authors of GLUE and SuperGLUE (Wang et al., 2019, 2020), we weigh each downstream task equally and provide a macro-average of per-problem scores as an overall score for a language. These scores are then averaged by CodaLab and displayed on the leaderboard as Rank.

---

[3] `https://celt.ucc.ie/publishd.html`

[4] `http://corpas.ria.ie/index.php`

[5] `http://www.stgallpriscian.ie/`

[6] `https://wuerzburg.ie/`

[7] `https://github.com/sigtyp/ST2024/blob/main/list_of_text_sources.md`

[8] BERT (Devlin et al., 2019) was pretrained on BookCorpus, a dataset consisting of 11,038 unpublished books, and English Wikipedia, which contains 6,780,526 articles as of February 2024: `https://huggingface.co/bert-large-uncased`

[9] `https://github.com/Synkied/hanzipy`

[10] `https://universaldependencies.org/format.html`

[11] `https://doi.org/10.5281/zenodo.10655061`

[12] Unconstrained track: `https://codalab.lisn.upsaclay.fr/competitions/16818`
Constrained track: `https://codalab.lisn.upsaclay.fr/competitions/16822`

As is common in evaluation benchmarks (Wang et al., 2020; Hu et al., 2020; Ruder et al., 2021), we use multiple metrics for every problem (e.g. F1 and Accuracy @1 for POS-tagging) except for morphological annotation. This helps to smooth out shortcomings that individual metrics may have and to make the evaluation scenario more forgiving for complicated problems (e.g. combining Accuracy @1 and Accuracy @3 for lemmatisation). Accuracy @1 is usually referred to as simply 'accuracy' and calculated as a ratio of correct predictions to all predictions. While Accuracy @1 verifies if the top prediction is correct or not, Accuracy @3 is a milder metric that checks if the correct answer is among top-3 predictions.

In the case of morphological annotation, we calculate a macro-average of Accuracy @1 per tag, and also introduce punishment for predicting incorrect features. For example, if a token should only have two morphological features, and a system predicts the correct value for one, but the incorrect value for the other, and then also suggests a feature that this token should not have at all, the score achieved for this token will be $1 + 0 - 1 = 0$.

The evaluation scripts for both constrained and unconstrained tracks are available on the Shared Task GitHub.[13]

Task	Metrics
POS-tagging	Acc@1, F1
Detailed morphological annotation	Macro-average of Acc@1 per tag
Lemmatisation	Acc@1, Acc@3
Filling the gaps (word-level)	Acc@1, Acc@3
Filling the gaps (character-level)	Acc@1, Acc@3

Table 4: Evaluation metrics.

6 Baseline Models

Baselines were provided for the three challenges which are shared by both the constrained and unconstrained tracks. As the aim of this Shared Task was to provide a benchmark for embedding models, multi-layer perceptron network models were developed to classify token data for each of the three challenges. For the sake of ensuring simplicity across the baseline models and results, model design and input data format was kept as similar as possible across all challenges. Slight variation was tolerated, however, depending on the requirements of each specific challenge.

Specific models were trained for each of the 13 languages for both the POS-tagging and lemmatisation challenges. By contrast, the approach taken for the morphological annotation challenge was to train a language-agnostic model for each of the 44 morphological features used across all languages in the dataset. This was found to produce better results than using language specific models, particularly for morphological features which were not common across all languages in the dataset. It also reduced model training time, as the alternative would have been to create a discrete model for each feature in use by each individual language, resulting in significantly more models.

Early stopping was applied during training of all models to avoid overfitting. Validation loss was used as a metric to determine when early stopping should be applied for POS-tagger and morphological feature analysis models. However, tracking validation accuracy instead was found to produce better results when training lemmatiser models. All POS-tagger and morphological feature analysis models used 64 neurons per hidden layer, as did lemmatiser models for smaller datasets, however, for languages with larger datasets this was found to be insufficient. To avoid hampering performance, lemmatiser models were created with up to 1024 neurons per hidden layer, depending on the size of the dataset.

Aside from the areas of divergence just mentioned, the design aspects common to all models are as follows:

- Hidden layers: 2
- Activation: ReLU
- Dropout: 20%
- Optimiser: Adam (Kingma and Ba, 2015)

6.1 Data Preparation

Text data was pre-processed before being used in model training for each of the three challenges. Feature engineering was carried out on the input data to ensure models would focus on the most valuable information to inform morphological analysis. For each token which would be used as input data across all three challenges, the following information was extracted:

1. The token itself (entirely in lower case letters)
2. The length of the sentence in which the token occurs (number of tokens)

[13] https://github.com/sigtyp/ST2024/

3. The length of the token itself (number of letter characters)
4. Whether the token occurred first in the sentence (Boolean: true or false)
5. Whether the token occurred last in the sentence (Boolean: true or false)
6. Whether the first letter of the token was capitalised (Boolean: true or false)
7. Whether the entire token was in all caps (Boolean: true or false)
8. Whether the entire token was in all lowercase (Boolean: true or false)
9. The first letter of the token
10. The second letter of the token
11. The third letter of the token
12. The last letter of the token
13. The second last letter of the token
14. The third last letter of the token
15. The previous token (entirely in lower case)
16. The following token (entirely in lower case)

In addition to the information listed above, language codes were also extracted for the morphological annotation challenge. This was necessary because the models themselves were not trained on individual languages for this particular challenge, but language information would nevertheless be useful in identifying morphological features. Once this information had been generated for each token, it was compiled and vectorised so that it could be used as input data in model training and validation.

POS-tags and lemmata associated with each token were extracted from the training and validation sets on a language-by-language basis. They were then encoded and set aside to be used as labels during model training. Generating label data for morphological annotation models was more complicated. First, the training data for all languages was combined, as was the validation data for all languages. Next, morphological features associated with each token across all of the combined languages were extracted. If a particular morphological feature was not used by a given token, a value of '_' was generated to indicate non-use. In the case of features common across many languages, this resulted in relatively balanced training and validation datasets. However, for uncommon features this could result in less than 1% of labels having values other than '_'. This would result models simply learning to classify every token as '_' for that feature. To overcome this issue, if more than 80% of labels in any training or validation set had the value '_', the size of the dataset was reduced by dropping random instances of '_' values until at least 20% of the dataset had labels with other values. Finally, these were encoded for model training.

7 Submitted Systems

There were 14 registrations in total, of which three teams submitted to each track. Out of these six submissions, two systems were successful in the constrained setting and another two in the unconstrained setting, and four system description papers were submitted by different teams.

We expected that participants would use the same pre-training technique for every problem, as is common in benchmarking, but the winning teams applied different pre-training approaches to different problems. At the same time, all participants leveraged various transformer architectures, with RoBERTa (Liu et al., 2019) and its modifications being the most popular one.

While all participants outperformed our baselines for morphological feature prediction with the best average result about 96% across 13 languages, only the winning teams beat the baselines for POS-tagging and lemmatisation, achieving average results of 95.25% and 93.67% respectively in the constrained setting, and 96.09% and 94.88% in the unconstrained setting. Baselines were not provided for the mask filling problems which formed a part of the unconstrained track only. At the word level, the winning team could not achieve a higher average accuracy across all 16 languages than 5.95%, with the best result for an individual language being 16.9% for Medieval Icelandic. This outlines the particular difficulty of this specific problem. At the character level, the best average result over 16 languages was 55.62% and the best result for an individual language was 74.59% for Gothic.

The combined results of the constrained and unconstrained settings for problems 1-3 are provided in Table 5. Table 6 shows results for problem 4 from the unconstrained track. Finally, average results across all problems for each track can be found in Table 7. These tables are provided in the Appendix A.

7.1 Constrained Setting

For the constrained subtask, participants were not allowed to use anything apart from the provided datasets, but they could reduce and balance them if they saw fit. Our intention was to avoid any cross-lingual transfer in the constrained setting, including the transfer between the languages within the provided dataset. However, we seem to have failed to communicate this properly, and one of the systems submitted to this track made use of cross-lingual transfer within the dataset. Nevertheless, the system with embeddings pre-trained for each language individually achieved a better result.

7.1.1 Heidelberg-Boston

The winning team in the constrained track, representing Heidelberg University and Sattler College, submitted a system that uses a combination of contextual word and character embeddings pre-trained from scratch for each language in the dataset individually[14] (Riemenschneider and Krahn, 2024). Bringing together the hierarchical tokenisation method (Sun et al., 2023) and the DeBERTa-V3 architecture (He et al., 2023) for POS-tagging and morphological feature prediction, and using character-level nanoT5 models (Nawrot, 2023) for lemmatisation allowed the team to be on par with the winners of the unconstrained track, achieving the average score of 95.25%, 93.67% and 96.18% across 13 languages for POS-tagging, lemmatisation and morphological feature prediction respectively.

7.1.2 Team 21a

The team representing Allen Institute for Artificial Intelligence pretrained a multilingual transformer model, LiBERTus,[15] that follows RoBERTa's pretraining architecture (Liu et al., 2019) and takes inspiration from Conneau et al. (2020) regarding the scaling of BERT models to multiple languages. The authors point out that their model struggles with multiword expressions in Coptic and Ancient Hebrew (Miranda, 2024), which most likely refers to composite characters and vowel markings. Despite the use of cross-lingual transfer, the model's average score falls about 10% behind that of the winning team, reaching the average of 82.47%, 81.98% and 90.70% across 13 languages for POS-tagging, lemmatisation and morphological feature prediction respectively.

7.2 Unconstrained Setting

For the unconstrained subtask, participants could use any additional data in any language, including pre-trained embeddings and LLMs. Surprisingly, the winning team did not make use of embeddings at all in problem 4b, although this shared task was specifically dedicated to embedding evaluation. Still, we accepted this submission in full as the variety of approaches the team tried may be insightful for the reader.

7.2.1 UDParse

The winner of the unconstrained track is the UDParse team from Orange Innovation. To solve problems 1-3, the team trained their own UDParse parser[16] with the use of openly available contextualised embeddings: multilingual mBERT (Devlin et al., 2019), XLM-RoBERTa (Conneau et al., 2020) and GPT2 (Radford et al., 2019), and language-specific slavicBERT (Arkhipov et al., 2019) for Old Church Slavonic and Old East Slavic and heBERT (Chriqui and Yahav, 2022) for Ancient Hebrew. The team used distilBERT (Sanh et al., 2019) for word-level mask filling and an embedding-less n-gram based model for character-level mask filling (Heinecke, 2024). They achieve the average score of 96.09%, 86.47% and 96.68% across 13 languages for POS-tagging, lemmatisation and morphological feature prediction respectively. Their average results across 16 languages for word-level and character-level mask-filling are 3.77% and 55.62% respectively.

7.2.2 TartuNLP

The TartuNLP team from the University of Tartu submitted a system based on the adapters framework (Poth et al., 2023) that uses parameter-efficient fine-tuning (Dorkin and Sirts, 2024). They applied the same approach uniformly to all tasks and 16 languages by fine-tuning stacked language- and task-specific adapters for XLM-RoBERTa.[17] Although their system, achieving the average of 85.67% and 88.14% across 13 languages in POS-tagging and morphological feature prediction, is outperformed by UDParse, this is probably explained by the effectiveness of the UDParse morphological parser rather than by the quality of embeddings employed by either team. At the

[14] `https://github.com/bowphs/SIGTYP-2024-hierarchical-transformers`

[15] `https://github.com/ljvmiranda921/LiBERTus`

[16] `https://github.com/Orange-OpenSource/udparse`

[17] `https://github.com/slowwavesleep/ancient-lang-adapters/tree/sigtyp2024`

same time, TartuNLP outperforms UDParse in lemmatisation by 8.41%, achieving 94.88% on average across 13 languages, and in word-level mask filling, achieving 5.95% on average across 16 languages. The team's results for character-level mask filling generally concede 10-15% to the winner, which highlights an interesting observation: a very simple character-based n-gram model can be more effective in a low-resource setting than cutting edge approaches.

8 Discussion

Analysing results of the competition, we made a few interesting observations. First of all, data scarcity does have an effect on sequence labelling tasks, such as POS-tagging and morphological feature prediction, but this effect is not as dramatic as one might expect. Thus, the difference between the smallest corpus of 21K tokens (Vedic Sanskrit) and the biggest corpus of 599K tokens (Medieval Latin) is only 9.5% on average for POS-tagging and 11.3% for morphological feature prediction. The same is true for lemmatisation; however, models trained for this task seem to be more susceptible to orthographic variation and lexical variety in the data, as well as to the morphological complexity of a language. Thus, we see poorer results for lemmatisation across all languages despite the milder metrics.

Cross-lingual and cross-temporal (i.e. from modern languages to their ancestors) transfer could have played an important role in the systems that used XLM-RoBERTa. However, Riemenschneider and Krahn (2024) showed that similar results can be achieved with pre-training on modestly sized monolingual data without any transfer.

Mask filling tasks appeared to be much harder than we expected even for SOTA models. The problem could be attributable to the following reasons, or to some combination thereof:

- High lexical variety
- Orthographic variation
- Relatively short sentences
- Code-switching (e.g. Latin in historical Irish texts)
- Data scarcity (mask filling requires more training data than, for example, POS-tagging)
- Composite characters and vowel markings in Coptic and Ancient Hebrew
- Non-trivial character decomposition in Classical Chinese

9 Conclusion

The Shared Task on Word Embedding Evaluation for Ancient and Historical Languages attracted participants from five major research institutions and was an important step towards creating a universal multilingual evaluation benchmark for embeddings learned from ancient and historical language data. The best average results across 13 languages for POS-tagging, lemmatisation and morphological feature prediction were 96.09%, 94.88% and 96.68% respectively. However, participants only managed to achieve an average of 5.95% at word-level and 55.62% at character-level across 16 languages in more challenging mask filling tasks.

The dataset and evaluation scripts are available on our GitHub,[18] and the post-competition phase on CodaLab will remain open for anyone interested in testing their approach on our data. We are planning to further expand the dataset with more languages and add more downstream tasks in the next release of the benchmark. We would appreciate any suggestions and collaboration from both computer scientists and historical linguists.

Acknowledgements

This shared task was in part supported by the Irish Research Council under grant number IRCLA/2017/129 (CARDAMOM – Comparative Deep Models of Language for Minority and Historical Languages[19]) and co-funded by Science Foundation Ireland (SFI) under Grant Number SFI/12/RC/2289 (Insight) and SFI/12/RC/2289_P2 (Insight_2). We would also like to thank Universal Dependencies, University College Cork, the Royal Irish Academy, and HAS Research Institute for Linguistics for providing the source data.

References

Acadamh Ríoga na hÉireann. 2017. Corpas Stairiúil na Gaeilge 1600-1926. Retrieved: June 10, 2022.

Mikhail Arkhipov, Maria Trofimova, Yuri Kuratov, and Alexey Sorokin. 2019. Tuning multilingual transformers for language-specific named entity recognition. In *Proceedings of the 7th Workshop on Balto-Slavic Natural Language Processing*, pages 89–93, Florence, Italy. Association for Computational Linguistics.

[18]https://github.com/sigtyp/ST2024

[19]https://www.cardamom-project.org/

David Bamman and Patrick J. Burns. 2020. Latin BERT: A contextual language model for classical philology.

Bernhard Bauer, Rijcklof Hofman, and Pádraic Moran. 2017. St. Gall Priscian Glosses, version 2.0. Accessed: February 14, 2023.

Aleksandrs Berdicevskis, Gerlof Bouma, Robin Kurtz, Felix Morger, Joey Öhman, Yvonne Adesam, Lars Borin, Dana Dannélls, Markus Forsberg, Tim Isbister, Anna Lindahl, Martin Malmsten, Faton Rekathati, Magnus Sahlgren, Elena Volodina, Love Börjeson, Simon Hengchen, and Nina Tahmasebi. 2023. Superlim: A Swedish language understanding evaluation benchmark. In *Proceedings of the 2023 Conference on Empirical Methods in Natural Language Processing*, pages 8137–8153, Singapore. Association for Computational Linguistics.

Giuseppe G. A. Celano, Daniel Zeman, and Federica Gamba. 2014. The Ancient Greek and Latin Dependency Treebank 2.0. Accessed: February 08, 2024.

Avihay Chriqui and Inbal Yahav. 2022. HeBERT & HebEMO: a Hebrew BERT model and a tool for polarity analysis and emotion recognition. *INFORMS Journal on Data Science*.

Alexis Conneau, Kartikay Khandelwal, Naman Goyal, Vishrav Chaudhary, Guillaume Wenzek, Francisco Guzmán, Edouard Grave, Myle Ott, Luke Zettlemoyer, and Veselin Stoyanov. 2020. Unsupervised cross-lingual representation learning at scale. In *Proceedings of the 58th Annual Meeting of the Association for Computational Linguistics*, pages 8440–8451, Online. Association for Computational Linguistics.

Alexis Conneau and Douwe Kiela. 2018. SentEval: An evaluation toolkit for universal sentence representations. In *Proceedings of the Eleventh International Conference on Language Resources and Evaluation (LREC 2018)*.

Oksana Dereza. 2024. ACHILLES: Ancient and Historical Language Evaluation Set.

Oksana Dereza, Theodorus Fransen, and John P. Mccrae. 2023a. Do not trust the experts: How the lack of standard complicates NLP for historical Irish. In *The Fourth Workshop on Insights from Negative Results in NLP*, pages 82–87, Dubrovnik, Croatia. Association for Computational Linguistics.

Oksana Dereza, Theodorus Fransen, and John P. Mccrae. 2023b. Temporal domain adaptation for historical Irish. In *Tenth Workshop on NLP for Similar Languages, Varieties and Dialects (VarDial 2023)*, pages 55–66, Dubrovnik, Croatia. Association for Computational Linguistics.

Jacob Devlin, Ming-Wei Chang, Kenton Lee, and Kristina Toutanova. 2019. BERT: Pre-training of deep bidirectional transformers for language understanding. In *Proceedings of the 2019 Conference of the North American Chapter of the Association for Computational Linguistics: Human Language Technologies, Volume 1 (Long and Short Papers)*, pages 4171–4186, Minneapolis, Minnesota. Association for Computational Linguistics.

Aleksei Dorkin and Kairit Sirts. 2024. TartuNLP @ SIGTYP 2024 Shared Task: Adapting XLM-RoBERTa for ancient and historical languages. In *Proceedings of the 6th Workshop on Research in Computational Linguistic Typology and Multilingual NLP (SIGTYP 2024)*, St. Julians, Malta. Association for Computational Linguistics.

Adrian Doyle. 2018. Würzburg Irish Glosses. Accessed: February 14, 2023.

Loïc Grobol, Mathilde Regnault, Pedro Ortiz Suarez, Benoît Sagot, Laurent Romary, and Benoît Crabbé. 2022. BERTrade: Using Contextual Embeddings to Parse Old French. In *13th Language Resources and Evaluation Conference*, Marseille, France. European Language Resources Association.

HAS Research Institute for Linguistics. 2018. Old Hungarian Codices.

Dag T. T. Haug and Marius L. Jøhndal. 2008. Creating a parallel treebank of the Old Indo-European Bible translations. In *Proceedings of the Second Workshop on Language Technology for Cultural Heritage Data (LaTeCH 2008)*, pages 27–34.

Brandon Hawk, Antonia Karaisl, and Nick White. 2018. Modelling Medieval Hands: Practical OCR for Caroline Minuscule. *Faculty Publications*, (416).

Pengcheng He, Jianfeng Gao, and Weizhu Chen. 2023. DeBERTav3: Improving deBERTa using ELECTRA-style pre-training with gradient-disentangled embedding sharing. In *The Eleventh International Conference on Learning Representations*.

Johannes Heinecke. 2024. UDParse @ SIGTYP 2024 Shared Task: Modern language models for historical languages. In *Proceedings of the 6th Workshop on Research in Computational Linguistic Typology and Multilingual NLP (SIGTYP 2024)*, St. Julians, Malta. Association for Computational Linguistics.

Hai Hu, Patrícia Amaral, and Sandra Kübler. 2021. Word embeddings and semantic shifts in historical Spanish: Methodological considerations. *Digital Scholarship in the Humanities*, 37(2):441–461.

Junjie Hu, Sebastian Ruder, Aditya Siddhant, Graham Neubig, Orhan Firat, and Melvin Johnson. 2020. XTREME: A massively multilingual multi-task benchmark for evaluating cross-lingual generalization. In *Proceedings of the 37th International Conference on Machine Learning (ICML 2020)*, pages 4411–4421.

Kyle P Johnson, Patrick J Burns, John Stewart, Todd Cook, Clément Besnier, and William JB Mattingly. 2021. The classical language toolkit: An nlp framework for pre-modern languages. In *Proceedings of the 59th annual meeting of the association for computational linguistics and the 11th international joint conference on natural language processing: System demonstrations*, pages 20–29.

Diederik P. Kingma and Jimmy Ba. 2015. Adam: A method for stochastic optimization. In *3rd International Conference on Learning Representations, ICLR 2015, San Diego, CA, USA, May 7-9, 2015, Conference Track Proceedings*.

Kevin Krahn, Derrick Tate, and Andrew C. Lamicela. 2023. Sentence embedding models for Ancient Greek using multilingual knowledge distillation. In *Proceedings of the Ancient Language Processing Workshop*, pages 13–22, Varna, Bulgaria. INCOMA Ltd., Shoumen, Bulgaria.

Kentaro Kurihara, Daisuke Kawahara, and Tomohide Shibata. 2022. JGLUE: Japanese general language understanding evaluation. In *Proceedings of the Thirteenth Language Resources and Evaluation Conference*, pages 2957–2966, Marseille, France. European Language Resources Association.

Yuxian Liang, Nan Duan, Yizhe Gong, Nan Wu, Fangxiang Guo, Weizhen Qi, Ming Gong, Lin Shou, Daxin Jiang, Gang Cao, Xinyu Fan, Ruofei Zhang, Rishabh Agrawal, Emo Cui, Siqi Wei, Tanmay Bharti, Yu Qiao, Ji-Hong Chen, Wei Wu, and et al. 2020. XGLUE: A new benchmark dataset for cross-lingual pre-training, understanding and generation. In *Proceedings of the 2020 Conference on Empirical Methods in Natural Language Processing (EMNLP)*, pages 6008–6018.

Yinhan Liu, Myle Ott, Naman Goyal, Jingfei Du, Mandar Joshi, Danqi Chen, Omer Levy, Mike Lewis, Luke Zettlemoyer, and Veselin Stoyanov. 2019. RoBERTa: A robustly optimized bert pretraining approach.

Bryan McCann, Nitish Shirish Keskar, Caiming Xiong, and Richard Socher. 2018. The natural language decathlon: Multitask learning as question answering. *arXiv preprint:1806.08730*.

Wouter Mercelis and Alek Keersmaekers. 2022. An ELECTRA model for Latin token tagging tasks. In *Proceedings of the Second Workshop on Language Technologies for Historical and Ancient Languages*, pages 189–192, Marseille, France. European Language Resources Association.

Lester James V. Miranda. 2024. Allen Institute for AI @ SIGTYP 2024 Shared Task on word embedding evaluation for ancient and historical languages. In *Proceedings of the 6th Workshop on Research in Computational Linguistic Typology and Multilingual NLP (SIGTYP 2024)*, St. Julians, Malta. Association for Computational Linguistics.

Piotr Nawrot. 2023. nanoT5: Fast & simple pre-training and fine-tuning of T5 models with limited resources. In *Proceedings of the 3rd Workshop for Natural Language Processing Open Source Software (NLP-OSS 2023)*, pages 95–101, Singapore. Association for Computational Linguistics.

Leonard Neidorf, Madison S. Krieger, Michelle Yakubek, Pramit Chaudhuri, and Joseph P. Dexter. 2019. Large-scale Quantitative Profiling of the Old English Verse Tradition. *Nature Human Behaviour*, 3(6):560–567.

Donnchadh Ó Corráin, Hiram Morgan, Beatrix Färber, Benjamin Hazard, Emer Purcell, Caoimhín Ó Dónaill, Hilary Lavelle, Julianne Nyhan, and Emma McCarthy. 1997. CELT: Corpus of Electronic Texts. Retrieved: March 15, 2021.

Clifton Poth, Hannah Sterz, Indraneil Paul, Sukannya Purkayastha, Leon Engländer, Timo Imhof, Ivan Vulić, Sebastian Ruder, Iryna Gurevych, and Jonas Pfeiffer. 2023. Adapters: A unified library for parameter-efficient and modular transfer learning. In *Proceedings of the 2023 Conference on Empirical Methods in Natural Language Processing: System Demonstrations*, pages 149–160, Singapore. Association for Computational Linguistics.

Alec Radford, Jeffrey Wu, Rewon Child, David Luan, Dario Amodei, Ilya Sutskever, et al. 2019. Language models are unsupervised multitask learners. *OpenAI blog*, 1(8):9.

Frederick Riemenschneider and Anette Frank. 2023. Exploring large language models for classical philology. In *Proceedings of the 61st Annual Meeting of the Association for Computational Linguistics (Volume 1: Long Papers)*, pages 15181–15199, Toronto, Canada. Association for Computational Linguistics.

Frederick Riemenschneider and Kevin Krahn. 2024. Heidelberg-Boston @ SIGTYP 2024 Shared Task: Enhancing low-resource language analysis with character-aware hierarchical transformers. In *Proceedings of the 6th Workshop on Research in Computational Linguistic Typology and Multilingual NLP (SIGTYP 2024)*, St. Julians, Malta. Association for Computational Linguistics.

Sebastian Ruder, Jonathan H. Clark, Alexander Gutkin, Maheswaran Kale, Mengting Ma, Massimo Nicosia, Shyam Rijhwani, Patrick Riley, Joudy-Maysaa Abdel Sarr, Xiyang Wang, John Wieting, Nitish Gupta, Anna Katanova, Christo Kirov, Daniel L. Dickinson, Brian Roark, Bitan Samanta, Chen Tao, David I. Adelani, and et al. 2023. XTREME-UP: A user-centric scarce-data benchmark for under-represented languages. *arXiv preprint: 2305.11938*.

Sebastian Ruder, Noah Constant, Jan Botha, Aditya Siddhant, Orhan Firat, Jie Fu, Pengcheng Liu, Junjie Hu, Dan Garrette, Graham Neubig, and Melvin Johnson. 2021. XTREME-R: Towards more challenging and nuanced multilingual evaluation. In *Proceedings of the 2021 Conference on Empirical Methods in Natural Language Processing*, pages 10215–10245.

Victor Sanh, Lysandre Debut, Julien Chaumond, and Thomas Wolf. 2019. DistilBERT, a distilled version of BERT: smaller, faster, cheaper and lighter. *arXiv preprint:1910.01108*.

Tatiana Shavrina, Alena Fenogenova, Emelyanov Anton, Denis Shevelev, Ekaterina Artemova, Valentin Malykh, Vladislav Mikhailov, Maria Tikhonova, Andrey Chertok, and Andrey Evlampiev. 2020. RussianSuperGLUE: A Russian language understanding evaluation benchmark. In *Proceedings of the 2020 Conference on Empirical Methods in Natural Language Processing (EMNLP)*, pages 4717–4726, Online. Association for Computational Linguistics.

Eszter Simon. 2014. Corpus Building from Old Hungarian Codices. In Katalin É. Kiss, editor, *The Evolution of Functional Left Peripheries in Hungarian Syntax*. Oxford University Press, Oxford.

Pranaydeep Singh, Gorik Rutten, and Els Lefever. 2021. A pilot study for BERT language modelling and morphological analysis for ancient and medieval Greek. In *Proceedings of the 5th Joint SIGHUM Workshop on Computational Linguistics for Cultural Heritage, Social Sciences, Humanities and Literature*, pages 128–137, Punta Cana, Dominican Republic (online). Association for Computational Linguistics.

Rachele Sprugnoli, Marco Passarotti, Flavio Massimiliano Cecchini, and Matteo Pellegrini. 2020. Overview of the EvaLatin 2020 evaluation campaign. In *Proceedings of LT4HALA 2020 1st Workshop on Language Technologies for Historical and Ancient Languages*, pages 105–110, Marseille, France. European Language Resources Association (ELRA).

Rachele Sprugnoli, Marco Passarotti, Cecchini Flavio Massimiliano, Margherita Fantoli, and Giovanni Moretti. 2022. Overview of the EvaLatin 2022 evaluation campaign. In *Proceedings of the Second Workshop on Language Technologies for Historical and Ancient Languages (LT4HALA 2022), Language Resources and Evaluation Conference (LREC 2022)*, pages 183–188.

David Stifter, Bernhard Bauer, Fangzhe Qiu, Elliott Lash, Nora White, Siobhán Barret, Aaron Griffith, Romanas Bulatovas, Francesco Felici, Ellen Ganly, Truc Ha Nguyen, and Lars Nooij. 2021. Corpus PalaeoHibernicum (CorPH). Accessed: 19-02-2023.

Silvia Stopponi, Saskia Peels-Matthey, and Malvina Nissim. 2024. AGREE: a new benchmark for the evaluation of distributional semantic models of Ancient Greek. *Digital Scholarship in the Humanities*.

Li Sun, Florian Luisier, Kayhan Batmanghelich, Dinei Florencio, and Cha Zhang. 2023. From characters to words: Hierarchical pre-trained language model for open-vocabulary language understanding. In *Proceedings of the 61st Annual Meeting of the Association for Computational Linguistics (Volume 1: Long Papers)*, pages 3605–3620, Toronto, Canada. Association for Computational Linguistics.

Zuoyu Tian, Dylan Jarrett, Juan Escalona Torres, and Patricia Amaral. 2021. BAHP: Benchmark of assessing word embeddings in historical Portuguese. In *Proceedings of the 5th Joint SIGHUM Workshop on Computational Linguistics for Cultural Heritage, Social Sciences, Humanities and Literature*, pages 113–119.

Sergio Torres Aguilar. 2022. Multilingual named entity recognition for medieval charters using stacked embeddings and bert-based models. In *Proceedings of the Second Workshop on Language Technologies for Historical and Ancient Languages*, pages 119–128, Marseille, France. European Language Resources Association.

Gorka Urbizu, Iñaki San Vicente, Xabier Saralegi, Rodrigo Agerri, and Aitor Soroa. 2022. BasqueGLUE: A natural language understanding benchmark for Basque. In *Proceedings of the Thirteenth Language Resources and Evaluation Conference*, pages 1603–1612, Marseille, France. European Language Resources Association.

Alex Wang, Yada Pruksachatkun, Nikita Nangia, Amanpreet Singh, Julian Michael, Felix Hill, Omer Levy, and Samuel R. Bowman. 2020. SuperGLUE: A stickier benchmark for general-purpose language understanding systems. In *Proceedings of the 33rd Conference on Neural Information Processing Systems (NeurIPS 2019)*.

Alex Wang, Amanpreet Singh, Julian Michael, Felix Hill, Omer Levy, and Samuel R. Bowman. 2019. GLUE: A multi-task benchmark and analysis platform for natural language understanding. In *Proceedings of the 7th International Conference on Learning Representations (ICLR 2019)*.

Alexander Wettig, Tianyu Gao, Zexuan Zhong, and Danqi Chen. 2023. Should you mask 15% in masked language modeling? In *Proceedings of the 17th Conference of the European Chapter of the Association for Computational Linguistics*, pages 2985–3000, Dubrovnik, Croatia. Association for Computational Linguistics.

Krzysztof Wróbel and Krzysztof Nowak. 2022. Transformer-based part-of-speech tagging and lemmatization for Latin. In *Proceedings of the Second Workshop on Language Technologies for Historical and Ancient Languages*, pages 193–197, Marseille, France. European Language Resources Association.

Liang Xu, Hai Hu, Xuanwei Zhang, Lu Li, Chenjie Cao, Yudong Li, Yechen Xu, Kai Sun, Dian Yu, Cong Yu,

Yin Tian, Qianqian Dong, Weitang Liu, Bo Shi, Yiming Cui, Junyi Li, Jun Zeng, Rongzhao Wang, Weijian Xie, Yanting Li, Yina Patterson, Zuoyu Tian, Yiwen Zhang, He Zhou, Shaoweihua Liu, Zhe Zhao, Qipeng Zhao, Cong Yue, Xinrui Zhang, Zhengliang Yang, Kyle Richardson, and Zhenzhong Lan. 2020. CLUE: A Chinese language understanding evaluation benchmark. In *Proceedings of the 28th International Conference on Computational Linguistics*, pages 4762–4772, Barcelona, Spain (Online). International Committee on Computational Linguistics.

Ivan Yamshchikov, Alexey Tikhonov, Yorgos Pantis, Charlotte Schubert, and Jürgen Jost. 2022. BERT in plutarch's shadows. In *Proceedings of the 2022 Conference on Empirical Methods in Natural Language Processing*, pages 6071–6080, Abu Dhabi, United Arab Emirates. Association for Computational Linguistics.

Daniel Zeman, Joakim Nivre, Mitchell Abrams, Elia Ackermann, Noëmi Aepli, Hamid Aghaei, Željko Agić, Amir Ahmadi, Lars Ahrenberg, Chika Kennedy Ajede, Salih Furkan Akkurt, Gabrielė Aleksandravičiūtė, Ika Alfina, Avner Algom, Khalid Alnajjar, Chiara Alzetta, Erik Andersen, Lene Antonsen, Tatsuya Aoyama, ..., and Rayan Ziane. 2023. Universal dependencies 2.12. LINDAT/CLARIAH-CZ digital library at the Institute of Formal and Applied Linguistics (ÚFAL), Faculty of Mathematics and Physics, Charles University.

A Shared Task Results

		AVG	chu	cop	fro	got	grc	hbo	isl	lat	latm	lzh	ohu	orv	san
POS-tagging															
Baseline		92.76	93.36	94.98	91.57	93.73	90.33	94.07	94.00	92.39	97.22	90.91	93.59	90.33	89.37
Constrained	HDB-BOS	**95.25**	**96.57**	**96.92**	**93.10**	**95.41**	**96.39**	**96.68**	**96.08**	**95.54**	**98.43**	**92.92**	**95.98**	**94.46**	**89.71**
	Team 21a	82.47	94.62	42.65	85.14	93.48	93.49	27.26	93.85	92.43	94.41	81.79	94.42	91.23	87.32
Unconstrained	UDParse	**96.09**	**97.00**	**97.33**	**96.01**	**96.47**	**96.49**	**97.84**	**96.88**	**96.83**	**98.79**	**93.76**	**96.71**	**94.99**	**90.02**
	TartuNLP	85.67	66.35	60.99	94.51	92.72	95.72	94.15	96.67	95.86	**98.79**	83.28	75.14	75.67	83.83
Lemmatisation															
Baseline		91.95	89.60	95.74	91.93	91.95	91.06	95.28	93.78	92.08	97.03	98.81	89.43	84.44	84.24
Constrained	HDB-BOS	**93.67**	**94.49**	**95.07**	**92.63**	**93.31**	**94.08**	**97.29**	**96.63**	**96.00**	**98.46**	99.18	**85.92**	**90.09**	**84.59**
	Team 21a	81.98	79.59	46.32	83.32	90.79	88.30	61.75	94.58	92.35	97.22	**99.84**	69.97	78.44	83.21
Unconstrained	UDParse	86.47	59.56	74.78	92.47	92.81	**94.02**	96.85	**97.96**	96.74	**98.91**	**99.96**	63.43	68.55	88.10
	TartuNLP	**94.88**	**92.70**	**98.28**	**95.11**	**95.41**	93.39	**98.15**	97.23	**96.99**	98.69	99.91	**86.91**	**89.23**	**91.48**
Morphological feature prediction															
Baseline		33.32	85.07	47.41	28.27	18.95	25.10	42.78	35.83	18.17	30.94	43.58	23.20	25.55	08.34
Constrained	HDB-BOS	**96.18**	**96.04**	**98.60**	**97.87**	**95.32**	**97.46**	**97.46**	**95.29**	**95.17**	**98.68**	**95.52**	**96.30**	**95.00**	**91.58**
	Team 21a	90.70	94.06	80.47	94.08	93.96	96.50	71.20	94.79	93.31	97.98	85.98	94.64	92.16	90.00
Unconstrained	UDParse	**96.68**	**96.49**	**98.88**	**98.33**	**96.23**	**97.78**	**97.05**	**95.92**	**96.66**	**98.83**	**96.24**	**96.62**	**95.16**	**92.60**
	TartuNLP	88.14	67.14	74.86	98.01	92.40	97.33	95.14	95.53	95.91	**98.83**	88.75	75.62	80.00	86.33

Table 5: Results of the *SIGTYP 2024 Shared Task on Word Embedding Evaluation for Ancient and Historical Languages* for problems 1-3. The winner of each track (constrained / unconstrained) is marked in **bold**, and the overall best result is underlined. The team names are as provided by participants, except HDB-BOS, which stands for 'Heidelberg-Boston'. For language code reference, see Table 1.

	AVG	chu	cop	fro	got	grc	hbo	isl	lat	latm	lzh	ohu	orv	san	sga	mga	ghc
Mask filling: word-level																	
UDParse	3.77	**2.80**	0.00	3.28	2.67	**3.07**	**5.39**	3.42	3.51	4.73	6.10	**6.31**	5.03	3.86	2.79	**4.03**	3.29
TartuNLP	**5.95**	2.42	**1.87**	**7.22**	**3.40**	3.01	0.00	**16.90**	**11.45**	**14.39**	**10.46**	0.06	**6.05**	**4.79**	**3.21**	3.99	**6.00**
Mask filling: character-level																	
UDParse	**55.62**	**66.77**	0.00	**62.77**	**74.59**	**68.46**	**36.85**	**66.45**	**67.91**	**72.93**	0.00	**66.52**	**66.77**	**70.10**	**58.38**	**53.38**	**58.09**
TartuNLP	48.38	53.79	**45.10**	52.46	67.34	61.15	18.56	57.32	65.79	69.84	**0.25**	45.65	48.04	64.52	34.86	39.49	49.88

Table 6: Results of the *SIGTYP 2024 Shared Task on Word Embedding Evaluation for Ancient and Historical Languages* for problem 4. The winner is marked in **bold**, and the absolute best result across all languages is underlined. The team names are as provided by participants. For language code reference, see Table 1.

		AVG	chu	cop	fro	got	grc	hbo	isl	lat	latm	lzh	ohu	orv	san	sga	mga	ghc
	Baseline	72.68	89.35	79.38	70.59	68.21	68.83	77.38	74.54	67.55	75.07	77.77	68.74	66.77	60.65	–	–	–
Constrained	HDB-BOS	**95.02**	**95.70**	**96.65**	**94.54**	**94.68**	**95.98**	**97.14**	**96.00**	**95.57**	**98.53**	**95.88**	**92.73**	**93.18**	**88.62**	–	–	–
	Team 21a	85.05	89.42	56.48	87.51	92.74	92.76	53.41	94.41	92.69	96.54	89.21	86.34	87.28	86.84	–	–	–
Unconstrained	UDParse	**61.93**	**71.15**	**58.90**	**71.10**	**73.07**	**71.84**	**67.05**	71.98	72.38	74.79	**59.20**	**70.61**	**69.15**	**69.61**	**30.59**	**28.71**	**30.69**
	TartuNLP	55.74	49.85	51.52	68.93	69.74	70.25	60.94	**72.88**	**73.15**	**76.15**	56.54	51.98	55.66	65.51	19.03	21.74	27.94

Table 7: Overall results of the *SIGTYP 2024 Shared Task on Word Embedding Evaluation for Ancient and Historical Languages* averaged across all problems for a given language. The winner for each setting is marked in **bold**. The team names are as provided by participants, except HDB-BOS, which stands for 'Heidelberg-Boston'. For language code reference, see Table 1.

Author Index

Association for Computational Linguistics
209 N. Eighth Street
Stroudsburg, Pennsylvania 18360

ISBN 978-1-7138-9461-2

9 781713 894612

CURRAN ASSOCIATES INC.
proceedings.com